Beyond Monopoly

CRITICAL MEDIA STUDIES

Series Editor
Andrew Calabrese, University of Colorado

This series covers a broad range of critical research and theory about media in the modern world. It includes work about the changing structures of the media, focusing particularly on work about the political and economic forces and social relations which shape and are shaped by media institutions, structural changes in policy formation and enforcement, technological transformations in the means of communication, and the relationships of all these to public and private cultures worldwide. Historical research about the media and intellectual histories pertaining to media research and theory are particularly welcome. Emphasizing the role of social and political theory for informing and shaping research about communications media, Critical Media Studies addresses the politics of media institutions at national, subnational, and transnational levels. The series is also interested in short, synthetic texts on key thinkers and concepts in critical media studies.

Titles in the series

Beyond Monopoly: Globalization and Contemporary Italian Media edited by Michela Ardizzoni and Chiara Ferrari

Global Communications: Toward a Transcultural Political Economy edited by Paula Chakravartty and Yuezhi Zhao

Governing European Communications: From Unification to Coordination by Maria Michalis

Knowledge Workers in the Information Society edited by Catherine McKercher and Vincent Mosco

Democratic Communications: Formations, Projects, Possibilities by James F. Hamilton

Hegemony in the Digital Age: The Arab/Israeli Conflict Online by Stephen Marmura

Punk Record Labels and the Struggle for Autonomy: The Emergence of DIY by Alan O'Connor

From the Labyrinth of the World to the Paradise of the Heart: Science and Humanism in UNESCO's Approach to Globalization by Vincenzo Pavone

The Laboring of Communication: Will Knowledge Workers of the World Unite? by Vincent Mosco and Catherine McKercher

Cultural Studies and Political Economy: Toward a New Integration by Robert Babe

Patronizing the Public: American Philanthropy's Transformation of Culture, Communication, and the Humanities edited by William J. Buxton

Beyond Monopoly

Globalization and Contemporary Italian Media

Edited by
Michela Ardizzoni and
Chiara Ferrari

LEXINGTON BOOKS

A division of
ROWMAN & LITTLEFIELD PUBLISHERS, INC.
Lanham • Boulder • New York • Toronto • Plymouth, UK

Published by Lexington Books
A division of Rowman & Littlefield Publishers, Inc.
A wholly owned subsidiary of The Rowman & Littlefield Publishing Group, Inc.
4501 Forbes Boulevard, Suite 200, Lanham, Maryland 20706
http://www.lexingtonbooks.com

Estover Road, Plymouth PL6 7PY, United Kingdom

Copyright © 2010 by Lexington Books

All rights reserved. No part of this book may be reproduced in any form or by any electronic or mechanical means, including information storage and retrieval systems, without written permission from the publisher, except by a reviewer who may quote passages in a review.

British Library Cataloguing in Publication Information Available

Library of Congress Cataloging-in-Publication Data

Beyond monopoly : globalization and contemporary Italian media / Michela Ardizzoni and Chiara Ferrari [editors].
   p. cm. — (Critical media studies)
Includes bibliographical references and index.
ISBN 978-0-7391-2851-0 (cloth : alk. paper)— ISBN 978-0-7391-4267-7 (electronic)
 1. Mass media and globalization—Italy. 2. Mass media and culture—Italy. 3. Mass media policy—Italy. I. Ardizzoni, Michela, 1969- II. Ferrari, Chiara, 1975–
P94.65.I8B49 2010
302.230945—dc22   2009038877

∞ ™ The paper used in this publication meets the minimum requirements of American National Standard for Information Sciences—Permanence of Paper for Printed Library Materials, ANSI/NISO Z39.48-1992.

Printed in the United States of America

Contents

Foreword — vii
   Milly Buonanno

Introduction: Italian Media between the Local and the Global — xi
   Chiara Ferrari and Michela Ardizzoni

PART I: GLOBALIZATION, POLICY, AND TECHNOLOGY

1. Shaping Tomorrow's Television: Policies on Digital Television in Italy, 1996–2006 — 3
   Alessandro D'Arma

2. "Il Caso Canadese" and the Question of Global Media — 21
   Mark Hayward

3. Digital Terrestrial Television and Its Promises: Framing the Debate on the Transition to Digital Television in Italy — 37
   Cinzia Padovani

PART II: TELEVISION FLOWS AND FORMATS

4. Struggling for Identity: The Television Production Sector in Italy and the Challenges of Globalization — 57
   Flavia Barca and Andrea Marzulli.

5. Public and Private, Global and Local in Italian Crime Drama: The Case of *La Piovra* — 79
   Elisa Giomi

6	Dubbing *The Simpsons*: Or How Groundskeeper Willie Lost His Kilt in Sardinia *Chiara Ferrari*	101
7	A Peninsula in the Sea of TV Formats: Exploring Italian Adaptations of *Survivor* *Marta Perrotta*	129

PART III: NEW AND ALTERNATIVE MEDIA

8	E-democracy and Italian Public Administration: New Media at the Service of Citizens *Giorgia Nesti and Chiara Valentini*	151
9	Neighborhood Television Channels in Italy: The Case of Telestreet *Michela Ardizzoni*	171
10	Web-Based Technologies in Media and Cultural Production: Emerging Evidence from Italian Web-TVs and Web-Radios *Lorenzo Mizzau, Federico Riboldazzi, and Fabrizio Montanari*	185

PART IV: IMMIGRATION AND DIVERSITY

11	Missed Opportunities: The Debate on Immigrants' Voting Rights in Italian Newspapers and Television *Cristian Vaccari*	203
12	Globalization vs. Localization: Anti-immigrant and Hate Discourses in Italy *Rinella Cere*	225
13	Multiculturalism in New Italian Cinema: The Impact of Migration, Diaspora, and the Post-Colonial on Italy's Self-Representation *Alberto Zambenedetti*	245

Index	269
About the Contributors	277

Foreword

Milly Buonanno

I would like to take the liberty to start this brief foreword with a couple of personal anecdotes, which I would not cite if I did not regard them as being of wider symbolic importance. At the end of summer 2008 I was contacted by a Scandinavian television network about an interview to be broadcast as part of a new current affairs program. The interview focused on the hegemony exercised by Silvio Berlusconi on the Italian media, and the way in which this very "rare influence" affects both the Italian media system and the Italian public. Only a few weeks earlier I had found myself perforce engaged in the same topic; on that occasion, I had to give an opinion on a number of articles collected in an anthology about Italian media in the Berlusconi era, to be published in the United Kingdom.

I shall now abandon the field of personal anecdotes to draw attention to a case, which is, literally, before everyone's eyes, or at least of those who, being interested in cultural studies, are familiar with the scholarly journals that are published under this heading. When the authoritative *International Journal of Cultural Studies* embarked on its second decade of existence, it smartened up its cover. Starting with the June 2008 issue, the cover features a magnificent photographic composition by an artist (Patrick Nicholas) who likes to reproduce artistic masterworks of the past, reinterpreting them in modern style. The picture was inspired by Johann Heinrich Füssli's most famous painting, the sombre and disturbing "Nightmare" (1781). Like the original, the picture shows a sleeping girl in the foreground whose head and arms are hanging over the edge of the bed, her mind and body sunk in deep slumber. Unlike the original, however, the photograph does not have recourse to allegories of monsters to conjure up the oppressive fear of troubled sleep. The body of the sleeping girl stands out against a background of a tilted encircling wall, covered with television screens.

The present-day nightmare, then, is television: reality television in particular, as the title of the photo ("Reality") indicates and as is exemplified by the panoply of images displayed on the screens. And there is a remarkable and interesting detail: to illustrate the Gothic horror of reality shows, the creator has chosen to use images taken from Italian television programs. In presenting his new cover, which inspired him to an elegant reflection on the fact that we simultaneously instigate and revile the televisual nightmare, the journal's editor John Hartley attributed the choice made by the artist to the "unusually exuberant tradition of trash TV" in Italian television (*International Journal of Cultural Studies*, 11, 2: 132).

I offer these examples in support of the fact that Silvio Berlusconi's media power and "trash TV"—two things that are not infrequently regarded as inseparable elements of a symbiotic relationship or a causal connection—now seem to constitute the most conspicuous and pronounced features of the Italian media scene: more especially in the eyes of those who observe it from outside Italy. Without disregarding (and how could one!) the fact that the repeated rise of a media mogul to the head of Italy's government gives irresistible grounds for curiosity and interest and prompts questions that must be asked and asked again, and without denying or underrating the demeaning vulgarity of some of Italian domestic television, I do not conceal that I am somewhat disappointed by the reductionist obsession with Berlusconi and the perfunctory and ill-informed judgments made by quite a few observers or onlookers of the Italian media.

Fortunately, this does not apply to the chapters that are collected and introduced in this book. The editors and most of the authors are young Italian scholars, many of whom have studied and are now working in foreign universities and can therefore turn to good advantage the privileged position that the in-betweenness often confers. They offer us a well-structured, measured and competent discourse on present-day Italy's media scene in the grip of the globalization processes. They speak to us about television, cinema, the daily press, the policies of the digital and the new media; and they give us analytical and critical interpretations that do not necessarily bring into play 'evil geniuses like media moguls behind the scenes,' to quote Hartley's neat wording (ibid: 134). At least half the chapters do go beyond Italy's media monopoly and make no reference to it; this is refreshing.

Speaking to the sociologists who attended the ISA Forum of Sociology in Barcelona (5–8 September 2008), the great globalization scholar Saskia Sassen urged those present not to work only in the light shed by the master categories, such as the global and the national, but also to search in the shadows cast by their dazzling brightness. It is an effective method for capturing and bringing out of obscurity the articulations, the singularities, the details, everything that leads to a mapping of the territory that is perhaps less noticeable but more subtly nuanced. In a certain way, 'digging into the shadow' of the Italian mediascape is precisely what is suggested to us—commendably—in many of this book's pages.

It will be important to continue working in the same way in the future. Italy is a complicated and problematic country—more so, perhaps, than ever before—and the Italian media are both an expression and a multiplier of this intricate and confused state of affairs. We need to search deeply and to throw light into the opaque areas of society that the media all too often make no attempt to dissipate, but instead help to create and reproduce.

I will confine myself to quoting just one brief example, on which (not by chance) the last part of this book concentrates: the growing presence of immigrants among the population of Italy. The difficulty of formulating and implementing policies that address the phenomenon of migration in all its complexities is unquestionably a problem of Italian politics—just as the palpable presence in recent years of a climate of mistrust and insecurity, which is a potential breeding-ground for attitudes of closure toward "the other," is a problem affecting Italian society. Yet, most Italians are not racist or xenophobic, unlike what one might infer from the news media: whether from those that are allied with the political forces that find it easy to circulate a troublesome narrative of the presence of immigrants in terms of "security alarm," or those that, in adhering to a conventional position of political correctness, tend to the other extreme in frightening public opinion with reports of Italians' hostility toward foreigners.

"Italy is an odd country," wrote Primo Levi "in Italy foreigners aren't enemies. You'd think the Italians were more enemies to one another than to foreigners" (Primo Levi, *If Not Now, When?* Penguin, NY 1995, p. 323). Italy is indeed an odd and complicated country, and one that the media are not helping to render more transparent and easier to know (for both Italians themselves and others). This spells trouble for contemporary Italian media and society. The media moguls and "trash TV" are naturally part of the problem; but they are hardly the principal manifestation of it, let alone the cause.

September 2008
Milly Buonanno, Sapienza University, Rome

Introduction

Italian Media between the Local and the Global

Chiara Ferrari and Michela Ardizzoni

On May 28, 2008 the Italian government withdrew the amendment "Salva Rete 4" (Save Rete 4) from the legislative decree on digital broadcasting in Italy. This political move aimed at complying with the decision of the European Court of Justice, which, in January 2008, found Italy's system for allocating radio frequencies for television broadcasting in violation of EU law on communications.[1] The controversy over "Salva Rete 4" concerned the impossibility for channel Centro Europa 7 to broadcast on terrestrial analog frequencies, a right they legitimately earned in 1999 defeating Mediaset's Rete 4 in the competition. As a result, Rete 4 was supposed to switch its programming to digital transmission. Although the case has been brought to the attention of the EU, nine years after the decision in favor of Centro Europa 7, Rete 4 is still officially broadcasting on those terrestrial frequencies (the only ones available) and Centro Europa 7 is still struggling to go on the air. This situation has been possible because of the aforementioned "Salva Rete 4" amendment, which guaranteed Mediaset's channel its right to broadcasting "until found guilty of violating laws on digital technology and transmission."[2] The amendment was signed in December 2003 by Italy's Prime Minister Silvio Berlusconi, owner of Mediaset.

This brief description of a contemporary controversy in the Italia media landscape sheds light on numerous aspects of Italian communications: the close control of the State over Italian media; the anomaly of a Prime Minister who owns three of the seven television channels that broadcast nationally (Canale 5 and Italia 1, in addition to Rete 4); the difficulties of Italian media to embrace digital technology; and the uncomfortable role that Italy plays in the EU for its lack of clear laws against media monopoly. More generally, this example shows some of the struggles Italy has been facing in its attempt to embrace media globalization, while maintaining control over its national media industry.

Current trends of globalization have influenced the social, economic, and political framework of national media worldwide. In recent years, the field of media studies has focused on globalization as a phenomenon that has greatly impacted the production and reception of media formats. By reshaping local economies, diversifying societies, and introducing digital technologies, the globalization of media has enacted a process of re-definition of national and local broadcasting. This book examines the impact of globalization on contemporary Italian media. By engaging both the production and reception levels of different media, this anthology assesses the extent to which Italian media have been part of current trends of media flows and have responded to the centrifugal and centripetal forces of globalization. More specifically, the contributors to this edited volume touch upon issues as diverse as foreign ownership on satellite TV; the effects of digital technology on media policy making; the impact of guerrilla media channels against the thread of globalization; the impact of new media on local administrations; the analysis of international flows in media import, translation, and reformatting; the expansion of Italian public television in foreign markets; the representation of immigrants and immigration in contemporary Italian cinema; and the framing of "Otherness" in the news. These topics depict Italy as the scenery for multiple media outlets and suggest pluralism among the various channels of information offered to the Italian people. Conversely, and as the opening anecdote reveals, Italian media is characterized by an unusual concentration of power and control in the media (and political) sector. While this anthology explores diverse environments in the Italian media landscape, something needs to be clarified about Italy as the cradle of one of the most centralized empires in the hands of one single media mogul: Silvio Berlusconi.

Since the deregulation of the Italian broadcasting system in the late 1970s and early 1980s, it is difficult to discuss Italian media without mentioning Silvio Berlusconi and his media empire. The history of Italian television is one of a symbiotic relation between the media sector and the State or, more accurately, a relation between media and politics. Since the foundation in 1944 of the public broadcaster RAI—which was given exclusive broadcast rights in 1945 (but did not begin actual broadcasting until 1954)—television in Italy has been characterized and shaped by close governmental control.[3] In the two decades following the end of World War I, the main forces in the Italian political system, especially the Christian Democratic Party, made great use of national broadcasting for propaganda and established RAI as an official vehicle for ideological and political commentary. In that environment, the Italian Constitutional Court officially approved state monopoly for broadcasting in 1960, but also—paradoxically—expressed a desire for diversity. As a consequence of this tension, RAI 2 was founded in 1961 and added to the network's schedule of programming, which, until then, had only broadcast through its chief channel RAI 1. RAI 2 provided at first such diversity, by offering other political views and approaches. Nonetheless, since political monopoly ultimately continued and the Christian Democratic Party went on exerting its power through both of the national networks, in 1975 a specific commission created by the Parliament started to oversee RAI to assure political "pluralism" and "diversity."

It was only with the general deregulation in the European broadcasting system, however, that Italian media could finally breathe some fresh air through private cable TV and radio. Starting in 1976, at least thirty-five private television stations and about 150 private radio stations began to broadcast without a license. On the one hand this dynamics created confusion as well as a decrease in the quality of programming. On the other hand the situation suggested that diversity had always been lacking in the Italian broadcasting arena. The strong ties that the various political parties had developed with RAI were somehow "loosened" and RAI passed under parliamentary control, as opposed to governmental control. In this environment, Berlusconi entered the communication arena in 1980, by setting up his chief channel Canale 5, and soon began to establish his influence in the media sector by adding other media outlets (soon incorporating two additional channels, Italia 1 and Rete 4) and creating his Mediaset Group, which was officially founded in 1993, although it was not offered publicly on the board of trade until 1996.[4]

Since the 1990s Berlusconi's influence in Italian broadcasting and communication system in general has increased exponentially—including the ownership of the publishing company Mondadori and the film distribution company Medusa (part of his financial enterprise Fininvest).[5] This influence has also been translated into a stronger political role. Berlusconi, in fact, was elected Prime Minister of Italy in 1994, but his mandate only lasted nine months and he resigned at the end of the same year. In 2001, however, Berlusconi was re-elected, and this time he held power until 2006, when Romano Prodi, leader of the democratic opposition, became the new Prime Minister. However, after only two years of Prodi's leadership, as a result of a governmental crisis Berlusconi was re-elected in April 2008, starting his current and third mandate as Prime Minister.

Given the duopolistic nature of Italian television (RAI and Mediaset), considering the direct influence of the State (i.e. the Prime Minister) on the RAI administration, and bearing in mind that Berlusconi owns the Mediaset Group, the Italian media landscape reached, under Berlusconi's government, an unprecedented level of political control over media, not only in Italy, but also in any major Western democracy.[6] Such control over information was estimated to be close to 90% of all the information available to the Italian population, creating a situation that was brought to the attention of the EU because seriously threatening Italian democracy.[7]

Endless pages have been written and animated debates have been organized in Italy to discuss the evident "conflict of interest" implicit in Berlusconi's dual role in Italian society as both state leader and media mogul. Certainly Berlusconi represents a model for the study of contemporary trends of media globalization, because he exemplifies many, if not all, of the characteristics of corporate media capital. First of all, Mediaset and Fininvest represent a monopolistic concentration of multiple media products and outlets. Second, due to his centralized power in media, politics, and economics Berlusconi has awakened the interest (and the fears) of the EU, bringing a national case to the attention of a supra-national organization. Third, many alternative and local media manifestations in Italy have risen as a way to contrast Berlusconi's corporate media empire, including the use of both guerrilla broadcast media and new media. Finally, Berlusconi has facilitated, since the 1980s, the introduction of commercial television in Italy—the so-called Neotelevisione—characterized by high importation of American programs (at the level of media flows) and by an increasing embrace of "American" genres and narratives (at the level of media production).

These premises should provide a brief, yet precise overview of the dynamics of contemporary Italian media at the turn of the twenty-first century. While inevitably touching upon aspects of Berlusconi's empire, this book offers a collection of essays that explores contemporary Italian media in a wider variety of forms and perspectives. Unconventional media outlets include Web radios and Web TVs developed to provide alternative sources of information, and neighborhood television stations that have recently engaged in a type of local guerrilla broadcasting. As some of the essays will highlight, under the umbrella of Berlusconi's control over Italian media and politics lie parallel and even alternative forces that have shaped the Italian mediascape in its encounter with globalization.

Considering the contemporary scholarship that has discussed globalization beyond purely political economic terms, this collection considers the multiple aspects of international media flows and problematizes the idea of globalization as an inevitably and exclusively homogenizing force. In particular, this book moves away from the Neo-Marxist paradigm of cultural imperialism (Schiller, 1989 and 1991; Tomlinson 1991) that has considered international media flows exclusively in terms of cultural domination, to embrace current theories of globalization that have challenged this paradigm. Such theories include Joseph Straubhaar's idea of "cultural proximity" (1991); Marjorie

Ferguson's criticism of the myths of globalization (1992); Albert Moran's discussion of global media formats (1998); Milly Buonanno's theorization of the "paradigm of indigenization" (1999); Nancy Morris and Silvio Waisbord's discussion about media and globalization in relation to the State; and Timothy Havens' examination of media import/export in international markets (2006). These theories share the vision that the relation between media and globalization happens on multiple levels and many are the negotiations at play when national media industries import, produce, and sell media products for both global and local audiences.

In this respect, the Italian media landscape represents a particularly attractive case study to discuss the impact of globalization on contemporary media industries, as it offers multiple layers for cultural negotiations: not only does the anthology present the national as a vehicle to challenge the global, but it also examines the global embrace of local and regional elements that are fundamental aspects of Italian identity. In current discussions of media and nationality this approach is of particular interest as the notion of a unified concept of "the nation" has been recently criticized on various fronts as unable to address the multifaceted nature of single countries that increasingly include multi-ethnic and multi-racial communities within their national borders. Italy with its fervent regionalism and strong local manifestations of identity—but also with its increasing number of foreign immigrants—provides an insightful model to map and deconstruct the forces of globalization in national media markets, beyond national lines.

BOOK STRUCTURE AND ORGANIZATION

As we argued above, the Italian mediascape provides a complex and compelling example of the multiform shapes that media globalization can take in a Western context at the turn of the twenty-first century. While Italian media industries are booming, changing, and challenging audiences, the existing Anglophone literature on the subject is scarce. This volume aims at filling this gap by providing a collection of essays that engage with the most recent changes and trends in Italian media. As the reader will notice, several chapters discuss different aspects of television as the most popular medium in Italy and the one most easily influenced by globalization patterns. The attempt has been to provide a balanced anthology that embraces all important aspects of this national media context, hence the inclusion of analyses of contemporary cinema, alternative media, and online media. Yet, the emphasis placed on television in contemporary Italian media studies is reflected in the numerous essays included in this volume and is certainly indicative of a market that still considers traditional television making (and television viewing) as the pivotal force around which other media industries rotate. Clearly, like all edited volumes, our work does not claim to be comprehensive and exhaustive; its aim is rather to engage the reader with a selective series of critical essays that problematize the possible relationships between media and globalization in a national, ever-changing context.

In terms of its content, this book is divided into four sections. Part I, Globalization, Policy, and Technology, deals with the impact of new technologies and expanded borders upon the Italian television industry. In particular, Alessandro D'Arma's chapter analyzes the case of digital television to unravel the existence of two parallel trends in contemporary media: the intertwining of national media and political elites, and the tendency for domestic media to be controlled by private interests with close political ties. The timely and fascinating theme of digitization in the Italian television industry is further investigated by Cinzia Padovani, whose focus on the public debate about the so-called digital revolution asks important questions about the future of public-service broadcasting: will indeed the move to digital allow for more voices to be heard? As suggested by the incident of Rete 4 mentioned at the beginning of this introduction, the Italian public sphere in its mediatized form is still heavily subjected to the pulls of corporatization and concentration. Mark Hayward's study moves beyond the Italian national borders to examine the obstacles faced by RAI International in its attempt to penetrate the Canadian television market. This conflict shows how narratives about the relationship between state regulation, cultural identity understood as "ethnicity," and transnational communication networks are used to explain and justify the actions of cultural producers and the rights and needs of citizens.

Part II, Television Flows and Re-Formatting, discusses the industry of television formats and its adaptation in the Italian context. As a staple feature of most TV industries worldwide, global formats reveal the workings of current media trends and question issues of national, local, and global identities in a variety of forms. The first chapter in this section looks at the industry of formats and how it operates vis-à-vis (and within) Italian television. Here, Flavia Barca and Andrea Marzulli analyze the impact of both imported formats and imported final products on the programming of the major Italian broadcasters and, thus, evaluate the capacity of the Italian television industry to satisfy the domestic demand for programs across diverse genres and programming strategies. The three remaining essays in this section look more closely at specific programs of foreign origin and their adaptation for the Italian market. In particular, Elisa Giomi's study of the domestic drama *La Piovra*—a popular series on Mafia culture—allows for the exploration of the ways in which Italian crime drama has changed as a result of the influence of U.S.

programs. Through the process of transculturation, this program gradually incorporated U.S. crime series conventions, decontextualizing, reconfiguring and recontextualizing them in a way that they could appeal to the national audience. A similar process of adaptation is the one examined by Chiara Ferrari. Her chapter focuses on the translation and dubbing of the U.S. series *The Simpsons* in the process of "indigenization" of the text, in particular through the use of accents and regional expressions to identify the secondary characters of the show, re-territorializing them within the Italian context. What is particularly important, in this case, is the fact that the translation of *The Simpsons* in Italy highlights the lack of representation of Otherness on Italian television. Many of the characters portrayed as "Others" in the original U.S. version, in fact, lose their most genuine elements of Otherness by being re-inscribed within an Italian regional framework of reference that erases racial, ethnic, and national differences. As Part IV of this volume highlights, Italian media at large present evident struggles in how to deal with the Other. The last piece in section two draws a comparative analysis of one global format—*Survivor*—and its adaptation in three national contexts (Sweden, the United States, and Italy). Marta Perrotta's aesthetic and narrative analysis points to important cultural differences in the adaptation process of this format and paves the way for more cross-cultural studies of global formats.

Part III, New and Alternative Media, considers an aspect of Italian media that is rarely discussed in academic analyses: the emergence of non-traditional media, which can be read as a direct outcome of technological developments, as an attempt to counteract the overbearing monopoly of mainstream media, and as a need for more diversified voices to be heard. The chapters in this section address all these themes in their very different analyses. Chiara Valentini and Giorgia Nesti focus on the ways in which Italian municipalities use new technologies as a new medium to interact with citizens. Specifically, their study analyzes several Italian e-democracy projects, developed and implemented at local levels, in order to understand the impact of those projects in terms of restructuring and enhancing relationships between local administrations and its citizens. The democratic(izing) potential of alternative media is at the heart of Michela Ardizzoni's piece on the phenomenon of street television in Italy. The Telestreet project engages with an innovative social use of communication technologies: the traditional broadcasting approach of mainstream television networks is replaced by a process of narrowcasting that uses networked media to target selected groups and deal with local issues. Of particular interest for this collection is the convergence of old and new media that finds a very innovative expression in the Telestreet project. The last chapter in this section focuses the proliferation of web TVs and web radios in the Italian market. In their study, Lorenzo Mizzau, Federico Riboldazzi, and Fabrizio Montanari argue that both Italian web radios and web TVs are developing according to glocal patterns, whereby their success and popularity are tied to their coverage of local issues. As evidenced in this analysis, the global nature of a medium like the Internet is often counterpoised by the localized uses of some of its features.

The final part of the book, Immigration and Diversity, examines how Italian media have responded to the demographic and cultural changes that have characterized Italy in the past thirty years. Since the late 1970s, Italy has witnessed a steady increase in the number of immigrants from the East and South of the world. In an almost-overnight shift, Italy has thus changed from being a country of emigration to becoming a final immigration destination. Clearly, this ontological—but also economic and cultural—shift was received in different ways by the Italian society and the media. The chapters in this section deal with the multifarious responses to immigration and the construction of the Other. Cristian Vaccari's study looks at the institutional and political reaction to immigration. In particular, this chapter analyzes the 2003 debate on voting rights for immigrants and uncovers how print and broadcast news media covered the event. A similar focus on news making is shared by Rinella Cere's essay, which examines how immigrant groups have been portrayed in the news after September 11, 2001. Her focus is mostly on Muslim migrants—clearly the main targets after 9/11—but her study reveals how the same negative treatments are often extended to other minority groups as well. The concluding chapter by Alberto Zambenedetti provides a comprehensive look at contemporary Italian cinema, by examining how multiculturalism, immigration, and Otherness have been incorporated in recent Italian feature films. The several case studies included in this chapter reveal how contemporary Italian filmmakers have interpreted and expressed the need for a new representation of Italianness on the silver screen.

Once again, these discussions present the Italian mediascape as an arena for the interaction of diverse and multi-faceted aspects of media communications. This anthology, then, offers evidence of the complex balance between global, national, regional, and local content, between State monopoly and alternative media forces, between national and foreign production, between old and new media, and provides various case studies that shed light on current trends of globalization in contemporary media markets.

NOTES

1. Information about the Italian government's decision are available in English from CNBC online: http://www.cnbc.com/id/24868342/for/cnbc.

2. Information on the amendment and its initial approval are available from *La Repubblica* online: http://www.repubblica.it/2003/l/sezioni/politica/gasparri4/decre1/decre1.html.

3. Giovanni Bechelloni, "Italy." *The Museum of Broadcasting Communications.* Available from: http://www.museum.tv/archives/etv/I/htmlI/italy/italy.htm.

4. Information available from the Mediaset Corporate Group website: http://www.mediaset.it/corporate/chisiamo/storia_en.shtml.

5. Corporate information about Fininvest are available from: http://www.fininvest.com/_eng/indexeng.shtml.

6. Brian Barron, "Berlusconi: The Billion-dollar Question." *BBC News*, May 14, 2001. Available from: http://news.bbc.co.uk/1/hi/world/europe/1325466.stm.

7. Berlusconi's "dictatorial approach" towards the media in the years of his mandate as prime minister caused many of the most respected journalists and entertainers at RAI to be fired in a matter of days. In the sadly famous speech he addressed from Sofia in 2002, Berlusconi accused journalists Enzo Biagi, Michele Santoro, and Daniele Luttazzi of making a "criminal use of TV" when questioning Berlusconi's rise to politics, and they lost their jobs shortly after and were able to be back on the air only after Romano Prodi's victory in the 2006 elections for prime minister.

Part One
GLOBALIZATION, POLICY, AND TECHNOLOGY

Chapter One

Shaping Tomorrow's Television: Policies on Digital Television in Italy, 1996–2006

Alessandro D'Arma

INTRODUCTION

The story of digital television policies in Italy provides an interesting case-study to examine the interplay between domestic political dynamics and wider globalization processes in contemporary broadcasting policy-making. In particular, it serves well the purpose to illustrate certain constraints that national governments of advanced capitalist countries have faced in the context of broadcasting policy as well as some of the key strategic resources that they have deployed in order to maintain their control over the sector amid globalization processes.

In recent years, a body of literature has emerged that addresses these issues (e.g., Skogerbø 1996; Levy 1997a and 1999; Curran and Park 2000; Galperin 2000 and 2004; Morris and Waisbord 2001; Corcoran 2002; Ward 2002; Harcourt 2002 and 2005; Chada and Kavoori 2005). This growing academic interest reflects developments in the real world. Over the last twenty years national broadcasting policy-making has become increasingly exposed to the influence of non-domestic actors primarily as a result of technological change and the ideological shift toward neo-liberal policies. A general trend toward the marketization of national broadcasting systems has been widely detected and typically associated with globalization processes (Murdock and Golding 1999; Murdock 2000; Chada and Kavoori 2005). However, it is also the case, as it is generally acknowledged, that broadcasting policy remains deeply embroiled in national politics. National broadcasting systems are still primarily shaped by domestic political dynamics. David Levy has explained the limited impact of the European Union (EU) on the broadcasting reform processes undertaken in France, Germany, and the UK in the second half of the 1990s by referring "to the strong, national institutional structures and intense politicization that characterize the broadcasting sector" (Levy 1997a: 24), the latter in turn being a consequence of the "intense interest that politicians take in the cultural, political and—increasingly economic—impact of television" (Ibid.: 38).

This chapter purports to make a contribution to this debate. It provides an examination of how successive Italian governments have attempted to shape the structure of the emerging domestic digital television market by regulatory and other policy means. It first discusses developments in the area of digital satellite pay-TV in the second half of the 1990s, and recounts the failed attempt by the center left government to engineer the creation of the "single national platform" (1996–1998). Next, the chapter looks at the pro-active policies toward Digital Terrestrial Television (DTT) pursued by the Berlusconi's center-right government in the 14th Legislature (2001–2006), and the underlying agenda informing this policy.

DIGITAL SATELLITE PAY-TV: FROM THE "SINGLE NATIONAL PLATFORM" TO MURDOCH'S SKY ITALIA

In the majority of Western European countries, satellite television was the main door through which foreign operators entered the hitherto closed national markets. The borderless nature of satellite broadcasting made the new sector seemingly hardly amenable to the control of national governments pursuing protectionist policies (a textbook illustration of this being Murdoch's entry of the British television market in 1989). In the 1990s satellite television developed in most European countries as a multi-channel pay-TV service. This is perhaps even more important to explain the role of foreign operators. The large costs associated with the setting up of a digital pay-TV platform— involving leasing satellite capacity, setting up and managing conditional access systems, marketing new services, acquiring key programming rights, etc.—and uncertain consumer demand in the start-up phase meant that possibly only large multinational corporations could afford the risk of diversifying into this area (Humphreys and Lang 1998). In the mid-1990s, digital satellite pay-TV became the arena for frantic maneuvering among major multinational media groups—the likes of Kirch, Canal Plus, Bertelsmann, and News Corporation, each aiming to gain control of as many national markets as possible in the initial rolling-out phase (Olivi and Somalvico 1997: 325-386).

From a regulatory standpoint, the launch of digital satellite pay-TV services across Western Europe raised novel competition concerns, more akin to telecommunications regulatory concerns than to traditional broadcasting ones (Levy 1999: 126; Michalis 2002: 91; Galperin 2004: 139). Chief among these were concerns about monopolistic access to key bottleneck facilities associated with the new digital pay-TV business model, namely proprietary control of the gateway technologies embedded in the digital set-top-box (conditional access systems, application program interfaces, and accompanying electronic program guides), and exclusive access to premium content (major national sport events and Hollywood blockbusters) (see Cave 1997; Cawley 1997; Nolan 1997).

The European Commission (EC) was ready to address these policy concerns. In 1995, it adopted a Directive on Advanced TV Standard, whose stated policy objective was to establish a single market for digital TV services (Levy 1997b and 1999; Di Mauro 2006). The single market, however, did not materialize, primarily because, in the face of the opposition of established analogue pay-TV operators like Canal Plus and BKSyB, the Directive did not mandate common standards for conditional access systems. Rather than through a sector-specific regulatory initiative, therefore, it was through the application of EU general competition law (notably EU merger rules) that the EC managed to shape in a lasting manner the structure of the emerging digital satellite pay-TV markets of its member states. As recounted by several authors (e.g., McCallum 1999; Levy 1999: 86–95; Harcourt 2005: 41–61), between 1994 and 1999, the EC Competition Directorate, under the directorship of a determined commissioner (Karel Van Miert), took what has been described as an uncompromising stance toward proposed mergers and alliances in the digital pay-TV sector. In a number of decisions, most notably the two "MSG" cases in Germany in 1994 and 1998, the EC rejected deals which would have led to the creation of joint-ventures between national media and telecoms operators for the handling of the technical and business requirements for pay-TV digital platforms. The EC's rejection was motivated on the ground that, if implemented, such mergers would have entailed the joining of forces among players who were already dominant either in the upstream (content) or downstream (transmission) phase of the television supply chain, with detrimental effects on competition.

It is against the backdrop of these European-wide market and policy developments that back in 1996 the incoming Italian center-left government led by Romano Prodi embarked on an industrial policy effort motivated by concerns over both cultural sovereignty and national economic competitiveness. At around that time, the government started sponsoring the creation of what in the contemporary Italian political debate soon became known as the "single national platform." The government wanted the 'single platform' to be majority-owned by Italian companies. It envisaged that Telecom Italia, the then publicly owned monopolist provider of telecoms services, and RAI, the public service broadcaster, joined forces with Telepiù—the existing analogue pay-TV operator which at that time was about to fall under the control of French pay-TV group, Canal Plus—to manage the technical infrastructure through which pay-TV services and the future interactive services of the "Information Society" would transit. From the beginning, however, the debate over the "digital platform" in Italy was characterized by an underlying ambiguity. While it was clear that the government-backed new venture would handle technical aspects, including transmission and conditional access systems, it was much less clear whether the business and administrative requirements for pay-TV also fell under the definition of the single platform. As we will see, this was by no means a trifling issue from the standpoint of the EC Competition Directorate.

The attention that the center-left government began to give to the digital pay-TV platform toward the end of 1996 was, at least partly, a response to the industry's call for action. By the end of 1996, Canal Plus, Telecom Italia, and RAI had all come to look at the single digital platform as the best available option. The modest progress of Telepiù's satellite pay-TV services launched in September of 1996 prompted Canal Plus to search for an alliance with Italian partners. Telecom Italia and RAI, for their part, were keen to play a leading role in the development of the national digital pay-TV market but, at the same time, hesitated because of the large investments required (Menduni 1999).

Irrespective of the industry's call for action, the center-left government saw the single national platform very favorably. Influenced by the contemporary hype in European business and policy circles over the "information digital revolution," the incoming government saw the future of the digital TV industry as crucial for the national interest, both from an industrial and cultural perspective. Negotiations over the single digital platform started as early as the beginning of 1997 and went on for well over a year and a half. Throughout this period, the center-left government acted as a facilitator trying to restart negotiations every time they seemed to come to a standstill. Furthermore, in June 1997, the parliamentary majority succeeded in passing a government amendment to the new communications bill allowing Telecom Italia and RAI, which under the current legislation were banned from providing pay-TV services, to participate in the single digital platform.

A number of factors, however, eventually militated against the realization of the venture. Beyond the disagreement among the parties involved in the negotiations over the details of the operation—Canal Plus being reluctant to leave the majority control of Telepiù to its Italian partners—the main constraining factor was represented by the firm opposition to the project from both the national Competition Authority (AGCM) and the EC. While the new communications bill was still debated in Parliament, AGCM submitted a negative advisory opinion on the government amendment on the "single digital platform." Its rejection was motivated by the fact that the agreement for a single digital platform involving Canal Plus, Telecom Italia, and RAI, if implemented, "would cover not only technological aspects [something which was deemed acceptable from a competition perspective], but also organizational and commercial ones, as the collective management of clients and television programming" (AGCM Press Release, July 10, 1997). It is worth noting that since its establishment in 1990 AGCM had distinguished itself as a resolute free-market advocate and supporter of EC's liberalization policies across industrial and service sectors.

Notwithstanding AGCM's negative advisory opinion, the parliamentary majority and the government decided to go ahead with their plans. The communications bill became law in July 1997 with the inclusion of the single digital platform provision (Law 249/1997). After the passage of the law, the industry players proceeded with their negotiations with the backing of the center-left government, convinced that they could alleviate AGCM's competition concerns by committing themselves to a number of undertakings to be added to the final agreement. In the winter of 1997, the national single platform envisaged by the government seemed very close to materializing. Telecom Italia, RAI, and Telepiù, now together with Berlusconi's Mediaset and Italian film producer Cecchi Gori, signed a preliminary agreement. In line with the preferences expressed by the government, the majority-control of the single platform was left to national companies.

In a fatal blow to the prospect for the single platform, however, in March 1998, shortly after the preliminary agreement was signed, the EC Competition Directorate decided to intervene in the Italian affairs. It did so by sending an informal letter to Italy in which it broadly reiterated the objections on competition grounds raised by AGCM a few months earlier (the content of the letter is reported in EC 1999: 44). From the standpoint of European and national competition authorities, it was clear that the problem with the single national platform was that the proposed venture covered not only technological but also commercial aspects (Marra 1998: 925–926). The EC's warning against the single platform put virtually the final word to the negotiations. Unlike in Germany, where digital ventures similar to the one planned in Italy, had been vetoed by the EC through formal decisions, in Italy an informal letter sent by Commissioner Van Miert to the Italian government was sufficient to block the negotiations, already complicated by the lack of agreement among the interested parties.

In the summer of 1998, then, events took an abrupt turn. It was leaked in the press that News Corporation, Rupert Murdoch's media conglomerate was entering the fray and starting negotiations with Telecom Italia to take over Stream—the group's cable and satellite platform which had been operating on an experimental basis since mid-1996. Shortly after, it emerged that News Corporation was prepared to go for the highest bidder to acquire exclusive rights to all the Serie A soccer matches for a six-year period. The announcement of Murdoch's bid sparked a worried reaction from the government. Murdoch was seen by the center-left as the main agent of Italy's "industrial and cultural colonization." At the beginning of 1999, when Murdoch seemed close to finalizing the deal with Telecom Italia to acquire 80 percent of Stream, the center-left government adopted a decree-law on the mandatory sharing of the pay-TV football rights between Stream and Telepiù. This measure was seen by most observers as being clearly targeted against Murdoch.

If the objective was to curb Murdoch's ambitions in the Italian pay-TV market, however, the new regulation definitely missed its target. By mid-1999, the structure of the emerging Italian digital satellite pay-TV industry took a very different shape from what was envisaged by the center-left government. Rather than a single platform, two rival platforms were now operational. More importantly, the role played by Italian companies was not the leading one which the government had hoped for. The center-left policy in support of its 'national champions' (Telecom Italia and RAI) had found its way blocked by the EC as well as by the business strategies of Canal Plus and News Corporation. In December 1998, RAI signed an agreement with Canal Plus to take one percent stake in Telepiù. RAI committed itself to pool together a group of Italian investors to take over another 35 percent of Telepiù. Advanced negotiations were undertaken with the Italian energy group, ENEL, but no final agreement was ever reached (Menduni 2002: 174). Canal Plus was thus left with the full control of Telepiù. Telecom Italia and News Corporation, on the other hand, eventually reached an agreement in May 1999 after a one-year long negotiation. Telecom Italia retained only 35 percent of the shares in Stream, dividing the rest between News Corporation (35 percent), Cecchi Gori (18 percent) and SDS, a new company created by four soccer clubs (12 percent). Just a year later, however, Cecchi Gori and SDS exited from Stream, which then remained under the joint control of its two 'strong' shareholders, News Corporation, and Telecom Italia. Recounting years later the role played by the government in the negotiations over the single digital platform, the then Communications Minister, Antonio Maccanico, bitterly commented: 'We introduced in the law certain provisions to ease the digital platform, which in our view had to be a single one. We made great efforts to reach an agreement between RAI, Telecom Italia and Canal Plus. [. . .] I thought it right to make an attempt at ensuring that Italian companies played a leading role. But then it ended up exactly as I had feared' (Maccanico 2001: 28).

After the failure of the single platform project, the story of digital satellite pay-TV in Italy became, quite characteristically in Western Europe, that of two companies, Telepiù and Stream, fiercely competing for the leadership in the market while struggling to balance the books. Between 1999 and 2001, both Telepiù and Stream managed to increase the number of subscribers and their revenues. However, neither ever managed to become profitable. In line with a European-wide trend, operating costs for both increased more than revenues. In Italy certain country-specific factors worsened the situation even further, most notably widespread piracy.

Eventually, in the spring of 2001, it emerged that Vivendi Universal—the parent company of Canal Plus—had reached an agreement with News Corporation to buy Stream. It took more than two years before the merger between the two platforms was finalized, on terms, however, diametrically opposed to those initially agreed upon. In a sudden swapping of roles, in June 2002, Murdoch became the buyer and Vivendi, which in the meantime had precipitated into a serious financial crisis, the seller. Meeting the turnover thresholds set in the EU Merger Regulation, the transaction was to be scrutinised by the EC (Baccaro 2003; Mendes Pereira 2003). In April 2003 the European Competition authorities gave the green light to the merger. This was a widely expected decision. Since 1999, after the series of negative decisions in the mid- to late-1990s, the EC Competition DG had made no prohibitions in the area of digital TV mergers. According to Alison Harcourt (2005: 57), this was most likely due to a combination of factors including the reluctance of the EC to intervene in digital pay-TV markets following the European-wide economic crisis of the sector; the adoption of the EC new regulatory framework for electronic communications which had widened the definitions of communications markets; and possibly, the more condescending approach of the new Commissioner who inherited the competition portfolio from Van Miert in 1999 (the Italian Mario Monti).

The merger between Telepiù and Stream under the aegis of News Corporation was implemented in July 2003, three months after the EC's decision. The combined platform was renamed Sky Italia. Notwithstanding the harsh conditions imposed on News Corporation by the EC upon approval of the merger and the problems with piracy, the prospect for Sky Italia as of mid-2003 looked bright. The new operator enjoyed a virtual monopoly over the provision of pay-TV services in Italy. With the exception of Fastweb providing video-on-demand services to a very tiny number of subscribers via fiber-optic networks in Northern Italy, no other company at that time was marketing pay-TV services to Italian viewers (Mendes Pereira 2003: 36).

Within the space of six years, the control of what had at first appeared to the center-left government a communication resource of national interest had entirely fallen in the hands of Rupert Murdoch.

DIGITAL TERRESTRIAL TELEVISION AND DOMESTIC POLITICAL AGENDAS

Arriving in office in May 2001, the center-right government led by Silvio Berlusconi adopted what appeared to be a rather cool stance toward the events unfolding at that time in the area of digital satellite pay-TV. By the beginning of the new century, much of the attention of Italian policy-makers had already shifted to another related front, namely Digital Terrestrial Television (DTT).

Italy was by no means alone in promoting DTT in the early years of the new millennium. By that time, in fact, most industrialized countries had put the development of this new technology high on their policy agenda. The original impetus for national DTT policies must be traced back to a number of initiatives promoted by the U.S. administration and the EU since the mid-1980s. Back at that time, EU policy-makers had started advocating a process of radical restructuring of the technological basis of the broadcasting industry, first through the support of analogue high definition television (HDTV) and then, shortly after, through the sponsoring of digital television standards. According to Hernan Galperin (2004: 25–52), three interrelated "political-economic forces" explain the activism of both the United States and the EU in this area since the mid-1980s. First, especially in the first phase, the digital transition was seen by Western governments as an opportunity to revitalize the declining domestic consumer electronic industry and promote related high-tech sectors. Later, in the early 1990s, digital TV became a key component of what Galperin calls the "information revolution agenda." Originated in the U.S. and then rapidly spread on the other side of the Atlantic, the information revolution agenda called governments "to sponsor the development of new communications and information technologies in order to secure long term economic growth and promote social inclusion" (Galperin 2004: 14). Finally, in the late 1990s, the promotion of the digital transition found a new important rationale in the radio spectrum shortage created by the exponential growth of mobile telecommunication services (Galperin 2004: 43–51). The transition to digital TV, and DTT in particular, appeared to offer a convenient solution to the problem of accommodating the growing demand for spectrum-dependent services. Thanks to the adoption of digital compression techniques allowing several programs to be transmitted over a single frequency channel, digital broadcasting generates significant economies in the use of the radio spectrum (Cave and Nakamura 2006: 9–12).

When this general policy agenda emanating from the EU began to be translated by member states into concrete regulatory initiatives for the introduction of DTT, however, it became clear that motives other than the ones associated with the international 'political-economic forces' identified by Galperin were in some cases much more influential in persuading national governments of the need to move rapidly in the introduction of DTT. These other motives varied from country to country as they reflected the particular history and structure of each country's national analogue television system. Generally, the main reason why several governments backed DTT was to promote terrestrial broadcasting as a means of television distribution and ensure that analogue national broadcasters would continue to play a prominent role in the digital era. As a resource unambiguously falling under the jurisdiction of national authorities, DTT was seen by Swedish policy-makers, for instance, as a means to reassert their authority over content regulation (Brown 2005). One of the key rationales for introducing DTT in Sweden was to bring "the regulation refugees" (satellite channels targeted at the Swedish viewers broadcasting from London so to escape stricter domestic licensing constraints) back to the terrestrial network under national regulatory control (Brown 2005: 208). In Britain, one of the key policy goals pursued by the government through the establishment of the regulatory framework for DTT in 1996 was to challenge Rupert Murdoch's dominance of the pay-TV industry by stimulating platform competition through DTT (Galperin 2004: 165; Goodwin 2005: 157).

In Italy too both the center-left and the center-right governments favored the introduction of DTT with largely domestic concerns in mind. DTT policies were formulated under the center-left government during the XIII Legislature (1996–2001). From the perspective of the center-left, DTT offered a unique opportunity to introduce competition in the terrestrial television sector dominated by Mediaset and RAI. However, the DTT regulatory framework, which was adopted through primary legislation by Parliament toward the end of the center-left government's tenure (Law 66/2001), appeared to be patently inadequate to open up new spaces for prospective entrants.

In order to explain the failure of the center-left DTT policies, consideration must be given to the fact that the introduction of DTT in Italy found in the saturation of the radio spectrum a major technical obstacle. Differently from the situation in other countries, in Italy no spare capacity that the government could allocate administratively to incumbent and/or new broadcasters to start DTT services was readily available. Channel occupancy was very close to spectrum saturation due to the proliferation of private stations during a fifteen-year period of complete a-regulation.

Early on, AGCom, the new communications regulator, took on a leading role in the formulation of the DTT policies. AGCom deemed the commitment of established national broadcasters necessary in order to successfully and rapidly introduce DTT given the large investments required and the major structural obstacles. National broadcasters, in return for their endorsement of the digital transition plan, demanded reassurances that the new technology would not be used to threaten their dominance over the terrestrial television sector. AGCom's proposals were unveiled in 2000 in a White Paper (AGCom 2000). The White Paper advocated a market-driven solution to the problem of how to liberate sufficient frequencies to start DTT. It proposed that frequencies for DTT services would be made available by encouraging small local broadcasters to free up frequencies through financial incentives and by using the excessive frequencies allegedly held by the major national broadcasters.

Unsurprisingly, this solution found support with national broadcasters. More surprisingly, given the coalition's objective, the center-left government also stood behind the White Paper's industry-backed proposals. With general elections due in mid-2001, and having failed to pass a comprehensive piece of legislation on broadcasting over the preceding three years, the government probably saw the passage into the statute book of the regulation on DTT as an accomplishment in the area of television policy. In keeping with AGCom's 2000 proposals, the legislation adopted in March 2001 introduced the so-called frequency trading mechanism as a market-driven solution to the "spectrum scarcity" problem. It was decided that the frequencies to be made available for DTT would either be the excessive ones managed by major national broadcasters—which they, but not other operators, were entitled to use for DTT—or the ones to be traded among broadcasters (hence the denomination "frequency trading"). There was little doubt that, because of their financial strength, RAI and Mediaset would take the lion's share in the "purchasing campaign" of the transmission networks of the many cash-stripped local broadcasters. Ultimately, the new regulatory framework adopted under the center-left government left incumbent broadcasters with effective control over the DTT network.

At the general elections of May 2001, just two months after the introduction of the DTT legislation, the center-right coalition won a landslide victory. The task of implementing the DTT regulatory framework was therefore left to the incoming center-right government led by Silvio Berlusconi. The new government championed the rapid take-up of DTT, like the center-left had done in the past legislature, but it did so with diametrically opposed goals. Unsurprisingly, the broadcasting policies of the Berlusconi government

(2001–2006) were largely driven by the needs of Mediaset. Rallying behind the business interest of its leader, the center-right government actively promoted the rapid introduction of DTT initially as a means to bypass the enforcement of the 1997 media ownership rules forcing Mediaset to migrate one of its three analogue terrestrial channels to satellite (Rete4).

In November 2002, the Italian Constitutional Court ruled that the 1997 broadcasting law was unconstitutional, as it had assigned to an administrative authority (AGCom) the task of fixing the date for the termination of the transitory period during which the enforcement of 1997 media ownership rules was put on hold. The 1997 legislation had required AGCom to enforce the media ownership rules when it deemed that the development of satellite and cable television in the country was "congruent." In July 2001, AGCom had ruled that the time for a move of Rete4 to satellite would be warranted when at least 50 percent of all television households were able to receive multi-channel television and predicted, rather unrealistically, December 31, 2003 as the relevant date for this to happen, however subject to a further reassessment in the course of 2003. If by end-2002 multi-channel penetration was still less than 35 percent, as it appeared likely, then AGCom could have decided to postpone further the deadline. The Constitutional Court ruled that Mediaset was to move Rete4 to satellite by the end of 2003, irrespective of cable and satellite penetration.

The center-right government was far too ready to cope with the new threat that the Constitutional Court's decision had posed to Mediaset. In an attempt to pre-empt the effects of the decision, the government submitted a new broadcasting bill to Parliament in the autumn of 2002. For one thing, the Gasparri Bill—from the name of the proponent Minister—established new ownership thresholds valid for the analogue-digital simulcast period. These rules were designed in such a way to allow Mediaset to keep its three analogue terrestrial channels well after the Constitutional Court's end-2003 deadline. Importantly, the Gasparri bill, as revised in a later version in the course of the legislative process, established as condition for Mediaset to be allowed to keep Rete4's analogue frequencies that DTT would became rapidly available to a large section of the Italian population at an affordable price. In order to ensure that this condition was met, the center-right government promptly undertook a number of initiatives designed to expedite the successful roll-out of DTT. In particular, it moved resolutely to tackle what was the major obstacle to a rapid and successful introduction of DTT, namely the high costs of receiver equipments. In the budget law for 2004, the government allocated a total of 130 million Euros to subsidize the household's purchase of DTT set-top-boxes. Italy was the first European country to agree upon direct economic incentives on the demand side to expedite the roll out of DTT.

Throughout 2003, while the government was committed to create favorable conditions for the successful roll-out of DTT through regulatory and other means, incumbent national broadcasters—most aggressively Mediaset—embarked on a major "purchasing campaign" of local transmission plants so to be able to set up their DTT multiplexes by the deadline set in the Gasparri Bill (end-2003). DTT services were eventually marketed starting in December 2003 in keeping with the schedule fixed by the Gasparri bill. As of May 2004 there were twenty free-to-air television channels over five multiplexes with coverage of the population ranging from 50 to 60 percent. In the meantime, the Gasparri Bill, after one of the most difficult passages through Parliament in the history of the Italian Republic, became law (Law 112/2004). Mediaset was now allowed to keep Rete4's analogue frequencies in compliance with national legislation.

MEDIASET AND SKY ITALIA UNDER THE BERLUSCONI GOVERNMENT

As has been argued, the Berlusconi government initially championed the rapid roll-out of DTT primarily as a means to bypass the enforcement of the 1997 media ownership rules forcing Mediaset to migrate one of its three analogue terrestrial channels to satellite. Once the position of Rete4 was legalised through the promulgation of the Gasparri Law in May 2004, DTT came to be seen by the center-right government as serving another strategic goal. Now DTT was seen as the technology through which national free-to-air terrestrial broadcasters (Mediaset in particular) could mount a challenge to Rupert Murdoch's dominance of the Italian pay-TV market.

Since its launch in July 2003, Sky Italia had made considerable progress. In particular, the pay-TV operator had acted effectively to eliminate the phenomenon of illegal viewing by replacing the old Telepiù encryption system with the more secure conditional access system of News Corporation's own subsidiary, NDS. Also, the number of Sky Italia's subscribers had been growing steadily. By mid-2004, in short, it had became clear that, if not in the short-, certainly in the medium-term, Sky Italia could represent, if unchallenged, a serious threat to the business of established analogue terrestrial broadcasters. Enjoying a virtual monopoly over the domestic pay-TV market and backed by a company as financially strong and managerially expert as News Corporation, Sky Italia benefited from the ideal conditions to become a viable business overcoming the structural obstacles that up to that moment had constrained the development of pay-TV in Italy.

Aware of this, Mediaset and the Berlusconi government mounted a concerted challenge to Murdoch's Sky Italia. In the summer of 2004, Mediaset acquired the rights to broadcast on the new DTT platform the league home matches of the three most popular national football teams for the following three seasons. Mediaset's raid into the pay-TV business was made possible by the undertakings undersigned by News Corporation in order to obtain the EC's clearance of the acquisition of Telepiù in April 2003. Among the others, News Corporation had agreed to waive its exclusivity rights for premium content (movies and football) on means of transmission other than satellite and to limit the duration of football rights to two years (Baccaro 2003). With great business acumen, as well as exploiting some favourable regulatory provisions granted by the center-right government allowing the provision of subscription television services on the DTT platform, at the beginning of 2005 Mediaset launched an innovative pre-paid card system, modeled on pre-paid mobile phones, allowing DTT users to buy cards one match at a time from as little as 3 Euros without the need to pay a monthly subscription fee.

In the meantime, in the autumn of 2004, shortly after Mediaset had announced the acquisition of the DTT football rights, the center-right government had made public its intention to confirm the subsidy for the DTT set-top-boxes for another year. Importantly, as in the previous year, Sky Italia's set-top-boxes were excluded by the subsidy. Bruised by Mediaset's raid into its own territory, Sky Italia had started lobbying the Italian center-right government to extend the subsidy to its set-top boxes. In May 2005, then, having failed to convince the government, Sky Italia filed a complaint to the EC against Italy on the ground that the subsidy was violating the EU-enshrined principle of technological neutrality and thus distorting competition in the television market. In December 2005, the EC opened a formal investigation procedure under the state aid regulation on the subsidies provided by Italian government in 2004 and 2005 (Santamato and Salto 2006). Such a defensive move on the part of Sky Italia coincided with the most difficult period in the satellite platform's short existence. The financial results of the last three months of 2004 were disappointing: Sky Italia had lost 105 million Euros—roughly the same as the year before. The prospect of the break even point appeared still distant. Also, the pay-per-view football offer launched by Mediaset through DTT in January 2005 proved to be a hit. More than 500,000 cards were sold in the first month.

However, in spite of the Mediaset's successful raid into the pay-TV business, by the time Berlusconi was ousted from office (April 2006), Sky Italia had managed to overcome its problems and had become the first company in Italy to make money out of pay-TV. In the financial year ending in June 2006,

Sky Italia reported an annual operating profit of 32 million Euros. News Corporation's latest annual report made bullish forecasts about Sky Italia's future contribution to its parent company, estimating profits conservatively in the region of hundreds of millions of Euros in coming years (News Corporation 2006: 9).

As of mid-2006, therefore, two conclusions appeared inescapable. First, News Corporation had now become a key actor in the Italian television market, and, in turn, Italy an important province of Murdoch's global media empire. At the end of 2006 Sky Italia saw its subscriber base pass the four million mark (slightly less than 20 percent of the total number of Italian television households). Sky Italia's share of overall television revenues in Italy had reached 21.1 percent in 2006 (from 17.7 percent in 2005) (AGCom 2006: 78). In turn, Sky Italia now accounted for 10 percent of News Corporation's worldwide consolidated revenues (News Corporation 2006: 48).

The second conclusion is that by mid-2006 the medium-term business prospects of national free-to-air broadcasters, and Mediaset in particular, appeared good, despite Sky Italia's successful entry into the market. Sky Italia's near-monopoly over Italian pay-TV was now clearly something of the past. According to a recent estimate, over 3 million DTT pay-per-view cards had been sold by the end of 2006. The number of owners of DTT pay-per-view cards were expected to reach the number of Sky Italia's subscribers by the end of 2008 (cited in Key4biz 6.2.2007). Mediaset now accounted for 10 percent of the subscription revenues in the Italian pay-TV market, according to figures released by its Chairman (cited in Key4biz 8.3.2007). This represented certainly a minority but by no means a marginal share of the market.

The role of the center-right government in shaping this outcome was key. Most notably through the use of substantial public money to expedite the digital transition, the government had managed to make DTT a successful proposition. In relation to the transition to DTT in the UK and the U.S. Galperin has argued that national governments of these two countries have had "considerable autonomy to shape the transition in consonance with domestic policy agendas and protect established arrangements in the communications sector" (2004: 284). Certainly, this argument also appears to hold true when applied to Italy.

In January 2007, the EC notified its decision concerning the DTT subsidies granted by the Italian government in 2004 and 2005. The EC argued that as a result of the introduction of the subsidy scheme competition in the Italian TV market had been distorted, particularly in the pay-TV market. The subsidies violated the principle of technological neutrality and were therefore illegal under EU state-aid regulation. The broadcasters who had benefited most from the subsidies (i.e., those who provide pay-TV services via DTT, notably

Mediaset) were required to reimburse the state aid. Shortly after, Mediaset announced its intention to appeal against the ruling. Whatever the outcome of this complaint, it is clear that, as an ex-post remedy, the reimbursement that Mediaset and other operators are obliged to make is unlikely to substantially alter by themselves the position that in the meantime these operators have gained in the national pay-TV market.

CONCLUSION

This chapter has examined the dynamics that have shaped the structure of the Italian digital television market in the last ten years. The analysis has illustrated how Italian governments have continued to play a key role in shaping overall market dynamics in the broadcasting industry, primarily through the regulation of the terrestrial sector which has compensated for the partial loss of authority experienced by national policy-makers following the launch of digital satellite pay-TV services in the country in the second half of the 1990s.

In this area, the industrial and cultural policy ambitions of the center-left governments were frustrated by the EC threatening to enforce competition law to veto the government-sponsored "single national platform." Eventual market outcomes—Murdoch emerging in 2003 as the monopolistic provider of satellite pay-TV services in the country—ran obviously counter to the preferences of the center-left. In the following legislature (2001–2006), the center-right government led by Silvio Berlusconi managed successfully, albeit highly controversially, to promote a technology more amenable to national regulation like DTT in order to protect established arrangements, namely Mediaset's dominant position in the national television market. Initially, DTT offered a convenient means for the center-right government to bypass a Constitutional Court's decision forcing Mediaset to transfer one of its three analogue television channels to satellite by the end of 2003. After having secured the future of Rete4 through the enactment of new legislation, the center-right government continued to promote DTT heavily. Now DTT was seen as a means through which Mediaset could mount a successful challenge to Sky Italia, by entering the pay-TV business and thus adjust to European-wide trends in the economics of the television industry, namely, the saturation of the advertising market and the growth of revenues from direct payment. In the process, the center-right government made choices which were discriminatory against Sky Italia and contravened EU's state aid regulation.

In Italy, similarly to what has happened in other industrialized countries, the introduction of digital television from the mid-1990s onwards has prompted a process of industrial restructuring which has challenged established market and regulatory arrangements. Due to certain technological and economic characteristics associated with digital broadcasting, this process of industrial restructuring has created opportunities for non-domestic actors. News Corporation successfully entered the Italian market. There is also evidence of the EU exerting a greater influence on national policy agendas and outcomes. However, the analysis has also showed that the Berlusconi government had much room for maneuver to shape the transition to digital television in consonance with its policy agendas. The center-right successfully used DTT as a means to protect vested economic interests that long since have opposed any real democratization of access to the broadcasting infrastructure in the country, subordinating general industrial and socio-cultural policy goals associated with the transition to digital television to personal economic interests.

REFERENCES

AGCom. "Libro Bianco sulla Televisione Digitale Terrestre." 2000. http://www.AGCom.it/provv/libro_b_00/librobianco00.htm (accessed October 30, 2006).

AGCom. "Relazione Annuale sull'Attività Svolta e sui Programmi di Lavoro." 2006. http://www.agcom.it/rel_01/index.htm (accessed February 27, 2006).

Baccaro, Vincenzo. "The Commission Closes Probe into Pay-TV Industry in Italy Approving Newscorp/Telepiù Merger Deal." *Competition Policy Newsletter*, no 2 (2003): 8–11.

Brown, Allan. "Sweden: The Digital Threat to Cultural Sovereignty." Pp. 203–221 in *Digital Terrestrial Television in Europe*, edited by Allan Brown and Robert G. Picard. New Jersey: Lawrence Erlbaum Associates, 2005a.

Cave, Martin. "Regulating Digital Television in a Convergent World." *Telecommunications Policy* 21, no 7 (1997): 575–596.

Cave, Martin and Kiyoshi Nakamura. "Digital Television: An Introduction." Pp. 1–22 in *Digital Broadcasting: Policy and Practice in the Americas, Europe and Japan*, edited by M. Cave and K. Nakamura. London: Edward Elgar Publishing, 2006.

Cawley, Richard A. "European Aspects of the Regulation of Pay Television." *Telecommunications Policy* 21, no 7 (1997): 677–691.

Chadha, Kalyani and Anandam Kavoori. "Globalisation and National Media Systems: Mapping Interactions in Policies, Markets and Formats." Pp. 84–103 in *Mass Media and Society*, edited by James Curran and Michael Gurevitch. London: Edward Arnold, 2005.

Corcoran, Farrel J. "Digital Television in Ireland: Local Forces in a Global Context." Javnost/The Public 9, no. 4 (2002): pp. 49–64.

Curran, James and Myung-Jin Park. "Beyond Globalisation Theory." Pp. 3–18 in *De-westernizing Media Studies*, edited by James Curran and Myung-Jin Park. London: Routledge, 2000.

Di Mauro, Luca. "Regulation of Digital TV in the EU: Divine Coherence or Human Inconsistency?" in *Digital Broadcasting: Policy and Practice in the Americas, Europe and Japan*, edited by Martin Cave and Kiyoshi Nakamura. London: Edward Elgar Publishing, 2006.

EC (European Commission). (1999). Communication to the European Parliament, the Council of the Economic and Social Committee and the Committee of the Regions on The Development of the Market for Digital Television in the European Union, COM (1999) 540 final.

Galperin, Hernan. "Regulatory Reform in the Broadcasting Industries of Brazil and Argentina in the 1990s." *Journal of Communication* 50, no. 4 (2000): 176–191.

———. *New Television, Old Politics: The Transition to Digital TV in the United States and Britain*. Cambridge and New York: Cambridge University Press, 2004.

Goodwin, Peter. "UK: Never Mind the Policies, Feel the Growth." Pp. 151–180 in *Digital Terrestrial Television in Europe*, edited by Allan Brown and Robert G. Picard. New Jersey: Lawrence Erlbaum Associates, 2005.

Harcourt, Alison. "Engineering Europeanization: The Role of the European Institutions in Shaping National Media Regulation." *Journal of European Public Policy* 9, no 5 (2002): 736–755.

———. *The European Union and the Regulation of Media Markets*. Manchester: Manchester University Press, 2005.

Humphreys, Peter J. and Matthias Lang. "Digital Television between Economy and Pluralism." Pp. 9–34 in *Changing Channels: The Prospects of Television in a Digital World*, edited by Jeanette Steemers. Luton John Libbey Media, 1998.

Levy, David A. "Regulating Digital Broadcasting in Europe: The Limits to Policy Convergence." *West European Politics* 20, no 4 (1997a): 24–42.

———. "The Regulation of Digital Conditional Access Systems: A Case Study in European Policy Making." *Telecommunications Policy* 21, no 7 (1997b): 661–676.

———. *Europe's Digital Revolution: Broadcasting Regulation, the EU, and the Nation State*, London: Routledge, 1999.

Maccanico, Antonio. *Il Grande Cambiamento: Gli Anni della Liberalizzazione delle Comunicazioni Visti da un Protagonista*, Milano: Sperling & Kupfer, 2001.

Marra, Antonio. "La Televisione Digitale in Italia e le Regole di Concorrenza." *Il Mulino* 47, no 5 (1998): 921–932.

McCallum, Linsey. "EU Competition Law and Digital Pay Television." *Competition Policy Newsletter* 1 (February 1999): 4–16.

Mendes Pereira, Miguel. "Recent Consolidation in the European Pay-TV Sector." *Competition Policy Newsletter* no 2 (2003): 29–39.

Menduni, Enrico. "La Televisione Digitale in Italia." *Il Mulino* 48, no 6 (1999): 1119–1125.

———. *Televisione e Società Italiana 1975–2000*. Milano: Bompiani, 2002.

Michalis, Maria. "The Debate over Universal Service in the European Union: Plus Ca Change, Plus C'Est la Meme Chose." *Convergence* 8 no 2 (2002): 80–98.

Murdock, Graham. "Digital Futures: European Television in the Age of Convergence." Pp. 35–57 in *Television across Europe: A Comparative Introduction*, edited by Jan Wieten, Graham Murdock and Peter Dahlgren. London: Sage, 2000.

Murdock, Graham and Peter Goldin. "Common Markets: Corporate Ambitions and Communications Trends in the UK and Europe." *Journal of Media Economics* 12 no. 2 (1999): 117–132.

News Corporation. "Annual Report." 2006. http://www.newscorp.com/investor/annual_reports.html (accessed February 23, 2007).

Nolan, Dermot. "Bottlenecks in Pay Television: Impact on Europe Market Development." *Telecommunications Policy* 21, no 7 (1997): 597–610.

Olivi, Bini and Bruno Somalvico. *La Fine della Comunicazione di Massa: Dal Villaggio Globale alla Nuova Babele Elettronica*, Bologna: Il Mulino, 1997.

Schoser, Christof and Sandro Santamato. "The Commission's State Aid Policy on the Digital Switchover." *Competition Policy Newsletter* 1 (2006): 23–27.

Skogerbø, Eli. "External Constraints and National Resources: Reflections on the Europeanisation of Communications Policy." *Nordicom Review*, no 1 (1996): 18–26.

Waisbord, Silvio and Nancy Morris. "Introduction: Rethinking Media Globalization and State Power." Pp. vii–xvi in *Media and Globalization: Why the State Matters*, edited by Nancy Morris and Silvio Waisbord. Oxford: Rowman & Littlefield, 2001.

Ward, David. *The European Union Democratic Deficit and the Public Sphere*. Amsterdam: IOS Press, 2002.

Chapter Two

"Il Caso Canadese" and the Question of Global Media

Mark Hayward

A great deal has been written about the international distribution of media under the banner of globalization and transnationalization. The majority of this literature places this phenomenon in the context of the eventual demise of the nation-state as the principal model of social, political, and economic organization. Such an approach to the cultural, institutional, and economic relations of the present moment typically shows the way in which nationalism and ethnicity are being de-linked from states and territories and linked up with other kinds of globally diffused social organizations: networks, meshworks, markets, and so on. However, I would like to argue in this chapter that the destabilization of the territorial nation-state does not mean that the nation-state is necessarily on the way to disappearing. It is, however, being reconfigured and the goal of this chapter is to provide some indications about how we might begin thinking through this process as both citizens and scholars. This chapter is an attempt to map some aspects of the way in which the Italian state—its services, powers, and administrative functions—has evolved in relation to the various populations of "Italians," specifically those that reside outside the national territory.

In the pages that follow, I lay out the details of a conflict between representatives of the Italian and Canadian governments, the Italian state-owned broadcaster, a Canadian privately-owned cable network, various cultural intermediaries, and members of the Italian Canadian community. The conflict has come to be referred to by both the Canadian and Italian press as il caso canadese. At its simplest, this is a turf war. It is about the attempts of the Italian public broadcaster Radiotelevisione Italiana (RAI) to win a license for distribution on digital cable in Canada and the attempts made by Canadian Italian-language broadcaster, the Telelatino Network, to block the application. But, stepping back from the specifics of the disagreement over access, this conflict also shows how narratives about the relationship between state regulation, cultural identity understood as 'ethnicity', and transnational communication networks are used to explain and justify the actions of cultural producers and the rights and needs of citizens.

Making sense of the scandal, I would like to suggest that the conflict between RAI and Telelatino was organized by the circulation of discourses about "global media" and their role in processes of control and resistance. The events outlined below unfolded around ways of thinking about the dangers of external control of information and the problem of cultural homogenization that such control threatens to bring with it in a context where the meaning of national identity and state power are changing dramatically. For this reason, I believe the events discussed below must also be seen as part of broader trends in the regulation and organization of media production, distribution, and consumption both in Italy and elsewhere, particularly in the way in which they bring together talk about the economics of "global markets" with demands for cultural recognition.

However, I would like to avoid the common methodological pitfall that views "global media" as a singular and unified object of study that has various local instantiations open to empirical investigation. As Armand Mattelart (2002) reminds us, the term globalization in English invokes two meanings of the word "global." The first refers to a spatial conception that covers the entire surface of the planet, the globe itself. The second suggests a form of universality, a kind of knowledge present and self-evident regardless of position or situation. The globalization of Italian media and the tensions involved in this process are constitutive of global media rather than being the product of an abstract process (i.e., globalization) for this reason it is necessary to remember that the study of "global media" is always positioned in particular ways.

For this reason, rather than simply reproduce practiced logics of the "global," I would like to make use of this case study to examine the effectivities involved in the circulation of the understandings of the global. "Global media" is not merely descriptive of changes in the "real" world; it is productive. It is productive in the sense that it brings into existence (and is brought into existence by) a set of knowledges, objects, scales, and agents. In order to do this, I concentrate on the narratives offered by parties involved in the conflict in order to throw into relief the process through which the global is constructed. My aim, then, is not to reject the notion that there are actors and institutions that extend beyond the territorial boundaries of a single sovereign state (one of the constitutive territorializations of the "global"), but to show that these objects and agents are complex entities implicated in fields of material and discursive force that cannot simply be seen to operate within the smooth, pre-given space of the "global." The "global" is not simply the stage upon which these events unfold—a passive container—but is rather an active component in shaping understandings of our contemporary moment.

IL CASO CANADESE: A TALE TWICE-TOLD....

I would like to offer two tellings of the "same" story.

On November 17, 2002, Massimo Magliaro, the Director of RAI 2 (one of Italy's publicly-owned national networks) and acting director of RAI International (the international branch of the state broadcaster) delivered a keynote address at the Columbus Center, an Italian Canadian community center in Toronto, on the occasion of the second national meeting for italiani all'estero (Italians abroad) (see Maglio 2002). The speech was a strident call for solidarity among Italians around the world. The key point, which Magliaro repeated several times, was the importance of ensuring the distribution of RAI International in Canada rather than its re-broadcasting through Canadian proxies. "You will have RAI!" was the refrain that punctuated his comments (Magliaro 2002).

In a language evoking a reversal of the transcontinental journey made by hundreds of thousands of Italians to Canada in the previous century, the arrival of RAI International offered the possibility of a reunion with the "seeds that were sown long ago"—the Italian diaspora reconstituted digitally (Magliaro 2002). Canada was described as a "black hole" and a "lost continent." While acknowledging that Canadians were currently served by the Telelatino Network, a national cable channel that broadcast 55 percent RAI programming at the time (the other 45 percent of programming was in Spanish), as well as numerous local broadcasters that carried portions of RAI programming from Satellite sources, Magliaro lamented that Italian Canadians remained divided from Italy and the "Italian brotherhood" by the small-minded self-interest of Canadian broadcasters and a wall of short-sighted government regulation enacted in the distant past.

Magliaro's comments were framed by the attempt made by the Italian government to reach out to the millions of Italians living around the world (Serafini 2002). These initiatives have taken the form of international conferences gathering together Italians living abroad and their descendents, the creation of a government ministry, under the broad aegis of the Department of External Affairs, for italiani all'estero, as well as continued support for the network of istituti culturali around the world and an extensive subsidy programs for language education. However, perhaps the boldest and most surprising development has been the decision to grant voting rights to Italians living abroad and the allocation of twelve new seats in the lower house of the Italian parliament (and six in the senate) to represent Italians who no longer reside on Italian territory.

Returning to Magliaro's comments, all of these decisions are presented by him as part of a single initiative. In a complex metaphor bringing together soccer ("Serie A," the Italian equivalent of the English Premier League), the right to vote and the need for RAI International, Magliaro notes:

> You will have RAI because it's the right thing to do. You are citizens of Serie "A." And it's not enough that we say it, it's time that we do something about it. You cannot be recognized as Serie "A" citizens without the benefit of a public broadcasting system that includes both radio and TV from the country of origin, in this case, Italy. A country that allows you to vote in its elections must be able to provide you with information about those elections. (Magliaro 2002)

Taken together, Magliaro argued that the introduction of RAI International into the Canadian market, the extension of the vote to Italians living abroad and the new found sense of community among Italians around the world provide a provocative and inescapable example of the way in which political, social and economic boundaries have faded away. RAI International, and the Italian nation itself, must learn to ride the waves of information flowing around the world if they are to survive.

Moving from Magliaro's statements in Toronto to an article published in the Italian news weekly L'espresso seven months later, a very different version of the Italian broadcaster's interests in Canada is offered. Denise Pardo, the magazine's media critic, recounts the details of a meeting between the president of Telelatino, Aldo Di Felice, and Massimo Magliaro on July 4, 2003 in Rome. According to a fax sent to Pardo one week after the meeting, Di Felice claimed that Magliaro had arrived at the meeting "speaking and acting very aggressively." Magliaro's distaste for Di Felice reached its height with some "friendly advice" to the television executive. Paraphrased in Di Felice's letter, Magliaro is reported to have said: "If you continue in this way, you won't just be dealing with the power of RAI International, but also RAI Italia, the Italian government, and the Vatican. In five years, you won't be able to walk the streets of Canada" (Pardo 2003).

Attempting to limit the damage resulting from the story's circulation (picking up on the title of the article's subtext—"First we cut your programming and then we break your legs"), Magliaro phoned into a Toronto-based Italian language radio talk show the day after the story was published to defend himself saying: "Those who know me, know that I am not a mafioso" (Magliaro 2003).

Di Felice's letter to Pardo sharing Magliaro's behavior was only a part of a broader campaign launched by Telelatino in opposition to the move by RAI International into Canada. Making use of its ability to access members of the Canadian public directly, a series of informational announcements of various lengths were produced for broadcast. The longest of these, entitled "The Future of Italian Television in Canada," ran thirty minutes in length and featured various "experts" from the Italian Canadian community interviewed by Telelatino on-air personality Alf De Blasis, best known as host of the network's Sunday morning coverage of Italian soccer. One of these experts, Professor Francesco Guardini, who also serves as a member of the Committee representing Italian citizens residing in Toronto (Comites—Toronto), summarised the situation as follows:

> RAI through its representatives has defined TLN as an incompetent institution. From their standpoint, obviously this is the reason for announcing its divorce and making its case for a totally independent channel twenty-four hours a day. I think it would be a dangerous situation because the power would be in the hands of somebody who doesn't have a real interest in the Italian Canadian community but perhaps an interest in political votes or commercial interests. It wouldn't look good for Canada. This isn't the wild west after all. We are a country with governmental rules and regulations. If RAI didn't like the way TLN has broadcast their programs, they could have asked for changes. If the divorce must happen, let it happen. (Telelatino 2003)

At the heart of Guardini's retelling of the conflict between RAI International and Telelatino and Di Felice's recounting of the meeting with Magliaro in Rome is an appeal to order and, for lack of a better word, decorum. The outrageousness of RAI's behaviour is likened to the Wild West against which Canada—the Canadian state specifically—is positioned as the sheriff, a necessary protection for good citizens like Telelatino against external dangers. The protective aspects of community, through the invocation of the paternal nation-state and the social solidarity of community in Canada, are proposed as a rallying point by Telelatino against the savage capitalism of Magliaro and his cronies.

It is versions of these stories that received the widest circulation in the popular press. Very soon after RAI International made the decision to break off its ties with Telelatino, the Toronto-based Italian-language daily Corriere Canadese started to publish articles in support of the action, continually referring to arrival of the vote for extraterritorial citizens and the important educative function of the channel as necessary for the preservation of Italian culture in Canada. According to the editorial line presented by the Corriere, the continued absence of RAI from the Canadian broadcast universe was structured as the equivalent of cutting the Italian Canadian community from its lifeblood (Riondino 2003).

The story as picked up by the English language press was closer to the telling presented by Telelatino (probably a result of their closer ties with the Canadian media establishment). Comment pieces ran in Canada's two largest circulation dailies—*The Toronto Star* and *The Globe and Mail*—that concentrated on the incursion by a foreign power into Canada and the possibly dangerous effects this would have on Canada and its multicultural mosaic (Caldwell 2003, Ricci 2003, and Zerbisias 2003). Antonia Zerbisias concluded her article in *The Toronto Star* with the following, unpleasantly nativist note: "People, please check your ethnic, tribal, territorial, partisan, religious and assorted other conflicts at the Canada Customs door. Canadian culture rules. Otherwise ask yourself this: Why did you come here in the first place?" (Zerbesias 2003)

Taken together, these stories constituted the frame for the struggle over the hearts and minds of "the community"—the abstract and amorphous communities of "Italian Canadians"—that started in the fall of 2002 with the announcement by RAI International that it would be terminating its agreement with Telelatino. As the debate spread across the pages of Canada's Italian-language press in the months that followed, these narratives proved their ability to marshal feelings of belonging as a tool to repel threats deemed exogenous to the community. Social club meetings turned into shouting matches. Demonstrations were organized and petitions were circulated (Riondino 2003).[1]

As a tale of domination in the age of "global media," this is a conflict between two media organizations seeking to maximize their access to audiences (and profit) by attempting to control the flow of resources (programming). Given this read of the events, it is not surprising that the fact that the Corriere Canadese received considerable support from the Italian Ministry of External Affairs and that Telelatino was majority-owned by Corus Entertainment (the broadcasting arm of Shaw Cable, one half of Canada's cable television duopoly), became central to determining the authenticity of the broadcasters' interest in the "community" (see Barbetti and Bruno 2003). Could the Corriere be trusted to cover the events when its own survival was tied to funds from the same government ministry that was partly responsible for the management of RAI International? Did Telelatino have a right to claim the voice of the Italian Canadian community given that it was simply a niche-channel for one of Canada's largest media conglomerates? In both cases, the direct line between ownership and authenticity to the ideals of the community were called in to question in such a way that each side's accusations reinforced the view that Italian culture in Canada was in the process of being hi-jacked.

At the same time, these stories are tales of resistance. These issues pose important questions about the nature of community and the forms of belonging constituted through mediated communication within and beyond national territories. As I have already intimated, I believe that the disagreement represented in these tellings recounts the same story in different registers—they are narratives about the drawing of borders around communities. The primary difference between them revolves around a disagreement over the meaning of cultural homogenization. For Magliaro, the struggle against homogenization means resistance to English-language global dominance. For Di Felice and Telelatino, this same struggle is about absorption into centrally controlled Italian cultural space co-ordinated by Rome. As De Felice commented to The Ottawa Citizen in late 2003: "I think the question is, is Italian-Canadian culture or Italian-Canadian media going to be run from Rome or is it going to be run from Canada?" (Lofaro 2003).

However, it is necessary to note that the effectiveness of these stories was not unrelated to their limitations. Both tellings found themselves trapped in logics of what Paul Gilroy has called in another context "ethnic absolutism." RAI International, by linking its claim to the vote for citizens residing abroad and the centrality of the Italian language, ultimately excluded a vast majority of the 1.3 million people who self-identified themselves as Italian, whether by birth or affinity, in the last Canadian census, not to mention the vast majority of people living on Canadian territory. Similarly, the approach made by Telelatino, rooted in the specific hybridity of Italian Canadians, found itself in the uncomfortable position of invoking an idea of the Canadian nation that ultimately excluded the kinds of cultural diversity it relied on as a "multicultural" broadcaster.

Beyond simply increasing the level of acrimony among the broadcasters and the journalists covering the story, this situation also put the regulatory bodies of the Canadian state in a difficult position from which there seemed no easy exit. The Canadian broadcast regulatory body, the Canadian Radio Telecommunications Commission (CRTC) found itself caught in the middle, paralysed by one of the great tensions of Canadian politics over the past two decades, namely the re-articulation of the welfare state in response to the pressures of liberalizing global markets. Much of the regulatory regime currently in place in Canada is built upon an assumption about its ability to maintain regulated boundaries between the nation and its outsides. However, with the adoption of the Free Trade Act and NAFTA, as well as the trade negotiations at the WTO, there has been a move away from these policies toward the "open market" and a belief in self-regulation of capital and cultural flows.

Almost a year after the initial application of RAI to the CRTC in 2003, the Liberal government (at the time a minority government), sensing a potentially explosive situation in a community that had long been an important source of support in both Toronto and Montreal, realised the importance of the situation for retaining power in parliament. In the summer of 2004, Canadian Heritage Minister Liza Frulla commissioned a report on the status of third-language broadcasters in Canada from a three-person committee chaired by Quebec MP Clifford Lincoln entitled Integration and Cultural Diversity.

The report acknowledged that the present system of regulating ethnic television was no longer sufficient in an era defined by the rise of the digital distribution and the proliferation of services. The panel called for a more balanced approach in which existing Canadian services would not always be given preferential treatment. Essentially rewriting the existing policy on third-language broadcasting, the new regulations replaced the previous concentration on the development of Canadian services (the policy which had led to the creation of Telelatino Network in 1984) with greater interest in the development of competition. It also recommended a new definition of "public broadcaster," one no longer tied to public ownership, instead using the term to refer to any broadcaster that was the "principal broadcaster" in its country of origin. After these suggestions were accepted as policy, RAI International's license was granted in less than two months. Soon after Minister Frulla described these changes in a speech to a gathering of Canada's private broadcasters as "opening the door to progress."

Through this shift in policy, the Liberal government was able to shore up its support among ridings dominated by Italian community groups around Toronto and Montreal. But perhaps most important for this discussion is that these actions revealed the way in which the discourses about belonging and identity produced by RAI International and Telelatino were situated within understandings of the relationship between culture, economics and the nation in Canada. It is not simply that RAI International provided a more viable business model or more valid cultural mandate, but that the relation (or the relation of a non-relation) between the production of value and the production of culture was one in tune with emergent broadcast policy. And, more generally speaking, the RAI application could be effectively articulated with shifting understandings of the relationship between cultural production, multiculturalism, and the project of Canadian nationalism that is taking shape in the present moment.

RETHINKING THE BORDER. . . .

The goal of this chapter is not to establish the "truth" of these tellings, but to show how they "perform" dominant understandings of media's role in the global era. Both of the narratives of the conflict between RAI International and Telelatino outlined in the previous section attempted to change existing social relations by producing and marshalling various "truths." In the process, these narratives bring to light the emergent structure of political and social organization of discourse around questions of culture as articulated around the nation-state in the global era. However, I do not want to suggest that the events they recount are merely symptomatic of changes in other areas of state intervention. Such a position would be to repeat those arguments that relegate media and cultural policy to a secondary position of far less significance for understanding the way of the world than the more serious areas of government enterprise such as those involving the management of the economy and international affairs. Instead, I believe that the caso canadese shows the way in which media and cultural policy have become increasingly important areas for understanding a broad range of shifts in practices of governance.

The elaboration of the possibilities and limitations of a European citizenship elaborated by Etienne Balibar provides a useful way for thinking through these changes that does not relegate culture to the level of mere symptom. In his recent writings, he develops the idea of the border as the site through which to interrogate the logic and the limits, both literally and philosophically speaking, of the nation and ethnic communities (Balibar 2002: 75–86, Balibar 2004: 101–114). Through a detailed analysis of the way in which national identities and state apparatus are implicated in the production of community through processes of inclusion and exclusion, his approach also allows for greater attentiveness to the ways in which global or transnational media are implicated in national projects.

At the heart of Balibar's critique of the "border," understood as a clearly expressed dividing line between two discrete units, there is also a profound critique of sovereignty and identity (or nationality when understood in the terms of the nation-state). Furthermore, as Balibar shows, to trouble the certitude of borders is to trouble the very foundations of the modern subject as it has developed in Western Europe and North America. We are all, as Balibar notes quoting Fichte, "internal(ized) borders."

The disjoint between traditional notions of the absolutely sovereign nation and the reality of increasingly integrated world economic and cultural systems has resulted in sets of relations that have come to instantiate a kind of "global" apartheid (Balibar 2004: 3–45). This is a world in which two different but interrelated systems (with two distinct logics of circulation), corresponding to those who enjoy full rights of citizenship and those who do not (e.g., les san-papiers in France), exist at all times in all places with the former dominating the latter. Balibar's intervention, therefore, attempts to find a way out of the increasingly violent manifestations of state-form (such as police intervention both at "home" and abroad; the economic violence of the constitution and consolidation of international markets) through the positing of a new logic of inclusion, a logic based on the radical undecidability of the border as both a space of division and site of encounter—in his words, "a dialectic between 'constituent' and 'constituted' citizenship" (Balibar 2004: 77).

To discuss global media in light of Balibar's elaboration of the relationship between borders and citizenship (Balibar 2004: 51–77) would demand that our analyses go beyond simply remarking the extension of borders by means of communications technology. This would be to return to the uncritical view of globalization I evoked at the beginning of this chapter. Instead, it is necessary to develop a critique of the ways in which the borders that delimit a community are constituted. In the case study discussed above, the extension of the vote abroad by the Italian state and the rationalization of extraterritorial markets for the state broadcaster can be seen as the disaggregation of the concept of filiation through blood and national identity from its grounding in territory. These developments can be seen as involving the extension of borders while preserving the social and economic inequalities currently in existence.

Of course, there have always been some aspects of the Italian nation-state that have been transnational. For this reason, it is important to place these events in the context of a longer history of "state transnationalism"—a term under which I categorize the ways in which nation-states have sought to organize transnational populations—and that earlier forms of "state transnationalism" play an important role in shaping the contemporary moment. This is to move away from those understandings of transnationalism that declare that we are witnessing something for the first time ever. This is not to say that every moment has been the same, but that they are connected and that the way that they differ is important.

The contemporary form of "state transnationalism" clearly differs from earlier practices employed by Fascist Italy in which propaganda often took a back seat to physical coercion and the brute force of conquest. The kinds of relations and descriptions of relations that constituted Italian colonialism—and colonialism is undoubtedly a very widely diffused form of "state transnationalism"—ranging from the direct possession of territory, armed conquest, and a language of imperialism are for the most part absent from even the most extreme discourses about migration in contemporary Italy. In fact, it is one of the peculiarities of Italian popular and official memory that Italy's involvement in these earlier practices has almost totally been forgotten. Instead of territorial expansion, it is culture that comes to play an increasingly important role in the form of "state transnationalism" that has been at work in Italy since the end of the Second World War.

By working through the caso canadese, I have attempted to describe a situation that makes apparent the growing importance of cultural policy in the eyes of government, a shift foundational to the practices through which national heritage and the population itself are developed as an economic resource in the global era. This situation shows the emergent practices through which the nation-state binds transnational flows of capital (whether economic or informational) to particular bodies, bodies identified and organized according to the "cultural difference."

CODA: GLOBAL ITALY

On April 9th–10th, 2006, national elections were held in Italy. Being in Rome on election night, I walked from my apartment to Piazza del Popolo where Romano Prodi's center-left coalition had planned a massive victory celebration. Voting had closed a few hours earlier. Based on polls leading up to the election, the center-left had felt confident enough about the outcome that they announced earlier in the day that the evening's events would start at eight o'clock with the leaders of the coalition parties taking the stage together sometime before midnight. In spite of early indications that Prodi's "Democratic Union" coalition was heading toward certain victory, the piazza was almost completely empty and the stage dark upon my arrival at half past nine.

Curious as to what was going on, I walked back toward my apartment, stopping along the way in Piazza Sant'Apostoli where Romano Prodi's campaign headquarters were located. A crowd had gathered in front of the headquarters and were watching the results come in on a large projection television. The joyous mood of members of the center-left coalition that I watched earlier on television had now disappeared. Incoming reports from polls across the country (primarily the slow to report rural areas in the North and the provinces of the South) revealed that the left's sizeable lead had eroded almost completely. By 11 pm they were trailing in the senate.

As the hours passed, it became increasingly apparent to those gathered in front of television screens across the nation that the election would not be decided that night. In fact, the election would not even be decided in Italy. It would ultimately be resolved by the results from a handful of seats—newly created for this election—voted on by Italian citizens living around the world. The votes of the Italiani all'estero (Italians abroad) had been cast approximately a month before and mailed to Rome. They sat under lock and key at the Ministry of the Interior and were waiting to be counted.

On the evening of the 10th of April, the supporters of Romano Prodi did not take this as a good sign. Common sense was that the italiani all'estero were mostly conservative (if not openly fascist) and vehemently opposed to the parties of the left. They were, after all, the ones who had supposedly left Italy in previous decades because they opposed the leftist tendencies of the Italian state. Casting further shadow on the situation, the seats themselves had been the invention of Silvio Berlusconi's government in 2001, a pet project of the formerly fascist but now far-right (and center-moving) Alleanza Nazionale (National Alliance) to reward their longtime supporters abroad. As one commentator put it, it seemed as though the Italian left had once more managed to snatch defeat from the jaws of victory.

It was, therefore, surprising to many when it was announced the next day that the majority of seats abroad in both the lower house and the senate (of which there were twelve of the former and six of the latter) were taken by the center-left coalition. It solidified the center-left's majority in the Camera dei deputati, Italian parliament's lower house, and broke the deadlock in the senate. In a matter of a few hours, the role that non-resident Italians played in the country's political life—a question that had been seen as having symbolic but little actual importance for understanding how Italy was governed—became central to determining what kind of government would be formed. After all, a deciding vote in the senate was now held by an eighty-year-old industrialist who had immigrated to Buenos Aires fifty years earlier and who explained his party affiliations by saying: "Those of us from abroad do not have the luxury of sitting in opposition."

The instability of the newly formed government that emerged from the election, was matched by a public debate about the uncertainty of the meaning of these results. While the normal accusations of corruption were exchanged, many of these tensions were focused on the role of the italiani all'estero in the electoral process. Outgoing Prime Minister Silvio Berlusconi immediately began to question the validity of the vote from abroad, suggesting that there were irregularities in the elections overseas, and even sought to cast doubt on the legitimacy of the seats themselves. "They don't pay taxes," he remarked, "therefore, it is arguable that they should be able to vote" ("Berlusconi" 2006).

Meanwhile, those on the center-left were forced to quickly recalibrate several generations of received wisdom about Italians abroad. The Italiani all'estero were transformed from the mass of lumpen-proletariat with "cardboard suitcases" and proto-fascist tendencies into the undervalued conscience of the Italian nation, more finely attuned to the status of Italy in the world and the damage done by Berlusconi's time in office. The outcome of the election and its aftermath, from the adaptation of the center-left's views about Italians abroad to the rebuttal by the parties on both the left and the right of Berlusconi's attempt to delegitimize the extra-national electoral districts, mark an important step in the solidification of a new understanding of the Italian nation-state and its relationship to territory. Italy had gone global.

The extension of the vote abroad and the increased availability of Italian information services that are at the heart of the caso canadese have generally been treated as the recognition of rights long denied to citizens living abroad. I think this is mostly right, but it has also shown the way in which the modern nation-state, through media, institutional, and economic recognition, has reconfigured the lines between citizens and others. Balibar powerfully describes this process, writing:

> Sometimes noisily and sometimes sneakily, borders have changed place. Whereas traditionally, and in conformity with both their juridical definition and "cartographical" representation as incorporated in national memory, they should be at the edge of the territory, marking the point where it ends, it seems that borders and the institutional practices corresponding to them have been transported into the middle of political space. They can no longer function as simple edges, external limits to democracy that the mass of citizens can see as a barrier protecting their rights and lives without ever really interfering with them. (Balibar 109)

Ultimately, media matters in the Italian case because it is one of the places in which these divides are put into practice. There is a disturbing symmetry between the Roman living in Toronto who votes in Italian elections for the Left Democrats in the hope of ousting the neo-fascist National Alliance from the governing coalition and the Albanian living in Rome who falls victim to the draconian immigration policies of fortress Europe. It is difficult to ignore that the surfeit of rights enjoyed by citizens of the most developed nations finds its mirror image in the absolute absence of rights granted to an increasing percentage of the population of the rest of the globe.

For those of us outside of Italy—all'estero—it is important to see how the rights granted to some citizens can be brought into line with the politics of multiculturalism in ways that do not increase tolerance and openness. In both cases, the institution of a "global" understanding of the role that communication technologies and media production and consumption play cannot be allowed to simply re-instantiate the practices of exclusion already in circulation, but something new must be imagined and enacted. It is the radical indeterminacy in every invocation of community that must be acknowledged and the necessity of continual struggle for openness against exclusion. To ignore this project, and bury oneself in either the joy or despair of a global perspective stripped of its particularity, is not an option.

Understanding global media (and the possibility of global media studies) cannot simply involve a broadening of the bounds geographically. Such a project cannot be reduced to the addition of "others"—other places, other subjectivities—without radically reconfiguring the methods and conceptual tools used to describe this widening field of study. In this pursuit, I believe that the tools of media studies for discussing global media are inadequate if they do not also involve a thorough-going rethinking of the conceptual frameworks it offers for thinking about practices of group belonging and identity formation. This challenge is pressing for both academic and non-academic analyses of the media. The fact that the diffusion of media technology allows for the almost instantaneous message does not mean that the "global" has been constituted as a clearly delineated space of action. The caso canadese is only one of many sites in which these questions are being posed; questions whose answers become more urgent by the day and ever more difficult to find.

NOTES

1. The roots of this chapter lay in this period. At the time, I was working on contract for a company producing documentaries about the Italian Canadian community for Telelatino. In a matter of a few months, the changing relationship between Telelatino and RAI became a common subject of conversation. None of the projects I was working on dealt directly with the topic of Italian media in Canada, but I spent many afternoons in discussion about the new landscape for Italian television in Canada as I travelled around talking to people for various projects. In each of these discussions, it was the link between community, government regulation, and identity that were being interrogated. There is another article to be written about the struggles in the community.

REFERENCES

Adams, James. "Who's afraid of Al-Jazeera?" *The Globe and Mail*, February 14, 2004.
Appadurai, Arjun. "Disjuncture and Difference in the Global Cultural Economy" in *Modernity at Large*. 27–42. Minneapolis: University of Minnesota Press, 1996.
Balibar, Etienne. Politics and the Other Scene. London: New York, 2002.
———. *We, the People of Europe?: Reflections on Transnational Citizenship*. Princeton: Princeton University Press, 2004.
Barbetti, Luciana and Eugenio Bruno. "Giornali in cooperativa, corsa a 58 milioni di euro." Il Sole–24 Ore. August 31, 2003.
Barker, Christopher. *Global Television: An Introduction*. Oxford: Blackwell, 1997.
"Berlusconi: discutibile il voto all'estero," *La Stampa*, May 22, 2006.
Caldwell, Rebecca. "Fight for 24-hour Italian TV pits TLN against old country." *The Globe and Mail*. August 5, 2003.

Lofaro, Tony. "Italian Community Lobbies for Homeland Channel." *The Ottawa Citizen*. November 22, 2003.

Magliaro, Massimo. Speech to Second Annual Conference of Comites, 2002.

———. Interview on CHIN Radio. July 26, 2003.

Maglio, Antonio. "Rai lascia Telelatino." *Corriere Canadese*. November 18, 2002.

Mattelart, Armand. "An Archaelogy of the global era: constructing a belief." *Media, Culture and Society*. Vol. 24, No. 5, 591–612.

Morley, David and Kevin Robins. (1995). *Spaces of Identity: Global Media, Electronic Territories and Cultural Boundaries*. London: Routledge

Pardo, Denise. "Ti taglio le transmissioni e pure le gambe." *L'espresso*. July 25, 2003.

Parks, Lisa and Shanti Kumar. *Planet TV: A Global Television Reader*. New York: New York University Press, 2003.

Ricci, Nino. "Beware Silvio's Siren Song." *The Globe and Mail*. October 21, 2003.

Riondino, Francesco. "Telelatino ci ha traditi." *Corriere Canadese*. July 7, 2003.

Serafini, Dom. "Rai International contro il Canada." *America Oggi*. December 16, 2002.

Zerbisias, Antonia. "Italy sparks a local War of Words." *The Toronto Star*. December 11, 2003.

Chapter Three

Digital Terrestrial Television and Its Promises: Framing the Debate on the Transition to Digital Television in Italy

Cinzia Padovani

INTRODUCTION

The transition from analogue to Digital Terrestrial Television (DTT), a technology that uses the frequency occupied by analog broadcasters to deliver the digital signal, is a phenomenon of global dimensions. In the United States of America the date for the shutdown of analogue broadcasting was set for mid-2009. In South Africa and Canada, the deadline is 2011. Australia and most member states of the European Union (EU) are supposed to complete the conversion by 2012.

As various scholars have pointed out (Colombo 2007; Galperin 2004; Smith 2007; and Starks 2007), this transition has been dictated primarily by political and industrial interests, rather than, as often presented (Sartori 2004:13), by a desire to improve citizens' access to the digital world. Although an all-digital future is what is in store for billions of TV viewers around the globe, each national government has implemented its own policies to guide the transitional phase. Indeed, the conversion to DTT offers a unique opportunity to look at the role of national broadcasting legislation in the face of global forces (Galperin 2004: 3–24).

Likewise, the digitization of the TV sector in Italy provides the occasion to explore the reasons behind Italian governments' support of DTT. The conversion to digital terrestrial television is a window through which the echoes of such a global phenomenon on national legislation and industrial policies can be gauged, and offers an opportunity to observe how the interests of the operators in the "old" analogue broadcasting sector have influenced the digital television sector of the future.

In Italy, the analogue broadcasting market is characterized by a duopoly, which dates back to the mid-1980s, consisting of *RAI Radiotelevisione Italiana*, the public broadcaster, and Mediaset, the commercial TV broadcaster owned by media mogul turned politician Silvio Berlusconi. By the end of 2007, the two operators shared between themselves 84 percent of advertising revenues for television and 82.3 percent of national audiences (AGCOM 2008: 6).

THE PUBLIC DEBATE ON DIGITAL TERRESTRIAL TELEVISION

During the transition to digital TV (which, after being postponed various times in Italy, is scheduled to be completed in 2012), a plurality of sources to inform and engage citizens in a robust debate on issues surrounding the digitization process, including the legislation that will shape the future of the TV industry and the costs and overall benefits of the conversion, is crucial. In this regard, the public service broadcaster has an important role to play. Indeed, its mission should be that of providing a vibrant public sphere, where citizens can learn and share information, while deepening their understanding of digital technologies (how to use them, what to expect from them, etc.). During the time leading to the switch off of the analogue signal, not only should the public broadcaster position itself as a provider of quality content and services on its DTT channels, it should also offer a public forum open to a plurality of perspectives, where citizens, not just consumers, can be engaged in the process.

Is RAI fulfilling this mission? In particular, how has the broadcaster contributed to framing the nation's debate on DTT? What are the characteristics of that debate according to RAI's programs? How, if at all, are the interests of the RAI-Mediaset duopoly reflected in the coverage of the transition? How does the public discourse reproduce or sustain those interests?

In this contribution, I implement a qualitative methodology of textual analysis to study the broadcaster's coverage of digital television and, in particular, of DTT. Although the discourse surrounding the introduction of this new technology emphasizes, in Italy as elsewhere, the interactive and participatory potentials of digital terrestrial television, I am interested in finding out whether RAI's broadcasts have encouraged critical positions, alternative perspectives, and citizens' participation in their coverage and analysis, or whether those broadcasts have played into the political and industrial interests of the existing operators in the analogue TV market. In other words, I want to explore how, if at all, RAI has performed its role as a public sphere.[1]

Justifying DTT

The discourse on DTT in Italy resembles the broader debate on DTT in Europe and elsewhere. Since the late 1990s, the prevalent reason for justifying support of digital terrestrial television has been that such a technology is relatively inexpensive and user friendly. Only a decoder, or set-up box, is needed to update an existing TV set, and, thanks to DTT's interactive capabilities, everybody can join in and access the plentiful world of digital media.

Another reason for the widespread support of DTT is that this delivery technology allows for a better economy of frequencies in the management of a scarce resource, the radio spectrum (Galperin 2004; Richeri 2007).[2] Indeed, as a result of the explosive growth of wireless telephony and other telecommunications services in the 1990s, the spectrum bandwidth, granted through licenses by the governments to broadcasters, has become a prime real estate, and, therefore, a potential source of revenue for governments.

In Europe, where broadcasting remains a very sensitive sector and television continues to be perceived as an important medium for encouraging social cohesion, better representation, and to improve opportunities for democratic participation, the introduction of DTT has been applauded since the late 1990s, for its potentially positive social significance. The impetus behind European governments' support of the technology came after the March 2000 European Council meeting in Lisbon, when an agenda was put in place for the social and economic renewal of the Union. On that occasion, the heads of member states agreed that the EU would soon become "the most competitive and dynamic knowledge-based economy in the world," based on the establishment of an "information society for all" (European Council 2000). Whereas Personal Computers (PCs) and the Internet had failed to provide equal access to the Information Society, DTT, thanks to the ubiquitous TV sets, had the potentials to "guarantee [the] 'democratic' development . . . of the new technology" (Sartori 2004: 17) and to narrow the digital divide, while promoting the sort of inclusive digital literacy plan that the European Council had foreseen (Richeri 2007). Moreover, in countries known for their powerful public service broadcasters (PSBs), digital terrestrial television, a delivery technology capable of providing free-to-air digital content (the rest of digital platforms are pay TV channels), was also perceived as the natural continuation of the generalist TV channels of the analogue era, and as an opportunity for PSBs to reassert their "dignity and legitimacy" (Sartori 2004: 16).

The Case of Italy

With a history of belated innovations in the TV sector,[3] no Italian government could afford to miss out on the opportunity to present itself as technologically innovative and advanced. In line with the dominant discourse in Europe, since the late 1990s all governments supported the introduction of DTT: easy to install and fairly inexpensive, it was expected that the new technology would provide access for anybody with a decoder to the wonders of digital TV. Increased capacity for content, a more efficient use of radio spectrum, and new interactive possibilities, were the most important public objectives and perceived benefits of the new technology (Analysis, 2005: 47). Italian governments also envisioned sophisticated e-government applications: in a country where the penetration of Personal Computers and Internet remained low, "promoting access to new content and information without the need to own a PC [was] a key objective. . . . [Therefore,] given the high penetration of TV [sets], it [was] decided that interactive services may be best delivered via [television]" (AGCOM, quoted in Analysis: 50).

Digital Television and the Duopoly

There were, however, other, perhaps less lofty, reasons behind the choice of DTT. These reasons were related to the industrial and political interests of the dominant operators, RAI and Mediaset, both of which enjoyed powerful alliances inside the political establishment.

As discussed elsewhere (Padovani 2009), since the late 1990s, Italian governments had capitalized on the expectation surrounding the arrival of DTT as a justification not to intervene in the analogue broadcasting market. A more efficient use of the spectrum would have done what lawmakers had been unable to accomplish for decades: put an end to the duopoly. Given the laborious history of broadcasting legislation in Italy, characterized by a chronic unwillingness on the part of politicians to take a clear stance in favor of pluralism of information (thereby reducing the dominant position of the two broadcaster), the new technology was manna from Heaven.

The Legislation

Since the mid-1980s, RAI and Mediaset had been able to maintain full control of their market shares, while lawmakers had made only timid attempts to create a more pluralistic, and open, TV sector. Law August 6, 1990, no. 223, the first one to be passed after the duopoly had been *de facto* established, sanctioned the position of the dominant players by establishing *ad hoc* anti-trust limits: no operator could control more than 25 percent (or three) of all available national channels (Art. 15, comma 4). Three was exactly the number of channels RAI and Mediaset each controlled.

Not even Law July 31, 1997, n. 249, passed by the first Romano Prodi's center left government, the so-called Maccanico law (named after then Minister of Communications Antonio Maccanico), was able to resist the commercial and political interests of the two broadcasters. Although on that occasion lawmakers lowered the anti-trust limits to 20 percent of national channels (Art. 2, comma 6), they failed to establish a deadline by when each broadcaster would have to comply with those limits.

Certainly, if ever applied, the 1997 law would have considerably downsized both RAI and Mediaset. RAI's third channel would have had to either migrate to satellite, or stay on the air without advertising (RAI, since its early days, has been funded by mixed revenues of license fee and advertising money). Mediaset's Rete4 would also have had to migrate to the satellite, resulting in a significant loss of advertising revenue. Neither option was very popular, and no government was likely to impose such drastic measures.

The solution to the conundrum (to ensure pluralism, while protecting the duopoly), was to be found in a new delivery technology that could be developed in a short time. One that could also carry the aura of being socially useful would have been even better: DTT was the answer. The center left government of the late 1990s enthusiastically supported the new technology (in 1998 the first experimental transmissions were carried out in various cities) and established that, as early as 2006, Italy would be one of the first European countries to complete the transition from analogue to digital TV (Law March 20, 2001, n. 66, Art. 2-bis, comma 5).

Political support for DTT intensified during the following center right government of 2001–2006, when the interest for this technology "perfectly coincided with Berlusconi's specific interests" (Richeri 2007). Indeed, by the time Berlusconi began his second term as prime minister, both the Communications Authority (AGCOM 346/2001) and the Constitutional Court (466/2002), had agreed that December 31, 2003, was the deadline by which broadcasters had to comply with the anti-trust limits established by the 1997 law.

The prospective of losing one of Mediaset's lucrative channels was a strong motivation for the center right government to support digitization and, in particular, DTT. The expectations that digital terrestrial television could become a reality in a short period was enticing, as the new technology would eliminate any reason for forcing Berlusconi's media holding to shut down Rete4's analogue broadcasting. Indeed, with just one digital Multiplex, the number of national channels would have increased to the point where neither Mediaset nor RAI would have been in violation of anti-concentration regulations.

After long parliamentary debates, in May 2004, the Gasparri Law (named after Berlusconi's minister of communications at the time) was passed. In an effort to secure a fast and easy transition to digital television and encourage the take off of the new technology, Art. 25 determined that, by January 1, 2004, the public broadcaster's digital terrestrial channels would have to secure coverage of at least 50 percent of the population, 70 percent by January 1, 2005 (Law May 3, 2004, Art. 25 comma 2, a). As a tangible support for the new technology, the law foresaw a system of financial assistance (coupons) to purchase DTT decoders (Art. 25, comma 7). At that point, Italy was the only European country to offer such a contribution.

However, notwithstanding these efforts to promote a fast and efficient transition, consumers' interest did not develop as expected, due, at least in part, to the poor quality of content on DTT. Indeed, although the quantity of digital channels had grown considerably since DTT was first launched in January 2004, providing, at least theoretically, more choices for the viewers, the digital TV market was characterized, from the beginning, by a net separation between those who could afford pay TV (satellite and/or premium DTT) and those who couldn't. As various scholars had predicted (Marzulli 2006; Perrucci and Richeri 2003; Richeri 2000a), the market became polarized, with quality content migrating to Pay-TV and premium DTT channels, and programs of lower quality remaining on free-to-air DTT channels.[4] In 2005, the government finally acknowledged that the country was not ready for the transition and set 2008 as the new deadline for the shut down. Meanwhile, the duopoly remained untouched.

In May 2006, a center left government, led by Prime Minister Romano Prodi, was sworn in. In August of that year, Paolo Gentiloni, the new Communications Minister, pushed back to 2012 the date for the completion of the transitional period. In October 2006 the Council of Ministers approved the so-called Gentiloni bill, which foresaw a reform of the media and TV sectors, including the implementation of stricter anti-trust limitations and the migration of exceeding analogue broadcasting channels by the end of 2009 (the reform also foresaw changes in the governance and funding structure of the public service broadcaster in order to reduce its dependence on advertising revenues). The bill, however, was never converted into law. After the fall of Prodi's government in the winter of 2008, new national elections were held. In May of that year, Silvio Berlusconi became Italy's prime minister for the third time.

THE STUDY

In the next section I present the results of an analysis of RAI's programs that deal with digital TV and, specifically, with the transition to DTT. The research was conducted in the public broadcaster's multimedia archives in Rome, in the summer of 2007. I chose to focus on RAI's programs (instead of also including Mediaset's shows) because the public service broadcaster has a mission to provide citizens with a wide range of information and in-depth analysis on a variety of issues, including, one would expect, the conversion to digital terrestrial television.

Methodology

In order to get a sense of the trends in the coverage, to identify peaks of interest in the topic, and to orient my sampling of RAI's broadcasts, I did a pilot search of the free indexed archives of one of Italy's most influential newspapers, *Corriere della Sera*, using the key words "digital television" AND either "terrestrial/DTT," or "RAI" or "Mediaset." The time frame for the research of *Corriere's* database was 1993–2006 (1993 was the first year for which *Corriere della Sera*'s electronic archives were available; November 2006 was the time when the pilot search was conducted).[5] The results indicated three peaks of interest: one in 1998–1999, another in 2004, and the third in 2006.[6]

These three periods coincide with significant developments in digital TV as well as DTT. By the late 1990s, Rupert Murdoch had consolidated News Corp.'s control over satellite digital TV in various European countries, including the UK, France, and Germany, and was negotiating with Telecom Italia for the establishment of a satellite TV platform in Italy. The second period (2004) coincides with important events in the legislation and the industry. In the summer of 2003, Tele+ (the satellite TV platform established in 1991 by Silvio Berlusconi and Cecchi Gori) was acquired by Murdoch's Sky Italia, which became the sole digital satellite platform in the country. At the end of 2003, the so-called *decreto Salva Rete4* (a decree designed to postpone the migration of Rete4 to digital platform as ordered by the Constitutional Court and the Authority), was passed by the center right government (Decree-Law December 24, 2003). On January 1, 2004, the first DTT channels were officially launched. On May 3, 2004 the Gasparri law was passed. The third period (2006) coincides with Mediaset's controversial use of government subsidized DTT decoders as platforms to sell its own pay-per-view content, in particular *Serie A* live soccer matches, and with the Gentiloni bill of October 2006.

RAI's Broadcasts

In addition to those three main periods, I also decided to include the period from November 2006 to July 1, 2007, when searching the broadcasts. This was done because significant events, including parliamentary discussions concerning the Gentiloni bill, had occurred from the time the pilot search of *Corriere della Sera* was completed (November 2006) and the time when the search of RAI's archives was conducted (July 2007).

Critical Discourse Analysis

In order to understand the nature and quality of the debate, I implemented a qualitative methodology called Critical Discourse Analysis (CDA), a method which is distinct from traditional linguistics and takes as its unit of analysis not the sentence, but the entire "utterance" (e.g., a news bulletin, a public affairs program). This approach is closer to literacy and rhetorical criticism than the quantitative word-count of empirical content analysis.[7] The CDA is particularly appropriate to the objective of my research, which is to look at how the discourse on digital TV has been communicatively framed in relationship with political and governmental institutions, broadcasting institutions, and the media industry.

Sample

I conducted two separate searches using two key words: "televisione digitale" (digital television) and "digitale terrestre" (digital terrestrial). This was done in order to be as inclusive as possible. The search on "digital television" returned a total of 207 broadcasts (see table 3.1); the one on "digital terrestrial" returned 245 broadcasts (see table 3.2).

On the basis of the description and type of each show, I selected those programs that were relevant to my research. I wanted to look at the coverage and discussion of the political aspects of the transition, including the legis-

Table 3.1. Number of RAI broadcasts by year and genre using the keyword "digital television"

			Genre of Relevant Shows				
Year	Total Hits	Relevant (%)[a]	Talk Shows	Variety	Public Affairs	News[b] (P.T.)[c]	Edu.[d]
1998	10	5 (50%)	0	0	0	5 (2)	0
1999	43	23 (54%)	1	0	0	22 (14)	0
2004	93	25 (27%)	7	0	1	17 (5)	0
2006	42	16 (38%)	1	0	0	15 (5)	0
2007[e]	19	11 (58%)	1	0	1	9 (2)	0
Total	207	80 (39%)	10	0	2	68 (28)	0

Notes: (a) Percentage of total hits selected as relevant; (b) Total news broadcasts; (c) Number of news broadcasts on prime time (P.T.); (d) Educational programming; (e) This search period ended July 1, 2007.

lation related to digital TV and/or DTT, and aspects of the RAI-Mediaset duopoly discussed in relationship to digital TV/DTT. For this reason, from the hundreds of hits, I focused on: RAI's news bulletins (Tg1, Tg2, and Tg3, trying to eliminate those that were repeats in different time slots); public affairs shows; talk shows; variety shows; and educational/scientific programs. I eliminated from my sample all hits that referred to advertisements.

On the basis of these criteria, 39 percent of the results from the first search, or 80 shows, were relevant. Of these, ten were talk shows, two were public affairs programs, and 68 were news bulletins, of which, 28 were aired on prime time (table 3.1). For the second search, 29 percent of the results, or 70 shows, were relevant. Of these, five were talk shows, two were public affairs shows, 59 were Tgs (of which 20 were aired on prime time), two were educational programs, and two were variety shows (table 3.2). My entire sample was comprised of 150 shows.

I printed out the informational forms (*Anagrafia Programma*, also called *Sezione Dati Puntata*: they complement each archived broadcast) of all relevant shows. Those forms, compiled by RAI library personnel, contain quantitative as well as qualitative information, including name of the show, date, hour, and duration of the broadcast (or segment), type of show; the name of the host and a list of all guests, a description of the program (background, setting, footage, camera shots, etc.), and a summary of the topics presented or discussed.

Many of the shows selected were not available on digital support, and I was unable to obtain recordings (some shows, whose copyrights are cleared, can be recorded for a fee, but it is an expensive and lengthy process).[8] Therefore, I watched the programs that were available in the library and took notes of dialogues and of visual characteristics (backgrounds, colors, camera shots,

Table 3.2. Number of RAI broadcasts by year and genre using the keyword "digital terrestrial"

			Genre of Relevant Shows				
Year	Total Hits	Relevant (%)[a]	Talk Shows	Variety	Public Affairs	News[b] (P.T.)[c]	Edu.[d]
1998	0	0	0	0	0	0 (0)	0
1999	2	2 (100%)	0	0	0	2 (0)	0
2004	149	33 (22%)	4	1	1	25 (5)	2
2006	75	29 (39%)	1	1	0	27 (14)	0
2007[e]	19	6 (32%)	0	0	1	5 (1)	0
Total	245	70 (29%)	5	2	2	59 (20)	2

Notes: (a) Percentage of total hits selected as relevant; (b) Total news broadcasts; (c) Number of news broadcasts on prime time (P.T.); (d) Educational programming; (e) This search period ended July 1, 2007.

etc.). Given the qualitative nature of the methodology, I allowed themes to emerge inductively and asked the following questions of the broadcasts: How does the journalist approach the topic? Does he/she interview somebody? Who? Are opposing views expressed? What kind of catch phrases or key words seem to be repeated?

1998–1999: Foreign Monopoly or National Duopoly?

The late 1990s were times of great fervor around digital television: two main topics were covered in the news. One was Rupert Murdoch's negotiations with Telecom Italia on a new digital platform (the negotiations eventually failed), and the other was the struggle over broadcasting rights of live soccer matches. Fear of an invasion of foreign ownership and concerns over the skyrocketing cost of sports rights motivated the government to intervene with a decree in January 1999 intended to limit control over broadcasting rights in the hands of any one single TV operator (Decree-Law, January 30, 1999). A foreigner in control of the most Italian of all sports, soccer? That could not be! The opposition, at the time led by Silvio Berlusconi, complained that the government was not doing its best to prevent the formation of a monopoly over rights on pay-TV platforms (Tg2 at 8:30 p.m., December 13, 1999).

On the occasion of the first talk show ever devoted to discussing the implications and developments of digital TV, one of the guests, Communications Minister Salvatore Cardinale, framed the issue as one of national pride. He emphasized the need for Italian operators to stay strong to face market competition and warned that Italy could not "subject [itself] to Europe, rather [it] ha[d] to be a protagonist in Europe" (*Domenica In*, December 20, 1998). This was necessary, he insisted, if the country was ever going to show that there were "players [out there] able to offer [Italian] content" (*Domenica In*, December 20, 1998). Ignoring the fact that the very Italian-owned Mediaset TV had long been a main vehicle through which foreign content had flooded the country's households, implicit in Cardinale's argument was the notion that in order for Italian-owned broadcasters to be successful in the digital TV environment, they needed to be given time and resources to prepare.

Yes, of course: when asked about the duopoly at home, Cardinale would acknowledge that neither broadcaster should be left free to operate in a regime of duopoly, and said that, eventually, Rete4 would have to migrate to the satellite, while RAI3 would have to give up its advertising revenues (Tg2 at 8:30 p.m., July 20, 1999). However, the minister also underlined that "we need to find a point of equilibrium that will not damage *anybody* [emphasis added] and that will allow both operators to work . . . and to face the risks of the market" (Tg2 at 8:30 p.m., July 20, 1999). Of course, here Cardinale was not referring to just *anybody*: he was talking specifically about RAI and Mediaset. Perhaps, somewhere between the lines, the message was that an Italian duopoly was still better than a foreign-owned monopoly.

During the same show (a prime time news bulletin on RAI's second channel), the anchor confirmed that "Rete4 will go on the digital platform and RAI3 will not receive advertising revenues anymore. But—the journalist continued—the time frame for this is all to be decided" (Tg2 at 8:30 p.m., July 20, 1999). In a nutshell, the key message was to continue to pay lip service to the need for breaking the duopoly, while remaining vague with regard to the exact date of the migration.

Here It Comes!

Another theme that emerged early on in the coverage, and that continued through the next peak of interest in 2004, was a sense of urgency, of immediacy, with regard to the arrival of digital TV, first, and of DTT, later. As Communications Minister Cardinale had already declared in 1998, digital TV "will soon arrive" (*Domenica In*, December 20, 1998).

In 1999, as the discourse shifted from "digital TV" (which, in 1998, still included "the dish and cable TV," *Domenica In*, December 20, 1998), to "digital terrestrial," news bulletins insisted that the transition would happen very fast. Cardinale pointed out that it was necessary "to accelerate the development of DTT" (Tg2 at 8:30 p.m., July 10, 1999), while Vincenzo Vita, then the undersecretary for communications (Tg3 at 10:30 p.m., July 12, 1999), confirmed that the shutdown of the analogue signal would happen no later than 2006. "If anything—Cardinale echoed—such a date should be anticipated" (Tg2 at 8:30 p.m., July 20, 1999).

2004: Social Usefulness

Coverage of DTT intensified in 2004. On one public affairs show, aired one day after the Gasparri law had been approved, the choice of the new technology was defended by Berlusconi's Communications Minister Maurizio Gasparri, against criticism coming from representatives of the opposition questioning why the government had decided to focus only on DTT, as opposed to other technologies, including satellite and cable TV, and broadband (Stefano Passigli, in *Porta a Porta*, 4 May 2004). No answers were given to those requests for explanation: rather, the minister reported with pride that the new law had saved Rete4 from migration, that RAI was financially viable (therefore, the license fee did not need to be increased the following year), and that December 31, 2006, was still the deadline for the shut off of the analogue signal. On the same show, Carlo Sartori, head of RAI's DTT division, came to the defense of DTT, calling it the "Esperanto" of television, and saying that the new delivery technology was "the revolution of television, not at all a superfluous addition" (*Porta a Porta*, May 4, 2004).

Interactivity

Experts often emphasized the social usefulness of the new technology. Carlo Sartori, who was frequently interviewed on a variety of programs, depicted a future where the public broadcaster would partner with cities and other local governments to provide viewers direct interface with public institutions (*TG2 Mattina*, January 3, 2004). Again and again, interview after interview, the head of RAI's DTT division praised the new technology, which will "help us live better [lives]" (*Cominciamo Bene*, 13 February 2004), and without which, "generalist TV would only be good for the poor, for those in the third world" (Internet Café, 27 March 2004). DTT, Sartori insisted, "is the way for TV to get up to speed with the technology" (*Internet Café*, 27 March 2004).

DTT and Democracy

DTT was celebrated for its democratic potentials as well. According to Giovanni Sartori, a well known political scientist (not to be confused with Carlo Sartori), thanks to the introduction of DTT, "pluralism [of information] will increase" (*Visite a Domicilio*, April 21, 2004). The interactive possibilities of the new technology would also provide citizens with novel opportunities to learn "more about their voting rights [and about] new ways to participate in the [upcoming] European elections" (*Sette Giorni al Parlamento*, May 1, 2004). It might be relevant to point out that European elections are notoriously unpopular, and one has to doubt whether any technology could ever change that.

On this show, a weekly news magazine reporting on Parliament's activities, the launch of one of the first RAI interactive channels, RAI Utile, was also announced. The new channel focused on exchange of useful information between citizens and the public administration, civil and rescue services, and local public offices. RAI Utile, however, did not last long. Indeed, even in the digital world of interactive TV, ratings, rather improved democratic participation, are still the coin of the kingdom. RAI Utile, due to poor performance, was shut down in 2008.

2006: A Missed Opportunity

News coverage during this period focused on the controversies surrounding Mediaset's use of DTT decoders (those controversies had begun at the end of 2005), and on the new bill proposed by the Prodi government in October 2006. Ample resonance was given to Berlusconi's reactions after the center left government announced its plans to impose stricter anti-trust limitations over broadcasting. For Berlusconi, then the leader of the opposition, the bill was part of an "antidemocratic plan" (Tg1 at 8:00 p.m., October 12, 2006), designed to penalize his own TV channels (Tg1 at 1:30 p.m., October 12, 2006).

The introduction of the Gentiloni bill, and the discussions surrounding it, were opportunities for developing a debate about pluralism of information in Italy, the role of DTT, and about the need for the government to intervene in the analogue TV market. However, it is surprising to notice that only one talk show and one variety show discussed the topic of digital terrestrial television at length during this period. The search with the key word "digital television" returned only one talk show.

The First Half of 2007: What Was Missing?

From the end of 2006 until July 1, 2007, the search for "digital television" returned nineteen hits, of which eleven were relevant. Of these, one was a public affairs show, one was a talk show, and the rest were news broadcasts (only two of which aired during prime time). During the same period, the search for "digital terrestrial" returned 19 hits, of which six were relevant. Among these, there was one public affairs program, which covered a broad range of topics related to interactive communications, mentioning DTT only as a platform for interactive advertising (*La Storia Siamo Noi*, June 28, 2007). There were five news bulletins, only one of which reported news related to DTT on its prime time edition.

Whereas the perspectives of government and industry representatives continued to be often heard on news bulletins, citizens' voices were generally hard to find. One important exception was an episode of the popular *Mi Manda RAITRE* (May 25, 2007), which covered the plight of consumers as they attempted to recuperate unused credit from their expired premium DTT cards. Sympathetic with the consumers, this talk show pitted a representative of the European Consumers Council against Marco Leonardi, the director of Mediaset premium DTT (Mediaset is the leader in the premium DTT market in Italy). By highlighting the difficulties those consumers had encountered, the show also spoke to the fact that DTT technology was not that user friendly after all. This program represents the kind of engaging, useful, and entertaining forum for citizens groups, consumer advocates, and industry representatives to interact and express their positions, expectations, and needs; exactly what one might expect from a public service broadcaster.

CONCLUSION

According to the information analyzed in this contribution, public debate on digital television and the transition to DTT has been qualitatively poor. It has lacked critical examination and in-depth information, and the necessary exposure on prime time television. In an environment dominated by a duopoly in the analogue broadcasting sector, the interests of the two broadcasters were reflected in the shows. Those interests included: portraying only the positive sides of the transition; creating an expectation for a quick transition, when indeed the transition continued to be postponed; avoiding discussions on why other technologies were not receiving the same attention as DTT; and providing little in-depth coverage on public affairs programs and talk shows.

The result of the analysis shows a model of communication that is mostly top-down, acritical, rather than interactive and participatory. Rather than an enlightened debate, on RAI's broadcasts one often finds a celebratory monologue, where the new technology is presented as a given, rather than as something to be discussed and evaluated by the public.

More needs to be done to map the evolution of public discourse on DTT. A textual analysis of coverage of broadcasts on Mediaset channels might provide an important complement. A review of the print media is also necessary to add more depth to the study. Comparable data from other countries would help us gain a broader, historical perspective on how the global phenomenon of the digital transition has been framed and presented to the public in different national contexts.

NOTES

1. In critical media studies, public service broadcasting (PSB) has often been associated with the notion of the public sphere as an institution ideally protected from both the government of the day and commercial imperatives (Garnham 1983, 1986, 1992); a place where contrasting, independent perspectives can be expressed and where citizens can access and share information. Although the association between the public sphere and PSB has been criticized on both theoretical grounds (Keane 1995a, 1995b) and pragmatic grounds (Jacka 2003, Padovani 2005), it continues to be important as a normative tool for assessing the democratic quality of public media.

2. The frequency that it takes to broadcast one analogue channel can be used to broadcast several digital channels.

3. Here I am referring, for example, to the delay imposed by the Italian governments of the 1970s on the transition from black-and-white to color TV. See Peppino Ortoleva, *Un Ventennio a Colori, Televisione Privata e Società in Italia* (1975–1995). Florence: Giunti, 1995.

4. For in-depth analysis of the Italian digital TV market, see Giuseppe Richeri, "Le prospettive della televisione digitale alla luce dell'esperienza internazionale," in *L'industria della Comunicazione in Italia: Quali mercati dopo la crisi*, VII Report, Rosselli Foundation, Turin: Guerini & Associates, 2004, 16–25; by the same author, "La programmazione delle piattaforme digitali e le prospettive dell'industria audiovisiva," in *Rivista Electronica Internazional de Economia de las Technologias de la Informacion y de la Comunicacion*, Vol. II, No. 2, July/August 2000a, 4-22; and Richeri, "L'industria dei programmi verso la TV digitale," in *L'industria della comunicazione in Italia: L'Era Internet, V Report*, Rosselli Foundation, Turin: Guerini & Associates, 2000b, 39–49. See also Cinzia Padovani, "Digital Television in Italy: From Duopoly to Duality," in *Javnost/The Public*, Vol. XIV (2007), 1: 57–76.

5. *Corriere della Sera*'s archives have changed since the time this search was first conducted. In November 2006, only articles' titles and leading paragraphs were accessible for free; as of May 2009, articles' full texts became available electronically at no fee.

6. Based on the results of this pilot study, the precise dates chosen for the search of RAI's broadcasts were: November 1, 1997–October 31, 1999; November 1, 2003–October 31, 2004; and November 1, 2005–October 31, 2006.

7. See Ruth Wodak and Brigitta Busch, "Approaches to Media Texts," in *The Sage Handbook of Media Studies*, John D. H. Downing (editor-in-chief), London: Sage, 2004, 105–122.

8. I did not have the time or financial resources to watch the tapes of analogue broadcasts. In order to watch them there is a viewing fee and one must make appointments with library personnel located on a different premise. Consultation and viewing of digitized material, instead, is free and can be done from work stations in any RAI library.

REFERENCES

AGCOM (Italian Communications Authority). Annual Report on activities carried out and work programmes 2008. www.agcom.it/Default.aspx?message=download pdf&DocID=101 (accessed May 3, 2009).

———. Resolution n. 346/2001. "Termini e criteri di attuazione delle disposizioni di cui all'art. 3, commi 6, 7, 9, 11, Legge 31 Luglio 1997 n. 249." http://www.agcom.it/provv/d_346_01_CONS.htm. (accessed November 10, 2007).

Analysis. Public policy treatment of digital terrestrial television (DTT) in communications markets. August 26, 2005. http://www.anacom.pt/pdfrender.jsp?contentId=296289 (accessed February 15, 2009).

Colombo, Fausto, ed. *La Digitalizzazione Dei Media*. Rome: Carocci, 2007.

Constitutional Court. Sentence n. 466/2002. "Giudizio di legittimità costituzionale in via incidentale." http://www.uonna.it/466-2002-sentenza-corte-costituzionale.htm (accessed December 21, 2007).

European Council. "Lisbon European Council 23 and 24 March 2000 Presidency Conclusions." http://www.europarl.europa.eu/summits/lis1_en.htm (accessed April 22, 2009).

Galperin, Hernan. *New Television, Old Politics: the Transition to Digital TV in the United States and Britain.* Cambridge: Cambridge University Press, 2004.

Garnham, Nicholas. "Public Service versus the Market." Screen 5, no. 1 (1983): 6-28.

———. "The Media and the Public Sphere." Pp. 37–54 in *Communicating Politics: Mass Communication and the Political Process*, edited by Peter Golding, Graham Murdock, and Philipp Schlesinger. Leicester: Leicester University Press, 1986.

———. "The Media and the Public Sphere." Pp. 359–376 in *Habermas and the Public Sphere*, edited by Craig Calhoun. Cambridge, MA: MIT Press, 1992.

Italian Government Acts. Law August 6, 1990, n. 223. "Disciplina del sistema radiotelevisivo pubblico e private" [Regulations on the public and private broadcasting sector]. http://www.agcom.it/L_naz/L223_90.htm (accessed May 23, 2009).

———. Law July 31, 1997, n. 249. "Istituzione dell'Autorità per le garanzie nelle comunicazioni e norme sui sistemi delle telecomunicazioni e radiotelevisivo" [Institution of the Communications Authority and norms on the telecommunications and broadcasting systems]. http://www.agcom.it/L_naz/L_249.htm (accessed May 23, 2009).

———. Decree Law January 30, 1999, n. 15. "Disposizioni urgenti per lo sviluppo equilibrato dell'emittenza televisiva e per evitare la costituzione o il mantenimento di posizioni dominanti nel settore radiotelevisivo" [Urgent norms for a balanced development of television broadcasting and to avoid the establishment or the continuation of dominant positions in the radio television sector]. http://www2.agcom.it/L_naz/dl_300199_15.htm (accessed April 23, 2009).

———. Law March 20, 2001, n. 66. "Conversione in legge, con modificazioni, del decreto-legge 23 gennaio 2001, n. 5, recante disposizioni urgenti per il differimento di termini in materia di trasmissioni radiotelevisive analogiche e digitali, nonché per il risanamento di impianti radiotelevisivi" [Conversion in law . . . of decree-law 23 January 2001 . . . containing urgent dispositions regarding the transition of analogue and digital broadcasting]. http://www.camera.it/parlam/leggi/01066l.htm (accessed May 27, 2009).

———. Decree-law December 24, 2003, n. 352. "Disposizioni urgenti concernenti modalità di definitiva cessazione del regime transitorio della legge 31 luglio 1997, n. 249" [Urgent norms regarding the final deadline for the transitional period as of law 31 July 1997, n. 249]. http://www2.agcom.it/L_naz/DL_352_03.htm (accessed May 23, 2009).

———. Law May 3, 2004, no. 112. "Norme di principio in materia di assetto del sistema radiotelevisivo e della RAI-Radiotelevisione Italiana S.p.a., nonchè delega al Governo per l'emanazione del testo unico della radiotelevisione" [Norms of principles concerning the restructuring of the broadcasting system and of RAI]. http://www.comunicazioni.it/binary/min_comunicazioni/normativa/L112_2004.pdf (accessed May 23, 2009).

Jacka, Elisabeth. "Democracy as Defeat: The Impotence of Arguments for Public Service Broadcasting." Pp. 177–191 in *Rethinking Public Media in a Transnational*

Era, edited by Gerald Sussman. Special issue of Television and New Media 4, no. 2 (May 2003).

Keane, John. "Structural Transformations of the Public Sphere." *Communication Review* 1, no. 1 (1995a): 1–22.

———. "A Reply to Nicholas Garnham." *Communication Review* 1, no. 1 (1995b): 27–31.

Marzulli, Andrea. "Televisione." Pp. 37–54 in *L'Industria della Comunicazione in Italia, Dai Tradizionali produttori dei contenuti ai nuovi content aggregator, IX Report*, Rosselli Foundation. Turin: Guerini & Associates, 2006.

Ortoleva, Peppino. *Un Ventennio a Colori, Televisione Privata e Società in Italia (1975–1995)*. Florence: Giunti, 1995.

Padovani, Cinzia. *A Fatal Attraction Public: Television and the Party System in Italy*. Lanham, MD: Rowman & Littlefield, 2005.

———. "Digital Television in Italy: From Duopoly to Duality." *Javnost/The Public*, 14, no. 1 (2007): 57–76.

———. "Pluralism of information in the television sector in Italy: History and contemporary conditions." Pp. 289–304 in *Press Freedom and Pluralism in Europe: Concepts and Conditions*, edited by Andrea Czepek, Melanie Hellwig, and Eva Nowak. ECREA book series. Bristol: Intellect, 2009.

Perucci, Antonio, and Giuseppe Richeri, eds. *Il mercato televisivo italiano nel contesto Europeo*. Bologna: Il Mulino, 2003.

Richeri, Giuseppe. "La programmazione delle piattaforme digitali e le prospettive dell'industria audiovisiva." *Rivista Electronica Internazional de Economia de las Technologias de la Informacion y de la Comunicacion* 2, no. 2 (July/August 2000a): 4–22.

———. "L'Industria dei programmi verso la TV digitale." Pp. 39–49 in *L'industria della Comunicazione in Italia: L'Era Internet, V Report*, Rosselli Foundation. Turin: Guerini & Associates, 2000b.

———. "Le prospettive della televisione digitale alla luce dell'esperienza internazionale." Pp. 16–25 in *L'industria della Comunicazione in Italia: Quali mercati dopo la crisi, VII Report*, Rosselli Foundation. Turin: Guerini & Associates, 2004.

———. Interview with author, tape recorded. Rome, July 11, 2007.

Sartori, Carlo. "Digitale terrestre: la televisione alla riscossa. Una rivoluzione che cambia (in meglio) gli operatori, i programmi, i sistemi televisivi," *Nuova Civiltà delle Macchine Passati e presenti della televisione. TV e tecnologia in Italia, storia, presenze e scenari* 86, no. 2 (April–June 2004), RAI Eri: 11–19.

Smith, Paul. *The Politics of Television Policy: The Introduction of Digital Television in Great Britain*. Lewinston, NY: The Edwin Mellen Press, 2007.

Starks, Michael. *Switching to Digital Television UK Public Policy and the Market*. Bristol, UK: Intellect, 2007.

Wodak, Ruth, and Brigitta Busch, "Approaches to Media Texts." Pp. 105–122 in *The Sage Handbook of Media Studies*, edited by John D. H. Downing. London: Sage, 2004.

Part Two

TELEVISION FLOWS AND FORMATS

Chapter Four

Struggling for Identity: The Television Production Sector in Italy and the Challenges of Globalization

Flavia Barca and Andrea Marzulli

"Yes watching the sea I believe that if Europe is to have a future, a good future, it is what Edouard Glissant calls the Mediterranean Creole." —Izzo Jean-Claude. *Aglio, menta e basilico,* Roma: Edizioni E/o. 2006.

INTRODUCTION[1]

The relationship between globalization and television production is complex. In twenty years from now, the television industry will have completely modified not only its own system of financing but also the way it is articulated, as a result of both globalization and digital networks. The Internet is physically and conceptually transforming communications at a global level even though consumer habits take time to mature and resistance to traditional operators is still quite strong.

The effects of globalization within media industries are very articulate, and the television production sector is characterized by particularly complicated mechanisms, so an effort of synthesis is required to take into account the many variables at stake.

First, the context of the television market varies from country to country. In Italy the duopoly between the public broadcaster RAI and the commercial rival Mediaset has contributed to creating a highly homogeneous scenario, with little room for innovative content. The free play of market forces has therefore also made production homogeneous and has relegated Italy to the category of countries that import audiovisual products. In addition, public policy has not been able (unlike other countries such as the UK or France) to introduce solutions to the gaps in the market, namely an unbalanced negotiating playing field between broadcasters and producers, lack of incentives for original production and excessive reliance on imported formats.

The increased importance of assets such as intellectual property, and the circulation of creative ideas well received in global markets, has not yet been matched by a policy that encourages investment in research and development and releases risk capital to finance programs and ideas capable of crossing national borders.

In summary, Italian television today shows little inclination for risk-taking and has passively succumbed to the internationalization of television content. These risk-free formats,[2] tried and tested, give a sense of security to producers and broadcasters. 'Global' tends to prevail over 'local' owing to the complete inertia of local production: there is way too little original television content and it rarely travels across borders.

One consequence is that in the future local producers will no longer be equipped to face changes in demand and in the way TV is used. The only way to turn such a situation around, as the conclusion of this work will argue, is to make innovation a key goal in the entire sector over the next few years. We reach this conclusion in four steps. After a brief overview of the effects of globalization on the media industry and, in particular, on the television production industry and the format phenomenon (section 1), section 2 outlines the history of legislation in the Italian television production sector, focusing mainly on the ways Italian legislators have accepted the relevant EU regulations and their main effects, especially on TV drama production. Section 3 examines the characteristics of the production sector in Italy, while section 4 analyzes the main changes in the television market and their profound repercussions on content.

GLOBALIZATION AND TELEVISION PRODUCTION: THE FORMAT CONCEPT

Globalization has been accompanied historically by migration, the internationalization of capital, trademarks and firms, and the development of communication networks, which then become a platform for virtual migratory processes. The internationalization of capital, trademarks and firms have conditioned audiovisual products, and, as we shall see in greater detail, transformed them from quintessentially local merchandise into formats with the capability to travel to different cultures and markets. Communication networks comprise electronic and digital networks, conveying either money or knowledge, or both at the same time. With the globalization process underway, contents adapt themselves less to the means than to new forms of consumption. This paradigm shift from transnational to trans-cultural (the new dimension in which format is conceived and then developed) is on the verge of radically transforming television production as it has been known so far.

It could be said that an *ante litteram* type of format—in the sense of a foreign show being adapted to the taste of national viewers—already existed in Italian television in the 1950s, though there was no awareness of the phenomenon at the time. Entertainment programs such as *Lascia o raddoppia?* ("Pass or Double?"), one of the biggest Italian television successes of the fifties inspired by the popular American quiz *The $64,000 Question*, or *Il Musichiere*, again in the 1950s, created on the model of the NBC game show *Name that Tune* were surely formats.

It was, however, in the 1990s that globalization effects in the media industry really took off, creating a limited number of leading transnational enterprises, with horizontal and vertical concentration processes. Increasing competition, as well as a growing market deregulation, have led to standardization in products and services through the intense use of information and communication technologies not only to provide new services but also to attempt to optimize the production process. This standardization facilitates the global flow of content and allows repeatable and adaptable modules to be built for any context.

A repeatable and adaptable module is the definition of a format, the ultimate product of this phase of globalization. The format concept contrasts with the traditional idea of audiovisual goods, produced in a prototype industry (where costs are linked to producing an original) characterized by high *sunk costs* (irretrievable costs), as well as *experience good* (a service whose quality can only be known after its use). The main innovation of the format concept is that it can contain costs as a global product but at the same time it develops characteristics able to meet a local flavor (*glocalization*), after it has been tried within the original market.

The strategic role of formats in building a TV schedule is to fill whole strips of programming with a number of episodes, guaranteed by a single concept that can be identified immediately and repeated daily. This guarantees viewer fidelity for the broadcaster, while the standardization of the productive process saves resources. The cost-effectiveness of the concept is an advantage for the format originator, the producer and the broadcaster. While the mechanism was initially associated with entertainment programs, it was subsequently adopted for TV drama, and in particular for product series like sitcoms and soap operas.[3]

The format concept was thus already an important ingredient of international television in the 1990s,[4] but in the last decade it has developed significantly.

There are a certain number of economic variables that have contributed to the phenomenon. First, the growing number of television channels has created a significant increase in program demand. Second, the exponential growth of competitive pressure, owing both to the multiplication of channels and to the consequent audience fragmentation, has spurred television enterprises to look for less risky options. The adaptation of an already tested format for another market allows for a more reliable measurement of viewer shares and profiles.

The increasing need to optimize production times and costs has led television enterprises to prefer programs which can be made in less time, and the adaptation of formats allows for huge savings in production time owing to the standardization of the production process and therefore contains costs.

The analysis of the European audiovisual market could support the claim that the format concept has succeeded where co-production has failed. Since the end of the 1980s, it has been EU policy to give national markets incentives to open up to co-productions with other countries and to devise products with a potentially wider audience. A highly protected European market, with often-insurmountable cultural barriers, however, has often thwarted these initiatives. EU policy has thus had the effect of strengthening national production without creating a truly European audiovisual market.

One effect of globalization on the media industry, and, in particular, on the success of formats in television production has been a marked trend towards horizontal integration, while another one has been product and geographical diversification. Two big international production groups, Endemol and Fremantle Media, have developed in Europe,[5] both active in the most important markets with effective localization strategies. The main propellant in the internationalization strategies of these groups is the availability of rights for appealing programs, organized in a sufficiently diversified catalogue.

Yet, another effect of globalization has thus been to accentuate the importance of intellectual property in the economies of firms, especially communications and media companies. The circulation of knowledge exploits the originality of ideas and requires tools to safeguard intellectual property and copyright in order to defend investments in research and development, which generate competitive advantage. Competitive pressure has also promoted horizontal integration inside individual markets where groups of production companies strong enough to contrast international competition have formed, with the goal of overseeing different types of products (Imagina Media Audiovisual in Spain, All3Media in the UK, Magnolia in Italy, Carrère Groupe in France). These groups have also extended their activities to production for new media.

The question whether globalization in the media industry, and specifically in television production, has had a negative effect on national cultural identities, or has weakened creative national industries, is still open. In the case of the Italian industry, Section 3 will explore this matter further.

A BRIEF HISTORY OF THE TELEVISION PRODUCTION INDUSTRY IN ITALY

The Directive "TV without Frontiers" to Support a European Market

Protecting and promoting European audiovisual production in the 1980s was one of the guidelines of EU policy concerning television. An important reason for this was excessive reliance on imports (on the part of Fininvest in Italy as well as Rtl in Germany and the privatized Tfl in France). EU Directive 89/552/EEC, "TV without frontiers," introduced program and production quotas for European works and independent productions.

The articles of the Directive (later to be amended by Directive 97/36/EC) aimed to create a strong single European production market and declared the need for "measures to guarantee transition from national markets to common production and distribution markets which create the conditions for fair competition." They also enshrined the idea that adopting minimum standards for producing European audiovisuals from EU television programs, be they public or private, was a way to promote independent production and distribution that was complementary to other tools already being used or planned to be used in the future.

The development of a European production market generated an increase in national demand by imposing a percentage of programs that were required to be European and independent (art. 4 and 5 of the Directive). In the view of EU legislators an "internal" European Market could be built by grouping together the demands of national markets, in order to establish a sufficiently remunerative outlet for products as expensive as audiovisuals. In fact, the Directive stipulated that it was necessary to promote wider markets so that television production in member States could recover their investments, not only by adopting common standards, which would open national markets up to one another, but also by envisaging for European productions a significant proportion of television programs from all Member States.

In an attempt to combat over-reliance on imports, EU legislators used the tool of program and production investment quotas to stimulate internal demand. Furthermore, they set the goal of encouraging the development of a European axis in the production of television contents that would one day be strong enough to compete with U.S. production. This result should be obtained through the consolidation of an extremely fragmented sector, made up mainly of small- and medium-sized enterprises, and the promotion of their growth.

The financial tool accompanying the Directive was the Media Program, a fund to support the audiovisual industry set up in 1991. One of its main aims was to encourage co-productions involving producers and broadcasters of at least two member States as well as to circulate audiovisual works in European markets, with incentives for film and television distribution. According to the most recent comprehensive study promoted by the Directorate for Information Society and Media of the EU Commission, this goal has not been achieved. Out of television channels with shares above 3 percent (the so-called *primary channels*) programming featuring non-domestic European works only grew from 10.9 percent to 12.3 percent from 1993 to 2002 (Graham 2005).

The Italian Legal Framework for Television Production

EU regulations for television content production were not received very well in Italy. Rules to protect and promote production were either not enforced or applied lightly, thus reducing the onus on both public and private broadcasters. In fact, Italian Law 223 issued on August 6, 1990 (called the "Legge Mammì" after the Minister who proposed it) ignored regulations concerning independent producers. The idea of protecting European works was extended to safeguarding national production (in part based on the sub-quota model for works of "expression originale française"—or "eof" as the French called it) but only to "cinematographic films."

Italy did not come up with more precise regulations regarding programming and production of European and independent works until the April 30, 1998, Law 122, restructuring the 1997 version that had, in the meantime, come into force under the EU Directive. Article 2 of the new law, comma 1, declared that national broadcasters (free-to-air or pay), should dedicate "more than half" of their monthly programming to European products. Comma 3 of the same article established that 10 percent of "qualifying" programming should be devoted to European independent production, bringing it up to 20 percent of programming for the public service broadcaster. Comma 4 reiterated the criteria established in the 1997 Directive as far as independent producers and residual rights were concerned, but delegated regulation for attributing rights to the Communications Authority (Agcom).

After considerable procrastination, this regulation was approved on July 30, 2003 with Agcom Resolution 185/03/CSP. It was explicitly stated that payment for "independent producers can only be established by an autonomous private sector and by means of negotiation between the parties, respect-

Struggling for Identity

ing the criteria established by the Communications Authority as far as quotas for residual rights are concerned, in particular regarding time frames, the peculiarities of each typology of production, and in proportion to their participation in product development and creation." The time limit for re-attributing residual rights to producers was increased to no less than seven years for all genres, except for documentaries (five years). At the end of 2006, given the problems linked with managing exploitation rights, and the lack of benefits for the producers, the Communications Authority commissioned a survey in order to re-examine the rules for attributing residual rights (Resolution n. 164/06/CSP). In 2008, the Authority released a draft set of rules for exploitation rights which, as of March 2009, was still not approved.

The Effects on the Market and the Rise of TV Drama

The main effect of Law 122 on the production market in Italy was to spearhead the domestic TV drama market, though this took place later than in other European countries which had assimilated the EU 1989 Directive much more quickly. With the gradual increase of pay-TV and the migration of "premium" contents, such as cinema and sports, towards pay channels, TV drama took on a strategic role in terrestrial generalist broadcasters' schedules. TV drama attracted significant viewer attention and contributed to consolidating the broadcaster's own brand (great stories about national

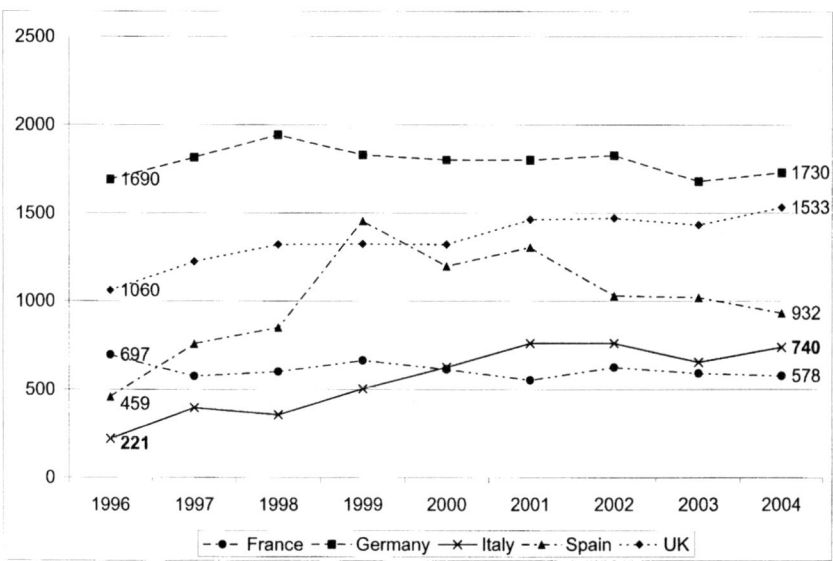

Figure 4.1. Original Domestic TV Drama Production (Hours), 1996–2004

identity for RAI, appealing stories about daily life for Mediaset). Since 1999, investments in TV drama for the two main national broadcasters (with the exception of 2002, one post-crisis year), continued to increase.

According to Eurofiction[6] the Italian market used domestic TV drama to partly close the gap with other major European markets in terms of hourly volume of original production.

The Duopoly Market Structure and the Weak Negotiating Power of Producers

The difficulties of the television production sector also stem from the market context. The Italian television market, in fact, at least until 2005, was duopolistic. The two broadcasters, RAI and Mediaset have control over 83 percent of national television frequencies, 84 percent of viewers and 85 percent of advertising revenue (Marzulli: 2006). It was not until 2005–2006, with the rapid rise of the satellite pay-TV operator, Sky Italia, created by merging the two platforms Telepiù and Stream and 100 percent under the control of News Corp., that the presence of a significant third actor re-balanced the market.

From the point of view of television production, however, Sky Italia has not yet altered the relationship between supply and demand of original contents. Sky Italia has made little effort to commission original television productions, owing partly to the fact that Law 122 for pay-TV operators calculates investment shares in audiovisual production based only on advertising revenues not including subscription revenues.[7] Only the strongest and most innovative Italian producers also work for the satellite platform.

Out of the absence of real competition for television products, and the homogeneous supply squeezed between the public service broadcaster and its main commercial competitor, a naturally imbalanced negotiation position has emerged between producers and broadcasters to the advantage of broadcasters. The fact that productions are almost exclusively financed by broadcasters, allows both RAI and Mediaset, during the negotiation phase, to perpetually hold all exploitation rights for all platforms. This leaves producers without a rights-portfolio to sell on other markets (international, new media, home-video): thus, they are unable to generate extra earnings, the capitalization of their immaterial assets is negligible or inexistent, and they lack the financial capacity to attract risk capital for production. The lack of readily available risk capital is what has triggered the vicious circle leaving the ownership of rights in the hands of broadcasters.

Furthermore, RAI and Mediaset exert strict editorial control as early on as in the development stage, often directly intervening in casting and carefully monitoring expenses. The fact that broadcasters intervene financially and conceptually supports their position in any legal wrangling with producers over the attribution of exploitation rights. The *producer fee*, or rather the producer's profit calculated as a percentage of production costs, represents the only source of profit for producers. While this profit source is secure, it does not stimulate producers' creativity, nor does it force them to take any real entrepreneurial risk. Product innovation and growth suffer without investment in research and development.

Italian producers are thus like contract consultants for programs commissioned by RAI and Mediaset and they are rarely independent. This is particularly true in the case of TV drama production, which is the most valuable area of 'external' television production. Entertainment is another matter. This is partly because lower production costs for a pilot give producers greater scope for investment. However, the main reason is that the popularity of imported formats steers negotiations between producers and broadcasters to follow established international licensing practices. The stronger negotiating force of originators and format distributors leaves licensed Italian producers with a limited rights package, which they, in their turn, are unable to cede to broadcasters.

The few documentary and animation producers with international appeal are different because their works are often co-produced. While in Italy the broadcaster nearly always retains rights, in the case of animation the product's ability to 'travel' internationally, as well as the excellent potential for supplementary revenue owing to licensing and merchandising spin-off deals, encourage producers to risk investing more heavily. When a product is successful, results contribute to the growth of the production company (as with Rainbow, the production company for the animation series *Winx*).

In conclusion, a policy to support television production was implemented with a significant delay compared to the growth of commercial TV, at a time—the end of the 1990s—when the early effects of globalization on the TV sector, as we shall see later, evidenced the need for greater regulation and intervention, in the direction of exploiting intellectual property assets to the full.

The Effects of Globalization on the Television Production Sector in Italy

Following Robert G. Picard's taxonomy of the effects of globalization on the television production sector in Italy,[8] this section will now examine in particular two significant factors: first, the interchange of television formats, with imports dominating over exports in Italy; second, the presence of branches of large foreign production groups (mainly Endemol and Fremantle Media), and their market strength, while, by contrast no Italian production company either wants or is able to open branches abroad.

This section will then go on to investigate the import and export of finished television products in Italy, for which data is scarce and surveys promoted by operators in the sector inexistent.

The Economic Dimension of the Sector: Weakness and Fragmentation

The turnover of the Italian industry betrays the backwardness of the sector in comparison with other international markets. The 423 (out of a total of 500 active companies) television production companies assessed in a recent study on television production in Italy (Barca, D'Urso, Marzulli: 2006) generated in 2004 700 million Euros from television production,[9] with an average per company of 1.7 million Euros.[10] In other countries with similar socio-demographic characteristics such as the UK and France, production turnover was significantly higher: 1.61 and 1.26 billion Euros, respectively. In Germany the figure was 2.2 billion Euros. Likewise, average turnover is decidedly higher in other countries: UK (3.2 million Euros), Sweden (3.1), Germany (2.8) and France (2.5) (see Ofcom: 2006b). The traditional fragmentation of the Italian market has thus contributed to its difficulty facing increasing competition from international markets.

Comparing the turnover of the top ten television production groups in Italy with the top ten British groups, it is evident that Italy's market is weak and undersized. The turnover ratio is near 1:4. Clearly the comparison is cruel, as the UK is the world's leading television exporter. However, what is significant is that strict regulation for managing exploitation rights (the UK *Codes of Practice* safeguard producers in the negotiation phase with broadcasters) has contributed to this result. British producers, furthermore, boast exports amounting to approximately one billion Euros, which include the various

Table 4.1. Independent production in main European countries: Main indicators, 2004

Country	Number of Companies	Average Turnover (M€)	Turnover (M€)	Total TV Market (M€)	% Production/ TV Market
France	500	2.5	1,261	8,223	15.3
Germany	800	2.8	2,221	12,340	18.0
Italy (total)	423	2.5	1,065	6,805	15.7
Italy (only TV revenues)	423	1.7	700	6,805	10.3
Sweden	30	3.1	93	1,620	5.7
United Kingdom	500	3.2	1,615	14,651	11.0

Source: authors' data elaborations from IEM, Italian Tax Office (Agenzia delle Entrate), Screen Digest, Ofcom.

Table 4.2. Top 10 television production groups in the UK and Italy, 2007

United Kingdom			Italy		
Group	Main shareholders	Turnover	Group	Main shareholders	Turnover
Img Media	Forstmann Little & Co.	324.0	Endemol Italia group*	Mediaset-Cyrte-Goldman Sachs	156.7
All3Media	Permira	295.9	Magnolia group	De Agostini-G. Gori	85.6
Endemol Uk	Mediaset-Cyrte-Goldman Sachs	233.8	Grundy Italia	Fremantle (Rtl Group)	68.5
ShineReveille	3i Private Equity, Sony, Newscorp.	213.4	Film Master Group	Castellani-Balich-Coffa-Marino	51.4
Hit Entertainment	Apax	208.5	Lux Vide	Bernabei-State Street-Ben Ammar	44.5
Talkback Thames	Rtl Group-Fremantle	204.6	Fascino Pgt	Mediaset-De Filippi	40.0
Rdf Media	D. Frank et al.	145.1	Cattleya	Tozzi-Chimenz-Stabilini	33.7
Shed Media	Cyrte-Newton et al.	104.9	Dap	De Angelis family	32.3
Entertainment Rights	in Administration	99.4	Taodue	Mediaset-Valsecchi	28.3
Tinopolis	Schroder Inv.	96.4	Ballandi Entertainment	Ballandi	28.2
Total		**1,926.1**	**Total**		**569.2**

Notes: in million Euro (average exchange UIC – Ufficio Italiano Cambi for 2007: 1 Euro = 0.6843 Pound Sterling); (*) 2007 data for Palomar, Mediavivere, Yam112003; 2006 data for Endemol Italia SpA.
Source: authors' elaboration on data from Iem, Mediatique, Broadcast, Televisual.

forms of licensing for different channels of audiovisual distribution that boost profits even further.

Moreover, it is worth noticing that British groups are often linked with investment funds. In the UK, the profitability of production has attracted venture capital investments, whereas in Italy this phenomenon is virtually non-existent because companies have limited capitalization.

ITALIAN TELEVISION'S DEPENDENCE ON IMPORTED FORMATS AND THE IMPORT/EXPORT BUDGET

The success of formats has thus revealed the fragility of Italian television production. Its fragility is not only due to the industrial weakness of the sector; it also suffers from lack of support and lack of incentives within a weak policy and regulation framework.

Producers' financial dependence on broadcasters as far as funding production is concerned has provided broadcasters with the negotiating power to hold rights in perpetuity. The fact that producers do not possess their own rights-portfolio means most production companies have little capital at their disposal and therefore cannot invest in research and development in order to create new appealing formats for foreign markets.

It is customary in the Italian market for broadcasters to reimburse costs incurred for research and development when they consider a format proposed by a producer that they think will be successful. At this point, however, the producer only can produce the program if he/she gives the broadcaster all the rights for the format. Producers are thus denied any chance of exploiting the format in the future. The result is that producers have no incentive to invest in innovation nor are they able to attract capital investments (growth is directly related to the possibility of optimizing one's library, or rather one's rights archive). This clearly has a very negative impact on creativity, while existing talents are not exploited to the full. In short, unlike other industries, television production companies are denied the opportunity to exploit their brand, their company name or their product. This obviously reduces their visibility at home, and, more importantly, abroad.

The result is that Italy's impact on the international format market is negligible. A study conducted by Screen Digest (2005) showed that the world market for formats has grown from 1.7 billion Euro in 2002 to approximately 2.2 billion Euro in 2003 and then to 2.4 billion Euro in 2004. Italy benefited marginally from this growth and holds a mere 1.5 percent share of the world market in formats.

The import/export balance of television programming hours based on formats is led by a small group of leading countries with highly profitable

Struggling for Identity

Table 4.3. TV formats global export, by country of origin (2002–2004)

Country	Hours	%
United Kingdom	10,471	32.1
Netherlands	6,811	20.9
USA	5,945	18.2
Australia	2,696	8.3
Sweden	1,161	3.6
France	932	2.9
Norway	623	1.9
Denmark	576	1.8
Italy	**500**	**1.5**
Argentina	456	1.4
Others	2,464	7.6
Total	**32,635**	**100.0**

Notes: format-based programming hours from 2002 to 2004.
Source: authors's elaboration on data from Screen Digest, Goldmedia, Frapa.

companies. In 2004, 3,800 hours of programming based on formats originating in the UK were produced in the world. By contrast, in the UK only 633 hours of foreign formats were broadcast. The balance is particularly positive also for the Netherlands and the United States. By contrast, in a handful of countries the capacity to export is minimal and reliance on imports is very high. These include France, Germany, Spain and, of course, Italy.

In the Italian market, only 3 percent of programming based on formats originates with Italian formats. Over-reliance on imported formats, however, is not an Italian prerogative: in most large television markets domestic formats are a minority, but in Italy this phenomenon is more evident than in other places and domestic products are particularly weak.

THE LIMITED INTERNATIONALIZATION OF PRODUCTION COMPANIES IN ITALY

By internationalization of production companies we mean the capacity to attract resources from television markets other than domestic markets. This can take place in a variety of ways:

- selling (directly or indirectly via distributors) programs, format rights or spin-off products (home-video, licensing) that have already been exploited in the Italian marketplace;

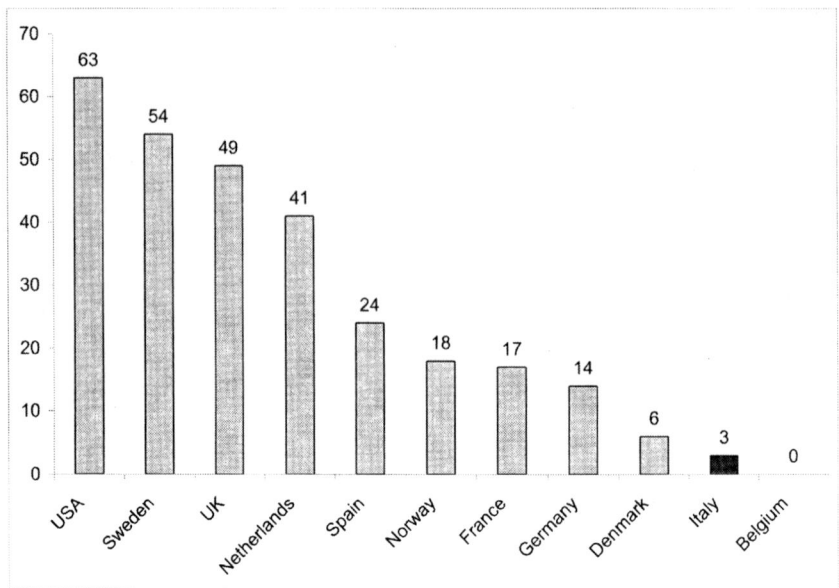

Figure 4.2. Democratic Format Programming out of a Total Format-Based Programming (% hrs.), 2004

- selling services to non-Italian broadcasters or entering foreign markets via companies created ad-hoc that are either completely controlled or in a joint-venture with local producers;
- attracting investments from foreign producers or broadcasters for co-productions originating in Italy but deemed to have international appeal.

In general, however, very little conceptual work originates in Italy, and Italian producers, with rare exceptions, do not generally play a role in the international market. The fact that producers do not hold rights-portfolios goes a long way, again, toward explaining this, and is also an underlying reason for limited product innovation.

A significant exception is the company Magnolia, founded in 2001 by Giorgio Gori and Ilaria Dallatana (former Mediaset managers), that specializes in developing and adapting formats as well as producing entertainment programs, in particular reality shows and talk shows for prime time, and game shows for access-prime time. In 2007, the Magnolia group (about ten companies) declared a turnover of 85.6 million Euros. At the beginning of 2007, 53 percent of the company was purchased by the publishing group De Agostini (which controls the Spanish channel Antena 3) for 100 million Euros. The group set up a company in Spain (Magnolia TV España), which works mainly for the Spanish network Telecinco (controlled by Mediaset), and which also managed to penetrate the French market by registering the company Magnolia France (initially with a 50 percent share of the production company Loribel, which later became part of the production group Unimedia, and then took 100 percent control of the company).

Aside from these companies, and the new company, Mondo TV France—part of the Italian group Mondo TV created to co-produce animation products—there are no branches of Italian audiovisual production companies or Italian groups active in markets outside Italy.

Some companies manage to fund their own production activities by participating in co-productions. This is true for Palomar (a company controlled by Endemol) and for Lux Vide. With their slate of projects based on the Bible or on important Italian historical figures, the latter has made international co-production one of its flagships since the 1990s and has attracted European and American capital as well as exporting Italian TV drama products to the international marketplace. While co-production could be problematic for a genre that does not travel well across borders such as TV drama, documentaries and animation, on the other hand, travel better. Most Italian animation companies create co-productions with foreign partners (usually with two different partners from different countries, with Rai financing 30 percent) to limit both costs and risks.

By contrast, since the beginning of 2000 Italy has represented a particularly interesting and fruitful market for international majors. Of the six biggest groups, representing in 2004 25 percent of the sector turnover, a substantial portion (more than 14 percent) was generated by companies that belong to the two international groups, Endemol and Fremantle.[11] The comparison of the turnover of international companies investing capital in Italy with the turnover of Italian companies on foreign markets yields a negative balance: 238 million Euro versus a mere 16 million Euro.

When Mediaset bought 33 percent of the Endemol group in 2007 (with two other identical fractions undersigned by Cyrte Funds, owned by the company's founder John De Mol, and by Goldman Sachs) the scenario was set to change. This takeover represents the largest investment in content ever realized by an Italian television operator. The level of integration accomplished launches Mediaset into international markets (though the main effects will be seen in markets where Mediaset already plays a role, such as Italy and Spain).

In conclusion, as far as direct exports of television products are concerned, the turnover of Italian production companies relies mainly on TV drama. This genre, on one hand, has proved to appeal to viewers' values (as audience results generally confirm); on the other hand, it does not travel well (and not just in Italy). Recently, owing to a process of "formatting" of the genre, as

Table 4.4. Foreign companies in Italy and Italian companies abroad, by group and turnover

Foreign Companies in Italy (origin group and country)	Turnover (year)	Italian Companies Abroad (origin group and destination market)	Turnover (year)
Endemol Italia (Endemol, Netherlands)	156.7 (2007)	Magnolia France (Magnolia Group, France)	16.0 (est. 2006)
Palomar Endemol (Endemol, Netherlands)		Magnolia TV España (Magnolia Group, Spain)	
Mediavivere (Endemol, Netherlands)		Mondo TV France sas (Mondo TV, France)	start-up in 2007
Yam 112003 (Endemol, Netherlands)			
Grundy Productions Italy (Fremantle Media, Germany)	68.5 (2007)		
Fbc Media (Fbc Group, UK)	4.6 (2007)		
Europroduzione (Europroducciones, Spain)	2.9 (2006)		
Polyvideo (Sinim, Switzerland)	2.7 (2007)		
Wilder (Fox Intl. Channels, USA)	2.5 (2005)		
Total foreign companies turnover in Italy:	**237.9**	**Total Italian companies turnover abroad:**	**16.0**

Notes: controlling stakes are often less than 100%.
Source: authors using data from operators and the Italian Tax Office (Agenzia delle Entrate).

we have seen, new possibilities for the internationalization of TV drama have begun to open up.

Currently, most Italian program exports pass through the commercial arm of the public service broadcaster, RAI Trade. This is because in many cases RAI holds all the rights for commissioned productions, and because most producers prefer to delegate commercialization of their products to RAI Trade, which they consider better organized for the task. Italian producers rarely sell programs or formats abroad and exports of television products do not generate more than 20–30 million Euros a year.[12] In comparison, French producers and broadcasters export 200 million Euros worth, while British exports generate a turnover of about 1,500 million Euros.

THE FIRST CRACKS IN THE TELEVISION SET: NEW MEDIA

The structure of the market, traditionally dominated by broadcasting as the sole output for production, is rapidly changing. This is not only because the proliferation of television channels and distribution platforms stimulates demand for more variety (largely satisfied by the big U.S. television producers). More importantly, it is because the model for exploiting audiovisual contents is being profoundly transformed owing to the boom of the Internet. A powerful distribution network of this kind has flanked mainstream professional audiovisual creation with a bottom-up production and dissemination model now universally referred to as user generated content. Audiovisual consumers, therefore, have become not only distributors (file sharing in various peer-to-peer technologies) but also content producers. The phenomenal success of video-sharing and social networking sites (YouTube and MySpace as well as video-blogs), has made the Internet a global distributor, while traditional television is competing against all odds for consumers' *mind-shares*, particularly among younger age groups.

The battle for advertising revenue thus sparks a chain reaction, varying as consumer habits in different markets evolve. First, there is a shift in turnover shares from generalist TV to thematic TV, while at the same time, advertising shares for the Internet increase compared with other media. Television channels, whose programming flows are highly structured, lose advertising appeal, while content producers can compete with broadcasters to reach and appeal to viewers and attract advertising investors. The expansion of fruition on demand, linked with content, encourages direct contact and communication between advertisers and producers. This means that commercial brands and content are inextricably linked, leaving no role for broadcasters or advertising concessionaries.

Thus, the most innovative television production companies aim to evolve their business model in the multi-platform sector. This entails both ad hoc content productions for different networks (mobile TV, IPTV, digital terrestrial TV) and content creation for different platforms. It also involves advertising investors in both the creative process and production (branded entertainment). Clearly, this strategic development is still very new, except for highly innovative companies (Magnolia, Einstein Multimedia).

The great unknowns that weigh on the television market are linked with the popularity and potential of so-called Internet videos, including user-generated content. These spontaneous products of the global network replace traditional audiovisual products commercially, geographically and culturally.

As a result market dynamics are radically altered. While the impact may seem potentially destructive for broadcasting as we know it, it is more difficult to foresee its impact on television production. The only thing that is clear is that opportunities will be limited if production continues to cling to the sinking ship of broadcasting with risks being dragged down with it. If at least the more innovative broadcasters begin to envisage business models that take into account user-generated content as an additional variable, producers who develop specific content types in a 'circular' exchange with viewers/program consumers could also follow suit.

Investments, imagination, and innovation are needed. Without these the audiovisual market will be ill equipped to tackle its challenges. A market as static and flagging as the Italian television production market runs the risk of succumbing to the defensive position of generalist broadcasters and therefore of submitting slowly but surely if not to their demise at least to their reshaping in the face of the competitive pressure of content creation and global platforms.

CONCLUSION: THE NEED OF A RADICAL CHANGE IN AUDIOVISUAL PRODUCTION POLICY

Globalization has radically altered the competitive environment and has brought increased risks and opportunities to all those involved. The analysis of the industrial sector of television production and its future outlook in international markets, yields, as we have seen, a negative balance with few exceptions, and there is little room for hope. The virtuous circle that increasing competition could trigger is still very uncertain. There are few Italian producers able to reinvest their profits in creating innovative products.

The television duopoly has spawned a highly self-referential production model and has not encouraged producers to create products that travel well across borders. Producers are in most cases little more than contract consultants for broadcasters, and, owing to the way rights are managed and held, they do not partake of supplementary or spin-off earnings and have little incentive to invest in production.

Competition for viewers among national broadcasters has triggered a race for risk-free tried and tested products, making imported formats even more popular given that innovative national formats are few and far between. Big international groups are thus free to exert their market strength pushing Italian formats into a corner. The risk adversion of Italian broadcasters and producers makes them unable to seize the opportunities inherent in the opening up of the competitive arena.

The format concept, and, more in general, globalizing forces have not succeeded in stimulating growth and product innovation in the Italian market. This is a symptom of a country that has no faith in its creative class and in the importance of strengthening its creative capital. This is essential not only for maintaining a competitive edge, but mostly for stimulating the socio-cultural and economic development of a country's human capital. In other areas of immaterial capital such as fashion, with a far smaller target impact, there are many strong performers and there is much more respect for, and protection of, the creative work involved. There is instead little of the same respect or protection for television production, even though it is by its very nature aimed at a mass market and its social influence is widely recognized. Also, although traditionally bound by national borders and national broadcasters, it is increasingly destined to travel over networks across borders.

In conclusion, globalization brings with it a promise of economic and social development of the production industry if at least three conditions are met. First, negotiating power of producers over broadcasters must be increased so that content producers can hold a rights portfolio. Second, a virtuous circle of sustainable, blended innovation that is open to contamination by outside influences in the audiovisual sector should be triggered. A blend of national and local identity best expresses Italian cultural roots when it meets other cultures, other forms of innovation and new devices, as well as an ability to experiment new technological frontiers with the help of a market with vision and enlightened government policy. Third, in part linked to the first, the television production sector needs to make a collaborative effort to become more visible in international markets. The overarching priority is to create a system. The main feature of Italian communications companies—whatever size they are—is their inability to communicate and to identify shared strategies. Associations in the sector are similarly unable to group together and form an effective lobby.[13]

Italy could change direction if it were able to tackle these three conditions. In television production, as well as in other areas of cultural industry, taking on a passive role (simply a buyer of cultural products) while globalization is radically altering the world around you, creates a disadvantage. In order to compete on the global market you need to have something to offer and innovation needs to be encouraged and supported. The weaker you are, the more powerful others can become.

NOTES

1. Several paragraphs of this article have been re-written on the basis of research undertaken regarding the television production industry in Italy. A position paper on

the subject was presented in March 2007 to the Communications Authority as part of an inquiry into the application of regulations concerning residual rights. We would like to thank the co-authors: Elio De Tullio, Federica D'Urso, Andrea Veronese. A paper on this subject has also been presented by the authors at the 8th World Media Economics and Management Conference (Lisbon, May 2008).

2. The format may be considered the set of the invariable elements within each episode of a TV series, from which to then produce variable elements. Siae, the Italian authors' collecting society, has recently defined it as a "work of genius having the original explicit structure of a show and complete in the articulation of its sequential and thematic phases, suitable to be performed on radio, television or in a theatrical form, immediately or through intervals of adaptation, or elaboration or transposition, also in view of the creation of multiples." A fundamental aspect of format, in fact, is that the concept is constantly applied and tried out. A format is made up also and mainly of its concrete implementations and from the continuous modifications it is subject to in light of the needs and characteristics of the different reference targets, in a process of fine tuning which is perfected in time.

3. In the case of the fiction format, the finished product is not commercialized but distributed internationally with adequately adapted concepts and plots, which may be more easily adapted on local tastes (starting with the choice of themes).

4. The most significant examples are the quiz *Who Wants To Be a Millionaire?* created by the British group Celador (1998) and the reality show *Big Brother* by the Dutch group Endemol (1999).

5. For a closer look at Endemol's strategies, see Zaccone et alia, 2003, p. 164. At the end of 2008 another pan-European production group, Zodiak Entertainment (controlled by Italian media group De Agostini), stood out as one of the biggest production players.

6. See *Eurofiction* reports, European Audiovisual Observatory, various years (1996–2004).

7. The Law has been amended at the end of 2007 and Sky Italia will calculate investments on its total revenues (subscriptions, advertising and other), excluding sport packages sales revenues.

8. According to the scholar Robert Picard (2005), globalization has taken different forms in the business strategies of active players. These include: direct export, or the shipping of goods produced in one country to another; selling rights and licenses to another country, to duplicate or translate the contents and produce local editions; format licensing, or selling rights to produce a consolidated television format in another country; joint-ventures, or partnership for the production of contents to be used in respective countries of origin (this is the case for co-productions); direct foreign investments, or company acquisition or opening of branches overseas, with the goal of building up the size and volume of business in a company.

9. Out of 1,065 million Euro in total revenue; the rest is mainly from film and advertising, services, and events organization.

10. Considering all activities the total becomes 2.5 million Euro.

11. The remaining 11 percent of turnover is produced by four groups of Italian companies: FilmMaster Group, De Angelis Group, Magnolia, and Einstein Multimedia Group.
12. In spite of limited information published, certain names are recurrent: Palomar and Lux Vide's TV drama, Magnolia's formats, Fbc's productions of branded entertainment amongst others.
13. There are four producers' bodies in Italy: Anica (comprising film producers), Apt (television producers), Doc/It (documentary producers) and Cartoon Italia (animation producers). In the UK there is one: Pact.

REFERENCES

Barca, Flavia, and Federica D'Urso, Andrea Marzulli. "L'industria della produzione televisiva in Italia" Pp. 191–304 in *L'industria della comunicazione in Italia. Nono rapporto IEM*, edited by Flavia Barca. Milano: Guerini & Associati, 2006.

David Graham and Associates Ltd. *Impact Study of Measures (Community and National) Concerning the Promotion of Distribution and Production of Tv Programmes Provided for Under Article 25(a) of the Tv Without Frontiers Directive. Final Report*, for Audiovisual, Media and Internet Unit, Directorate-General Information Society and Media, European Commission, 2005. http://europa.eu/comm/avpolicy/docs/library/studies/finalised/4-5/27-03-finalreport.pdf (accessed February 19, 2008).

De Grazia, Victoria. *Irresistible Empire*, Cambridge, MA: Belknap Press of Harvard University Press, 2005.

Eurofiction reports, European Audiovisual Observatory, various years (1996–2004).

Featherstone, Mike. "Cultura del consumo e postmodernismo" in P. Malizia (ed.), *Tracce di società. Sull'azione sociale contemporanea*. Milano: Franco Angeli, 2005.

Granieri, Giuseppe. *La società digitale*, Bari: Editori Laterza, 2006.

Hartley, John. "Television & Globalisation," in G. Creeber (ed.), *Tele-Visions: Concepts and Methods in Television Studies*. London/Berkeley: British Film Institute/University of California Press, 2006.

Izzo, Jean-Claude. *Aglio, menta e basilico*, Roma: Edizioni E/o, 2006.

Marzulli, Andrea. "Televisione." Pp. 37–54 in *L'industria della comunicazione in Italia. Nono rapporto IEM*, edited by Flavia Barca. Milano: Guerini & Associati, 2006.

Mediatique. *From the Cottage to the City: the Evolution of the UK Independent Production Sector*, report for Bbc, 2005.

Ofcom. *Review of the Television Production Sector. Consultation document*, 2006.

———. *The International Communications Market*, 2006.

Oliver & Ohlbaum Associates. *Uk Tv Content in the Digital Age. Opportunities and Challenges*, report for Pact, 2006.

Picard, Robert G. *Economia e finanza dei media*. Milano: Guerini & Associati (orig. ed. *Media Economics: Concepts and Issues*), 2005.
Robertson, Roland. *Globalization: Social Theory and Global Culture*. London: Sage, 1992.
Screen Digest, Goldmedia, Frapa. *The Global Trade in Television Formats*, London, 2005.
Zaccone Teodosi, Angelo, and Flavia Barca, Francesca Medolago Albani. *Mercanti di bisogni*, Milano: Sperling & Kupfer, 2003.

Chapter Five

Public and Private, Global and Local in Italian Crime Drama: The Case of *La Piovra*

Elisa Giomi

INTRODUCTION

This contribution explores the changes within Italian TV home-grown drama (that is, drama produced by Italian broadcasters) as a consequence of the liberalization of the TV market at the end of the 1970s. The rise of the private-owned network Fininvest (currently Silvio Berlusconi's Mediaset) in the 1980s introduced the principle of network competition within Italian broadcasting, previously under RAI's monopolistic control: this change radically affected the domestic TV output both in terms of program content and aesthetics. In this transition to the so-called Neotelevisione (Neotelevision) (Casetti, Odin, 1990), a major role was played by the increasing presence of U.S. formats and programs, which perfectly matched the specific features of the emergent commercial TV environment as well as those of Italian culture and society more in general. At the beginning of the 1980s, in fact, Italy underwent a process of radical transformation and shift from the collective-oriented values of the previous decade to a new symbolic asset, characterized, as I will show, by a consumerist and individualistic drift.

Nationally-produced drama constitutes a privileged terrain to explore the overall change that occurred both in Italian society and television in the 1980s. The first reason concerns drama as a genre, whose relationship to society and culture has been analyzed by several commentators since the early stage of TV studies. As Raymond Williams put it, "drama offers dramatic simulation of a wide range of experience," through which a given society represents itself to itself (Williams, 1992: 44); in John Tulloch's terms, drama should be viewed as a major site for the production of stories, or myths, about contemporary cultures and hence a site of struggle over the meanings of that culture (1990). According to Silverstone, too, TV stories fulfill similar functions as those of an oral culture (such as myths and folktales), "reflecting, refracting, resolving (or at least appearing to resolve) the major and minor dilemmas of life and belief in their host cultures" (1999, p. 44). All these statements point to the value of TV drama as a "document": a document which offers a truthful portrayal not of a society and its culture in a given historical period, but of the ways in which this society and culture make sense of the fears, desires, anxieties, and ideological tensions which are dominant in that period, elaborating them in the form of a common language. Clearly, when it comes to home-grown drama, which offers stories about the country where it was produced, the "reflexive" function individuated by Williams is even more accentuated.

As to the Italian case, drama can also be considered a 'document' with reference to the change that occurred within TV as a consequence of the liberalization of the market and the spread of U.S. programs. From the late 1970s to the mid-1990s, in fact, drama has been one of the areas where the influence of U.S. productions was mostly felt: rising costs and stagnant resources resulted in the arrested development of Italian programs and the purchasing of increasing numbers of foreign TV films and series (Menduni, 2006). The majority of imported programs came from Japan (cartoons), Latin America (Argentinean and Mexican telenovelas) and from the U.S. (soap opera, sit-coms, cop shows). As a consequence, notes Buonanno (2000:24), national TV's narrating voice, due to economic factors, weakened just at the beginning of the 1980s, when foreign drama started to burst into every single slot of schedules and to firmly place itself within the Italian audience's preferences. The presence of U.S. programs, however, did not affect Italian TV production only in terms of "quantity": U.S. imports proved to have a great qualitative influence as well, standing out as the major models in the production of Italian TV series.

In the 1980s, the global circulation of Western, and especially American, television, and the unbalance within TV transnational flows were discussed using versions of Herbert Schiller's Cultural Imperialism Theory:[1] with Hollywood as the world's center of production, American media were viewed as a threat to indigenous culture in developing countries and the fear was that the world media would be homogenized (a position known as Media Imperialism theory; Boyd-Barrett, 1977; Lee, 1980). In this vein, cultural commentators complained about the increasing presence of U.S. programs in the European schedules, and in some cases, such as France, the government went as far as trying to stop the broadcasting of *Dallas* (Ang, 1985). According to Liebes and Livingstone (1998), in the 1980s and 1990s fears about American media's leadership were so widely spread in television and media studies, that they formed a new "Paradigm" (the Americanization Paradigm).

As it has been noted, the Americanization Paradigm, grounded on purely quantitative data about communication flows, lacked a cohesive analysis of the actual ideological tendencies in media contents and of fieldwork on these contents' effects (McQuail, 2004). As research started to develop on the textual forms of nationally and regionally produced TV programs, as well as on the reception of both home-grown and global products by local audiences, things started to change. Different concepts were introduced, pointing to more complex dynamics in the relationship between cultures. Some scholars confuted the Media Imperialism thesis referring to the factors in program choice and consumption by local audiences, which, according to Straubhaar, are always driven by the principle of "cultural proximity" (Straubhaar, 1991; Straubhaar, La Pastina, 2005). Some other positions examined national, regional, and local audiovisual productions, elaborating notions that placed emphasis on cultural encounters and active processes of adaptation rather than on uncritical imitations of foreign recipes: for example, "indigenization" (Chan and Ma 1996; Buonanno 1999), "hibridity" (Kraidy, 1999), "transculturation" (Chan and McIntyre, 2002)

Emphasis on active processes of adaptation is the basis for my analysis of the qualitative influence of U.S. programs on the production of Italian drama. I believe that a very interesting case study is provided by the home-grown and well-known series *La Piovra*, which focuses on the struggle of a few Italian policemen against the Mafia in Sicily. Launched by the public-owned channel Raiuno in 1984, *La Piovra* was the first and only long-running series ever produced by Italian television at the time, and it is still one of the few Italian productions to have been exported internationally. The series debuted on an early stage of commercial TV broadcasting and retained a stable presence in the TV schedules for more than ten years. The concept of the program was originally inspired by local Italian narrative models and production traditions: among its main features, a strong commitment to social and political criticism, realism, and melodrama in terms of genre composition, and a sober visual style.

Over the years, though, *La Piovra* has increasingly assimilated with U.S. series' narrative and aesthetic features: components of action and romance were introduced, and the visual style became more 'glossy'. This series, therefore, allows for the exploration of the ways in which Italian crime drama on television has changed as a result of the influence of U.S. programs, but it also allows to grasp the dynamic of transculturation, described by Chan and Ma as "the process by which one culture is transformed by another for self-aggrandizement when they come into contact with one another" (Chan, Ma, 2002: 4). Transculturation, in particular, is the process by which *La Piovra* gradually incorporated U.S. crime series conventions, "decontextualizing, reconfiguring and recontextualizing" them in a way that they could appeal to the national audience.

My specific object of analysis is the hero representation in *La Piovra*, in particular that of chiefs of police Corrado Cattani (seasons 1–4) and Dave Licata (seasons 5–6). They can both be considered "glocal heroes," whose characteristics balance U.S. crime genre conventions on the one hand, and on the other, the more realistic representation of the Mafia in *La Piovra*, which has to account for the tragic reality of organized crime in Italy.

The first section of this chapter addresses the issue on a more general level, clarifying how Italian TV drama radically changed as a consequence of the rise of private-owned channels and the spread of the U.S. productions. Before the rise of commercial television in Italy, writers for TV drama used to take their subjects from theater masterpieces or nineteenth century national and European literature (Alessandro Manzoni's *Promessi Sposi*, Antonio Fogazzaro's *Piccolo Mondo Antico*, *Pride and Prejudice*, *Wuthering Heights*, *Le rouge et le noir*, *The Citadel*, *Le Comte de Montecristo*, to give some examples). These works were believed to express ethic and aesthetic values particularly consistent with RAI's pedagogic project. Characters were chosen that might function as role models for the audience, and stories were expected to offer 'moral parabolas.' A preference was found, in this period, for "epic" narratives, both in literary and metaphoric terms, given that ancient Greek tragedies, such as *L'Odissea* (*The Odyssey*, 1968), were screened as well. With Neotelevisione, plots gradually shifted to different thematic preoccupations such as ordinary people's existence, family and private problems, and to an inner-oriented perspective, paying special attention to the representation of the characters' feelings, passions and emotional life. As I will show, the symbolic order underpinning Neotelevisione's narratives has been deeply influenced by U.S. serials.

The second section provides an overview of the ways in which the Mafia was portrayed in TV series of the late 1980s and 1990s, and, *La Piovra* is specifically taken into consideration as a case study. I argue that Cosa Nostra is a particularly interesting subject to explore the pitfalls and possibilities of the politics of representation that Italian drama has been formalizing since the liberalization of the TV market. The one represented in many Neotelevisione series, such as soap operas and sitcoms, is a 'minimalist' world, where the focus on ordinary, private, and emotional aspects of existence is somehow a natural law; but what happens when TV storytelling leaves this world to venture in lands at the boundaries of fact and fiction, borrowing its topics from history and news stories? What happens when, as in the case of series about the Mafia, relevant issues of the public sphere are addressed? Are these narratives still informed by the 'private and emotional' poetics, and what are the consequences in terms of creation of meaning?

Finally, in the third section the analysis shifts to the gradual departure of *La Piovra* from its original concept and its drawing closer to U.S. police series. At the beginning, the series did not even seem to fall into the crime drama genre, but was labelled as "social melodrama" (Grasso, 2002): its main concern was not to create spectacular or intriguing crime/detection-based story lines, but to offer a realistic representation of the helpless struggle of the Italian State against the Mafia; later on, the series started to explicitly deploy crime drama's codes and forms, in order to invoke the Italian audience's familiarity with Hollywood programs. In highlighting their influence on *La Piovra*, I will focus on the hero construction and make the point that such representation is the result of a culturation process, intended to conciliate two opposite demands. On the one hand, those of Hollywood crime series, requiring the policeman to overcome crime, to restore justice and social order, and to ensure the safety of citizens; on the other, the demands coming from the local and realistic nature of *La Piovra*, which has to take into account the specificity of Italian civic culture. Such culture has always been deeply ingrained with a certain suspicion, even skepticism, towards justice, police, and the law, all believed to be unable to accomplish their tasks (Buonanno, 2002a: 71). Furthermore, skepticism towards institution and their representatives became true disillusion in the case of the State/Mafia conflict, particularly in the 1980s and 1990s, when the Mafia was stronger than ever.

NEW POETICS AND NEW HEROES IN ITALIAN TV DRAMA: SHIFTING FROM PUBLIC BROADCASTING TO COMMERCIAL TV

In the competitive environment produced by the rise of commercial broadcasting within the Italian TV system, both the private and public broadcasters found an important strategic resource in TV series produced abroad, such as Latin American telenovelas, Japanese cartoons, and U.S. soap operas. At least in the beginning, the public service network RAI displayed a more cautious attitude toward foreign imports, as it had to combine the need to maximize audience ratings with the necessity to construct a different—more "national"—brand image from that of its competitor, the private-owned network Fininvest. Fininvest, in fact, immediately became the most important conduit for U.S. commercial television—and consumerist culture—to spread in Italy (Menduni, 2002).

First of all, it was an economic factor that determined the increasing tendency to purchase foreign productions, as they perfectly met the needs of the emergent commercial TV. Advertising had always been the first source of income for Fininvest, and it now represented an important revenue for RAI too, which found it increasingly difficult to remain faithful to its public service principles and limit its programming to national content. Both RAI and Fininvest quickly ended up with a 24-hour schedule of programming per day, and their main goal became that of capturing the biggest audience possible for the longest possible time, thus maximizing advertising revenues. Broadcasters therefore had to fill in schedules at low cost and with content able to ensure the viewers' loyalty over time. U.S. series proved to meet these requirements at best: first, because being produced as serials according to Hollywood's traditional mode of TV production, they could be sold on the international market in packages of hundreds of episodes at a very competitive price; plus, U.S. series came out already "cut" for advertising to be inserted in (Menduni, 2006: 148).

In addition to their convenience in economic and programming terms, what contributed to the success of U.S. series in Italy was also their being perfectly suitable to the new features of Italian culture and society, which, like other European countries, were experiencing a consumerist and individualistic drift. "In Western countries"—Franco Monteleone argues—"the development of the cultural industry and the widespread economic welfare had made customers more exigent and attentive. Such a varied and creative cultural demand could not be satisfied by the Monopolistic television" (2003: 427). On the contrary, the new set of desires and fantasies that characterized Italian society in the wave of the 1980s hedonistic yuppie lifestyle were immediately intercepted by soap operas' glamorous, sparkling mise-en-scenes, by police series' spectacular actions, and by the more licentious humor of sitcoms. In short, Italy became enchanted with U.S.-style light entertainment values (Dyer, 1973) and rhetoric of self-made men, individual achievement, and power.

This factor played a major role in countries such as Italy and France. Once the huge mobilizations and demonstrations of the 1970s were over, once collective expectations for the "Big Reforms" were disappointed and terrorism started to shock public opinion, there was a gradual withdrawal to the safe, protected space of private and domestic life, made more pleasurable by the diversified cultural and media consumptions now available. Public values, in short, were substituted by interests, needs, and aspirations far less ideological and, moreover, rigorously individualistic. Thus, if Neotelevisione made large use of U.S. series, it was "moreover to endow TV broadcasting with the values, affections and emotions of everyday life, which are the true essence of American drama" (Menduni, 2006: 144).[2] As Françoise Dupont has noted, *Dallas*, along with all the other U.S. soaps, carefully avoids any reference to current affairs, to political or economic history: everything revolves around everyday and private conflicts of jealousy, envy, passion, and power (Dupont, 1993: 57).

Before the transition to a free market, RAI executives had followed the BBC motto "information, education, entertainment," believing that radio and television should aim to culturally and morally uplift their audience. In that period, Italian home-gown drama, too, reflected this concern; the humanistic roots of Italian culture and thought emerged in the choice of national and European literature and theater masterpieces as the main models for TV narratives. However, the strong tie that was created since the 1980s between the needs of the new competitive broadcasting environment and the features of U.S. serials resulted in the establishment of a new and precise role-model for TV drama: this shift started to influence also domestic production, whose aesthetic and cultural forms radically changed. The pedagogic, solemn attitude found in drama under the monopolistic control of RAI was gradually replaced by a more complicit, intimate tone: TV narratives no longer aimed to the social education of citizens, rather they meant to be their assiduous and discrete companions; instead of the national consciousness, TV dramas were now addressing the individual, aiming to exorcize his/her everyday problems and to share the joy of his/her family life.

Interestingly, adaptations of classic novels commonly found under RAI's monopoly were re-proposed by Neotelevisione and they aligned with the general transformation described above.[3] In comparison to the first adaptations, in fact, these new 'remakes' lacked any philological rigor, tending to shift away from their original literary sources and to establish their own representative features: authors were more concerned with emphasizing visual spectacle than with portraying social reality; stories are often set in an almost atemporal dimension, with historical references only serving the dramatic and universal appeal of the individual's inner feelings and private conflicts. This is precisely the discourse[4] which was constructed within the series produced by the Neotelevisione.

The underlying, minimalist poetics of home-grown drama after the liberalization of the TV market is particularly reflected in the typology of its heroes. The model proposed by these narratives is that of the everyman: a character with the same features of common people, with the same problems, abilities, and desires of the viewers. A figure "superior neither to other men nor to his environment; the hero is one of us: we respond to a sense of his common humanity and demand from the poet the same canons of probability that we find in our own experience. This gives us the hero of the low mimetic mode, of most comedy and realistic fiction" (Frye, 1957: 34). As I will show in the next section, this model is fundamental to characterize Mafia stories in the Neotelevisione.

LA PIOVRA AND THE
AESTHETICS OF NEOTELEVISIONE

Over the twenty-five years comprised between the first appearance of the long-running series *La Piovra* in 1984 and the present, five series focusing on the Mafia have been produced, showing how this subject retained a continuous, though intermittent, presence on Italian television. Mafia stories were numerous at the beginning of the 1990s, they considerably diminished later in the same decade, and, finally, since the beginning of 2000s, they have been enjoying a renewed interest on the part of both broadcasters and audience, especially over the last four or five years.

The first "wave" of TV Mafia stories coincided with the debut of commercial television, as *La Piovra* was launched in 1984–1985 by the public channel Raiuno. Nine seasons were produced and broadcast until 1997–1998, while the last one aired in 2000. Between the 1980s and the 1990s, other programs portraying Cosa Nostra were produced by both Fininvest and RAI: *Polizza droga* (Mediaset, 1988–1989), *Donna d'onore* (Mediaset, 1989–1990), *Per odio e per amore* (Mediaset, 1991–1992), *Un uomo di rispetto* (RAI, 1992–1993). They all proved successful, but the one which gained the highest ratings was *La Piovra*, with some episodes peaking to reach 16 million spectators.

The reasons behind the popularity enjoyed by this subject, according to Milly Buonanno, lay in its compatibility with TV drama's narrative logics: "Mafia posses the whole panoply of archetypes, topoi and ingredients of popular crime-based narratives: clearly identifiable heroes and villains, the ones opposed to the others" (1996: 28). Also, this is a topic, which allows TV to put into operation one of the most important functions of symbolic representation systems, that is, portraying and personifying evil. Between 1988–1989 and 1992–1993, as many as twenty series set in Southern Italy were produced, and all of them were enthusiastically greeted by the domestic audience. Along with the Mafia, these series focused on Camorra and Andrangheta (mafia-style organizations respectively based in Campania and Calabria, while "the Mafia" is officially based in Sicily), on violence, crime, and delinquency, and on easily recognizable enemies, likely to have a great emotional impact on spectators, but also likely to turn Southern Italy into a lawless "evil land," where justice is destined to succumb.

The Mafia stories produced in this period are characterized by very stable characteristics and recurring elements as well as by significant absences. The first striking absence is that of positive characters belonging to Southern Italy. The heroes either come from elsewhere (like chief of police Cattani, protagonist of *La Piovra*, who is from Northern Italy) or, if they are originally from the South, they return to Southern Italy only after spending most of their life in other places (and, metaphorically, after having freed themselves from the negative influences of that region, as it happens with Dave Licata coming back to Sicily from New York). The "good" characters from the South usually play secondary roles, and as a consequence their representation is quite stereotypical and scarcely incisive. Buonanno identifies two categories: the "predestined victim," a strenuous and generous opponent of the Mafia, who has no chance to survive, and the "good bandit"—another cliché of popular narratives—who goes in for a life of crime as the only possible existence given to him in such a deprived and depriving environment (1994: 164–166).

Another significant absence characterizes these years' narratives: that of civil society. The heroes struggling against the Mafia are always institutional figures, such as policemen, magistrates, lawyers. It can be argued that the first seasons of the series (1980s and 1990s) reflected the perception of the Mafia as a tentacular, unbeatable force—as the name *La Piovra*, Octopus, suggests—and the widespread pessimism and disillusion typical of that era. This climate also affected the construction and representation of the hero: the variety of hero "models" that later developed on Italian television can ultimately be traced back to the prototype elaborated in *La Piovra*. This model was first embodied by chief of police Corrado Cattani (played by actor Michele Placido), who represents a perfect synthesis of local elements and U.S. influences.

Cattani possesses many of the features of the "low mimetic mode" hero (the everyman), which, as I noted in the previous section, characterizes the programs of Neotelevisione. Great attention is paid to his psychological construction; the policeman's contradictions, doubts and failures make him an ordinary human being, absolutely similar to the common spectator. Cattani, however, is an ambivalent figure: he is completely devoted to his job, which he interprets as a mission—a mission for which he is willing to sacrifice any other dimension of his existence. Despite his being a tender and generous lover, Cattani is never seen to engage in a stable relationship, nor is he seen to allow himself any kind of personal pleasure. Private life is completely removed from his character, and a lonely, melancholic aura surrounds him.

This hero's construction might seem contradictory to the dramatic poetics of Neotelevisione, which, as discussed earlier, stresses the characters' private life (love affairs, family ties, and interpersonal relations). Nevertheless, the next section provides a twofold evidence: first of all, the private sphere does have a great importance in Cattani's construction as a hero, being at the very heart of his devotion to his job. This makes him a perfect product of Neotelevisione and draws him closer to U.S. programs' narrative values. Secondly, Cattani's liaison to U.S. TV cop shows is particularly evident in his taking the role of the "lonely avenger," a figure commonly found in American shows since the 1970s. This model, however, is decontextualized and reconfigured in a way that matches the features of Italian civic culture and the specific reality of the Mafia at the time the first season of *La Piovra* aired.

U.S. SERIES TRANSCULTURED: FROM THE LONELY AVENGER TO THE TRAGIC HERO

The first series of *La Piovra* was directed by Damiano Damiani, a prominent exponent of Italian militant cinema, a movement driven by civic values and social and political criticism.[5] These features transferred to the concept of *La Piovra*, and this is why the series has been classified as a "social melodrama": a label that shows the coexistence of social realism and the aesthetic values of Neotelevisione.

As the series progresses, though, it increasingly departs from its original concept, drawing closer to the U.S. serials. Under the direction of Luigi Perelli (who debuts in the third season and directs many, including the last one), suspense and a faster narrative pace are introduced, along with spectacular actions such as chasing and shooting, at the expense of the psychological elaboration of characters. The eighth and ninth seasons, respectively broadcast in 1996–1997 and 1997–1998 and directed by Giacomo Battiato, complete this process: the plot is no longer set in contemporary Italy but in the 1950s and 1960s Sicily, and it carefully avoids any reference to current issues; the portrayal of society becomes superficial and apolitical, storylines are stuffed with a great component of romance, explicitly winking to soap operas. "In short"—Aldo Grasso comments—"*Dallas* has not hit the Italian TV market in vain" (Grasso, 2002: "*La Piovra*").

At the beginning of the second season, Cattani's teenage daughter is kidnapped and raped by the Mafiosi he is trying to arrest. The event causes a deep rupture between Cattani and his family, both on a psychological and a more practical level (his daughter moves to Swizterland in a nursing-home to recover from the shock caused by the rape; his wife holds him responsible for it and leaves to take care of the girl). What ties Cattani to his work, therefore, is something more than an unqualified devotion: it is a ranging, desperate self-abnegation, an almost maniacal obsession, originated in the irreparable loss that he bears; his self-commitment to the fight against the Mafia seems to derive more from personal concerns than from professional deontology. Or, at least, it derives not only from civic values and sense of institution, but from family reasons as well. So, while *La Piovra*'s focus on the opposition State/Mafia could open up for a different and more political narrative, from the second season onwards the discourse constructed in the series becomes ultimately consistent with the symbolic universe of commercial television: the private sphere, though here "in absence," plays the major role, sometimes causing public values to fade in the light of the rhetoric of the lost family. The design of Cattani's character also proves that *La Piovra* had actually assimilated some of the U.S. serials' conventions—already largely circulated in Western Europe's schedules by the time the program was launched—at an earlier stage of its history: Cattani, as said, is a lonely man, he has no affective or family ties, he has nothing to lose, and this is why he is determined to pursue his goal by any means, even the most irregular ones. He is isolated also because of his hostility towards discipline and any rule dictated by formal justice—an attitude which makes him alien to the institutional context he belongs to. Moreover, he is completely isolated in his furious struggle against the Mafia, followed by a bunch of devoted collaborators only, ready—like him—to go for risky ventures.

These features clearly recall those of the lonely avengers, the 'politically incorrect' policemen commonly found in U.S. serials of the 1970s and 1980s. After the Watergate Scandal had put citizens' trust in the State into question, U.S. drama started to be "invaded" by "justice paladins," policemen or former policemen skeptical of the system's effectiveness in contrasting injustices and crime (*The Equalizer* is one of the most popular examples). What all the policemen and detectives in those series had in common was a self-righteous belief in the validity of their own methods, even if those methods involved a degree of violence and a bending of the rules (Pastore 2006: 99). The same trend is found in UK serials. Liz Cook has noted:

> In a decade in which the social consensus of the post-war years was breaking down . . . the ends justified the (often illegal) means. In an increasingly lawless society extreme tactics were sometimes needed by these fictional policemen in the performance of their "duty." In the "law and order" decade of the 1970s, television police series became an arena where the ideological and coercive work of the police was foreground as never before. (2001: 198)

These considerations also apply to Italian culture in the 1980s more in general: without having overcome the social problems that became evident with 1970s mobilizations, the 1980s see the decline of collective forms of belonging and values; underneath the patina of consumerist consensus and hedonism, stands an increasingly atomised, individualistic and anomic country. Spectators immediately identify with Cattani, as they "have the same feelings and the same frustrating experiences as him; they live in a complex and difficult social reality, where institutions do not work properly, where those who break the law and bribe win and those who perform their duty are never rewarded" (Livolsi, 1998: 98). In this context, Cattani's rage against those who have caused him to lose his family becomes a metaphor for the widespread feelings of resentment and powerlessness; bending rules becomes the only means to overcome the dictatorship of bureaucracy, perceived as a complicated system operating against the citizens' interests.[6]

Mobilizing the avenger stereotype, therefore, can be seen as a narrative strategy intended to resolve the spectators' anxieties and fears, thus offering them a symbolic compensation, one of the most important cultural functions of TV drama. As the series progresses, the construction of Cattani as an avenger and unconventional policeman is accentuated. This model, besides embodying the desire for ransom and justice diffused within Italian society, is made more and more popular with the domestic audience by the increasing circulation on Italian television of U.S. police series in the 1980s and 1990s. Along with very innovative and progressive programs, such as *Hill Street Blues* or *Cagney and Lacey*, more "conservative" police series were produced in the United States, which aligned to the 1970s model and were characterized by a "judicial emphasis" (Pastore, 2006: 138). Some of them featured extra-institutional figures, such as former CIA agent Robert McCall from *The Equalizer* (CBS; 1985–1989), who offered New York citizens his private services[7]; other programs, like *Hunter* (NBC, 1984–1991), focused on a tough, authoritarian policeman, inclined to unconventional methods and committed to punish criminals at any cost. This series was broadcast in Italy, first by RAI and then by Mediaset, in the same years as *La Piovra*, and gradually built up a cult following.[8]

In the 1990s, some of the most popular U.S. series in Italy adopted the model of *The Equalizer* as well as very telling titles modified in translation: *Swift Justice* (broadcast by Mediaset by the title of *Swift il giustiziere*, Swift the Avenger); *Vengeance Unlimited* (RAI, *Mr Chapel*); *Dark Justice* (RAI, *I giustizieri della notte*, that is Night Avengers). The latter's main character, lawyer Marshall, has a similar life story like that of Cattani: he begins to mistrust the system after his wife and daughter are murdered. On a general level, all the characters from these series are depicted as those who can succeed there where ordinary law and bureaucracy have failed.

This kind of hero construction clearly cannot be simply carbon-copied by *La Piovra*: its stories are not fictional, its evil characters are not just 'bad guys' nor common criminals. Its plot focuses on a real problem, one which is deeply rooted in Italian society, culture and politics, and an American-style "superhero," compensating for the failures of institutional justice and restoring order, would be totally unrealistic here. The writers of *La Piovra* therefore have to find a balance between crime drama as a global form of entertainment, and the cultural specificities of the program in the Italian context. This is a particularly difficult adaptation process, because of the generic patterns the series' concept draws on and because of the specific issue it deals with. As a social melodrama, in fact, *La Piovra* has to maintain a considerable degree of truth to reality, and this is hard to conciliate with positive and encouraging representations, given the role of the Mafia in Italian news.

Once again, the tension produced by these two opposite demands was resolved by glocalizing (Robertson, 1995) the avenger prototype that *La Piovra* borrows from U.S. police serial. As a result of this process, which can be understood as "the global production of the local and the localization of the global" (Chan and McIntyre, 2002:227), Cattani appears quite different from his U.S. colleagues. He is a complex figure, engaging viewers in a constant oscillation between hope and disillusion: like other cop-heroes, he is a projective character, provided with incredible strength, courage, and abilities; yet, unlike them, Cattani does not flatter himself on having real chances to overcome his enemies: he is constantly ringed by a halo of defeat, a direct expression of the feeling of impotence characterizing 1980s Italy. In a context where the dominant values are wealth, success, and ephemeral pleasures, a few policemen and magistrates are the only ones struggling to death against crime, which flourishes thanks to political protections and widespread indifference, or "omertà." People's courage and civic virtues, if not subsided, for sure fade before daily news broadcast reporting on Mafia's slaughters. Spectators, therefore, identify with Cattani and support him, knowing that even though he wins a battle, he is not going to win the war. The policeman's death, "killed by a spray of bullets (necessary to kill a hero, not a man)" (Livolsi, 1998:99), is perfectly in line with these premises. Cattani's nature as a hero is re-established once and for all: he is a tragic hero, a loser.

At a closer look, however, the notion of "glocalization" fails to effectively describe the essence of the operation undertaken to adapt the narrative structures and icons of U.S. police series to the specific Italian context of this series, and of the Mafia's slaughters of the 1980s and 1990s. A theoretical formation, which seems to better grasp this narrative and generic adaptation is that of "transculturation." This can be seen as a process "by which a culture is transformed by another in their mutual encounters" (Chan, 2002: 225). Far from being simply carbon-copied or transplanted, borrowings from other cultures and media productions are always reconfigured. If we examine the development of *La Piovra* after Cattani's death, other evidence can be found of how transculturation works in terms of active deconstruction, appropriation, and indigenization of generic patterns. Again, the main site of this reconfiguration is the protagonist's narrative trajectory, which, as in the case of Cattani, is paradigmatic of the overall discourse produced in the series.

In the fifth season, aired in 1990, Cattani is replaced by Dave Licata (played by actor Vittorio Mezzogiorno). Like his predecessor, Licata is an outsider, in every sense: he is an ex-policeman and he arrives to Sicily from New York. The codes of American action movies and TV series are deployed to a larger extent than in the Cattani-based editions, and the stereotype of the policeman who bends rules and uses unconventional methods is reworked in a more radical way: Licata embodies the isolated violent cop-as-hero in an alienated and anomic world commonly found in 1970s and 1980s U.S. and UK police series (Tulloch, 1990: 71).

At the same time, Aldo Grasso argues, Licata is just "born to counteract the inefficiency of law and justice and to make us daydream": he is an imaginary hero, occupying the same fictional space as James Bond, where everything seems possible and where the limits and obstacles that real policemen have to face in their struggle against the Mafia can be overcome. Too many people had already been killed by the Mafia at the beginning of the 1990s, and a cathartic representation was somehow needed. The world inhabited by Cattani was the real one, with its everyday necrologies: for this reason, he could only canalize the audience's sense of injustice, but was bound to succumb. Licata's world, on the contrary, which seemed to offer a true symbolic compensation for the threatening reality of the Mafia.

This reading, surprisingly, is contradicted by the last episode of the sixth series. There seems to be a continuous negotiation between the attraction to U.S. narratives, on the one hand, and the influence of indigenous models on the other. With Licata, the American police series' cliché of the avenger is accentuated, yet, once again, this cliché has to be decontextualized, reconfigured and recontextualized (Chan and Ma, 2002: 234) in order to fit in with *La Piovra*'s claim for social realism: in the end, Licata, too, is killed, and his death will tragically resonate with the (real) death of Giovanni Falcone and Paolo Borsellino, the two magistrates who, together with their colleagues, had started a "New Deal" in the struggle of the State against the Mafia, creating a dedicated Pool (the Pool Antimafia) and managing to summit hundreds of criminals to court. Ironically, their murders carried out by the Mafia in 1992, happened a few months after Licata's fictional murder.

CONCLUSIONS: *LA PIOVRA* AND BEYOND

In the first part of this contribution, I mapped out the features of the politics of representation developed by Italian drama as a consequence of the liberalization of the TV sector and the circulation of U.S. productions. My aim was to show how the portrayal of Italian policemen's struggle against the Mafia in the 1980s and 1990s series conformed to these features and to pin down the consequences of it in terms of public and private values articulation. I used the case of *La Piovra*, whose long-standing presence in the schedules allowed to analyze the ways in which this topic has been addressed over the years.

My conclusion is that, despite the strong component of social and political criticism found in the program's original concept, the discourse produced in it was gradually and increasingly affected by the individual-oriented perspective of Neotelevisione TV drama as well as by its emphasis on private problems and inner feelings as the main thematic preoccupations. The series of *La Piovra* featuring policeman Cattani and aired after the first one clearly shows this: private concerns are foregrounded as the ultimate reasons for the protagonist's heroism and involvement in the struggle against the Mafia, so that the political force of the program is partially blunted. Obviously, this is also due to the competitive broadcasting environment in which *La Piovra* was born and the consequent concern of the network to gain a mass audience. This imposes to: (a) smooth controversial issues and align representations to mainstream values and orientations; (b) propose contents likely to appeal to the whole TV audience: articulating shared meanings and common experiences (love, emotions, interpersonal relations, everyday family life, etc.) is the best narrative strategy in order to attract spectators of any age and from the most varied socio-cultural backgrounds as possible.

Anyway, this "private-bias" seems to be a systematic and long-standing one in Italian home-grown drama, and its persistence and manifestations cannot simply be traced back to the nature of TV as a generalist, profit-driven medium globally embedded in the domestic and private context of the household. An interesting confirmation can be found if we briefly examine domestic police series. As the production of homegrown drama started to increase in European countries since the 1980s, these were more and more able to devise their own approach to this genre[9]: Italy, for instance, created a truly indigenous variant of this species, called "poliziesco all'italiana" (Italian-style police drama), firstly developed in cinema and then carried into TV production.

A large part of recent productions, such as *Il Maresciallo Rocca* and *Carabinieri*, still explicitly draw on the Italian comedy model, adding to the detection/crime component those of melodrama and humor (with conflicts always being recomposed, happy end assured, a parochial touch and a consistent degree of euphemism); other programs, inspired by foreign formats, are far more realistic and characterized by darker and more tragic tones: this is the case of *La Squadra* (inspired by the British series *The Bill*); *La Omicidi*; *Ris* (an attempt to indigenize the popular American *CSI* format); *Distretto di Polizia* (again, inspired by the U.S. series *New York Police Department*). Anyway, in both types of Italian police series, a common discourse is produced: the cases of deviance and delinquency, the antisocial behaviors which police officers have to face are always presented as caused by private, individualistic reasons, so that criminality appears easier to localize and be dealt with (Natale, 2005: 75). The emphasis of these narratives is never on the system but always on the individual; they never call into question society, focusing exclusively on the single person (either the policeman or the criminal). Like a mincer, these dramas mill any public/political ingredient and turn it into a private matter, which is easier to metabolize.

La Piovra was broadcast over the two decades in which U.S. series and serials firmly established within Italian audience's consumer habits and TV narrative universe: the second aim of my contribution was to show to which extent and in which ways the program assimilated some of the features of U.S. police and action series. First, Cattani (the main character in series form the first one to the fourth one) and Licata (fifth and sixth series) explicitly recalled the isolated, controversial, even violent policemen featured in many U.S. series; secondly, as the years passed, the component of melodrama increased, with storylines revolving around emotional conflicts and love affairs; finally, the presence of light entertainment values was accentuated as well: action scenes, a faster narrative pace were introduced, along with a varnish of glamour recalling the "slick" style of some Hollywood police series.

The word "Hollywood" within the context of popular culture studies is always likely to evoke the threatening scenarios predicted by 1960s and 1970s analysis of unequal media flows, when the dominating notions were "media imperialism," "cultural imperialism," and "cultural dependence." The fear that world media would be homogenized or that we would assist to a domination of Hollywood in the media world were later replaced by other theoretical formations, such as "asymmetrical interdependence," taking into account the "variety of possible relationships in which countries find themselves unequal but possessing variable degree of power and initiative in politics, economics, and culture" (Straubhaar, 1991: 39).

"Transculturation" is one of those notions, and by employing it I showed that *La Piovra*'s borrowings from U.S. police series, far from being simply transplanted, were actively recontextualized in a way that they could appeal to the national audience. Dominant global motifs were creatively combined with local preferences, cultural forms were transfigured, foreign was rendered indigenous: the narrative was transcultured for its own purposes. These purposes are clear: providing a portrayal of the struggle between the forces of the law and Mafia likely to exorcise the audience's fears without giving up the program's claim for social realism. "The more contextualized is a story, the more believable it will be" (Chan and Ma, 2002: 234): contextualizing, here, means turning the tough and unscrupulous avenger found in U.S. action and police series into a tragic hero, like Cattani, conscious of being a loser but still determined.

This leads to a conclusive consideration on the discourse constructed in TV drama and in police series in particular. These operate as an integral part of the historical moment they are framed by, working its ideological tensions, anxieties, and fantasies into fictional forms (Tulloch, 1990: 71). The way this working is performed, as it happens in all TV drama, can also be contradictory because discourses cannot be aligned with a single axis of power. In comparison to the series portraying Cattani, those based on Licata depict an even more Manichean moral order, where evil and good characters are easily recognizable. This can be seen as a discourse of compensation for the experience of real Mafia made by the Italian audience. Though, as noted by Christine Gledhill about melodrama—a genre equally characterized by clear cut-oppositions personified in the conflicts of villain, hero, heroine—the stable fictional world these figures inhabit, and the actions they perform, must be filled out in popular drama by reference to social discourses if they are to be seen as realistic (1988: 75–76).[10]

This is an even more powerful demand in the case of *La Piovra*, given its concept oriented to social realism. Licata appears as a fantasy figure similar to James Bond, a figure able to fulfill the audience's desires and expectations (the series based on this character were watched by 12.4 million spectators on average); at the same time, a counter-discourse was produced, as storylines were seen to recover the original interest for social and political criticism inspiring *La Piovra*'s concept: witness is that the fifth and sixth series gave rise to heated debates on the part of Italian politicians, irritated by the explicit references found in the plot to actual events and prominent exponents of the national public scene (Grasso, 2002: "*La Piovra*").

In this sense, the eight and ninth series of *La Piovra*, set in 1950s and 1960s Sicily, giving up any attempt to draw a realistic portray of contemporary Mafia and stressing the ingredients of romance, melodrama and action instead, can be linked to the diffusion of U.S. aesthetic and narrative values in the Italian TV schedules. It is worth noticing, anyway, that the home-grown Mafia stories broadcast over the last ten years reverted this trend and went back to more indigenous and social realism-oriented formulas: twelve out of the fifteen series aired between 1998–1999 and 2006–2007 were factual, that is based on characters and events from current affairs or recent Italian history.

This can be located at the crossroad of two specific trends emerged over the last years in Italian TV drama production: the first one is the shifting of a consistent part of the TV narrative universe toward the past, with an increasing number of productions focusing on key-events and/or characters from recent Italian history (Buonanno, 2007); the second one is the renewed attention for topics on current affairs, which, not by accident, was a major editorial line also between the 1980s and 1990s (a period when this subject was very popular too).[11]

• • •

In 2001, RAI aired *Brancaccio*, dedicated to Don Puglisi, parish priest of Brancaccio, the most degraded district of Palermo, who was killed at the beginning of the 1990s because of his opposition to the Mafia and attempt to promote legality values among local youth. With this mini-series, noted Stefano Munafò, at that time Head of RAI Fiction, "RAI definitively broke up with *La Piovra* model." In his opinion, since 2001–2002, "both RAI and Mediasest started to avoid spectacular actions carbon-copied from America, preferring an investigative-journalism/biographical style and basing the programs' scripts on instant books by journalists specialized in Mafia coverage."

On a more general level, the ways in which the approach to the narration of the Mafia evolved since *La Piovra* to contemporary series can be seen within a gradual move of the television drama sector towards a more industrial production. From the mid-nineties onwards, the quantity and features of the domestic programs dramatically changed: their content and language were molded to the form of native values and models, directly reflecting national society. Mafia stories, therefore, offer a confirmation that Italian television has fully regained the original role of the medium: that of a "central storytelling system" of its own community (Newcomb, 1988).

NOTES

1. In the 1950s and 1960s, the global reach of U.S. programs and their "invasion" of less developed countries was understood in terms of Cultural Imperialism: according to Schiller (1969), the export of cut-price television programs (and of other cultural goods), by means of the images of the affluent Western lifestyle that they portrayed, spread consumer culture all over the world and therefore promoted the commercial interests of American corporations, thus supporting the political and military interests of the West (Bignell, 2004: 69).

2. "In the 1950s and 1960s"—Paul Ginsborg argues—"middle class people, attracted by the shining lights of consumerism and by the chances of social and economic achievement, became stable promoters of a moderate and democratic status quo. It is possible to argue that in the 1980s this consensus was extended to the whole society. In other words, traditional family-values melted with those of parliamentary democracy and capitalist consumerism. These values became dominant in almost any sector of society. Italy's greatest transformation, therefore, was to adapt to the model of modernity first emerged in the age of 'economic miracle': a model strongly

infused with American influences, which was intensely contrasted between 1968 and 1973, but which seemed to have found its 'golden age' in the 1980s" (Ginsborg, 1989: 575–576).

3. *Promessi Sposi* (1989); *Le rouge et le noir* (1997–1998), *Le Comte de Montecristo* (1998–1999), *Piccolo mondo antico* (2000–2001), *The Citadel* (2002–2003), *Wuthering Heights* (2004–2005).

4. The notion of "discourse" I refer to in this essay comes from the work of Michel Foucault, according to whom a discourse is a set of statements or beliefs which produce knowledge that serves the interests of a particular group or class. Though discourses operate in a very similar way to ideology, the axes of power on which they operate will not be identical or unified, and they may interact in ways, which can be complex and sometimes contradictory (Thornham and Purvis, 2005: 83). This explains the 'appeal' that the notion of discourse had on TV studies and on drama studies in particular: it allowed to separate the concepts of narrative and genre from that of ideology, thus proposing a rather less monolithic relationship between ideology and television drama.

5. Many of the movies produced in these years focused on the Mafia: see Albano, V. (2003), *La Mafia nel cinema siciliano. Da In nome della legge a Placido Rizzotto*. Manduria, TA: Barbieri.

6. It is worth noticing that a discourse in part similar characterizes the popular UK series *The Sweeney*, focusing on the most secret aspect of the police work, the flying squad, and aired since 1975 to 1978. According to Tulloch, this series positions the individualistic/entrepreneurial Regan, the main character, in terms of oppositions that describe the current "problem" of the police as one largely of inflexibility and bureaucracy rather than corruption (Tulloch, 1990: 70). Of course, in *La Piovra*, corruption too is a problem.

7. The series was aired in Italy by both RAI and Mediaset under the name of *Un giustiziere a New York* (An Avenger in New York)

8. In 1989, Hunter was viewed by 2,718,000 spectators on average; in 1990–1991, it gained the first position in the police series hit parade (with 3,615,000 viewers); in 1992, viewer ratings picked up to reach 4,356,000 spectators and, in 1993, more than 6 million (Pastore, 2006: 139).

9. An overview of the different features of TV police series in England, France, Spain, Italy, and Germany is provided in Buonanno, 2002b.

10. So, for example, the contemporary detective hero may be female; her outline will be "filled in" with references to contemporary discourses about social equality, the independent woman and femininity, some of them arising from feminism.

11. Ultimo, broadcast by Mediaset in 1998–1999, and its sequels (*Ultimo 2 — La sfida*, 2000–2001 and *Ultimo 3 — L'infiltrato*, 2003–2004) focused on Captain Roberto Di Stefano, who managed to arrest Mafia boss and super-latitant Totò Riina; RAI produced a collection composed by the miniseries *Brancaccio* (2001–2002), *Donne di Mafia* (dedicated to Mafia bosses' wives who rebelled to Cosa Nostra) and *L'attentatuni* (reconstructing the arrest of the people who organized the bombing killing judge Giovanni Falcone, his wife and 5 people from his police escort); *Paolo Borsellino* (Mediaset, 2004–2005) and *Giovanni Falcone* (RAI, 2006–2007), focusing on the life

of the two judges who had a prominent role in contrasting the Mafia; *A voce alta* (RAI, 2005–2006), the true story of a shipyard worker and unionist in Palermo who, in the 1980s, fought against Mafia infiltrations within his workplace; *Joe Petrosino* (RAI, 2006–2007), dedicated to the life of this historical character; *L'ultimo dei Corleonesi* and *L'ultimo padrino*, both broadcast in 2006–2007 respectively by RAI and Mediaset and telling the arrest of forty-years-latitant Bernardo Provenzano in 2006.

REFERENCES

Albano, Vittorio. *La Mafia nel cinema siciliano. Da In nome della legge a Placido Rizzotto*, Manduria, TA: Barbieri, 2003.

Ang, Ien. *Watching Dallas: Soap Opera and the Melodramatic Imagination*, London: Methuen, 1985.

Bignell, Johnathan. *An Introduction to TV Studies*, London: Routledge, 2004.

Boyd-Barrett, Oliver. "Media Imperialism: Towards an International Framework for the Analysis of Media Systems." Pp. 116–135 in *Mass Communication and Society*, edited by James Curran, Michael Gurevitch, and Janet. Woolacott, London: Edward Arnold, 1977.

Buonanno, Milly, ed. *La bella stagione: La fiction italiana/l'Italia nella fiction Anno XVIII*, Roma: Edizioni VQPT- RAI, 2007.

———. *Le radici e le foglie: La fiction italiana/l'Italia nella fiction Anno XVII*, Roma: Edizioni VQPT-Rai, 2006.

———. *Lontano nel tempo: La fiction italiana/l'Italia nella fiction Anno XVI*, Roma: Edizioni VQPT-Rai, 2005.

———. *Storie e Memorie: La fiction italiana/l'Italia nella fiction Anno XIII*, Roma: Edizioni VQPT-Rai, 2002a.

———. *Eurofiction 2001: La fiction tv in Europa V Rapporto*, Roma: Edizioni VQPT-RAI, 2002b.

———. *Ricomposizioni: La fiction italiana/l'Italia nella fiction Anno XI*, Roma: Edizioni VQPT-Rai, 2000.

———. *Indigeni si diventa: Locale e globale nella serialità televisiva*, Milano: Sansoni, 1999.

———. *La Piovra: La carriera politica di una fiction popolare*, Genova: Costa & Nolan, 1996.

———. *Narrami o diva: Studi sull'immaginario televisivo*, Napoli: Liguori, 1994.

Casetti, Francesco, and Roger Odin. "De la paléo à la néo télévision. Un approche sémiopragmatique." *Communications*, n. 51 (1990): 9–26.

Casey, Bernadette, and Neil Casey, Ben Calvert, Liam French, Justin Lewis. *Television Studies: The Key Concepts*, London: Routledge, 2002.

Chan, Joseph M. "Dysnefying and Globalizing the Chinese Legend Mulan: A Study of Transculturation." Pp. 225–247 in *In Search of Boundaries: Communication, Nation States and Cultural Identities*, edited by Joseph M. Chan and Bryce T. McIntyre. London: Ablex, 2002.

Chan, Joseph M., and Eric K. W. Ma. "Asian Television: Global Trends and Local Process." *Gazette 58*, no. 1 (March 1996): 45–60.

Chan, Joseph M., and Eric K. W. Ma. "Transculturating Modernity: A Reinterpretation of Cultural Globalization." Pp. 3–18 in *In Search of Boundaries: Communication, Nation States and Cultural Identities*, edited by Joseph M. Chan and Bryce T. McIntyre. London: Ablex, 2002.

Chan, Joseph M., and Bryce T. McIntyre, eds. *In Search of Boundaries: Communication, Nation States and Cultural Identities*, London: Ablex, 2002.

Cook, Liza, "The Police Series." Pp. 122–123 in *The Television Genre Book*, edited by Glen Creeber. London: British Film Institute, 2001.

Creeber, Glen, ed. *The Television Genre Book*, London: British Film Institute, 2001.

Dupont, Françoise. *Da Omero a Dallas*, Roma: Universale Donzelli, 1993.

Dyer, Richard. *Light Entertainment*, London: British Film Institute, 1973.

Frye, Northrop. *Anatomy of Criticism: Four Essays*, Princeton: Princeton University Press, 1957.

Ginsborg, Paul. *Storia d'Italia dal dopoguerra ad oggi: Società e politica 1943–1988*, Torino: Einaudi, 1989.

Gledhill, Christine. "Pleasurable Negotiations." Pp. 64–89 in *Female Spectators: Looking at Film and Television*, edited by Deidre E. Pribram. London: Verso, 1988.

Grasso, Aldo, ed. *Enciclopedia della Televisione*, Milano: Garzanti, 2002.

Hall, Stuart. "The West and the Rest: Discourse and Power." Pp. 275–331 in *Formations of Modernity*, edited by Stuart Hall and Bram Gieben. Cambridge: Polity Press, 1992.

Kraidy, Marwan M., "The Global, the Local and the Hybrid: A Native Ethnography of Glocalization." *Critical Studies in Mass Communication* 16, no. 4 (December 1999): 456–476.

Lee, Chin-Chuan. *Media Imperialism Reconsidered: The Homogenizing of Television Culture*, Beverly Hills, CA: Sage Publications, 1980.

Liebes, Tamar, and Sonia Livingstone, "European Soap Operas: The Diversification of a Genre." *European Journal of Communication* 13, no. 2 (June 1998): 147–180.

Livolsi, Marino. *La realtà televisiva: Come la televisione ha cambiato gli italiani*, Roma-Bari: Laterza, 1998.

McQuail, Dennis. *Mass Communication Theory*, London: Sage Publications, 2005.

Menduni, Enrico. *I linguaggi della radio e della televisione: Teorie, tecniche, formati*, Roma-Bari: Laterza, 2006.

——. *Televisione e società italiana 1975–2000*, Milano: Bompiani, 2002.

Monteleone, Franco. *Storia della radio e della televisione in Italia: Un secolo di costume, società e politica*, Venezia: Marsilio, 2003.

Natale, Anna. Lucia. "Ieri e oggi. L'Italia nella fiction." Pp. 65–80 in *Lontano nel tempo: La fiction italiana/l'Italia nella fiction Anno XVI*, edited by Milly Buonanno. Roma: Edizioni VQPT-Rai, 2005.

Newcomb, Horace. "One Night of Prime Time: An Analysis of Television's Multiple Voices." Pp. 88–112. *Media, Myth and Narrative*, edited by James Carey, London: Sage, 1988.

Pastore, Renato. *Sulle strade delle fiction. Le serie poliziesche americane nella storia della televisione*. Torino: Lindau, 2006.

Silverstone, Roger. *Why Study the Media?*, London: Sage, 1999.

Straubhaar, Joseph. D. "Beyond Media Imperialism: Asymmetrical Interdependence and Cultural Proximity." *Critical Studies in Mass Communication* 1, no. 8 (March 1991): 35–59.

Straubhaar, Joseph D., and Antonio La Pastina. "Multiple Proximities between Television Genres and Audiences: The Schism between Telenovelas' Global Distribution and Local Consumption." *Gazette* 67, no. 3 (June 2005): 271–288.

Thornham, Sue, and Tony Purvis. *Television Drama: Theories and Identities*, Basingstoke: Palgrave Macmillan, 2005.

Tulloch, John. *Television Drama: Agency, Audience and Myth*, London: Routledge, 1990.

Williams, Raymond. Television: *Technology and Cultural Form*, Hanover: Wesleyan University Press, 1992.

Chapter Six

Dubbing *The Simpsons*: Or How Groundskeeper Willie Lost His Kilt in Sardinia

Chiara Ferrari

Given the international popularity of *The Simpsons* from the 1990s to the present, one might assume that the show does not require significant changes when exported abroad because of the familiarity that audiences worldwide have with the characters. In September 2005, however, executives at the Arab network MBC, felt that the Arab world needed a version of *The Simpsons* more in line with the feelings and beliefs of Islam, and they launched an "Arabized" hybrid of the series called *Al Shamshoon*. MBC altered the original text by changing some elements of the show through the Arab voiceover that substitutes for and translates the English soundtrack into Arabic. As a consequence, Homer Simpson becomes "Omar Shamshoon," hot dogs became Egyptian beef sausages; donuts are turned into Arab cookies called kahk; and, most unexpectedly, the omnipresent Duff beer became simple soda.[1] This is a particularly revealing example of how television executives aim at making a foreign product familiar (and "proper") to appeal to domestic audiences and maximize profit. MBC's adaptation of *The Simpsons*, in fact, is only one instance of many transformations the series has undergone when exported. Indeed, if audiences worldwide are familiar with the yellow animated characters from Springfield, most likely it is because they have watched a dubbed or subtitled version of the show rather than the original episodes. The importance given to the translation of *The Simpsons* is confirmed by the attention that FOX and Gracie Films (co-producers of the series) have paid to every phase of the show's international distribution. As Marion Edwards (Executive Vice President of FOX International Television) reveals in an interview with the author, the two production companies have been directly involved in the choice of translators and voiceover actors in most of the countries where the series has been exported. In Italy, in particular, Gracie Films has worked in collaboration with Mediaset to find voices for dubbing that match those of the original American actors as closely as possible. Furthermore, Gracie Films was directly involved in the choice of the Italian translator for the series.[2]

Such close attention to the exported product is explained, first of all, by the fact that through merchandizing and DVD sales, *The Simpsons* remains one of the most profitable shows on U.S. television. But because the animated series created by Matt Groening is replete with cultural and political references specific to the United States, close attention must be paid to achieve a successful translation. Cultural content is so relevant that, at times, even small visual details can create problems in foreign markets. Marion Edwards explains, for example, how the show received a cold welcome when first exported to Japan because all the characters in the series have four fingers. Variety reports that "having fewer than five digits in Japanese culture could signal a lower-class status (as in a butcher's occupational hazard), and thus a tough-sell to glamour-loving Japanese auds" (Swart, 1998). Furthermore, Bart's disrespectful attitude toward his parents and every type of authoritarian figure has also been difficult to sell in Asian countries where respect for one's elders is a cultural tradition. The solution found at FOX, in this case, was to market *The Simpsons* in Asia focusing on Lisa's intellectual character, instead of Bart's more "hip" attitude (Swart, 1998). These examples, together with that of MBC's *Al Shamshoon*, support the idea that translations are bridges between different cultures, not only between different languages. Furthermore, audiovisual translations not only modify the actual text; considered in a broad sense, they also provoke a systematic reorganization of programming and marketing strategies, a process that in itself represents a form of translation.

On this basis, the Italian translation of *The Simpsons* is an adaptation that involves not only linguistic and cultural factors but also aspects of programming. The modifications included in translation, in fact, far from depriving the show of its humor, have allowed the series to become particularly successful in Italy. This essay explores some of the changes made to the program and poses the following questions regarding the strategies employed to make *The Simpsons* more appealing to Italian audiences: (1) How does the translation of *The Simpsons* modify the characters and re-contextualize its archetypical and stereotypical features within a national framework of reference? (2) How does the translation reproduce the ethnic and racial multiplicity of *The Simpsons* within Italy's borders? And, more generally, (3) How does Italian television translate and adapt the many cultural references in *The Simpsons* to recreate the show's humor, satire, and irony? These particular questions arise when one realizes that in the many adaptations of *The Simpsons* abroad, two main elements emerge that, when "indigenized," increase the show's appeal: its references to popular culture and the stereotypical depiction of the characters. Italy is no exception in this respect. The translation relocates most of the cultural allusions to a new national (Italian) context and re-territorializes the characters according to domestic stereotypes.

What is most interesting and challenging in an analysis of *The Simpsons* is the fact that the show has been strongly identified with postmodern America and praised for its pungent and precise satire of contemporary American society. How, then, can it be localized for other parts of the world? Duncan Stuart Beard discusses the American-ness of the show, focusing on the difficulties involved in the translation of a type of satire "whose intent is locally directed" (Beard, 2004: 288). Beard examines *The Simpsons* to consider what happens when satire travels abroad and might get lost in translation:

> What the satirical elements of *The Simpsons* are ultimately involved in is an analysis of American socio-cultural practices and their relation to American notions of American identity. It is when viewed in this manner that its satire is at its most effective. Its interrogation of American identity assumes what is, for American audiences, an intuitive understanding of unspoken (and unspeakable) issues, primarily concerning what it means to be American. (289)

Although *The Simpsons* is undoubtedly rooted in specific references to American culture, Beard also argues that the show is successful worldwide because it manages to go beyond the constraints of its specific local irony. In particular, Beard contends that "what *The Simpsons* presents is not a form of global culture, but of local culture with a global reach" (290). He argues that *The Simpsons* is popular at home for its local satirical elements and successful abroad for the global themes and stereotypes it presents and ultimately "works best in directing its satiric energies against that mass media that is so often seen as threatening us with an increasingly homogenized cultural experience" (290). Expanding upon Beard's analysis, this chapter argues that *The Simpsons* is successful abroad not only for its global reach but also for the possibilities it offers for re-contextualization and local adaptation for international markets. In other words, what makes *The Simpsons* particularly popular worldwide are the many adaptations it has undergone, adaptations that have "indigenized" the text for international audiences.

The Italian translation of *The Simpsons*—*I Simpson*—is an all-encompassing process that includes changes to the characters' names and accents, acronyms, jokes, catch phrases, cultural references, signs, billboards, advertising jingles, songs, and episode titles. All the changes included in the translation of the series testify to the efforts made by the network (through the translator and the dialogue writer) to domesticate the program for Italian audiences. In this respect, the Italian adaptation of *The Simpsons* becomes particularly creative in its depiction of the show's secondary characters. The series is filled with minor figures who represent the entire population of Springfield in all its idiosyncrasies and stereotypical institutional roles: the reverend, the chief of police, the school principal, the bartender, and others. While the original U.S. voiceovers tend to play more with the tone of the characters' voices, often inspired by the famous actors and actresses who play them, the Italian translation adds regional accents to the characters, re-territorializing them across Italian geographical and stereotypical lines. In this regard, it is paramount to clarify one aspect of the adaptation: *I Simpson* is still based in Springfield and the characters are still "Americans," as in the original U.S. version. Having the characters speak with various Italian accents, however, corresponds to specific cultural stereotypes and represents a conscious effort to indigenize and domesticate the series for distribution in Italy. The following sections explore the significance of these modifications, from the domestication of the ethnic attributes of the characters to the adaptation of the many cultural references in the series to support an argument that there is a direct correspondence between the efforts made toward indigenization and interest in maximizing profits from the series' distribution in Italy.

GLOBAL REACH VS. LOCAL APPEAL: A FEW GENERIC CONSIDERATIONS

The discussion concerning the domestication of some of the show's characters in the Italian adaptation of *The Simpsons* requires a brief introduction about the role of these characters in the original U.S. version. It is also useful to discuss pertinent issues related to genre. Establishing the generic nature of *The Simpsons* and FOX's original idea about its intended audience is important as a foundation for understanding the corresponding Italian conception about the program and its targeted audience. It has been argued extensively that *The Simpsons* is stylistically and generically a combination of animation and family sitcom. The argument in favor of animation is fairly straightforward—*The Simpsons* is indeed an animated series. The idea of the show as a sitcom, however, might not be as obvious. Communication scholar Megan Mullen traces the origins of *The Simpsons* back to Hanna-Barbera's cartoons (*The Flintstones* and *The Jetsons*), the magicoms of the late 1960s (*Bewitched* and *I Dream of Jeannie*), and working-class and "socially relevant" sitcoms (*The Honeymooners*, *All in the Family*, and *Roseanne*, among others). The series' similarity with *The Flintstones* and *The Jetsons* certainly depends on its use of animation to convey irony but also rests on the legacy of these earlier animated series and the decision to air them on prime time, as well as marketing these series more as family sitcoms made for adults than as cartoons for children.[3] Mullen clarifies these influences on *The Simpsons*:

> The creators of *The Flintstones* and *The Jetsons* had exploited the unique potential of animation as a device to convey irony in an innocuous way, a strategy inherited and further developed by *The Simpsons*' creators decades later. While the sitcom genre itself offers a way to pack stories about common human experiences into less than thirty minutes, animation eliminates any need to meet expectations of verisimilitude. As with children's cartoons, viewers approach these "adult" cartoon sitcoms with suspended disbelief, and in the process absorb significant social commentary. (Mullen, 2004: 82)

The kind of witty humor and cultural critique that characterizes *The Simpsons* clearly testifies to FOX's intention to target a more adult audience, despite using animation as the stylistic and narrative mode. The schedule of programming in which *The Simpsons* originally aired provides further evidence that the series was considered a sitcom and not merely a children's cartoon. Indeed, FOX scheduled *The Simpsons* in direct competition with NBC's *The Cosby Show*, which, although in decline when *The Simpsons* premiered, had been one of the most popular family sitcoms on American television (Robins, 1990: 39).

Among the various elements that define *The Simpsons* as a sitcom, there is one factor that is particularly relevant for the analysis of the indigenization of the series: the presence of an innumerable cast of minor characters who participate in the development of the story in significant ways. Horace Newcomb closely examines the dramatic function of secondary characters in traditional sitcoms and argues that their role goes beyond that of mere foils. Newcomb writes: "The supporting characters live somewhere between the improbable world of the central characters and the world as most of the audience experiences it. . . . These supporting characters serve a crucial function in that they stand, dramatically, closer to the value structure of the audience than to that of the central characters" (Newcomb, 1974: 37–38). In this respect, *The Simpsons* not only follows the conventions of traditional sitcoms, but it also pushes their possibilities to the extreme. Newcomb's analysis, in fact, could not be truer for *The Simpsons*, whose number of secondary characters is much higher than those found in live-action sitcoms. Don Payne, writer and co-executive producer of *The Simpsons*, explains how some of the secondary characters were developed during *The Tracy Ullman Show* (where *The Simpsons* originally aired as a series of thirty-second animated shorts). Payne contends that part of the longevity of the show is indeed based on the many secondary characters for two fundamental reasons. First of all, they rise at times to the role of protagonists, therefore introducing alternative narrative into the overall family plot. Second, the minor characters are defined by very specific stereotypical traits that can provide quick and recurrent jokes. Payne confesses, in fact, that writers in *The Simpsons* "certainly embrace cultural stereotypes"—a factor that allows Italian translators to "play" with and adapt specific cultural conventions to the new context (Payne, 2007). Other characters, however, were created when the series premiered as an autonomous program in 1989, and others were added even later in following seasons.

Given the variety and number of characters, then, *The Simpsons* is able to explore most of the social and cultural types with which the audience is familiar. The series portrays a greedy and obnoxious boss (Mr. Burns), a corrupt Mayor (Quimby), an incompetent chief of police (Wiggum), an immigrant who fights for his rights as a citizen (Apu), a reverend more interested in material goods than in spiritual guidance (Lovejoy), and so on. Clearly enough, these are figures with whom viewers deal on a daily basis and whose attitudes either reflect ours or remind us of someone we know. In addition, these characters are not only depicted in their respective institutional roles in society. They are also strongly defined by specific social, cultural, and ethnic stereotypes, whose significance is increased by the precise environment—small town Americana—in which they function. The importance of the secondary characters is increased by the fact that the central characters of the show—mainly Bart and Homer—often come out as particularly "improbable" for their exaggerated lack of discipline (Bart) and lack of intelligence and common sense (Homer). As Newcomb contends, "[The central characters] are, in some way, out of touch with our day-to-day sense of how things happen, with the set of laws that allows us to predict the outcome of our actions" (36). The protagonists, therefore, do not usually provide the more realistic solutions to the problems that the audience is likely to have experienced.

In this respect, something needs to be clarified about the central characters in *The Simpsons* and their narrative roles. Accepting the idea that Bart, at first, and later Homer have been considered the main characters of the show, something must be said about their identity in relation to the plot. As Brian Ott argues: "Bart's identity privileges image over narrative. In contrast to Lisa, Bart has no political commitments and subsequently he can stand against anything. Bart offers a prepackaged image of rebellion, an identity largely independent of the show's weekly narratives" (Ott, 2003: 69). Similarly, Jerry Herron contends: "[Bart] has no history to bind him to a particular race or class or ethnicity, so he is semiotically up for grabs, and up for grabbing opportunities that await us all" (Herron, 1993: 19). Bart, with his easy catch phrases, his highly visual presence, and his detachment from any specific ethnic, racial or political identity, represents that "global reach" and appeal that Duncan Stuart Beard discusses. In this respect, then, age or generational diversity seems to sell better globally than ethnic diversity, as it is clear how Bart appeals to audiences across age, gender, race, and ethnicity (perhaps with the exception of East Asia, as discussed in the introductory paragraphs). The audience laughs at the disastrous outcomes of Bart's actions because they often entail slapstick comedy that is not based on his ethnic identity, but on his "age identity" as a disrespectful kid.

A way to indigenize Bart, therefore, is through the localization of his actions, which can become very culturally specific, even if not related to a particular ethnic or political identity. An interesting example of this type of indigenization is the voiceover that translates Bart's punishments in the opening credits of each episode. The punishment always consists of having Bart write on the school blackboard a different repeated phrase that corresponds to the action done in class—action for which he has been punished in the first place. Bart's rebellious personality is introduced right in the credits, since the audience is presented each show with a different form of insubordination that causes him to stay after class. As indicated earlier, the original U.S. version has Bart write (in English) on the board, with no need for voiceover to explain what he is writing. The Italian version, however, maintains the original visuals, but has the voiceover "translate" what is on the board for the Italian-speaking audience. Most times this is a translation of what Bart is actually writing, but there are a few instances in which the translation adapts and modifies the action for which Bart is being punished. In the pilot episode, "Bart the Genius," Bart writes: "I won't waste chalk." The wasting of chalk is not too serious an action in itself, but the joke lies in the fact that writing ad nauseam on the blackboard is certainly a waste of chalk, so the punishment makes less sense than the action being punished. The Italian version, however, seems less focused on the preservation of the original joke and more interested in establishing Bart's character as a brat (which is also an anagram of his first name) from the very beginning, given that this is the pilot. The translation changes the cause of the punishment, and while Bart writes "I won't waste chalk" the voiceover says "Non disegnero' donne nude in classe" (I won't draw naked women in class), an action much more serious, especially for a ten-year-old. The dubbed version, then, portrays Bart as almost erotically deviant, employing a cultural (global) stereotype often associated with Italians as overtly sensual and sexual. Italian "supposed sensuality," in fact, is stereotypically constructed for Italian audiences as well, and based on a more international idea of Italian-ness than on a truly Italian notion of Italian-ness. Clearly, Bart's indigenization is based less on specific ethnic and regional stereotypes than it is on more general characteristics, which concern Italian-ness in a more global sense. Bart's global reach, indeed, offers translators a fairly easy task when it comes to adapting the character for foreign audiences, as the Italian case demonstrates.

Homer is very similar in this respect, but for different reasons. Ott again provides an insightful explanation: "[Homer] furnishes a vehicle for endless intertextual reference and exemplifies a radical postmodern multiplicity—an extreme rejection of boundary, stability, historicity, and any concept of a cohesive self. In essence, Homer models an anti-identity; his being critiques the modernist idea of a unified, coherent subject (Ott, 2003: 66). By defying the reassuring idea of a unified subject, Homer's personality becomes hard to fully embrace and, consequently, hard to localize in its social, ethnic, and national individuality. Conversely, Homer's very lack of personal specificity has been a major factor in his becoming such an icon of global popular culture. Certainly several factors make Homer easily "up for global grabs." Like Bart, he is the cause of the slapstick aspects of the show, and also serves as the engine for the improbable complications of the plot. These elements add to his more universal appeal, since the humor is often based on the visuals. In addition, one of the traits that more strongly defines Homer's character is his habitual dependence upon consumption. Homer is particularly sensitive to deceptive commercial advertising, a factor that often turns into a narrative mechanism that triggers the action. To relate this aspect back to issues of identity, Homer is defined essentially by "what he buys" more than "what he is" or "what he says" (with the exception of his world renowned "D'Oh!"). A more effective way to localize Homer, then, is through the indigenization of what he purchases, instead of through the way he expresses himself. An example of this strategy is at play in an episode from season nine, "Lisa's Sax." The Simpson family is having a conversation in the living room when Marge asks Homer to hold Maggie and put her to sleep. Homer thinks that an effective way to get Maggie drowsy is to give her some beer and puts the can of Duff in her mouth while crooning "Come on Maggie, It's Miller time, it's Miller time." Homer dialogue recalls both a specific and real brand of beer— Miller—and its renowned American commercials, extolling "It's Miller time." The real reference, then, is to American popular culture, as the famous commercial tag line was coined in the 1970s and has been re-purposed in various forms to this day.[4] One of Homer's most characteristic features is his love for beer; indigenizing this habit, then, is an effective strategy to localize Homer maintaining his identity intact.

The Italian translator takes the cultural reference into consideration, and looking for an appropriate alternative, has Homer say: "Maggie... birra, e sai cosa bevi!" (Maggie... beer, and you know what you're drinking!) The catch phrase, easily remembered by any adult in Italy, refers to a popular 1980s commercial in which Neapolitan actor, TV host, and musician Renzo Arbore promoted and guaranteed the quality of Italian beers. While not related to any specific brand, the reference to the beer commercial and what it represents is precise, and targets the same adult audience in both countries. Homer, therefore, becomes "local" in his consumerist traits, which are not based on ethnic, racial, or political factors, but on more global aspects of popular culture. Like Bart's indigenization, Homer's transfer to the Italian context is fairly straightforward and based on comical and cultural characteristics that translate easily abroad. This is not to say that their characters remain "untouched" when the series is exported, but their indigenization is less based on linguistic and ethnic translation than the indigenization of secondary characters.

In contrast, many of the secondary characters in *The Simpsons* are depicted through their national, racial, and ethnic characteristics and idiosyncrasies, more locally specific than Bart's and Homer's attributes. Such specificity is what challenges translators the most, but it is also what offers them concrete and creative possibilities for indigenization. In this respect, Beard points out the importance of such secondary characters to the original U.S. version, but he also argues that their portrayal created several problems when the series was exported abroad:

> The eccentric cast of characters who constitute *The Simpsons*' heterogeneous vision of the American public provides a solid foundation upon which to base its critique of numerous elements of American life. In regard to the massive success of the show in foreign markets, however, this factor has also created interpretative problems for international audiences, particularly concerning the show's satiric intent. (Beard, 2004: 275)

As Beard observes, what is particularly significant about the importance given to secondary characters is the fact that they represent the kind of society that *The Simpsons* ultimately criticizes. Hence, not only does the series make ironic statements about idiosyncrasies related to institutional and social figures, but it also shows those figures in all their autonomous and precise stereotypical traits.

As mentioned in the introductory section, the Italian adaptation of *The Simpsons* becomes particularly creative and insightful when it re-territorializes these characters and their traits within an Italian frame of reference. The way in which this process of indigenization is achieved is mainly through the use of various Italian accents and dialects to dub the voices of the show's secondary characters. In so doing, the translation of *The Simpsons* for Italian audiences not only maintains the global appeal of these ironic portrayals (as Beard argues), but it localizes them, transferring the humor to a new national context. For example, considering the influence of the Catholic Church and the common tendency to criticize it, Italians are certainly familiar with religious figures who do not quite play their role as God's ministers but use the Church to attain personal benefits (like the show's Reverend Lovejoy). Similarly, many stereotypes in Italy are related to the corruption of politics and the police, and therefore characters such as Mayor Quimby and Chief Wiggum find fertile ground in the Italian context.

Furthermore, given the diversity of regional intonations and corresponding cultural types that Italian society offers, the small town of Springfield is imaginatively transferred to the Mediterranean peninsula fairly easily and effectively. To clarify, *I Simpson* (the Italian title of the series) is not geographically transported and based in Italy, but the stereotypical traits of its citizens are. Tonino Accolla, dialogue writer and director of dubbing for *I Simpson*, confirms and describes the conscious efforts made to depict the characters in terms of certain stereotypes. As he contends, this goal is often achieved in Italy through the use of regional accents: "In *I Simpson* I used many different accents. Accents from Chieti, from Venice, from Naples, from Calabria. Accents in Italy immediately recall precise personalities" (Accolla, 2005). In this respect, Accolla's comments fit particularly well with Antje Ascheid's theorization about the "re-writing" of new characters through dubbing: "These new characters are uttering a translated, which always also means interpreted, appropriated, and recreated new text, thus undergoing fundamental shifts in the construction of their national and cultural identity and context"—shifts that are fundamental to understand the Italian version of the animated series (Ascheid, 1997: 33).

While *The Simpsons*' characters do not become literally Italian, through their "linguistic indigenization," they are able to reflect some aspects of the new cultural and national context in which they are imported. The following section analyzes the most relevant examples among the show's secondary characters that have been modified through adaptation. Closely examining their linguistic peculiarities demonstrates how the translation utilizes Italian stereotypes to re-create familiar characters for the new audience.

INDIGENIZING CHARACTERS: ACCENTS, STEREOTYPES, AND THE "OTHERS"

Writing about the translation of *The Simpsons* in France, sociolinguist Nigel Armstrong claims that "the relative leveling of French pronunciation puts difficulties in the way of the oral translation of some social-regional accents that are used with rather subtle effect in *The Simpsons*" (Armstrong, 2004: 34). While not entirely judging the value of the translation per se, Armstrong's study examines the effectiveness of the adaptation of *The Simpsons* from

English into French. His examples show how the lack of a wide variety of accents in the French language creates difficulties in attempts to localize the program because the many accents of the original dialogue cannot be properly transferred into the French context.[5]

In this respect, the Italian case is opposite to that of French. Italy offers a greater range of accents and inflections than does the U.S., and therefore the translator is presented with several possibilities for indigenizing the text. The Italian translation, in fact, not only reproduces the use of accents in the American version in a new national and regional context, but it also adds accents where they were not originally present. The result is a picturesque community of characters whose linguistic peculiarities increase their appeal for the Italian audience. What follows are discussions of two groups of secondary characters from *The Simpsons* who have been linguistically localized following and re-proposing conventional regional stereotypes.

REGIONALIZED CHARACTERS

The first group includes those characters (Fat Tony, Moe Szyslak, Otto Mann, and Chief Wiggum) whose indigenization is based on ethnic stereotypes and personalities "within the nation," but whose characterization does not present (both in the original and in the translated version) any form of racial or foreign "Otherness." These characters are localized and domesticated for the Italian context through the use of familiar Italian regional accents, which also directly correspond to the American stereotypes employed to create the original characters.

Anthony D'Amico (Fat Tony)

Fat Tony is the typical Italian American mobster, a figure that has become popular as a result of the worldwide distribution of gangster genre narratives. As a consequence, his character is easily recognizable in the United States and abroad because of global exposure to American gangster movies and television series from the 1930s gangster movies to The Godfather saga and, more recently, *The Sopranos*. Fat Tony is involved in several criminal activities from his involvement in the dairy industry that provides rat milk to Springfield Elementary School passing it off as regular milk ("Mayored to the Mob") to the forgery of immigration documents that he provides to Apu when the latter risks being deported ("Much Apu About Nothing"). Dubbed by Italian American actor Joe Mantegna in the original series, Fat Tony's voice and tone evoke those of many Italian American gangsters portrayed in the media. The regional accent chosen by the Italian translators for Fat Tony is Sicilian, this because it is immediately associated with illegal activities related to the Mafia. The accent, therefore, conventionally associates Fat Tony with the mob, and it is significant here because it demonstrates how the use of Southern Italian accents for mobsters is a well-established and very common practice in Italian audiovisual translation.

Moe Szyslak

Moe Szyslak is the bartender and owner of Moe's Tavern, Homer's favorite location in Springfield. Moe is characterized, in the original U.S. version, by a consistent ambiguity regarding his downwardly mobile life and his suspect origins. His actions are usually dubious, and few are the instances in which the audience is informed about details of his life. One such example is an episode from season seven, "Much Apu About Nothing," which will be discussed in more detail during the analysis of Apu's character. This episode focuses on a referendum proposed by Mayor Quimby for the approval of a new anti-immigration law. In order to remain in the country, Apu must apply for citizenship and take a written and oral exam to prove his knowledge of American history, culture, and politics. In the citizenship classroom, Moe is shown hiding behind a fake moustache taking the test together with Apu and Willie (originally from India and Scotland, respectively). Consequently, we can legitimately assume that Moe is not a legal U.S. citizen.

In the Italian translation, Moe is localized on two separate levels. First, his given name is changed from Moe to Boe. While such a change might seem neither relevant nor necessary, it actually represents an interesting and creative way to indigenize the character. The name "Boe" does not exist in Italian, but it sounds like "Boh," a very common Italian expression, which means "I don't know." On the one hand, as *The Simpsons*' translator Elena di Carlo reports, the change to Boe is a comical mechanism because Italians use the expression "Boh" very frequently with amusing nonchalance (di Carlo, quoted in Bologna, 2005–2006: 59). On the other hand, however, given that the audience does not know much about the character, Boe turns into a humorous expression that also highlights the character's ambiguity. In addition, Boe occasionally speaks with a Sicilian accent. The fact that he expresses himself with a regionalized inflection (an element not present in the original U.S. version) only in a few episodes also increases his ambiguity and the curiosity of the audience. Through the choice of his first name and his occasional localization as a Sicilian, the Italian translation highlights Moe/Boe's tendency to hide information about his life, which is the most distinctive trait of the character in the original U.S. version. The indigenization, therefore, ultimately aims at re-creating an impression about the character similar to that of the American series.

Otto Mann

Otto Mann is the school bus driver, whose "stoner" incompetence and lack of any sense of responsibility often get him into trouble. Otto incarnates a "slacker" version of the "Peter Pan Syndrome"; he is a thirty-year-old male who lacks ambition and only wants to play the guitar (this last attribute is highlighted in Italian by a change to his last name from Mann to Disc). The "Peter Pan" stereotype translates well in Italy to the figure of *mammone* (mama's boy). One of the most recurrent jokes about Italian men (in Italy and abroad) concerns their inability to leave the parental home and care. Although not particularly dependent upon his parents, Otto presents some of the characteristics and stereotypical traits of those young adults who refuse responsibility, much like the *mammone*. The stereotype associated with *mammone* does not depend on particular regional traits but spreads throughout the peninsula. The Italian writers, however, chose a Milanese accent for Otto's voiceover. The choice of this accent adds humor to the depiction of the character not because Otto fits the cultural stereotype associated with Milano but because he contradicts it completely. Milano is the most industrialized and residential city in Italy, thus the Milanese stereotype is of people who are snobbish, pretentious, ambitious, and very efficient. Otto could not be further from this description. The humor and irony, then, lies in setting certain expectations through the use of a specific accent that evokes a certain regional type and then in challenging those same expectations with a character who contradicts them all.

Clancy Wiggum

Clancy Wiggum is Springfield Chief of Police. He is overweight, a factor highlighted by an enormous belly, and his character is defined by his continual eating, incompetence, lack of intelligence, and corrupt practices. In the original U.S. version, the actor plays with Wiggum's voice in an imitation of actor Edward G. Robinson. A Jewish immigrant from Romania, Robinson became hugely popular in the 1930s for his portrayal of Italian American gangster Little Caesar in Melvin Leroy's film *Little Caesar* (Rhodes). In the U.S. version, the irony is based on the use of a generic "funny" voice (for a young and less educated audience) and, more specifically, on the parody of Edward G. Robinson (for older and more acculturated viewers).

In Wiggum's case, the Italian translation is particularly creative and effective. The character's last name is changed from Wiggum to Winchester, after the famous rifle and shotgun brand, to mock American police officers' ease with weapons. The Italian voiceover actor dubbing Wiggum also speaks with a marked Neapolitan accent, which, as a matter of convention, makes the character sound amusing. The Neapolitan accent is particularly loved in Italy and, as Milly Buonanno contends, theater, film, and television have traditionally accustomed Italians to associate the Neapolitan accent and dialect with comedy (Buonanno, 1994: 163).[6] In addition to speaking with a Neapolitan accent, Wiggum's jargon is also strongly based on the Neapolitan dialect. The Chief of Police usually addresses criminals as guaglio' (short for guaglione), one of the most authentically Neapolitan expressions, translatable as "kid." Finally, his corrupt practices as a police officer evoke common labels associated to organized crime in Naples; therefore, Wiggum fits the characteristics of Neapolitan stereotypes on multiple levels. His accent, the specific words he uses, and the conventional portrayal of Neapolitan police as corrupt imaginatively re-territorialize Wiggum within the Italian context and symbolically "send" the Italian audience home.

DIVERSITY ITALIAN STYLE

Different from the first group of characters—Fat Tony, Moe Szyslak, Otto Mann, and Chief Wiggum—whose representations remain within the realm of national (and regional) stereotypes, the second group involves two characters—Willie and Apu Nahasapeemapetilon—whose stereotypical representations include strong elements of racial and foreign "otherness" (both in the American and Italian versions). Even in this case, these characters are indigenized so that their "otherness"—as well as their more familiar traits—is geographically and linguistically transferred and made comprehensible in the Italian context.

Willie: National "Other"

Willie is the groundskeeper at Springfield Elementary School. He is usually solitary and aggressive, and he often mentions his rural upbringing in Scotland, his native country. The fact that he is Scot is highlighted both linguistically and visually. Willie, in fact, speaks with a marked Scottish accent and often wears a kilt. Both elements place Willie as an outsider in Springfield since he speaks differently and wears "strange" items of clothing. For these reasons he is often the target of jokes planned by the kids in school.

What needs to be re-created in the Italian translation are Willie's Scottishness and his alienation from the Springfield community, a community that speaks and acts differently from the groundskeeper. In this regard, the fundamental difficulty that the Italian translator and dialogue writer encountered was the fact that the Scottish stereotype in Italy does not correspond to the characteristics that Willie presents. Scottish people are considered, in the Italian imaginary, as greedy and particularly prone to drinking. While the Italian idea about Scots might somehow "justify" Willie's aggressive attitude, it does not justify Willie's constant references to his rural lifestyle, which Italians do not associate with Scotland.

The solution chosen involves a drastic transfer of Willie's stereotypical (Scottish) character to a similar Italian personality, one possessing the same characteristics and idiosyncrasies as Willie. Willie becomes, in fact, an immigrant from Sardinia, which with Sicily is one of the two Italian island regions. Although Sicily is more integrated in the Italian imaginary, both because of the Mafia and the media (through movies, television fiction, and the news), Sardinia still remains isolated in the stereotypical view of Italians and is seen as very rural and almost "primitive" for the particularly arid nature of its landscapes. In reality, Sardinia is one of the most exclusive and expensive locations for tourism in Italy, attracting thousands of Italians and foreigners every summer, vacationers who are eager to enjoy the beauty of its beaches, the Gennargentu National Park, and many pre-Roman archeological sites. Nonetheless, traditional and stereotypical representation of people from Sardinia, especially in the media, figures a rustic lifestyle and stubborn people usually working as shepherds. In the Italian context, therefore, the Sardinian stereotype fits Willie more appropriately than the Scottish stereotype. Willie as a Sardinian ultimately creates in the Italian audience associations about the character that are analogous to what the American audience associates with him as Scottish. As for most of the characters, translator Elena di Carlo reveals that such a change was not made in the actual translation phase, but in a later phase, during the adaptation of the dialogue for the screen, by the dialogue writer and director of dubbing as they were rehearsing with the actors (Bologna, 2005–2006: 59). It seems that, at the level of actual translation, the changes involve primarily the use of specific words, names, and catch phrases. Later, in the subsequent level of adaptation for the screen, the accents come into play to complete the cultural transfer of the characters.

The process of indigenization that Willie undergoes is a significant example of domestication and re-territorialization and in his case not only on an imaginative level (as the characters described so far). In the Italian version, in fact, Willie not only speaks with a marked Sardinian accent (as harsh as the Scottish inflection in the U.S. version), but in the show he explicitly comes from Sardinia. With the exception of one ambiguous episode described later, Willie is literally transferred to Italy, geographically, culturally, and linguistically. The ambiguity of Willie's re-territorialization, at times, creates problems of credibility, but overall it works for the Italian audience that finds in Willie one of its favorite characters, precisely because of his Sardinian accent and temperament.

One of the major obstacles to overcome in the Italian adaptation, however, is visual: Willie often wears a kilt, which is an undeniably Scottish reference. When not ignored in the Italian translation, the kilt is often referred to as a regular skirt and simply considered as an element that adds to Willie's oddity. Overall, then, Willie's wearing a kilt/skirt only increases his strangeness for the Italian audience, but such a trait is detached from any national or ethnic aspect of his personality with the exception of one episode, "Monty Can't Buy Me Love," in which Mr. Burns, Homer, and Willie travel to Scotland, and both Willie and Homer wear kilts. Willie's origin from Sardinia is discussed in a few instances in the Italian version, mostly in correspondence to his depiction as Scottish in the U.S. version. Two episodes in the tenth season, in particular, make specific references to Willie as a Scotsman (in the U.S. version) and as a Sardinian (in the Italian version): "Lard of the Dance" and the aforementioned "Monty Can't Buy Me Love." The episodes are interesting because they provide information about Willie, confirming his origin from Scotland in the U.S. version, but creating problems, contradictions, and ambiguity in the Italian translation.

"Lard of the Dance" (Tanto va Homer al lardo che . . .) is less problematic because every piece of information or joke about Willie is based on language, and therefore fairly easily translatable through dubbing. In the episode, Homer discovers that he can make money by entering the grease recycling business. After many failed attempts, he decides to steal the school's fat waste with Bart's help. They successfully sneak into the school and start vacuuming the grease out, but Willie discovers them. Homer tries to defend himself pretending to be an exchange student from Scotland. After hearing that Homer is also Scottish, Willie becomes excited and asks Homer where he is from. Homer replies he comes from "North Kilt Town" and Willie gets even more excited because he comes from the same city and asks Homer if he knows Angus McLeod. The humor of the conversation is further increased by Willie's exaggerated Scottish accent.

The entire dialogue is translated and transferred to the Italian context by substituting every reference to Scotland with a reference to Sardinia. Homer pretends to be an exchange student from Sardinia and to come from "Nord Pecurone" (literally North Big Sheep Town). Excited, Willie asks if Homer knows Salvatore Udda, and the whole conversation is conducted in strong

Sardinian accents. The correspondence between North Kilt Town and Nord Pecurone, between Angus McLeod and Salvatore Udda, and between the accents is very precise. In the first case, the name of Willie's hometown is created based on very stereotypical traits: the kilt for Scotland and the sheep for Sardinia. Similarly, the reference to Angus McLeod and Salvatore Udda is comical because the two names respectively sound undeniably from Scotland and Sardinia. Hence, the conversation is directly transposed into Italian employing very stereotypical assumptions about Sardinia that correspond to similar assumptions about Scotland. What makes the Italian dialogue even funnier than the American version, however, is the fact that, in translation, Homer starts speaking with a strong accent from Sardinia as well, to better pretend and fool Willie. The consequences of the episode also correspond for the American and Italian audiences: Willie's hometown is confirmed to be Scotland (in the U.S.) and Sardinia (in Italy), even if the names of the two towns mentioned are clearly invented.

A later episode, "Monty Can't Buy Me Love" (Monty non può comprare amore), is analogous with "Lard of the Dance" in re-establishing Willie as a Scotsman in the U.S. version. The Italian version becomes ambiguous, however, because in this episode Willie claims to be born in Scotland as well (as opposed to Sardinia), thus contradicting and confusing all previous information about his character. In the episode, Homer's boss Mr. Burns, travels to Scotland to look for the Loch Ness monster, capture it, and take it to Springfield in order to finally be loved and appreciated by his fellow citizens. Mr. Burns forces Homer, Willie, and Professor John Frink to follow him and help him in the monster's capture. Once at the lakeshore, the Professor starts operating complicated machinery to detect the monster in the water, and a curious crowd gathers. Homer notices an older couple in the crowd who bear significant reseamblance to Willie. The groundskeeper confirms that they are his parents, who own a tavern nearby as well as the pool table where he was "conceived, born, and educated." For the American audience, used to hearing Willie speaking with a Scottish accent and seeing him wearing a kilt in Springfield, this episode simply adds information about the character and his comical representation.

The Italian adaptation of this episode presents many challenges for the translators. First of all, the visual references to Scotland are abundant and very explicit, and therefore hard to modify through the voiceover. Second, the older couple shown in the crowd looks unquestionably like Willie, and thus the translation needs to justify the presence of Willie's parents in Scotland even though he speaks with a Sardinian accent. Instead of clarifying information about the character, then, the Italian dialogue increases the ambiguity about Willie. Difficulties such as those in this episode of *The Simpsons* are not isolated cases. These problems arise when choices and changes are made at the time a series is first imported and adapted, and later translators need to be consistent with those initial narrative modifications even if the visuals contradict them completely. In this case, the challenge is to re-justify Willie's origin from Sardinia even though his family lives in Scotland. The translation changes Willie's origin back to Scotland in this episode, contradicting what previously had been said about his Sardinian origin, but makes every Scotsman in the crowd speak with a Sardinian accent, as if there were a direct–yet imaginative–correspondence between being Scottish and being Sardinian. In addition, right after revealing that he was born in Scotland, Willie makes two precise references to Sardinia that immediately transfer him back to the Italian context. First, once Homer goes underwater to look for the monster and does not reappear on the surface for a while, Willie claims that Homer shows more "stubbornness" than a "goat from Gennargentu," a renowned National Park on the east coast of Sardinia. Later in the episode, after Mr. Burns manages to capture the monster by himself, Willie defines him as being "stronger than Gigi Riva." Gigi Riva is a famous retired soccer player, a major star of the Italian national team and leading scorer in the 1970 World Cup, who played for the Cagliari team (the major Sardinian city) for about fifteen years until he retired. Willie's character, therefore, is re-confirmed both as an Italian for his passion for soccer, the Italian national sport, and ultimately as a Sardinian by making reference to Gennargentu and Riva.

At the risk of falling into a "dangerous" example of self-referentiality that might estrange viewers, the translators opted for two strong narrative reminders that re-establish Willie as a Sardinian. Thus, the importance of both episodes, "Lard of the Dance" and "Monty Can't Buy Me Love," lies in the fact that, against all (visual) odds, Willie is re-territorialized within Italian geography by translating a precise cultural stereotype into a more general Italian one. The Sardinian accent and language sound particularly harsh and therefore represent a good correspondence to the Scottish accent. Linguistically, in fact, the transfer works particularly well because Sardinian (which consists of two major subgroups, Logudorese and Campidanese) is the only idiom in Italy that is not a dialect, but an actual language. Sardinian is autonomous as compared to other modern languages derived from Latin, and is practically incomprehensible to other Italians (De Mauro, 1979: 89). Thus, Willie's difficulty in belonging to the community in which he lives is highlighted by the use of an insular idiom, geographically and linguistically detached from mainland Italy. In the translation, therefore, Willie emerges as an outsider, which is ultimately his U.S. role in Springfield as a foreigner from Scotland.

Apu Nahasapeemapetilon: Racial "Other"

While Willie presents features that differentiate him from the rest of Springfield in terms of his nationality, Apu Nahasapeemapetilon is represented both as a foreigner and as a racial "other." Apu is Indian and originally came to the U.S. to pursue a doctorate in computer science. Once in college he began to work at Kwik-E-Mart to pay off his student loans and never left his convenience store job even after he received his degree. Apu is married to Manjula, an Indian girl whom his parents chose for him, as is the custom in India. Apu speaks proper English with a strong Indian accent and maintains his cultural heritage and religious beliefs by displaying in the store the statue of Ganisha, an Indian divinity in the form of an elephant. Apu's representation mixes various common stereotypes associated with immigrants from India: from being particularly good at engineering and computer science to working 24-hours a day in convenience stores. Although racially different from most of the people in Springfield, Apu is generally well accepted in his community with the exception of one episode, "Much Apu About Nothing," in which he risks deportation. Mayor Quimby, in fact, proposes a referendum for the approval of a new law that would force all illegal aliens to leave Springfield and America. In order to avoid the possibility of being deported, Apu first turns to the local mobster Fat Tony to provide him with fake documents. When Apu thanks him humbly, Fat Tony promptly replies, "Cut the courtesy, you're an American now!" and suggests that he "act American" if he does not want to look suspicious. As Fat Tony's dialogue reveals, the episode is as much about the stereotypical representation of Apu's Indian heritage as it is about the American lack of tolerance for immigrants. The mocking of America becomes more explicit later on in the episode when Homer sees Apu showing off American flags, a cowboy hat, and a Mets jersey, as he is now an "American." Apu invites Homer to "take a relaxed attitude for work, and watch the baseball game." Homer is surprised by the changes in Apu, but welcomes the substitution of "that goofy sacred elephant statue" with American magazines in the Kwik-E-Mart. Apu, pretending to agree with Homer, replies, "Who needs the infinite compassion of Ganisha, when I've got Tom Cruise and Nicole Kidman staring at me from *Entertainment Weekly*?"

In a brief conversation, the writers of the series manage to reduce America to a country made of cowboys and baseball fans whose cultural superficiality is highlighted by their reading of Hollywood entertainment magazines. Apu, however, has not only assimilated into the stereotypical American culture of sports and film stars. An additional change that Homer notices in Apu is in the way he talks. Apu has almost completely erased his Indian accent and makes use of American slang such as "Hey there, Homer. How is it hanging?" Apu, therefore, assimilates into American vernacular and culture in order to fit in a society that might expel him for his foreignness.

While this stereotypical depiction turns out to be undeniably comedic visually, a profound critique of Americans' attitude toward assimilation remains barely hidden behind the humor. Apu's *performed* American-ness is based more on appearance and stereotypical symbols of patriotism than on actual manifestations of cultural identity. After all, Fat Tony himself suggests all Apu has to do is to *act* American—not necessarily to *be* American. And it is precisely his performed and artificial identity that soon brings Apu to reassume his Indian heritage. Ashamed at having betrayed his family and roots, he decides to take the official test to become a legal citizen and to become an American without repudiating his own Indian identity.

Clearly, this episode refers to the 1994 elections when Californians voted for Proposition 187, a ballot initiative aimed at preventing illegal immigrants from accessing health care benefits and public education. After Apu passes his citizenship exam and is convinced that it is wrong to vote for the new law, Homer organizes a party to celebrate Apu finally obtaining American citizenship and makes a speech to his neighbors. Homer claims that many "official Americans" take this country for granted while immigrants like Apu are the glue that really holds the society together. Notwithstanding Homer's popularity after his touching speech, the new law passes in Springfield. As a consequence, many are to be deported, most notably Willie, who closes the episode being forced to leave on a ship. In the meantime, Apu cries over receiving a notice for jury duty, considering it a true sign of his new citizenship rights. Soon enough, however, he throws the notice in the trash as an even truer sign of being American and taking his rights for granted.

The episode mocks many stereotypical and problematic American idiosyncrasies when it comes to immigrants and immigration policy. While America has been historically considered a country developed via immigration, Italians have most commonly been known for emigrating to foreign countries, particularly at the turn of the twentieth century. This tendency has changed in the last twenty years when waves of immigrants, especially from Northern and West Africa, China, Latin America, and Eastern Europe, have begun to move to and settle in Italy. Italy, therefore, has been undergoing a significant process of change, but the actual full inclusion of immigrants in society is still problematic and controversial. In translation to the Italian context, Apu and this episode in particular symbolize the new Italy dealing with immigration issues and struggling to understand its own emerging identity. The translation has Apu speaking Italian with a marked Indian accent, as in the original. In addition, his grammar is poor and his Italian broken and incorrect. Once he tries to pass as a citizen, however, Apu's Italian becomes impeccable and almost without any foreign accent. The solution found in the adaptation matches the common stereotype perpetuated in Italy about immigrants who can never really master the national language and can only express themselves in a very limited and comical fashion. With this linguistic choice, the Italian translation seems to perpetrate not only a stereotype of exclusion for immigrants but also the idea of Italian superiority, as immigrants are seen as incapable of grasping one of the most elementary aspects of their acquired national identity—language—unless faking it.

"WE ARE NOT RACIST, WE JUST DON'T LIKE THE SOUTH": CONCLUDING REMARKS ON RACE, STEREOTYPES, AND REPRESENTATION

The idea of national belonging both in the American and Italian example just described seems to be related to linguistic assimilation, demonstrating once again that language indeed represents a strong marker of cultural and national identity. Italians identify themselves primarily along regional lines as opposed to national lines. Technically, therefore, to really be considered "Italian," foreigners and racial "others" should be able to assimilate in a regional context both culturally and linguistically. In this respect, the reaction that Umberto Bossi (the leader of Lega Nord, the right-wing Italian party that promotes Italian regionalism, federalism, and xenophobic sentiments) had in 2003 about voting rights for immigrants is significant. After then Vice Prime Minister Gianfranco Fini's proposal of a new law that would grant the right to vote to immigrants for municipal elections, Bossi commented that he was going to endorse Fini's proposal only for those immigrants who could speak the dialect of the area in which they were going to vote (see Cristian Vaccari's discussion in chapter 11 of this anthology).

The Simpsons and its Italian translation offer an insightful example of this tendency through the character of Carl Carlson. Carl is one of Homer's colleagues at the nuclear power plant. He is an African American who, in the original version, is linguistically integrated within his working and social environment; he was born and raised in the U.S. and yet represents racial (and, implicitly, gay) diversity. The Italian dialogue writer decided to have Carl speak with a Venetian accent, a factor that both increases the humor and seems to suggest "genuine" belonging. Even if racially diverse from the stereotypical idea of the Italian people, in fact, Carl is characterized by a regional inflection, which immediately raises his status to "real Italian." This is different from Apu who does not speak with any regional inflection and therefore does not really fit in as "Italian." The choice of the Venetian accent for a Black character, however, perpetrates as well a stereotype of Italian superiority toward immigrants. In her dissertation, Federica Bologna hypothesizes about the choice of Carl's accent and argues that the Venetian inflection might depend on historical events. During the Fascist regime before WWII, many unemployed Venetian men were hired by different Italian companies and sent to the Italian colonies in East Africa to teach the natives jobs of the specific company that had hired them. As a consequence, the African people in the colonies not only learned manufacturing skills from the Venetian trainers but also absorbed their dialect and accents (Bologna, 2005–2006: 64).

The complex representations and linguistic translations of Apu and Carl lie at the core of contemporary debates about who should be "properly" and "officially" considered Italian now that foreign immigrants have started to mix with the White population. An exemplary case of such a debate has been the discussion that divided the media and the public opinion in 1996 after the election of Miss Italia. That year, the beauty pageant was won by Denny Méndez, a Black Latina originally from the Dominican Republic who had immigrated to Italy after her mother divorced her biological father and married an Italian man. Although Méndez won the popular election of those who were voting from home, the official judges in the competition were divided. There were those who did not believe that Méndez's traits and physical characteristics represented "Italian" beauty. This view championed Sophia Loren and Gina Lollobrigida as true Mediterranean beauties who could legitimately represent Italy and Italian women around the world. The opposing faction argued instead that Denny Méndez symbolized, on the contrary, the real identity of the contemporary Italian population, which was quickly changing. According to this view, therefore, Méndez was the face of the new country and was no less Italian than Sophia Loren or any other "proper" Mediterranean beauties.

The controversy over the 1996 election of Miss Italia and the sporadic and very stereotypical, if often extremely derogatory, representations of immigrants on television are central issues that are slowly influencing Italian television executives to support more realistic depictions of foreigners and racial "others." Since the late 1980s, a few programs on RAI have been produced to sensitize public opinion to immigration issues. Three examples are particularly interesting: *Non Solo Nero* [Not Only Black] (1988–1994), *Un Mondo a Colori* [A World in Colors] (1998–2003), and *Shukran* ["Thank you," in Arabic] (1999–present). Communication scholar Michela Ardizzoni contends that the three aforementioned programs have shaken and transformed the landscape of Italian television allowing for discussions on diversity. However, she also discusses how, in reality, these initial efforts have not been followed by concrete strategies aimed at including diversity in the daily programming of either RAI or Mediaset—the public and private poles of Italian TV, respectively (Ardizzoni, 2005: 526). In terms of televisual representation, in fact, what is more significant is that rarely, if ever, are immigrants featured in national productions of fiction. In other words, *Non Solo Nero*, *Un Mondo a Colori*, and *Shukran* are news programs that inform the audience about concrete issues concerning immigration, but there are almost no corresponding representations of immigrants in television fiction. Minister for Internal Affairs Giuliano Amato has highlighted this negligence at the conference on immigration issues held in Genoa in September 2006. Amato denounced the problematic and almost non-existent representation of immigrants on Italian television and invited network executives and producers to create TV fiction that can better and more realistically represent the role of immigrants in contemporary Italy. Significantly, Amato complained that, although audiences can see Black characters portrayed as doctors or other highly respected professions on American television, on Italian television "we are stuck to representations such as that of Mammy from Gone with the Wind, when blacks used to speak like Ciriaco De Mita" (Pieracci, 2006). Amato refers here to the aforementioned stereotypical depiction of racial "others" as incapable of mastering the Italian language, a factor that perpetuates the inferiority of immigrants as compared to native—White—Italians. What is even more significant, however, is that Amato compares this supposed linguistic "inability" of foreign immigrants to the common—and highly stereotypical—belief that Southern Italians also have difficulties in speaking proper Italian, free from regional expressions and inflections. Ciriaco De Mita, in fact, is an Italian politician from the area surrounding Naples, who is famous for his marked accent and his unsophisticated style of public speaking.

Italian racism has manifested itself in the profound division between North and South long before the arrival of foreign immigrants. While acts of racism against racial "others" in Italy are still frequent, these acts are usually criticized now as unacceptable, and campaigns promoting diversity and multiculturalism have been initiated both at the national and European levels. The separation between Northern and Southern Italy, however, is both accepted and hard to overcome not only because it is rooted in Italian history but also, and more problematically, because such separation is perpetuated in the stereotypical and often comical representation of Southern characters. Thus, ironically, what should be a division to be overcome becomes one of the most successful sources of "humor" on Italian television, whether nationally produced or imported from abroad and dubbed. *The Simpsons* is but one television show that confirms this tendency of the Italian media. Most of the characters that have been indigenized through the use of regionalized accents are re-territorialized in the Southern areas of Italy. While not all of them are discussed in this study, visually mapping all of these characters within the Italian peninsula gives further evidence of the North-South division and its consequent impact on media representations. Below is a map of Italy to which I have added the symbolic origin of the regionalized characters in the Italian version of *The Simpsons* (the line represents the separation between what are perceived as "the North" and the rest of the country).

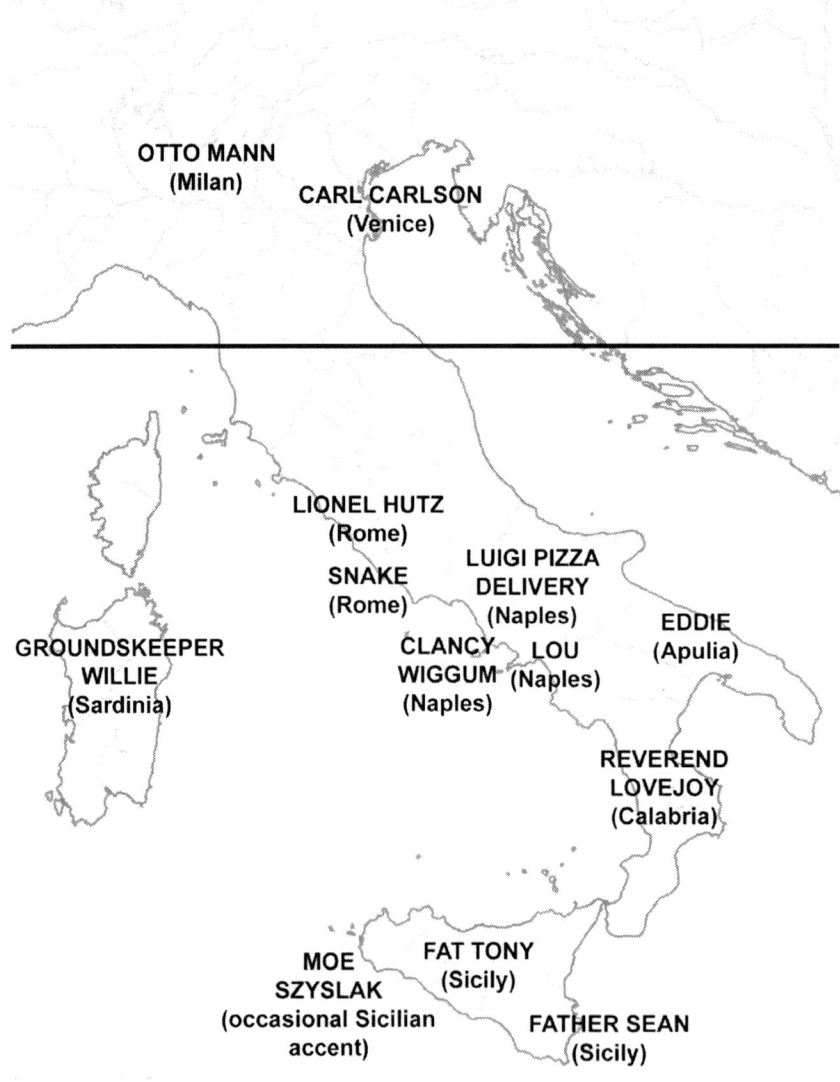

Figure 6.1

The map highlights how the geographical distribution of most of the indigenized characters in *The Simpsons* reinforce the idea that Southern accents and stereotypes in Italy still represent a very common strategy creating humor on television—humor based on problematic and clichéd assumptions about the South. More specifically, the majority of characters re-territorialized in the South are either symbolically from Naples or Sicily, the two areas most profoundly and stereotypically identified with Southern Italy. Wiggum's corruption and Fat Tony's mob affiliation, therefore, could not find a more "proper" ground for indigenization because the recurrent representations and discourses in Italy about the South usually fit these very images, which turn out to be profitable because they are familiar and embedded in Italian culture.

The translation of *The Simpsons*, then, exemplifies the tendency of TV networks to use national and cultural stereotypes to re-territorialize characters and the overall narrative according to familiar and profitable patterns. As American writers embrace cultural stereotypes in their creation of the original episodes, so do writers in Italy when they translate them. *The Simpsons* represents a challenge for adaptation because it is deeply rooted in American popular culture, so it is inevitable that comical references are altered and adapted for new audiences. In this case, in particular, additional attention (and money) has been invested in the distribution and dubbing of the series because of the considerable economic interests involved in the series' merchandising abroad. As a consequence, the original American TV network was actively involved in the processes of translation, dubbing, and adaptation—a situation that rarely occurs in international distribution. In Italy, the particular attention reserved to the series has allowed for all the official and proper phases of dubbing to be respected—a practice not adopted for less profitable shows—from the different professional roles involved to the quality of translation, screen adaptation, voiceover actors, etc. The conclusion here seems to be that high quality in translation and dubbing directly depends on the money invested by both the original networks and the distribution companies, and such investments depend on the expected profits of both domestic and international sales. For this reason, attention is also dedicated to the particular programming strategies that can more properly and profitably sell a program abroad. Ultimately, the animated nature of *The Simpsons* convinced Italian Mediaset to market the show for children, even if in the U.S. the target audience is clearly adults, and to air the program in an afternoon schedule because animation is not usually "prime-time material" for Italian television. This shift is significant because targeting the program to a younger audience allowed for massive merchandising sales to children and teenagers, a factor that further justifies the U.S. producers' interest in the reception and marketing of the show in Italy.

Ultimately, therefore, the dubbing of the *The Simpsons*, which is considered here as a form of cultural adaptation more than a simple translation, along with strategies of programming have facilitated the reception of the series in Italy. *The Simpsons* has been extremely successful and well received in Italy both because of its global cult status and for the specific national characteristics that it has gained in the adaptation. This study has demonstrated how television dubbing, one specific case of reformatting, allows for globally distributed programs to be indigenized for local audiences. More broadly, however, these findings suggest a reconsideration of the commonly held interpretation of global media processes: that there is a direct relation between one country's (specifically the U.S.) economic supremacy in media export and its correspondent cultural domination over other nations. In fact, if it is true that America is a leading producer and distributor of television programs worldwide, it is also true that these shows need to be adapted, translated, and re-marketed for new national audiences in each new environment in which they are imported. Thus, instead of considering international media flows in the light of the cultural imperialist paradigm, this research indicates that complex cultural and industrial negotiations are at play when individual countries import globally distributed programs. In taking this approach, this study has focused on linguistic issues of audiovisual translation to argue that dubbing provides a rich array of tools that allow national media industries to domesticate distributed television texts for national audiences.

NOTES

1. El-Rashidi reports how some Arab viewers in Dubai, especially the younger generations, were upset at the adaptation because they had already been exposed to the original American version, therefore they knew the characters in their American setting. She explains how "Many Arab blogs and Internet chat sessions have become consumed with how unfunny 'Al Shamshoon' is. "They've ruined it! Oh yes they have, sob. . . . Why? Why, why oh why?!!!!' wrote a blogger." Even more interestingly, another blogger comments on how the network, given the significance of the changes made, should have simply produced an original Arab series set in an Arab country: "I am sure the effort (of) the people who made this show to translate it to Arabic could have made a good original show about an Egyptian family living in Egypt, dealing with religion, life and work and trying to keep a family together. That way they can proudly say Made in Egypt, instead of Made in USA Assembled in Egypt." These quotes seem to suggest that adaptations can be meaningful and successful in a new national context as long as the programs adapted are not phenomena of popular culture such as *The Simpsons*, a series that by 2005 when it was imported to Dubai was certainly already very well known by its target Arab audience.

2. Mediaset Ludovica Bonanome explains how translator Elena di Carlo was chosen among three translators after a blind test proposed by FOX and Gracie Films. Once the translator was chosen, Tonino Accolla was appointed by Mediaset as dialogue writer and one of the several directors of dubbing that have rotated throughout the series. Tonino Accolla, renowned dialogue writer and voice over actor for film dubbing, also plays Homer Simpson's Italian voice. Tonino Accolla and Ludovica Bonanome. Interviews with author: Rome, Italy: July and September 2005.

3. The choice of turning to animation to renew brand image and to increase viewers was a strategy employed both by ABC and FOX respectively in 1966 and 1989. FOX was in fact in the same position at the end of the 1980s as ABC was in the 1960s. In fact, "both *The Flintstones* and *The Simpsons* appeared on fledging networks that were trying to distinguish themselves through counter-programming strategies." (Wendy Hilton-Morrow and David T. McMahan: 74).

4. As the Modern Brewery Age magazine reports: "The 'Miller Time' concept was coined in the 1970s for Miller High Life beer, but it was applied to Miller Lite for the first time in ads that started in 1997, which featured quirky situations created by a fictional adman named Dick. That campaign that used the theme 'Anything can happen at Miller Time' was aimed at introducing the brand to younger adult drinkers but was criticized by Miller distributors as being self-absorbed and ineffective." Quote from: "Miller revives 'Miller Time' theme for Lite." *Modern Brewery Age*, March 13, 2000. Available from: http://findarticles.com/p/articles/mi_m3469/is_11_51/ai_61622724.

5. The French translation of *The Simpsons* offers further evidence of the cultural specificity of the show. Canadian linguist Eric Plourde explains how, given the precise references in *The Simpsons*, the show is one of the few programs that are still translated and dubbed in two different versions for France and Québec, although they share French as the official language. Plourde explains how "France and Québec have different linguistic contexts, and this has an influence on dubbing. In fact, analysis reveals that the main divergence of the practice is that Québec cartoons target a young audience, resulting in censorship or mitigation of some subversive discourse, a strategy not apparent in French dubbing" (Plourd: 128).

6. Two major examples that come to mind are Neapolitan actor Totò, unanimously considered the "prince" of Italian comedy in film, and Eduardo De Filippo, whose theatrical plays written in the Neapolitan dialect are considered among the most genuine expressions of comedy Italian-style.

REFERENCES

Accolla, Tonino. Interview with author. Rome, Italy: July 12, 2005.
Ardizzoni, Michela. "Redrawing the Boundaries of Italianness: Televised Identities in the Age of Globalization." *Social Identities* 11.5 (September 2005): 509–530
Armstrong, Nigel. "Voicing *The Simpsons* From English Into French: A Story of Variable Success." *Cahiers AFLS* 10.1 (Spring/Summer 2004): 32–47.

Antje Ascheid. "Speaking Tongues: Voice Dubbing in the Cinema as Cultural Ventriloquism." *The Velvet Light Trap* 40 (Fall 1997): 32–41.

Beard, Duncan Stuart. "Local Satire with Global Reach. Ethnic Stereotyping and Cross-Cultural Conflicts in *The Simpsons*." *Leaving Springfield:* The Simpsons *and the Possibility of Oppositional Culture.* Ed. John Alberti. Detroit: Wayne State University Press, 2004.

Bologna, Federica. Dissertation: I Simpson, *La Traduzione di un Fenomeno Culturale.* Istituto Superiore Interpreti e Traduttori, Milano, 2005–2006.

Buonanno, Milly. *Narrami O Diva*. Napoli: Liguori Editore, 1994.

De Mauro, Tullio. *L'Italia delle Italie.* Florence, Italy: Nuova Guaraldi Editrice, 1979.

Edwards, Marion. Interview with author. Los Angeles, CA: March 17, 2006.

El-Rashidi, Yasmine. "D'oh! Arabized Simpsons not getting many laughs." *Wall Street Journal* (October 14, 2005). Available online from: www.post-gazette.com/pg/05287/588741.stm.

Herron, Jerry. "Homer Simpson's Eyes and the Culture of Late Nostalgia." *Representations* 43 (Summer 1993): 1–26.

Hilton-Morrow, Wendy and David T. McMahan. "*The Flintstones* to *Futurama*. Networks and Prime-Time Animation." *Prime-Time Animation: Television Animation and American Culture.* Eds. Carol A. Stabile and Mark Harrison. London and New York: Routledge, 2003: 74–88.

Mullen, Megan. "*The Simpsons* and Hanna-Barbera's Animation Legacy." *Leaving Springfield:* The Simpsons *and the Possibility of Oppositional Culture.* Ed. John Alberti. Detroit: Wayne State University Press, 2004: 63–84.

Newcomb, Horace. *TV: The Most Popular Art.* Garden City, NY: Anchor Press, 1974: 37–38.

Ott, Brian. "'I'm Bart Simpson, Who the Hell Are You?' A Study in Postmodern Identity (Re)Construction." *Journal of Popular Culture* 37.1 August 2003: 56–81.

Payne, Don. Interview with author. Los Angeles, CA: April 23, 2007.

Pieracci, Alessandra. "Datemi un medico nero in tv." *La Stampa* September 19, 2006.

Plourd, Eric. "The Dubbing of *The Simpsons*. Cultural Appropriation, Discursive Manipulation, and Divergences." *Texas Linguistic Forum* 44.1: 114–131. Proceedings from the Eighth Annual Symposium About Language and Society. Austin, TX April 7–9, 2000.

Rhodes, Joe. "Flash! 24 Simpsons Stars Reveal Themselves." TV Guide (October 21, 2000). Available from *The Simpsons* Archive: www.snpp.com/other/articles/flash.html

Robins, J. Max. "Programming Guerillas: Rebels with a 'Cos'?" *Variety* 339.9, June 6, 1990: p39+.

Swart, Sharon. "World Gets a Kick Out of Twisted U.S. Family." *Variety* 23 April 1998. Available from: www.snpp.com/other/articles/worldkick.html.

Vaccari, Cristian. "Missed Opportunities: The Debate on Immigrants' Voting Rights in Italian Newspapers and Television." *Globalization in Contemporary Italian Media.* Eds. Michela Ardizzoni and Chiara Ferrari. Lanham, MD: Lexington Books (forthcoming, 2009).

Chapter Seven

A Peninsula in the Sea of TV Formats: Exploring Italian Adaptations of *Survivor*

Marta Perrotta

GLOCALIZATION OF A REALITY TV FORMAT

The contemporary global television landscape is witnessing a growing international program market in which formats are increasingly playing a central role. TV formats are not cheap alternatives to proper programs but useful tools for the global production trade as well as an effective response to changes in international broadcasting culture.

Formats are intended to be generic and to be applied in every context. Moreover, instead of coming directly from American models and practices, some of their concepts have been developed in European countries (UK, the Netherlands, Scandinavia); this applies particularly to one of the more recent trends of global factual entertainment,[1] that is reality game show television. As Waisbord points out,

> many Western European companies are copyright holders of recent hit formats. The trade press has dubbed Europe "the leader of reality programming" [Fry 2000]. (2004: 361)

As one of the latest crazes in the whole television system in the last ten years, reality television has been defined as a global genre "associated with anything and everything, from people to pets, from birth to death" (Hill 2005a: 1), but particularly concerned with, at least, a couple of characteristics, "such as minimal writing and the use of nonactors" with the promise of a "nonscripted access to 'real' people in ordinary and extraordinary situations," (Murray, Ouellette 2004: 2) and the pursuit of authenticity deriving from the observation of common people.

Whether the setting is a TV studio or an exotic location, an ordinary house or a farm, reality programs build new social spaces, whose models are written in one of the first reality game shows ever conceived: *Survivor* (first run 1997 in Sweden as *Expedition Robinson*[2]). In fact, the complex social interactions between contestants and competitors, have involved audiences across the world and have in some ways inspired producers of the global television industry, possibly including Endemol, who, shortly after *Survivor*, created and broadcast the blockbuster format *Big Brother* (first run 1999 in the Netherlands). Whether *Big Brother* infringed upon the *Survivor* format or not,[3] it is clear that their key components, "certainly similar" (Bignell 2005: 21), have been studied thoroughly by media scholars all around the world, as global pillars of a "new generation of reality TV" (Menduni 2006: 182; my translation).

Since cross-national analyses of comparable media products is an undeveloped area of international media research, the purpose of this work is to compare the production of the reality show *Survivor* in three main national contexts: Sweden (where it was born), the United States (where it was a huge success), and Italy (where it initially failed).

This study presents a comparative aesthetic analysis of the basic elements of the show (title, airing formula, introductory clips, presentation, host, shooting techniques and editing style, use of sound and music), the contextually different production choices (pre-production or live transmission, televoting), and the semiotic[4] oppositions appearing in the format (time and place, different narrative programs, points of view, passions and rituals on stage). The comparison is developed taking into consideration the first seasons of both series (*Expedition Robinson* on SVT2 and *Survivor*: Borneo on CBS) as well as the first (and only) Italian season, aired by the private commercial channel Italia1.

This chapter is then intended to explore further implications of cross-country outcomes of the same format, focussing on Italian evolutions of the program into a celebrity show named *L'isola dei Famosi*, based on *Celebrity Survivor*[5] and produced for four seasons by the public service channel RAI2 and Magnolia.[6] Following the large insight provided by the comparison of this program to its forerunners, this study shows how Italian reality television entertainment has reacted to the convergence of global TV formats and takes a broad view of the place of scripted and non-scripted formats into Italian television programming of the twenty-first century.

FROM UK TO SWEDEN: *EXPEDITION ROBINSON* (FALL 1997)

Expedition Robinson has been one of the all-time biggest and most controversial television successes in Scandinavia. Its format, *Survive*, was invented in 1994–1995 by the English television producer Charlie Parsons (Castaway Productions Limited), who at first couldn't find any interest for it among the major broadcasters within the UK market. In 1996, the format was finally optioned[7] by the Swedish production company Strix Television, which produced it for the first time in 1997 with the Swedish public service SVT.[8]

Expedition Robinson is just about survival. For forty-nine days, sixteen strangers are stuck on a desert island, with the sole purpose of remaining on it while gradually being tried in a test of physical and emotional endurance.

The contestants have to survive more than the forces of nature, as *Expedition Robinson* is at heart an elimination competition. In the first half of the series the participants are divided into two groups who compete against each other in various challenges. They cope with a "reward challenge," a competition between two groups, in which the winners receive a luxury item to supplement island living (such as pillows, cold beers, clean clothing, a phone call or a hot shower). Then they deal with the "immunity challenge," a further competition where the winning group is immune from attending the "Council" and having to vote a contestant off the island. The losing team, on the other hand, must travel to the Council and vote one member off. Immunity is valid for one Council only.

In the second half of the game (after six eliminations) there are no more teams and the challenges are individual. Each episode climaxes with the tense drama of the Island Council where *Survivor*s meet to be interviewed by the host and to vote one of their group members off by secret or overt ballot. One person is eliminated in each episode. The islander who remains at the end of the seven-week period is declared the ultimate *Survivor* and awarded the grand prize—a large sum of money.

The big original idea behind *Robinson*, since the first series was produced, is the issue of voting and elimination. In classic quiz and game shows, the opportunity to win or lose is tied to an answer to a question, which could be either right or wrong. The winner is the person who answers questions correctly and has the largest score at the end of an episode, while contestants with lower scores are eliminated.

> "Voting off" is a crucial component of *Survivor*, which introduced the concept of eliminating not just one's fellow competitors, but one's actual team-mates (since seen on *Greed* and *The Weakest Link*). "*Survivor*s" are thereby invited to analyse each other, assess each other's relative worth to the team, evaluate the threat each poses, and build alliances that enable them to remain in the game as long as possible. (Douglas et alia 2001)

Its distinctiveness is probably the reason why *Expedition Robinson* has been produced and aired by SVT2 for a number of seasons. In 1997, the Swedish public service broadcaster was trying to make a revolution in its schedule, because "it was having quite a few years of entertainment production that didn't succeed" (personal interview with Johan Linden, 2005). SVT managers thought they had to do something completely different, something that could make an impression and could compete with commercial terrestrial and satellite broadcasters.

After seven seasons in 2004, in spite of its big success, SVT has decided to stop Robinson and change. In 2005 and 2006 the program has been on TV3 (a private commercial network), but in terms of audience ratings "it hasn't got the same reach anymore" (personal interview with Frida Åberg, 2005). However, "the success of the series contributed to a literal explosion of the genre, which meant that every channel had to profile themselves with a docusoap." (Hadenius and Weibull 2003: 430).

Robinson's migration started from Sweden toward Northern and Central Europe (Denmark in 1998; Norway and Switzerland in 1999). Furthermore, in 2000 the format premiered in Germany, Austria, Belgium, the Netherlands, and Spain. Since then it has traveled overseas, being produced at the same time in Argentina, Brazil, and the United States.

THE FIRST TRIP OVERSEAS: *SURVIVOR* IN THE UNITED STATES (SPRING 2000)

Viewers in the United States showed unanimous enthusiasm for *Survivor*.[9] From the beginning the man behind the U.S. version of the program has been Mark Burnett,[10] an executive producer with a long history of unconventional, outdoor competitions (Eco-Challenge Lifestyles), who had seen prototypes for the show on Swedish and Dutch television. His creativity and experience are the key to understanding the success of the CBS version of *Survivor*, whose ratings have been growing for several seasons and have driven CBS to be competitive against its rival NBC on Thursday nights. For seven editions, from 2001 to 2004, the series never averaged fewer than 20 million viewers each season. In particular, the second installment of *Survivor*: The Australian Outback, aired from January 2001 to May 2001 on CBS, was so popular that it gained the highest average Nielsen rating for the 2000–2001 seasons.[11]

A comparison of the basic elements and production choices of the two versions (U.S. and Swedish) reveals that the rules of the game are almost the same as well as the role of the host, the features of the location, the formula chosen to air the program (a one-hour prime-time weekly event). However, viewers who watch episodes of both first series would find many differences. This analysis compares features of different performances of the same format, focusing on the way elements like time and place, symbols and allegories, shooting and editing, music and dialogue, appear at a very simple level, through shooting techniques and editing style.

The first noticeable production difference is the final prize: the U.S. winner wins a million dollars, while in Sweden the sum of money was a thirtieth (about 25.000 Euro). This is a key element to understand the different choices in staging and dramatizing participants' relationships and dynamics in challenges and on "ordinary" days.

Secondly, the emphasis on the rules and the vocabulary removes the program from the linguistic realm of a standard game show. A primitive allegory invests every single feature of the U.S. version: contestants are called "*Survivors*"; they gather in "tribes" with proper nouns like "Tagi" and "Pagong," instead of teams simply called North and South. In addition, the symbolism of the show is particularly emphasized: the tribal council (with its elaborate set on a rocky outcrop) is conceptualized as emblematic and primordial:

> it is referred to as a "ceremony," with its connotations of the sacred. [. . .] It is highly ritualised, with *Survivors* possessing a torch that symbolises their "life in the tribe." If they are voted off, their torch is extinguished, and Probst [the host] solemnly utters the words, "The tribe has spoken." (Douglas et alia 2001)

Besides, when a *Survivor* or tribe wins a challenge that prevents their elimination, they are given not just immunity, but an "immunity idol," a sort of local god that the tribe is supposed to worship in the following days, to be supported in their mission. This metaphor was used in *Expedition Robinson* too, but it referred to a different semantic dimension which included "fellowship" and "family" sense-worlds and a simpler and more down-to-earth way of describing the situation: this becomes particularly clear when the host interviews the contestants during the council, asking them to describe how they feel about the missed immunity; in these discussions the immunity is mostly depicted as a practical opportunity to strengthen the relationships among the contestants, because it keeps the group from losing one member.

Thirdly, if we compare the first season of Robinson with the U.S. *Survivor*: Borneo we immediately feel they have different goals: the U.S. show is quicker, with fast cutting and short scenes;[12] it is, in some ways, conceived to be more entertaining than the Swedish one, whose documentary aesthetics produces a strong reality effect on the episodes of the series.

The choice of a more entertainment-oriented editing is not due solely to *Survivor* being aired on a commercial network (CBS) and Robinson on public service television (SVT2). What we feel looking at the Swedish show is a sense of closeness, of intimacy, of being involved in something very intimate, a sort of home video taped by a group of friends, almost relatives, who are sharing the same, extreme situation. The American show disregards any link with that handheld "Dogma" style that marks some episodes of the Scandinavian program. Instead, it presents a more formatted and professional flow of images, whose quality damages possible reality effects in order to stress adventure and fear factors.

> Clearly, the choice and use of music, clothing, picture composition and the like in *Survivor* all follow classical Hollywood narrative structures and techniques. Similarly, *Survivor* employs a number of conventions, such as voice-over narration, titles, and direct address, that are commonplace in television; thereby facilitating discussion of these conventions and their associated meanings. Finally, *Survivor*'s relationship to earlier programs illustrates how genres evolve over time. *Survivor* owes as much to game shows and soaps, as it does to the castaway premise of *Gilligan's Island*,[13] and the contrived social arrangements of *The Real World*. (Douglas et alii 2001)

This point is highlighted also by Haralovich and Trosset, who quote the trade magazine Variety's assessment of the show[14]:

> Burnett knew American viewers expect top-notch production values in primetime programs, so he eschewed the cheap-is-better convention of most reality shows and gave *Survivor* a virtually cinematic look that made the show look as good as (if not better than) the typical network drama. Indeed, the logistics of production justify Burnett's description of *Survivor* as "epic." (2004: 76)

Swedes and Americans have been producing the program for several seasons, reciprocally grabbing inspirations and ideas about new competitions, possible twists and surprises to shock contestants. Strix authors claim that Swedes look at the American productions because

> they're very good in making a big bombastic show, and especially in the first episode, when we have what we call "the landing," when the contestants arrive on the island. We want that moment to be shocking, it should look expansive, it should be huge, a grand opening of the show, and you need to vary that, and then we look at their *Survivor* quite a lot, because even though they have a bigger budget, the ideas we can take from that and actually adjust to our version are many. (Personal interview with Frida Åberg, 2005)

This, however, does not mean that the American and the Swedish styles have merged, but this hidden cooperation has certainly reduced their stylistic differences. Both of them, in fact, make a strong use of objective shootings and try to make the storytelling as neutral as possible, while in some recordings, like in the confessionals, they catch the contestants while they express their feelings and impressions, as if they were answering questions—requested by hidden interviewers—with the result of a subjective narration of the events. This continuous swinging between objectivity and subjectivity, that sometimes widens and sometimes limits the audience's viewpoint, is one of the favorite narrative devices of both format productions, and it is found in the Italian version as well.

SURVIVOR FOR BEGINNERS: THE ITALIAN ADAPTATION (SPRING 2001)

The first and only Italian season of *Survivor* was produced by Endemol and aired by Italia1[15] in February 2001, immediately after the first Italian *Big Brother* series, trying to exploit the big media storm that followed that program.

Contrary to all expectations, *Survivor* did not convince the Italian audience. The first episode gained a 17.2 percent share and the ratings have fallen down from the second episode on: the total audience for the season has been 7.1 percent (1,888,339 viewers) (Auditel 2001). Despite its poor performance the show was not pushed to a late-night slot or eliminated, because Endemol was confident in the format's broadcast history, expressed in terms of previous ratings and audience demographics, to repeat the program's original success.

What are the reasons of this failure? Some Italian scholars (De Maria et alii 2002) have given an answer to this question with the help of socio-semiotic tools of analysis. Here, I update some of their findings, making use of their point of view on the narrative structure of the Italian show.

In addition to that, my analysis focuses on textual aspects of the Italian adaptation, on its dramaturgical, narrative, and visual structure (how the show is put on stage), on direction, frames, music and editing (how the show results on the screen), on the modes of address to the viewer and on the promise of engagement with the viewer. A chart collects the results of the analysis carried out and is intended to help the reader in the comparison of the three examples (see Appendix—Table 1. Glocalization of a reality TV format: *Survivor*).

A Weak Hybrid

Italian *Survivor* could be considered a weak hybrid of an observational reality program, with surveillance cameras recording sixteen castaways marooned on a deserted island, a realistic narration of their adventures, that is more factual than fictional entertainment, and a prime-time talk show, with in-studio host, guests like parents, relatives, and friends of the contestants, but also food experts, psychologists, and other people invited to talk about emotions and events.

Therefore, each episode is divided into two parts: the first one shows the film taped during one week on the island (challenges and council included), ending with the person voted off leaving the location. The second part is a spin-off talk show about the film, where host and guests provide live comments on what they have seen.

While the Swedish and the American programs have a single set, the space in the Italian *Survivor* is divided into two main places: the island, place of the surviving game; and the studio, place of the interpretation of the events. The island (with its camps, beaches, water) is consequently the main stage of the story. It is probably an active character of the story. Sometimes it acts like a natural pure environment,

> filmed with evocative and sometimes stereotyped shots (white sandy shores, coconut palms, beautiful sunsets); sometimes it represents a prison for the contestants, their main obstacle to the survival, a place filled with more or less hidden perils. (De Maria et alia 2002: 117, my translation)

But even if the island works as the antagonist of the story,[16] its place is an "elsewhere" in comparison with the "here and now" of the studio. Events on the island happen in a far and different place and time: the threshold between the two worlds is the big screen in the background of the studio set, through which the audience in the studio and the viewer at home can enter the island. Hence the studio is where the story is told, where emotions are discussed, where different opinions of experts, relatives, friends, and voted-off contestants meet and aim to mirror audience's opinions.

PLOT AND FABULA: WHERE ARE THE BORDERS?

In terms of shooting techniques and points of view, in every adaptation of *Survivor* there must be a severe distinction between the fabula (what really happens) and the plot (what the audience can see on television). This is partly due to the features of the location (it is impossible to set up footage of the contestants as if they were shut in a house, like in Big Brother); but it is also due to the reality and objectivity effect the program needs to attain.

Besides the Italian *Survivor* made a strong use of confessionals as well. As in the American and Swedish series, the confessionals are carefully edited to further enforce the values of the program itself and to provide two notable effects: first of all, to confirm rather than challenge the images of the contestants and their relationships with one another; second, as Douglas and others (2001) suggest, to validate the common popular image of the show as the enviable challenge of a lifetime. Hence, we could consider confessionals as moments in which the viewer is in a seemingly favorable position in relation to knowledge of the players and the action. "Confession is a privileged discourse of the contemporary era, and thus *Survivor* employs this device as part of its strategy to constitute a relationship between player and viewer" (Douglas et alii 2001).

In relation to this, the most meaningful moment in the Italian series is when a sudden event reveals the backstage of the production, suggesting a third point of view on the program: one of the castaways, at nightfall, has stolen a lighter from the television crew camp (a fact that, of course, is not shot at all) and the affair engenders discussions among contestants (filmed and shown in the second episode of the series). The fact is explained by the host in the in-studio talk show, in order to clarify words heard by contestants. A picture of the cameramen's camp is shown, disclosing a secret actor of the storytelling and actually undermining the strength of the narration itself. This revelation seems risky for the balance of the program: we have evidence of this in the Swedish "model," where the presence of the production is accidentally revealed just once, only in the twelfth episode of the seventh run, when one of the participants challenges the regularity of a game in progress and the game is stopped to let the contestant have a chat with the authors. Until that moment, the Swedes had avoided any explicit reference to the existence of a production team (authors, cameramen, and loggers) in the narration of the events, in order to make the narration stronger and more realistic.

Where is the border between plot and fabula if the in-studio talk show jumps smoothly from one to the other and accepts to bring into the plot additional points of view and elements of the fabula? This practice can be considered a technical error, like a "blooper," a visible microphone in a movie, something that doesn't make any sense. Reality television is prevalently built on a silent "non-interaction agreement" between contestants and production teams. In this case, the agreement is broken by both parties: on the one side, the contestants talk to the production, with direct gazes at the camera; on the other side, the producers decide to leave this incident uncut in the final editing of the episode, clashing with the suggested reading rules embedded in the reality genre.

ROLE PLAY AND GROUP DYNAMICS: "CONTESTANTS" AND "SURVIVORS"

As argued about its format, *Expedition Robinson-Survivor* is, generally speaking, a reality game show where oppositions between contestants take place in the small world of the island (without any "intrusion" from the outside—like telephone polling or text-messaging voting of many other reality game shows). Contestants build their identities, roles, and coalitions in front of the cameras: this set of social skills leads them to face different competitions and councils which form the actual development of the game, whose psychology gets more and more interesting as the show goes along and tiredness, lack of food, and bad weather amplify differences between participants.

In the Swedish Robinson the predominant opposition is that between castaways and wilderness conditions, and for the U.S. *Survivor* it is given by "the diverse demographics of age, race, sexuality and gender" of the cast which "intensify the relationships between participants" (Haralovich and Trosset 2004: 78). In the Italian version, the most significant opposition on stage turns out to be the one between:

> people who claim to be on the island in order to experience the "real" emotion of being wrecked, and people who say they're just taking part into a TV game show. Some of them are looking for real adventure, while others live their residence on the island in function of the game, the show, so expecting the program to be a "not very faithful" simulation of wreckage. (De Maria et alia 2002: 122, my translation)

Since the second episode (February 20, 2001), in fact, contestants of one team appear divided into two groups, each one representing opposite feelings toward the game, either accepting or rejecting it. Phrases like "this is not a game" or "this is just a TV show" occur several times and explain the swinging positions of some leading elements of both groups. This conflict gradually evolves into an opposition between contestants and the game-show mechanism itself. Some participants appear reluctant to follow the rules (as was the case with the contestant who stole a lighter); others start to boycott the program through mutinies, carefully recorded by Endemol cameramen.

Some contestants refuse to be taped, others say they're being held captive by the television crew and start threatening legal actions, questioning the contract with the production company and the broadcaster. As for them, Endemol producers decide to show every single moment of the mutiny, no matter what the audience could see of the backstage; they prefer to support reality of events by documentary evidence instead of trying to hide the events themselves. In the final editing they also add subtitles to let the viewer catch every single word of contestants speaking far from the camera or behind it, turning *Survivor* into a documentary about the "making of" a reality game show.

BREAKING WITH CONVENTIONS

Even if the choice to show the backstage of the Italian *Survivor* could be considered revolutionary, it ends up revealing the mechanism of the format and weakening its lure among viewers:

> the power and popularity of reality programming depends on the authenticity of the contrived reality. As Jeremy Butler remarks, some nonfictional programs "invite us to suspend our distrust of television's 'devious' ways. For their impact these programs depend on our belief in the television producer's non-intervention." (Haralovich and Trosset 2004: 79)

When castaways are shot while having discussions about their agreement with the broadcaster, a social and televisual contract with the audience is broken. Although the disclosing of the format's mechanisms is a good way to affirm its effectiveness—its being a "reality" format and transform contestants' lives—it is probably the worst and most contradictory way to involve the audience at home.

Like other reality game shows, the Italian *Survivor* opens its diegetic world to the viewer with confessional videos only. For the rest of the action, the program is intended to be sealed, with characters inside the narration, addressing one another and not gazing at the camera. On the contrary, one of the Italian participants is shown pointing his finger at the camera saying "This is the enemy! We are playing their game."[17]

Trying to understand the possible reasons behind *Survivor*'s failure in Italy I agree with De Maria et alii (2002) who argue:

> *Survivor* has been a reality game show for its (sometimes overexcited) contestants but not for the audience. The feeling watching it is that it is really hard to get involved in such far and unnatural situations, so distant from our everyday life. Although some of the format's themes and values (for instance, the clash between team values and individualism) could be of interest to the Italian audience, the majority of them (like the idea of surviving, loyalty and betrayal, sacrifice and competition against nature) were probably less important for Italian viewers than they had been for the Swedes or the Americans, whose cultures probably share a stronger interest in the frontier and the challenges connected to it. (De Maria et alii 2002: 124; my translation)

Since "formats are de-territorialized, they have no national home, they represent the disconnection between culture, geography and social spaces that characterizes globalization," (Waisbord 2004: 378) it could be just a matter of filling the format model, in which signs of cultural territories are removed, with local "colors" so that the local audience can feel at home watching it.

This did not happen with *Survivor* in Italy. In addition to that, however, the program did not appeal to the imagined (local) audience because of its self-disclosure to the viewers, who were informed about the making of a reality program without, for instance, being involved in the game show mechanism and being given the opportunity to vote contestants off, or, at least, vote for their favorites.

Moreover, unlike *Big Brother* (*Grande Fratello* in its Italian translation), *Survivor* was not designed as a media event by the broadcaster: quite the opposite, Italia1 limited the program inside the spin-off talk show studio and did not plan any kind of programming decision or strategy, like official websites or magazines, forums or text messaging platforms, where the borders of the program could be expanded through different texts and discourses.

GOING TO THE ISOLA

We may never be able to give explanations of *Survivor*'s outcome in Italy. Several elements contributed to a general disappointment about it, including the absence of a live emotional component with games and audience participation, and also the weirdness of a cast completely alien to viewers and new to television (as requested by the original format, which needs extreme and divergent characters). These same elements have been taken into consideration after the program's failure, in order to reformulate it in a different way, with the help of the international know-how of the format.

Trying to keep one of the hallmarks of reality television, its unscripted or "documentary" feel, and to lose its reliance on "ordinary people" rather than professional actors, Charlie Parsons' Castaway developed a Celebrity version of its *Survivor*, produced in Spain with the title of *La Isla de los famosos*, and in Italy as *L'isola dei Famosi*, aired by the public service channel RAI2. Besides, in 2002 Granada[18] launched *I'm A Celebrity . . . Get Me Out of Here*. When the U.S. channel ABC broadcast it, CBS supported a claim for infringement of copyright-protected elements of the format *Survivor*. Even if a substantial similarity did exist, the United States District Court rejected the claim.

All of a sudden, a new wave of celebrity formats is on air all over the world. When celebrities enter a reality format

> the "characters" are already familiar with showbiz and, therefore, with acting in front of cameras. This leads the genre one step further from the documentary preoccupation to show people "as they are," but it greatly adds to the viewer appeal. (Dhoest 2005: 232)

This is further increased as the cameras are allowed to penetrate deeply into the characters' most private life. Moreover, the viewer can feel a heightened sense of exhibitionism, on the one hand, and voyeurism, on the other, as contestants are not typical celebrities at the summit of their careers. Contestants are chosen because they were famous in the past and are in need of a mediatic push. The genre's explicit claim to "veracity" and "authenticity" here relies more on the observation of celebrities' attempts to get back on the top than survive the harsh situation.

The program has taken advantage of Italian viewers' curiosity about celebrities' lives (as Goffman puts it about differences between front stage and backstage in everyday presentation of the self). This has also been possible (and believable) with a live interaction between the life on the island and the audience at home, who could vote off contestants with short text messaging from mobile phones.[19] The audience's power of elimination has been crucial to the allure of the *L'isola dei Famosi*, not merely because of its obvious appeal to some viewers' competitive, even sadistic tendencies, but because of the sense of empowerment it offers the audience.

This new wave in reality game shows proves attractive for the audience: *L'isola dei Famosi* reached a 31 percent market share in the last episode of the sixth run (2005); despite the success, this type of programming doesn't solve the problem of producers: "contestants in reality game shows learn how to behave from previous series, and there can be an element of parody to their performances" (Hill 2005a: 34).

Year after year, in fact, producers of all reality game shows need to come up with new twists to shock the contestants in some ways, who are able to foretell the possible developments of the game at the expense of their involvement and spontaneity. During the first season of both the U.S. *Survivor* and *Robinson*, contestants were perceived to be "real" people playing for the money-prize; now, all of the contestants seem eligible for the rewards (and costs) of celebrity. Fame has become the primary reason for participating. And this is even more truthful in the case of *Celebrity Survivor—L'isola dei Famosi*.

Finally, *L'isola dei Famosi* is a successful adaptation of *Survivor*, both from the producers' point of view and from the audience's perspective. On one hand, in fact, producers choose this programming formula (celebrity shows) because they are particularly cheap and profitable in the tight Italian television market. There are two main broadcasters, RAI and Mediaset, which compete for the 90 percent of the television audience. Then we have four or five major format licensors/brokers/producers—Endemol, Fascino, Magnolia, Einstein Multimedia Group, Ballandi Entertainment—which control the national format business. Finally, only four agents manage the main characters of the star system and decide their participation in one show or another, while also supervising the rest of the casting process.

On the other hand, the audience is more and more involved into this kind of entertainment, primarily because it combines the interest of the viewer in the private life of the celebrities with cooperation-competition dynamics typical of reality game shows. As stated by an anonymous Swedish twenty-eight-year-old male viewer, "I often think there's a lot of delight over other people's misfortune, I guess that to some extent is the definition of a docusoap, that you're supposed to be able to sit at home in your TV sofa and then you're allowed to let your malicious delight out, which you never get to show in every day life" (Hill 2005b: 21); as far as the Italian audience is concerned, since the contestants chosen for *L'isola dei Famosi* are mostly wannabe-celebrities or stars affected by the "sunset boulevard" syndrome, it seems clear that viewers enjoy watching famous people getting exposed to tests and humiliations more than watching normal persons in similar situations.

CONCLUSION

The reading of these adaptations of *Survivor* format can only be partial and doesn't take into account several key elements, like audiences habits, programming decision, production routines and values, second and following runs, national/local cultures and tastes.

The features I analyzed here, however, are more concerned with the basic concepts of television, that is how it appears in its form and content, and they may give us a description of how the worldwide famed format *Survivor* has evolved through different stages of adaptation and localization. Paraphrasing the famous motto of the American series, which used to say goodbye to voted-off contestants with the words "the tribe has spoken," this is how the format itself has spoken into different languages.

The analysis of this format in three different countries, in fact, highlights a limited degree of variety in the results of the adaptation choices: *Survivor* comes out as a not very flexible format. However, the first Italian adaptation was so hard and unlucky because of the lack of experience of the production which altered its core concept.

As stated by Waisbord, "format television shows 'glocalization' at work—that is, the merits of a business 'multicultural' strategy that is 'sensitive' to cultural diversity" (2004: 378). Global television industries need to get through flops and failures in order to learn from errors and develop new well-built programming strategies. As for the Italian TV landscape, the *Survivor* experience was a sort of initiation with which the broadcasters and the production companies learned what reality television is not about.

Table 7.1. Globalization of a Reality TV Format: *Survivor*

Where	Sweden	USA	Italy
When (1st season)	Fall 1997	Spring 2000	Spring 2001
Title	*Expedition Robinson*	*Survivor*	*Survivor*
Reward	250.000 SEK (25.000 EURO) (roughly 1/30 of the American prize)	1 million dollars	Half Billion Lire (250.000 EURO) (more or less 1/4 of the American prize)
Number of Locations	One	One	Two
Location Description	*The Island*: place of the surviving game, active character of the story; it acts as pure natural environment but represents a prison for contestants	*The Island*: place of the surviving game, active character of the story; it acts as pure natural environment but represents a prison for contestants	*The Island*: place of the surviving game, active character of the story; it acts as pure natural environment but represents a prison for contestants
Studio: place of interpretation of events
Time	Present	Present	Past/Present
Dichotomy on Stage	Man/Nature	Man/Adventure	Man/Game
How Game Rules Are Presented	Playfully	Seriously	As a constraint
Use of Language	Social/Family allegory (Team instead of Tribe; North/South games; Island council)	Primitive allegory (Tribe instead of Team; Survivors instead of contestants, Tribe council)	Primitive/Military allegory (Tribe instead of Team; Survivors instead of contestants, Island council)

(*continued*)

Table 7.1. (continued)

Emphasis on Symbols	Low	High	High	High
Name of Council	Assembly	Ceremony	Ceremony	Duty
Point of View	Objective storytelling by eyewitness & subjective confessionals	Objective storytelling by eyewitness & subjective confessionals	Objective storytelling by eyewitness & subjective confessionals	Objective storytelling by eyewitness & subjective confessionals & external proofs
Details About Contestants	From confession booths	From confession booths	From confession booths	From confession booths and investigations during spin-off talk shows
Prevailing Filming Style	Light handheld/home-video/ "Dogma"	Classic Hollywood narrative techniques		Light handheld/home-video
Prevailing Editing Style	Continuous shots Documentary	Fast-cutting Adventurous/Dramatic		Continuous shots Documentary
Use of Music	Soft	Strong		Soft
Timing of Music	On challenges, on snapshots of the island	Throughout the episodes as narrative device		On challenges, on snapshots of the island
Address to the Viewer	Through natural shooting (sense of closeness and intimacy, being involved in the experiences of a group of friends)	Through emotional editing (formatted and professional flow of images whose quality heightens adventure and fear factors)		Through conversational discourses (discussion of the issues and the role-playing that emerge in the viewing experience)

Through the international format industry, moreover, reality television is growing and widening its genre definition. Many of these formats, especially the ones dealing with celebrities, have blurred the conventional boundaries between fact and fiction, between drama and documentary: as a result, reality shows are becoming less an exploration of veracity of ordinary people participating, but more the promise of the disclosure of what the reality of reality television is.

NOTES

1. "'Factual entertainment' is a category commonly used within the television industry for popular factual television, and the category indicates the marriage of factual programming, such as news or documentary, with fictional programming, such as gameshows or soap opera. Indeed, almost any entertainment programme about real people comes under the umbrella of popular factual television" (Hill 2005a: 14).

2. A Castaway format, produced in Sweden by Strix TV with the title of *Expedition Robinson* and aired by the public service SVT.

3. As reported by Bignell, "after the success of *Big Brother* in Europe, the owners of the *Survivor* format initiated a legal case against Endemol, arguing that it infringed the *Survivor* format" (2005: 21). "The Dutch Supreme Court in the Hague in its decision of 16th April 2004 rejected the appeal of Castaway Television Production and Planet 24 against the judgment of the Amsterdam Court of Appeal on 27th June 2003. In its judgment the Dutch Supreme Court agreed with the Court of Appeal that on the one hand the format *Survive* [*Survivor*] was indeed a copyright protected work, but on the other the format *Big Brother* was not an imitation which infringed copyright." In particular, "the court found that, to the extent that elements of the *Survive* format are similar to the *Big Brother* programmes, these elements together do not satisfy the requirement of originality" (Fey *et alii*, 2005: 70).

4. See De Maria *et alii*, 2002, in particular pages 115–124 and 261–265.

5. In 2002 Granada, UK's biggest commercial television producer has launched *I'm A Celebrity . . . Get Me Out Of Here* on the market. When ABC broadcasted it, CBS supported a claim for infringement of copyright-protected elements of the format *Survivor*. Even if a substantial similarity did exist, the United States District Court refused the motion.

6. Magnolia is one of the leading Italian independent production companies and a format licensor specialized in entertainment formats for the global market. One of its founding partners, Giorgio Gori, has been working in Mediaset as editorial manager of the network Italia1. Among its most successful formats are *Camera Café* and *Milano Roma*. See also www.magnoliatv.it.

7. In the global trade of formats, a company interested in producing a program will looks for an option, giving it time to test market the format before spending money to acquire the rights. Usually an option may have a limited term of 3 to 6 months, to prevent licensee from blocking the format within the territory.

8. Strix has produced (Spring 2006) the 10th run, which will probably be the last one in Sweden for some time. Meanwhile, however, the format has been sold by Castaway to more than sixty countries, from Australia, to Russia, to Japan, but especially in the United States where the twelfth season is being aired by CBS. During the past 9 years, Strix has enriched the format's bible with its skills in producing the program in Sweden and abroad and selling its expertise when required.

9. The United States was the exception to the global rush to *Big Brother*. All the countries that commissioned first runs witnessed unprecedented audience ratings, while in the United States the program scored average ratings.

10. Burnett's personal point of view on the meaning of *Survivor* into popular culture and products context is clearly expressed in two "companion books" written during the first and the second U.S. seasons: BURNETT, Mark. 2001. *Survivor II, A Field Guide*. New York: TVBooks and with DUGARD, Martin. 2000. *Survivor, The Ultimate Game*. New York: TVBooks.

11. For an interesting table showing reality television programs by year and Nielsen ratings see also BAKER, Sean, 2003. From *Dragnet* to *Survivor*. Historical and Cultural Perspectives on Reality Television, edited by Matthew J SMITH, and Andrew WOOD, 57–71. *Survivor Lessons: Essays on Communication and Reality Television*. Jefferson, NC: McFarland, p. 61. At the time of writing, CBS is airing the 12th *Survivor* seasons and will produce seasons number 13 and 14 until the end of 2007. The host of the program, who has never changed, is Jeff Probst, famous anchorman turned TV host.

12. See the analysis of *Survivor-Expedition Robinson* shooting techniques in Taggi, 2003: 423.

13. *Gilligan's Island* is an American sitcom about a group of people and their failed attempts to get off the deserted island where they have been shipwrecked. It was aired on CBS in the Sixties, then it has become a reality series launched in 2001 entitled *The Real Gilligan's Island*. In this reality game, very similar to *Survivor*, two groups of people are placed on an island and have to survive while acting as the characters of the sitcom.

14. Unexpectedly, *Variety* aligns *Survivor* with episodic drama rather than reality television.

15. Italia1 is a private commercial channel owned by Berlusconi's media group Mediaset. This channel primarily attracts young viewers with its pronounced entertainment offering. Its target audience consists of both teenagers (during the day) and young adults (in the evening).

16. "The one that makes the story begin and become attractive and appealing for the audience. Every challenge is a challenge to conquer something useful to live on the island, to make it more comfortable and civilized: under this challenge we can see an archetypal value and topic opposition between man and nature" (De Maria *et alia* 2002: 117, my translation).

17. Second episode, 20th of February 2001, (my translation).

18. UK's biggest commercial television producer.

19. As Henry Jenkins points out (2006: 59), televoting has been one of the main drives of some reality shows. Besides that, it has finally lead to a deep spread of text

messaging practices in the United States, where with *American Idol*, for instance, phone companies were "happy because they have been trying to find a way to get Americans more excited about text messaging, which hasn't taken off in the United States the way it has in Asia and northern Europe."

REFERENCES

Bignell, Johnathan. *Big Brother: Reality TV in the Twenty-first Century*. Basingstoke Hampshire: Palgrave Macmillan, 2005.

Casetti, Francesco, and Di Chio, Federico. *Analisi della televisione*. Milano: Bompiani, 1997.

Corner, John. Documentary Values, edited by Anne Jerslev, 139–158. *Realism and 'Reality' in Film and Media*, Copenhagen: Museum Tusculanum Press, 2002.

Curran, James, and Park, Myung-Jin. *De-Westernizing Media Studies*. London: Routledge, 2000.

De Maria, Cristina, Grosso, Luisa, and Spaziante, Lucio. *Reality TV: La Televisione ai Confini della Realtà*. Roma: RAI-ERI, 2002.

Dhoest, Alexander. "The Pfaffs are not like the Osbournes. National inflections of the celebrity docusoap." *Television & New Media* 6 (2): 224–245, 2004.

Douglas, Kate, and McWilliam, Kelly (eds). "'Must-see' Reality TV." *M/C Reviews. Culture and the Media*. N. 12, http://reviews.media-culture.org.au, 2001.

Fetveit, Arild. "Reality TV in the Digital Era: A Paradox in Visual Culture?" *Media, Culture and Society* 21: 787–804, 1999.

Feyles, Giuseppe. *La Televisione secondo Aristotele*. Roma: Editori Riuniti, 2003.

Hadenius, Stig, and Weibull, Lennart. *Mass media. A Book about the Press, Radio and TV*. Falkenberg: Albert Bonniers Förlag, 2003.

Hill, Annette. *Reality TV: Television Audiences and Factual Entertainment*. London: Routledge, 2005.

Hill, Annette, Weibull, Lennart and Nilsson, Åsa. *Swedish Factual and Reality Television Audiences*, Jönköping: Jönköping International Business School Research Reports No. 2005–2004, 2005.

Jerslev, Anne (ed.). *Realism and 'Reality' in Film and Media*. Copenhagen: Museum Tusculanum Press, 2002.

Jenkins, Henry. *Convergence Culture. Where Old Media and New Media Collide*. New York: New York University Press, 2006.

Jost, François. *L'empire du loft*. Paris: La Dispute, 2002.

Malbon, Justin and Moran, Albert. *Understanding the Global TV Format*. Bristol, Intellect, 2006.

Menduni, Enrico. *I Linguaggi della Radio e della Televisione. Teorie, Tecniche e Formati*. Roma-Bari: Laterza. 2006.

Moran, Albert. *Copycat TV. Globalisation, Program Formats and Cultural Identity*. Luton: University of Luton Press, 1996.

Murray, Susan, and Ouellette, Laurie (eds.). *Reality TV. Remaking Television Culture*. New York: New York University Press, 2004.

Perrotta, Marta. Il format televisivo. *Caratteristiche, Circolazione Internazionale, Usi e Abusi.* Urbino: Quattroventi, 2007.
Taggi, Paolo. *Il Manuale della Televisione.* Roma: Editori Riuniti, 2003.
———. *Morfologia dei format televisivi.* Roma: RAI-ERI, 2007.
Waisbord, Silvio. "McTV. Understanding the Global Popularity of Television Formats." *Television & New Media* 5 (4): 359–383, 2004.

Part Three

NEW AND ALTERNATIVE MEDIA

Chapter Eight

E-democracy and Italian Public Administration: New Media at the Service of Citizens

Giorgia Nesti and Chiara Valentini

INTRODUCTION

It is widely recognized that the process of globalization has been facilitated and made possible by the development of new media (Castells 1996, 2000). According to Flew and McElhinney (2002) three dimensions of new media are at the core of globalization. First, new media constitutes the technologies and service delivery platforms through which international flows are transacted. Second, new media industries are leaders in the push towards global expansion and integration. Finally, new media provides informational content and images of the world through which people seek to make sense of events in distant places (ibid.: 289).

New media, intended as technological forms used to communicate messages, influences the communicative practices of individuals and institutions, and this in turn influences societies and cultures. Coleman and Gøtze (2001) discovered a correlation between globalization, new media, and political representation in developed democracies: in correspondence to a general crisis of traditional forms of representation they found a spread of new tools of communication (ibid: 4). As Norris states: "It has become common place to suggest that the Western public has become more and more disenchanted with the traditional institutions of representative government, detached from political parties, and disillusioned with older forms of civic engagement and participation" (ibid., 2000: 2). These positions suggest that citizens perceive democratic institutions as opaque and detached from their living space and experience, and find themselves highly disengaged from the policy process. In this sense, globalization has affected the ways by which democratic institutions produce policies, services and public goods. Market interdependency and the rise of more complex economic and social demands have profoundly altered the context for policy-making. Increased policy complexity has forced governments to find new organizational and procedural arrangements that have altered traditional institutional boundaries. The creation of "authorities" and committees of experts and the rise of networks for public/private policy involved along all the stages of the policy-making process are only a few examples of how this transformation is occurring. What is emerging is a system of governance where the political power is dispersed and/or re-allocated among public entities neither directly accountable to citizens nor connected to traditional representative institutions. No room, therefore, for civic engagement and public deliberation seems to be possible. In this respect, new media opens up more spaces for interaction between citizens and policy-makers.

The use of new media is believed to have the potential to increase levels of trust and solidarity which are prerequisite of political and civic participation (Putnam 2000; Putnam et al. 1993). Recent studies provide an indication of the potential of new technologies to enhance local community interaction and communication (a sort of "social capital"). These are studies of communities in which a majority of residents use new technologies (Wellman and Haythornthwaite 2002; Huysman et al. 2003). For instance, an example of a community where the use of new technology has created more interaction and communication is Blacksburg, Virginia, a town in the United States. During the mid-1990s Blacksburg received relevant technology investment to allow the local community to become by 2001 a "wired community" with more than 75 percent of local businesses having their own websites, more than 80 percent of residents having internet access and more than 120 non-profit organizations having subscribed to different internet services that included information sharing software (Kavanaugh and Patterson 2002).

New media facilitates interaction between source and receiver of information and to certain extents it creates forms of cyber-dialogues. Especially for internet and related computer technologies it is possible to detect a real revolution of the way in which individuals and organizations communicate. Holtz (1996) argued that two fundamental models of communication have been altered by the ability to communicate and access information via computer: the first model concerns who provides information, the second addresses how audiences get the information they need. Since anyone with a computer and a modem can access and distribute information, often directly and with no gatekeepers involved, the sender-based information model has changed to a receiver-based model (Springston 2001: 604). Proponents of the decline of traditional mass media believe that the success of these new forms of communications lies precisely in the possibility to bypass national contexts and timeframes, in the rapidity of diffusion, and in the opportunity to escape from the traditional information gatekeepers' interpretation of facts. Not only people using new media can make their own news and present their own facts, but they can also interact among themselves (peer interaction) and with different entities (institutional interaction). New media and, in general, Information and Communication Technologies (ICT) offer "a possibility of a new public communication environment which is interactive, relatively cheap to enter, unconstrained by time or distance, and inclusive" (Coleman and Gøtze 2001: 5). They have, in sum, a great potential in broadening participation within the political process that will in turn enhance and enrich democracy. This is the reason why several Western democracies have made considerable efforts toward the definitions of what are commonly labeled as "e-democracy policies," that is, initiatives aimed at promoting civic engagement by means of ICTs and internet. This trend is also visible within the Italian context.

In the last ten years Italy has been facing socio-economic challenges, which required structural reforms of its institutional public apparatus. Such reforms aimed at coping with the citizens' pressing requests for participation in policy-making and with the necessity of remaining economically competitive. At the same time, Italian mass media has shifted towards global communication trends, characterized by an increasing development of new forms of mediated communications and a related change in the way of doing communication. While traditional mass media such as television, radio, and newspaper continue to be important sources of information, other forms of communications via internet, satellite, and mobile phones have emerged in the Italian media landscape.

This chapter explores the ways in which Italian public administration has been using information and communication technologies as new media "tools" to interact with citizens for example by creating websites, such as Iperbole, MO-Net/Unox1 and Partecipa.net, where citizens can interact with public officers upon local policies through online forum discussions or they can request specific services by submitting online documents, for instance, for school applications and so on. After a brief presentation of the importance of new media in relation to democracy and public participation we will describe the Italian approach to e-democracy within the context of international and European programs. We will then analyze a few case studies of Italian e-democracy projects developed and implemented at the municipal levels in order to understand the impact of those projects for restructuring and enhancing relationships between local administrations and their citizens. Finally, we compare Italian e-democracy initiatives with international and European experiences in order to assess the level of interactivity between citizens and public administrators and whether it is possible to see the creation of social capital within the Italian online communities.

NEW MEDIA AND NEW FORMS OF PUBLIC INTERACTIONS

Current democratic systems are increasingly marked by highly complex characteristics. Public organizations need to cope with emergent challenges of globalization that hamper them from ensuring effective and legitimate policies. When the expectations of citizens on political responses are not satisfied, public support and trust in government progressively decline. Inglehart (1999) explains this dynamic in terms of distrust in traditional sources of authority and in hierarchical forms of power, which are perceived as unable to respond to the needs of citizens. It is precisely the gap between public expectations and political responses that seems to affect citizens' trust. It emerges as an increasing demand for new forms of representation and civic engagement to replace traditional channels of participation. In this environment, information and communication technologies promise tools for re-casting the relationship between governments and citizens in a more deliberative and active way (Blumer and Coleman, 2001). Information and communication technologies create alternative forms of public discourses on the net and open up new channels of public participation through internet forums, weblogs, and web communities. Internet can promote civic dialogue through online simultaneous exchanges of experiences and opinions. Its mechanisms for interactive exchange enable a greater symmetry of communicative power than one-way communication flows of the press and broadcasting media (Schultz 2000). The use of internet also lowers the cost of obtaining information. Citizens and groups with few resources can undertake acts of communication and monitor what previously was the exclusive domain of resource-rich organizations and individuals (Bimber 2000).

This "civic" potential of internet has encouraged political institutions (at the international, national, and municipal levels) to incorporate information and communication technologies into their governance activities. It appears that the approach of public institutions in Western countries has changed more and more towards e-democracy and e-governance.[1] E-governance refers to the use of information and communication technology by governments to exchange information and services with citizens, businesses, and other governmental offices. The most important benefits include improving the efficiency, the utility, and the accessibility of public services. E-democracy comprises the use of electronic communication technologies in enhancing democratic processes. More precisely, for e-democracy we intend "the use of information and communication technologies and strategies by democratic actors (government, elected officials, the media, political organizations, citizens/voters) within political and governmental processes that involve local communities, nations, and the international sphere. E-democracy suggests greater and more active citizen participation enabled by the internet, mobile communications and other technologies in today's representative democracy, as well as through more participatory or direct form of citizen involvement in addressing public challenges" (Clift 2004: 38). Typically, the kind of enhancements sought by proponents of e-democracy are framed in terms of making processes more accessible; making citizen participation in the decision-making of public policy more expansive and direct so as to enable broader influence in policy outcomes (as more individuals involved could yield smarter policies); increasing transparency and accountability; and keeping the government closer to the consent of the governed, while increasing its political legitimacy.

In particular, the applicability of ICTs to e-democracy is perceived as a tool for promoting a worldwide community of informed, inspired, committed citizens who are actively engaged in confronting the challenges humanity faces in all its aspects (Blumer and Coleman 2001; Clift 2004). Generally speaking, what ICT practices and brings into policy-making and democratic processes are: trust in and accountability of government actions; a better understanding of government structures, functions, and programs (i.e., civic education) that provide legitimacy and strength to democracy; active participation of citizens to policy-making through input and consultation; knowledge about citizen satisfaction and service delivery; reachable and equitable access for the public; and, last but not least, engagement in public life and deliberation among citizens on relevant issues (Clift 2004; OECD 2001).

THE ITALIAN APPROACH TO E-DEMOCRACY BETWEEN INTERNATIONAL EXPERIENCES AND NATIONAL ADMINISTRATIVE REFORMS

Since 1990, the Italian government has promoted an intense process of institutional and administrative reform,[2] mainly as the result of internal and external pressures. Internal pressures manifested at the end of the 1980s when the explosion of the fiscal deficit called for downsizing of public spending and staffing (Capano 2003). External pressures were characterized by the development of a new international public management approach, which promoted a greater privatization of public services towards an output-oriented approach, typically used by private sectors (Hood 1999). These trends in public management generated processes of copying and mimesis across the OECD (Organisation for Economic Co-operation and Development) countries including Italy.

The international movement towards a more effective and quality-based public sector with the adoption of ICTs as top of the agenda was launched in the early 2000s by the OECD, and it was based on the decisive e-democracy experiences of Canada, the United States, Australia, Sweden, Finland, and the UK.[3] Information and communication technologies have been conceived as a means to reform public service delivery, whereas citizens have been considered customer and, thus, active partners of a dialogic interaction with the public (Eskelinen 2005). Several legal acts carried out between 1990 and 2000 state that citizens are at the core of public administrators' actions[4] and that information and communication technologies are crucial in order to deliver transparent, effective, and customer-oriented services.

In the last decade this idea has also been the core of Italian strategy for building a national information society. A first action has been taken in 2001 when the Ministry and the Department for Innovation and Technologies (MIT and DIT) were established with the specific commitment to coordinate all initiatives carried out in the field of e-government and e-democracy. For their technical and organizational tasks, the MIT and DIT are supported by the CNIPA (National Center for Public Administration Informatics). The MIT focuses on the local dimension of e-activities, by decentralizing more and more at the municipal level the decisions of public administrations on such activities, and by strengthening the participation of citizens into local policy-making processes. Localized community-based programs have assumed a strategic importance on participation actions, above all because of the proximity between citizens and institutions (vertical subsidiarity) and for the direct possibility of collaborations and interactions between different groups of civil society (horizontal subsidiarity). Moreover, Italian institutional reforms towards e-democracy and e-governance have stressed the importance of active citizenry as contribution to local development and improvement of the general conditions of communities and their municipal governments.

The increment of projects on e-democracy and e-governance in the Italian context should be regarded as one of the results of institutional reforms aiming at decentralizing part of national government competencies towards regional and local administrations, and at the same time they should be considered the Italian response to the emergence of analogous initiatives in other countries. Laws 142/1990 and 59/1993, and the recent laws 1/1999 and 3/2001 have introduced relevant modifications on the Italian Constitution by strengthening the role of regional and municipal institutions. Directly under the national government there are twenty regions and below them are 107 Provinces and nearly 8100 Municipalities. Each level of government has an independent administrative policy-making and enjoys a good degree of financial autonomy. Regions, provinces, and local municipalities share competencies in the field of agriculture, tourism, environment, infrastructures, immigration, education, economic development, health, and social care. Municipalities are also responsible for urban planning. All the three levels of government are also responsible for innovation and R&D investment to improve internal administrative competencies and capabilities.

While international organizations such as the OECD, the UN, and the Commonwealth, have played a crucial role in disseminating good practices and policy recommendations on e-democracy and e-governance projects, several Western countries have started to put in place more and more policies for their diffusion. For instance, Italy frequently refers to policies on an Information Society developed by the EU. Since the Lisbon Council, in fact, the EU has assessed the importance of a digital, knowledge-based economy for the future of Europe and has acknowledged the strong impact that information and communication technologies have—or should have—on the life of all Europeans. Within the general reforms of the public sector, it has been recognized that new media improves the quality of public services towards citizens as much as its effectiveness and working conditions (CEC 2001; 2003; 2006).

In accordance with the EU recommendations towards the creation of an Information Society, the MIT published the Government Guidelines for the development of an Information Society in the Legislature in 2002, with the aim of specifically strengthening e-government practices and improving e-democracy in Italy. As the official document indicates, the process of administrative modernization is strictly joined with the decentralization of public decisions at the regional and municipal levels, and e-government collaborations between the MIT and regional and municipal governments are endorsed by co-financial mechanisms. In practice, all the activities and projects concerning the use of new information and communication technologies are monitored at the national level, but they are planned, developed, and implemented at the regional and municipal levels. Although the Italian government has proposed certain guidelines concerning the development of an information society, it is the responsibility of each regional administration to decide when, what, and how to implement these activities, as a consequence of their administrative and budgetary duties.

Similar to the MIT project, the DIT launched, in the same year, a call for proposal, First e-government program for regional and local authorities, where 134 projects were selected and co-financed (for a total amount of 120 million Euros) to promote local e-government initiatives. Coordinated activities between the Ministry, regional authorities, and other local organizations were assigned to the new-born Regional Competence Centers for E-government and Information Society (RCCs), a network of local entities, whose main task was to give technical and organizational support to municipal authorities.[5]

The second phase of the Italian e-government program started in 2003. This program outlined further areas to be included within the actions on e-governance, such as: local infrastructures, public services for business and citizens, organizational support for small municipalities, e-democracy, and public participation. In April 2004, the MIT launched the national call for selecting projects to promote digital citizenship to encourage public participation into local policy-making through ICTs. In 2005 a Commission of experts selected 57 projects among the 129 submitted by regional and local public administrations to be co-founded by the central government (for a total amount of 9,500,000).[6]

As a consequence of these reforms, both co-financed projects and e-democracy initiatives at the regional and municipal levels cover a wide spectrum of policy areas. Some projects deliver more traditional online services such as mailbox, chats, newsletter and forums, and they also allow users to update information about local events. Some municipalities are giving great relevance to e-democracy practices as an opportunity to better involve the public in the definition and discussion of problems and in identifying alternative solutions to critical questions related to social and environmental sustainability, territorial planning, allocation of budget, and industrial development. In most cases, citizens' opinions are then collected and analyzed during town councils and, in a few cases; online voting is made possible about relevant local questions.[7]

EXAMPLES OF ITALIAN E-DEMOCRACY PROJECTS: THE EMILIA-ROMAGNA CONTEXT

In this study we analyze three e-democracy projects in Italy as case studies: Iperbole, MO-Net/Unox1, and Partecipa.net. Iperbole was developed by the municipality of Bologna, MO-Net/Unox1 was implemented by the municipality of Modena, and Partecipa.net is a regional level project organized by the Region of Emilia Romagna and involving different partners. Iperbole, MO-Net/Unox1, and Partecipa.net are thus all localized in Emilia Romagna,[8] an area where the use of ICTs and new media is quite well spread both in private and public sectors. We chose the Region of Emilia Romagna as an example of the effects of e-democracy projects on citizen involvement because this region has historically been one of the most active in terms of proposing, developing, and implementing new forms of public involvement. This is in part the result of a long lasting policy effort made by regional authorities towards the adoption of information and communication technologies in the public sector so as to transform Emilia Romagna in a "digital region" where all services can be electronically provided.[9] But Emilia Romagna represents also a good model because the strong tradition of digital citizenship has lead to the development of effective and user-friendly tools for civic participation. In this region the use of information and communication technologies within public administrations has been particularly original and the governance approach for local policy-making has been innovative in terms of building strong partnerships between municipal government and associations of civil society.

We assess the quality of these three Italian projects by looking at two types of parameters: the strategies of their organization and the level of citizen participation. For each public organization we analyze the goals, communication strategies, target groups, and the types of tools and messages these public organizations employ. As far as the level of interactivity achieved, we consider whether and to which extent citizens can obtain relevant information and carry out various online procedures. Typically, these online procedures include applications and registrations of pupils in schools, requests of birth and marriage certificates, announcements of moving, registrations of a new company, car registration, and many others.[10] In addition we take into consideration the technological channels employed for enhancing citizen involvement. Specifically we verified which channels people mostly used to communicate, give feedback, ask questions, make complaints, exchange information, and build relationships with public administrators.

The level of participation was measured in relation to the frequency of access to internet webpages, the number of subscriptions to the newsletters, and the actual participation to discussion lists or forums. The goal is to assess the effectiveness of these projects on e-democracy by looking at their ability to create e-public spheres. Miani (2005) claims that new media can help the process of democratization when it is able to create virtual public spheres, where people can discuss about anything in synchronic or asynchronic time. This virtual public sphere, known as "e-public sphere," requires four basic consequential elements: (1) it needs a medium enabling the exchange of information; (2) this medium should have a social use and stimulate public discussions; (3) public discussions in this medium need to be rational; and (4) they should have some influence in political decisions.

Iperbole is the first e-democracy initiative developed in Italy. It officially started in 1995 with the creation of a specific webpage containing information of public interest for people and institutions in the area of Bologna. The aim was to connect citizens with public and non-profit organizations, to discuss and participate in municipal activities and policies. At the beginning

Iperbole's webpage only provided documents and information about the city, but subsequently it also supplied virtual spaces for discussions in forums, email accounts, and some internet spaces for private organizations, associations, and other institutions.

MO-Net/Unox1 is a project of the municipality of Modena that was created in 2002 as a tool for enhancing and improving public administration-citizen relationships. After a registration on Unox1 portal, citizens can receive to their email accounts tailored information according to their interests, can write and get direct answers to their questions and participate in different surveys and forum discussions. Through Unox1 services, public administrators of Modena aim at better knowing their citizens' interests and opinions, to enhance public participation and discussion in the political decisions of the city.

Partecipa.net started in September 2005 with the intent to extend fruitful e-democracy experiences already made available in different public administrations. The aim of this project is to manage all institutional services in a more efficient manner, and to facilitate and increase citizen participation in the very definition of regional policies. Partecipa.net's outcome is the creation of an "e-democracy kit," a complete tool available to all public organizations for developing and implementing the use of ICTs into their services and to create better relationships between public administrations and citizens.

These three projects have many similarities in terms of organizational strategies applied. First, they have similar goals: they aim at enhancing public participation in political decisions via internet and other technologies, improving public services' efficacy and efficiency, and developing trustful relationships and dialogues among public administrators and between public administrators and citizens. Second, they follow a chronological continuum for innovation. New technologies and approaches have been implemented after the evaluation of existing e-democracy programs. For example, Iperbole is one of the first projects on e-democracy produced in Italy, which has been regarded as a case study for other following initiatives including MO-Net/Unox1 and Partecipa.net. These projects started from the experience of Bologna and later developed additional specific solutions on the basis of their own needs. On the other hand, Iperbole's main organization has also changed since the beginning, after the development of new strategies of e-democracy carried out by MO-Net/Unox1 and Partecipa.net. At present, in fact, Iperbole includes some common features of the other two projects, such as online surveys, forums, boards, mailing lists, and newsletters.

We can thus claim that these three projects have many common features, which are the expression of the willingness of different public administrations to share their know-how and experiences to improve their services.

The similarities are also visible when considering their main communication strategies. All three initiatives have developed different solutions, but have sent similar messages to their specific publics. Although Iperbole was created only for citizens, during the last few years it has added many links and interactive systems aimed at involving other types of users, such as: civil servants, public officers, politicians, stakeholders, and other private and public organizations. Especially for Partecipa.net the involvement of external publics such as private and public organizations has been fundamental. As a regional portal, Partecipa.net contains a direct link to each city webpage and to other organizations within the region, which are providers of public services. Thus, Partecipa.net has tailored its messages to each group of users promoting a collaborative dialogue among people within local organizations, and among public administrations and citizens.

In terms of tools developed, all three projects offer two different types of instruments. Public and private organizations, such as schools, libraries, health care institutions, non-profit associations, and NGOs are given some free space in the portal. There they can publish their information, and/or ask to be linked as external sources. Citizens can obtain information on different public services and general policies, and, for certain of them, they can even obtain a full assistance via the net. Citizens can also register in thematic newsletters, mailing lists and acquire information via telephone and GPRS. MO-Net/Unox1 enables the user to select and receive information, to interact with public officers through a user-friendly board, and to download different forms. Finally, citizens can register with Unox1 and receive newsletters on various subjects. The number of registered users and newsletters has continuously increased together with the range of topics and editorials.[11]

Citizens can also discuss policy or particular matters in specific web areas dedicated to public discussions, but for all three projects a registration is required to access forums. MO-Net/Unox1 and Partecipa.net have adopted a profile filtering system during the registration. A new user needs to describe his/her interests by picking from a list and the software rejects anything that does not match what the portal offers. In MO-Net/Unox1 there is also the possibility to obtain specific information by clicking on a list without logging in, but for receiving emails, newsletters and participating in online forums and surveys registration is mandatory. The procedure for registering to Iperbole is rather complicated. First a new user needs to download a form, send it by mail or give it directly to a specific office at the local municipality, and then he/she can obtain a login account and password.[12]

Generally the forums and boards have a moderator who decides the topic of discussion and provides some indications on the aims.[13] The online debate is quite structured and the high level of participation reveals that a public discussion is taking place in the web community. Additionally, a public community can emerge over time when its members help one another by sharing their own experience with the problem at stake; create trust and a feeling of belonging to the community, which, as a result, increases the social capital of the participants. In these cases it is the technology that creates communities and improves the social capital of its members. It is not a coincidence perhaps, that the online forums on Partecipa.net focus on technical matters. These discussions represent spaces of communication among public officials on issues related to the implementation of the e-democracy toolkit more than an arena for public debates on local policy issues. Partecipa.net's "e-democracy Kit," in fact, is a complete set of tools that can be easily adapted to different organizations for online debates, and the acquisition and publication of decision-making results.

These three projects, even if at an early stage, are enhancing e-democracy practices. The high frequency of access to web pages, the high number of downloaded files, the e-mail traffic, and the moderately high involvement of citizens in forums seem to testify to the fact that Partecipa.net, Iperbole, and MO-Net/Unox1 are dynamic and interactive communication spaces. Moreover, information related to offline activities can help us depict a more complete picture of the projects and draw some conclusions about e-public sphere.

Partecipa.net is particularly interesting because it is the first attempt in Italy to promote and co-ordinate e-democracy initiatives on a regional level. It is built on a strong multi-level partnership among the region, provinces, municipalities, and local civic organizations of Emilia-Romagna. Its mission is particularly innovative because Partecipa.net is primarily aimed at promoting civic engagement into decision-making throughout a new cultural approach. Habermas's idea of public sphere is frequently recalled by Partecipa.net public administrators, and some of the project's keywords are: participation, dialogue, integration, innovation, listening, and trust (RER 2006).

In 2005 Iperbole created the new web area "Bologna Noi" (Bologna Us) in order to strengthen public participation. Here information about ongoing "participating process"—such as the local energy program or municipal regulatory plans—are available. On "Bologna Noi" six "participatory laboratories on urban planning" are also available where citizens can gain information about ongoing initiatives (working groups, assembly) and download relevant documents. The initiative is aimed at actively involving citizens in local policy-making through the adoption of a twofold online and offline strategy. Participation on MO-Net/Unox1 is enhanced by a multi-channel approach: forums, e-mail, online answers, and polls. A couple of experiments were made in 2003 and 2004. At the first poll answered 13 percent of the sample citizens considered. In the second one, the percentage of respondents raised to 21 percent. The overall result was modest, but the increment in citizen participation was encouraging.

Partecipa.net, Iperbole, and Mo-Net/Unox1 have created a virtual space that enables the exchange of information and stimulates public debates among citizens. In particular, discussions on forums are structured and, to some extent, rational, which testifies to the true interests of the citizens in participating in such debates. According to data illustrated above, the three projects represent good e-democracy practices since their results are quite positive. Though the level of participation is still low, online engagement is increasing. What is still unclear is the real impact exercised by e-democracy practices into political decisions.

CONCLUSION

Italian municipal governments have recently adopted a more participatory approach to policy-making decisions, recognizing the importance of active citizenry as a contribution to local development and improvement of the general conditions of municipal communities. Citizen panel, forums, focus groups, are only a few examples of innovative methods already experimented in municipal politics. This was partly due to EU regulations, which have set the parameters for extending the use of new information and communication technologies in all the member states and to the spread of analogous initiatives within Western countries supported by the OECD and other international organizations. But this was also due to the decisions of the Italian government to reinforce public participation and civic engagement as necessary governmental strategy for advancing Italian economic and social standards. The necessity to satisfy both projects on active citizenry and programs on bureaucratic modernization generated an increasing interest among local administrations in creating different community-based projects on e-democracy, which were developed according to varied and innovative technological solutions and hybrid communication tools.

Italian initiatives on e-democracy—and particularly to projects delivered in Emilia Romagna—are qualitatively good compared with those in other Western countries. Although Italian initiatives on e-democracy are at a young stage, this situation is rapidly changing. This tendency is shown by the high profile of some of these case studies. For instance, two of the projects discussed in this chapter have received much attention by citizens and the Italian national government. The Partecipa.Net and Iperbole project are increasingly popular websites. However, there are still substantial differences between Italian regions in creating, developing, and implementing projects on e-democracy. Law 59/1997 has given regional administrations more independence and thus more power on decision-making in relation to the activities and policies concerning their regional jurisdiction, including the adoption of ICTs and the development of related services. According to this law each regional administration can decide which activity to implement and how, while the national administration provides part of the financial resources for them. It comes that for certain regions, projects on e-democracy and e-governance have more relevance than other activities and thus the regional administrations invest more money and resources. Emilia Romagna has been one of the regions where the large investment of resources in ICTs has developed active citizenry. This is the result of combined factors, including the general high standards of the regional services, a strong and well established network of associations, federations and non-profit organizations, which have pushed to implement even more online services, and a generally high standard of ICT education among the population. The case of Emilia Romagna has gained great recognition at the European level and it has frequently been mentioned as a good model for studies on virtual communities. For example, Dell'Aquila (1998) cites the experience of Emilia Romagna upon projects on e-democracy as an example where the creation of virtual communities has determined the establishment of associations of public services whose goals are to connect groups of people and to allow them to confront each other about questions on their real community. The function of information and communication technologies should be that of enhancing more civic networking in a specific real community. Also being a member of civic network means to have access to resources that non-members do not have. Proponents of the importance of ICTs in local community interaction and communication believe that it is exactly this aspect of value gained from being a member of a network that characterized the concept of social capital. Social capital refers to networked ties of goodwill, mutual support, shared language, shared norms, social trust, and a sense of mutual obligation from which people can derive value (Huysman and Wulf 2005: 83). Considering these factors, the experience of e-democracy in Emilia Romagna can be regarded as a form of civic networking within a virtual community where social capital is, to certain extents, developed between the members of municipalities.

However, not the same level of ICT penetration is available in all Italian regions. Thus, the same possibilities to create social capital between public administrators and their internal and external users are not equal throughout the nation. Looking at Italy as a whole, the possibility of using information and communication technologies is fragmented, with still a large division between the northern and southern regions. In fact, the use of ICTs in the northern regions has generally reached the average European standards, while in the southern regions the process of innovation towards an information society is still slow.[14]

Regions proposing projects on e-democracy are also experiencing problems either related to the lack of adequate ICT infrastructures or with the incapacity of or lack of interest in using them. In this respect, there are two main contradictions in the globalization of the Italian use of new media within public administrations. First, the interest of the local administrations in developing e-democracy projects is not always followed by a corresponding delivery of services in the specific geographical areas. Second, the high request of local users for better, faster, and more interactive online public services is not necessarily followed by a real use of the online services. Nonetheless, within these contractions it is possible to notice some progress towards a global use of new media and thus an increase in the digitalization of different public services in Italy, including services enhancing e-public sphere and public participation.

NOTES

1. The adoption of e-democracy and e-government practices is clearly correlated to the diffusion of ICTs within a country. Namely, the main factors that seem to positively influence the use of ICTs are high levels of education among citizens, high percentage of GDP expenditure in R&D, and low costs for hardware, software, and internet access charges (Norris, 2001; Sartori, 2006). Moreover, a relevant role is also performed by the implementation of Public Administration reforms triggered by NPM theories. These factors would, in fact, give a plausible explanation of the reason why pioneers in e-democracy experiments were mainly Scandinavian and North-American countries. The lack of empirical reliable data on ongoing e-democracy experiences across the world, however, makes it extremely difficult to explain variances among countries.

2. Administrative reforms concerned: (A) *structures*: introduction of departments and agencies at the central level; decentralization and re-allocation of power at the regional and local levels; (B) *processes*: introduction of managerial accounting, budgeting control and management by objectives; de-legislation and simplification of administrative acts; promotion of transparency and accessibility to public acts; (C) *personnel*: "privatization" of public employment; public management reform. For more details see Gualmini (2003) and Natalini (2006).

3. An overview of relevant international experiences is collected in the OECD report *Promise and Problems of E-Democracy. Challenges of Online Citizen Engagement* (2003).

4. Law no. 142/1990, law no. 241/1990 are related to transparency and access to administrative acts; law no. 127/1997, law no. 50/1999, and law no. 340/2000 concern

simplification and de-regulation; law no. 59/1997 and law no. 150/2000 deal with communications and public relations between public administrators and citizens.

5. For more details on RCCs see http://www.crcitalia.it.

6. More information about these projects is available at URL: http://www.cnipa.gov.it.

7. For an overview of Italian e-democracy experiences see MIT (2004a; 2004b) and OECD (2003).

8. Emilia Romagna is a central region with a population of approximately 4.1 million where 1.6 million of families live. Each family is composed on average of 2.4 people. In terms of age 22.4 percent of all population is over 65 years old, 11 percent is over 75 years old, and 14 percent is under 18 years old. The level of education of those between 14–19 years old is quite high, 93 percent of them is officially enrolled in a high school program. For economical developments, Emilia Romagna has one of the most positive situations in Italy in terms of level of salaries, consumptions, and employment rates. The majority of industrial realities are small and medium sizes. In recent years a growing number of larger companies has emerged in this territory, especially in the industrial and commercial fields.

9. The region offers 214 free internet access points in public administrations, public offices, libraries, employment offices, and youth centers. 42 percent of all municipalities have at least one internet access point and 72 percent of all the population lives in municipalities which have at least one internet access point.

10. The public services analyzed were twelve for citizens and eight for businesses. Both measurement scale and list of public services taken into consideration were used by Cap Gemini Ernst & Young for the analysis of the eEurope project about the availability and quality of public services online. They have been widely used as the principal methods of evaluation of online services (Wauters and Van Durme, 2005: 7).

11. As far as MO-Net/Unox1 is concerned, in February 2007 there are 43,400 registered users and 4,200 newsletters are sent out and so far 77 different topics have been featured. In the same period, the total amount of access to Partecipa.net was 43,320 while people connected to Iperbole were 18,162, i.e. almost 5 percent of the whole population of Bologna (372,505 inhabitants). In January 1995, users connected to Iperbole were 172; in December they were 2,123. Between 1996 and 1998 they rose from 6,200 up to 14,163. At the end of 2000 they were 15,776. Hence, users have been growing exponentially in ten years.

12. The procedure is more complicated since a public officer needs to check the residence of the applicant before giving free access to the service. In fact, for the online services of Iperbole it is required to be a resident in the city of Bologna, while for the other projects it is not a prerequisite to access.

13. In MO-Net/Unox1 there are actually four categories of forums: about "general information and spare time"; "professional life"; "politics and public administration"; "associations and public organizations." In Iperbole, there are two main forums, one about "building and constructions" in the city and the other issues related with "urban planning."

14. Excluding some cases such as the city of Catania in Sicily and the Region of Sardinia, which have well-known and relatively well-developed projects, although they are arguably less-robust in terms of their democratic impact (Peart and Diaz, 2007: 23).

REFERENCES

Alexander, Cynthia. (1998). *Digital Democracy*. Oxford: University Press.
Bentivenga, Sara. (2005). *Politica e nuove tecnologie della comunicazione*. Bari: Laterza
Bimber, Bruce. (2000). "The Study of Information Technology and Civic Engagement," *Political Communication*, 7 (4): 329–333.
Blumer, J. G. and Coleman, S. (2001). "Realizing Democracy Online: A Civic Commons in Cyberspace" in *IPPR/Citizens Online Research Publication* No. 2, March.
Capano, Gilberto. (2003). "Administrative Traditions and Policy Change: When Policy Paradigms Matter. The Case of Italian Administrative Reform during the 1990s," in *Public Administration*, 81(4): 781–801.
Casalegno Federico. and Kavanaugh, Andrea. (1998). "Autour des communautés et des réseaux de télécommunications. » *Sociétés: Revue des Sciences Humaines et Sociales*, 59.
Castells, Manuel. (1996). *The Rise of Network Society*. Oxford: Blackwell
Castells, M. (2001). "Information Technology and Global Capitalism." In W. Hutton and A. Giddens (eds.), *On the Edge, Living with Global Capitalism*. London: Jonathon Cape
CEC (2006). 2010 *eGovernment Action Plan: Accelerating eGovernment in Europe for the Benefit of All*. COM 173 final.
CEC (2003). *The Role of eGovernment for Europe's Future*. COM 567 final.
CEC (2001). *eEurope 2002: Creating an EU Framework for the Exploitation of Public Sector Information*. COM 607 final.
Clift, Steven. (2004). *E-government and Democracy. Representation and Civic Engagement in the Information Age*. Available at www.publicus.net/e-government. Consulted on November 2006.
Coleman, Stephen and Norris, Donald F. (2005). "A New Agenda for E-democracy." Oxford Internet Institute, Forum Discussion Paper No. 4, January.
Coleman, Stephen. and Gøtze, John. (2001). *Bowling Together: Online Public Engagement in Policy Deliberation*. London: Hansard Society. Also available at www.bowlingtogether.net/bowlingtogether.pdf.
Comune di Modena (2004). *Citizens Relationship Management nel Comune di Modena*. Il sistema Unox1, Modena.
Dell'Aquila, P. (1999). "Critical Consumption and Virtual Communities: Some Observations." *Paideusis—Journal for Interdisciplinary and Cross-Cultural Studies*, 2/1999.
Doheny-Farina Stephen. (1996). *The Wired Neighborhood*. Yale: University Press.

Eskelinen, Sari Maarit. (2005). *Citizens' Attitude and Involvement in Public Consumer Information*. Unpublished Licentiate Thesis. Jyväskylä: University of Jyväskylä.

Flew, Terry and McElhinney, Stephen. (2002). "Globalisation and the Structure of the New Media Industry." In L. A. Lievrouw and S. Livingstone (eds.). *Handbook of New Media: Social Shaping and Consequences of ICTs*, 287–306. London: Sage Publications.

Government Online International Network (2001). *Online Consultation in GOL Countries*. Initiatives to foster e-democracy. Project report 6 December 2001.

Gualmini Elisabetta. (2003). *L'amministrazione nelle democrazie contemporanee*. Bari: Laterza

Hacker, Kenneth. L. and Jan. van Dijk (2000). *Digital Democracy: Issues of Theory and Practice*. London: Sage.

Hoff, Jens., Ivan, Horrocks and Pieter, Tops (2000). *Democratic Governance and New Technology: Technologically Mediated Innovations in Political Practice in Western Europe*. London: Routledge.

Holtz, Shel. (1996). *Communication and Technologies: The Complete Guide to Using Technology for Organizational Communication*. Chicago: Lawrence Ragan Communications.

Hood, Christopher. (1991). "A Public Management for all Seasons?" in *Public Administration*, 69(1): 3–10

Huysman, M., Wenger, E. and Wulf, V. (2003). *Communities and Technologies*. Dordrecht: Boston, Kluwer Academic Publishers.

Huysman, M. and Wulf, Volker. (2005). "The Role of Information Technology in Building and Sustaining the Relational Base of Communities." *The Information Society*, 21(2).

Inglehart Ronald. (1999). "Postmodernization Erodes Respect for Authority, but Increases Support for Democracy," in P. Norris (ed.), *Critical Citizens. Global Support for Democratic Government*. Oxford: University Press.

ISTAT (2006). *Le tecnologie dell'informazione e della comunicazione: disponibilità delle famiglie e utilizzo degli individui*. Roma: Rapporto dell'Istituto Nazionale di Statistica, Dicembre.

Kamarck, Elaine C. and Joseph S. Nye (2002). *Governance.com: Democracy in the Information Age*. Washington, DC: Brookings Institution.

Karakaya, Rabia. (2003). The Internet and citizen participation: How institutional environment impacts upon the strategy of a local authority? Paper to ECPR General Conference, Marburg, Germany, 18–21 September.

Kavanaugh, Andrea L. and Scott, J. Patterson (2002). "The Impact of Community Computer Networks on Social Capital and Community Involvement in Blacksburg." In B. Wellman and C. Haythornthwaite (eds.), *The Internet in Everyday Life*, pp. 325–344. Oxford, UK: Malden, MA, Blackwell Publishing.

Longo, Antonio; Barbanera, Sara; Mancini, Lucilla; Mancini, Rocco; La Grotta, Mariangela.; Corvino, Valentina; Caracciolo, Valentina.; Dal Poz, Marco. (2005). Cittadini on line. Indagine sulla comunicazione via internet della Pubblica Amministrazione. Report for Movimento difesa del cittadino. Roma, June.

Miani, Mattia. (2005). *Comunicazione pubblica e nuove tecnologie*. Bologna: Il Mulino.

MIT- Ministro per l'innovazione tecnologica (2004a). Linee guida per la promozione della cittadinanza digitale: e-democracy, a publication of the Italian Department for the public affairs—Formez.

MIT—Ministro per l'innovazione tecnologica (2004b). E-democracy: modelli e strumenti delle forme di partecipazione emergenti nel panorama italiano, a publication of the Italian Department for the public affairs—Formez.

Muzi Falconi, Toni. (2007). The perception of country identity in social media. Speech made at the Summit on "Enhancing Britain's global reputation—the challenges for business and public relations." Organized by Charted Institute of Public Relations, London, 26–27 February.

Natalini, Alessandro. (2006). *Il tempo delle riforme amministrative*, Bologna, Il Mulino.

Norris, Pippa. (2001). *Digital Divide, Civic Engagement, Information Poverty and the Internet Worldwide*. Cambridge: University Press.

OECD (2003). Promise and Problems of E-Democracy. Challenges of Online Citizen Engagement.

OECD (2001). Citizens as Partners—OECD Handbook on Information, Consultation and Public Participation in Policy-Making.

Peart, Michael N. and Diaz, Javier. R. (2005). Comparative project on Local e-democracy initiatives in Europe and North America. A study of the e-Democracy Centre Research Centre on Direct Democracy, Faculty of Law, University of Geneva, Switzerland.

Putnam, Robert D., Leonardi, Robert, Nanetti, Raffaella. (1993). *Making Democracy Work: Civic Traditions in Modern Italy*. Princeton, NJ, Princeton University Press.

Putnam, Robert D. (2000). *Bowling Alone: America's Declining Social Capital*. New York, Simon & Schuster.

RER—Regione Emilia-Romagna (2006), Partecipa.net. Piano di Comunicazione, Bologna.

Sartori, Laura. (2006*). Il divario digitale*, Bologna: Il Mulino

Schultz, Tanjev. (2000). *Mass Media and the Concept of Interactivity: An Exploratory Study of Online Forums and Reader Email. Media, Culture and Society*, 22 (2): 205–221.

Springston, Jeffrey K. (2001). "Public Relations and New Media Technology: The Impact of the Internet." In R. L. Heath (ed.). *Handbook of Public Relations*, pp. 603–614. CA: Sage Publications.

Wellman, Barry and Haythornthwaite, Caroline A. (2002). *The Internet in Everyday Life*. Oxford, UK; Malden, MA, Blackwell Pub.

Wauters, Patrick and Van Durme, Pascale. (2005). Online availability of public services: how is Europe progressing? Web based survey on electronic public services. Report of the 5th measurement, October 2004. Prepared by Capgemni for the European Commission Directorate General for Information Society and Media.

URL ADDRESSES OF THE THREE PROJECTS

Iperbole, www.comune.bologna.it
Mo-Net/Unox1, http://unox1.comune.modena.it
Partecipa.net, www.partecipa.net

Chapter Nine

Neighborhood Television Channels in Italy: The Case of Telestreet

Michela Ardizzoni

Citizens,
The televisual ocean in which we swim is beginning to reek of monoculture.
Only one species of fish dominates the infosphere.
The communicative biodiversity risks being erased.
The banana-fish is eating up all the other fish.
LISTEN CAREFULLY,
You, strong fish, who still love to swim freely, liberate your hearts from any forms of anxiety and depression.
It's time to get out of the fish tank.
May fantasy and creativity find again their power,
May friendship and challenge guide us towards the open space,
Because in danger dwells salvation.

This manifesto of civic (dis)obedience adorned some streets of Bologna in Northern Italy in June 2002. The poster with the metaphorical call to action reported above was created to launch the first neighborhood television channel in Italy. Orfeo TV, named after the street in which it originated and broadcast, had a footprint of 164 yards and was on the air for two hours a day. The first program was an interview with a local bartender.

Despite its humble beginnings, Orfeo TV paved the way for the creation of more than 150 street television channels that have developed across the country in the past five years. Intended as community media, these neighborhood channels aim at expanding local citizens' access to information by using simple technology for viewers to engage in the production and consumption of television programs. While Italian street TV channels differ in their goals and scopes, they all share a similar concern about the arbitrary consolidation of media in the hands of a few companies in Italy and the repercussions this system has on the kind of information viewers can access.

Since the early 1980s, Italian television has been characterized by a duopolistic system that juxtaposes RAI (the public network) and Mediaset (the private pole), which dominate 90 percent of the television market. This problematic concentration of television production by only two networks is further exacerbated by the unusual ties that bind the public and private sectors of television. Indeed, the private network Mediaset is owned by Silvio Berlusconi, who was elected prime minister of Italy in 1994, 2001, and again in 2008. In his position as head of the government, Berlusconi played a central role in nominating RAI's administrative boards and, vicariously, shaping the ideological and political slant of RAI's most popular channels. The period of the second Berlusconi government between 2001 and 2006 was defined by acts of mediatic censorship, a trend of convergence of public and private programming, and a loosening of ownership rules that favored Mediaset companies and its affiliates.

Concerns over Berlusconi's stranglehold on Italian media have been expressed by a variety of ideologically diverse sources both in Italy and abroad. The International Federation of Journalists, for instance, called on the European Union former President Romano Prodi to take action against the "unacceptable and intolerable conflict of interest [that] runs counter to the principles and policies of modern democracy which require that the administration of media is independent and professional" ("Journalists Call for European Union Leaders to Act Over Media Mogul Berlusconi's Conflict of Interest"). The Committee on Culture, Science, and Education of the European Union expressed similar signs of discomfort at the inextricable ties between politics and media in Italy: the committee officially urged Italy to deal effectively with the clear conflict of interest and call media owners to address their respective responsibilities. In this light, the position of the Italian government and media is seen as an anomaly within Europe that must be resolved in as timely a fashion as possible in order to "give a positive international example by proposing and supporting initiatives within the Council of Europe and the European Union and promoting greater media pluralism at the European level" ("Monopolisation of the electronic media and possible abuse of power in Italy," 2004).

In 2003, the Italian television market witnessed also the entrance of a major global media player, Rupert Murdoch's News Corporation, that has come to dominate the Italian satellite platform with Sky Italia. Through a pay-TV system, Sky Italia has been presented as the alternative to free-to-air, mainstream channels and has stipulated agreements to incorporate all satellite channels–whether private or public–in its platform. Sky Italia is to date the only satellite provider in Italy and has full control of pay television.

What I have briefly outlined above is the mediatic and cultural background against which neighborhood television channels have reacted. It is indeed no coincidence that Orfeo TV began in 2002 and most of the other channels developed shortly thereafter. The extreme concentration of television output in the hands of large conglomerates clearly resulted in programming with mass appeal that often marginalized community and local issues. The trend of convergence of public service and commercial programming that characterizes several media markets worldwide has affected Italian television as well and has resulted in the omnipresence of global formats, reality-based shows, game shows, and foreign television series.

In this chapter, I examine the creation of street television channels and their participation in the Telestreet network. The first part of the analysis focuses on the origins of neighborhood television in Italy by highlighting their programming, their objectives, and their unique use of new and old technologies. In the second section of the chapter, I articulate the contours of alternative media in the Italian context. Through the use of the theoretical framework provided by Downing, Jenkins, Schudson, Castells, and others in their work on alternative/radical media and media convergence, my aim is to understand the role of Telestreet in contemporary globalization processes that challenge notions of national and local identities, while also providing alternative outlets of communication and information. The Italian case of Telestreet proves particularly interesting in delineating recent global trends of civic journalism and the horizontal development of mass communication.

CONTOURS OF THE PHENOMENON

The phrase "street television" refers to a micro television channel with a very small footprint and realized through the use of inexpensive, accessible technology. Street television indeed operates in the empty frequencies left between regularly licensed channels. In this sense, street television does not take over the frequency allotted for another broadcaster; at the same time, though, its operations are not legally licensed through the Ministry of Communication. As the creators of Orfeo TV insist on specifying, street television is not legal, but is certainly legitimate and sanctioned by Article 21 of the Italian Constitution, which proclaims citizens' freedom of expression with any means of communication and prohibits censorship except for cases of public indecency.

The technology used to set up a street television is quite simple, almost rudimentary, and consists of three elements: a modulator to find the empty frequency; an amplifier for the transmission of the signal; and an electrical feeder. The signal is then transmitted through a regular television antenna placed on a roof or balcony.[1] Clearly, the set-up of street television relies on traditional broadcasting means, but its operations are supplemented by the use of the Internet as a locus of exchange of technical information, video clips, and news relevant to all street televisions. Technical details about the transmission and its costs can be found at Radio Alice website; the Telestreet network site (www.telestreet.it) provides updates on legislative changes that affect the existence and legality of street televisions in Italy and records the launch of new broadcasting operations in the country. The non-profit organization New Global Vision (www.ngvision.org) collaborates with the street television project by collecting video clips downloadable on tape or DVD in VHS quality: as a digital video archive, the New Global Vision project frames its mission as follows:

> [W]e are under the pressure of a pervasive and powerful information system, that points exclusively to consensus manipulation and political support. We think information is something different: to fight mainstream dis-information we need to implement the effectiveness of the tools we're able to immediately develop or quickly build up (www.ngvision.org/index.en.html).

The archive features hundreds of videos about environmental issues, gender and sexual identity, international conflicts, migration, religion, hacking, G8 meetings, and globalization. By embracing Telestreet's concern about the status of media in our times, this project has become a useful site of reference for street television producers who aim at relating the localism and communitarian scope of street television to the broader spectrum of global life and international issues. In this sense, the street television phenomenon sees the convergence of old and new media technologies for the creation of a project that is easily situated between the local and global of today's existence.

Another aspect that makes street television an accessible and attractive project is its cost effectiveness. The purchase of antennas, modulator, amplifier, and feeder is calculated to amount to 1,000 Euros (about $1,500) to which one must add the price of a computer and broadband Internet connection. Clearly, the limited costs involved in the creation of a street television become even less burdensome when the instruments are bought and used by a group of individuals, as it is often the case with street televisions in Italy. Indeed, to my knowledge, all street televisions were created by a group of two or more people and were never individual undertakings. The moderate expense and limited technical skills required to launch a street television allow a wide variety of citizens to become active participants in the communication process and decision-makers in the flow of information related to their local communities.

Since the very beginning, the Telestreet experiment has focused on the local as a site of identity, of creativity, and territorial affiliation. While this scope can be certainly linked to the limited footprint each street television has—often reaching only a few streets or a small neighborhood—this localism must be also understood as an attempt to re-center previously marginalized local issues that are indeed vital to the existence of communities throughout the country. For instance, Insu^TV from Naples features programs on the problem of trash-filled streets in the city and its surroundings, an obvious emergency for local communities. Telestreet Bari from the Southern region of Apulia gives voice to local writers and poets with interviews and live performances. Telecitofono from the North-West (Reggio Emilia), instead, straddles the global/local divide by engaging community-bound issues such as Saturday-night car accidents and Eastern European migrations westward.

As mentioned in the opening paragraph, Orfeo TV was the first instance of street television in Italy and emerged from the ashes of the 1970s' free radios, an earlier attempt at embracing the airwaves to promote the freedom of expression guaranteed by the Italian constitution.[2] Arguably, the most famous free radio in Italy was a left-wing political station, Radio Alice, based in Bologna and created by Franco Berardi (aka "Bifo")[3] and other students/political activists. Launched in 1976, soon after the liberalization of the airwaves for commercial uses, Radio Alice was on the air for one year before it was shut down by the police and his members were arrested for suspected connections with the extreme Left (Downing, 2000). At a time when television was dominated by the state broadcaster RAI, radio transmission appeared as the only medium through which alternative voices could be heard. In fact, in 1976 the city of Rome recorded a total of 74 free radios, among which Radio Radicale and Radio Città Futura were the most prominent (www.musicaememoria.com/le_prime_radio_libere_in_italia.htm). Thirty years after their creation, many free radios are no longer on the air, but their spirit is preserved in the Telestreet project. This evident connection between the two eras and two media is emphasized by Radio Alice's website that opens with a pop-up window alerting visitors: "it's not a coincidence that Orfeo TV was created by the Radio Alice team." As indicated in many street TV websites, in the twenty-first-century communication and information are hardly dissociable from the visual power of television, and this medium is perceived as the ideal tool to reach different groups of citizens/consumers.

The geography of the Telestreet network is still vague, and precise data on local street television stations are contradictory and changing rapidly. At the end of 2007 Italy had around 130 street televisions: some of these have been on the air for a few years, while others had a short-lived existence of just a few months. What matters for the purposes of this study, though, is their quick proliferation in different parts of the country and their creation among ideologically diverse groups of citizens. Thus, the leftist angle of most 1970s free radios has given way to a variety of ideological perspectives that have opted to use the Telestreet network to promote their views and re-claim access to information. In the next section, I will briefly describe the programming and goals of two street televisions that are emblematic of the diversity of themes covered by the Telestreet project.

INSU^TV FROM NAPLES

Insu^tv from Naples began in 2002 as an attempt to create means of mediated communication that could be shared and produced by the public. Nicola Agrisano, one of the founders of Insu^tv, defines the goals of this project as follows: "[our goals is] to create media that are produced by the same number of people that watch them. We like to call this 'proxyvision,' a space in osmosis with the reality of daily life."[4] It is particularly the convergence between the public sphere of television and the local space of daily, urban life that is at the heart of Insu^tv's programming. Like other street projects, this Neapolitan channel arose from dissatisfaction with the lack of representation of local issues in mainstream national media and the stereotypical portrayal of the Italian South as regressive and indolent. The reality of urban living in Naples' neighborhoods is often neglected by national media, which privilege a spectacle-like lens to filter commercially viable news of the area. Thus, the problems, but also the opportunities, presented by some areas of the city never reach the national stage and are consequently ignored by local populations as well. The creative idea behind Insu^tv aims at filling this lacuna by catering to local communities that are often voiceless in the national media.

Unlike other street channels that focus on some selected topics, Insu^tv does not limit its programming to specific issues, but rather follows the trajectories and the narratives that shape Neapolitan life over time. In this respect, one of the main contributions of Insu^tv is the space dedicated to migrants' issues. The trend of globalization that has accelerated the flows of migrations from the South and East of the world towards the West has heavily impacted Naples' urban life. Compared with other Italian cities, Naples is a relatively newer destination of migration for foreigners, who began moving into the city in the early 1990s. In 2007, the urban population of Naples was about 1,000,000, 6% of which are legal migrants.[5] To address the problems and obstacles faced by immigrants in Naples, Insu^tv created an alternative newscast, "Tg Migranti," that features stories shot and narrated from the migrants' perspective. Thus, instead of trying to capture the difficulties of migrant life through the eyes of a privileged native Italian—a viewpoint often adopted on national television—"Tg Migranti" hands the camera and the microphone to immigrants, who choose to report in their native language (subtitled in Italian) to narrate the shackles of their path to Europe or their views on the most recent laws on immigration. A program like "Tg Migranti" is alternative and innovative in two essential ways. First, the underprivileged and the powerless are allowed to speak and they do so by using the linguistic and ideological codes with which they feel most comfortable; this approach collides with the more paternalistic view of national newscasts, where immigrants are featured mostly in cases of criminality or lack of integration and their differences from traditional notions of Italianness are underscored by their limited knowledge of the language.[6] Second, "Tg Migranti" focuses on the interdependence between the local and the global in today's world. In this program, the national level is muffled by a more pragmatic look at how the international reality of migration patterns to Naples has impacted the city and, conversely, how the Neapolitan identity is increasingly re-centered by virtue of being exposed to a globalized world.

As the case of this program highlights, people of different ethnic, economic, and educational backgrounds participate in the creation of the channel and the promotion of its programs. While no official data exist on the viewership, Agrisano confirms that Insu^tv reaches a footprint of about 500,000 people living in the area where the channel is accessible. This reach is expanded in their website, which involves audience participation through polls and blogs and allows visitors to view the programs originally broadcast on television. As in most other street TV projects, what we witness here is a convergence of old and new media to target different sections of the audience and maximize the reach of their message: "give voice to the voiceless."

TELEOSSERVANZA FROM CESENA

The low-cost advantage of street television has also been appealing to some Italian churches whose priests see it as an opportunity to extend their reach beyond the hours of mass and into the intricate everyday life of their neighborhood. Teleosservanza, a street initiative of a church in the town of Cesena in Northern Italy, has been on the air and online since 2006 covering a neighborhood of about 4,000 people. Its founder, twenty-eight-year-old Giacomo Andreucci, has dubbed it "the television of hope" because its objective is to make the church socially and culturally relevant through alternative programming that stresses salvation through social work and "spiritual reflection." Besides live and recorded broadcasts of daily mass, Teleosservanza features daily newscasts, home improvement shows, local sports coverage, and investigative documentaries on local issues rarely covered by conventional media. According to the producers, the combination of old and new media through television and the Internet works effectively to connect older and younger generations in unprecedented ways. Free web video training through the channel is an appealing feature for many youth, who, while learning a critical skill to fulfill their digital needs, end up committing their time to church work and outreach projects.

One interesting fact about the Telestreet revolution in Italy is the militant resistance that animates its grassroots media producers at various levels. These channels have become propitious sites to challenge the hegemony of institutional Italy both in public and private media. Eventually, every broadcast of Telestreet is a political act wielded to put a halt to the dominance of private interests in Italian political and social life. In 2003, for instance, four street televisions (Teleaut, SpegnilaTV, OrfeoTV, AntTV) teamed up to retaliate against the forced suspension of Disco Volante, a street TV from Senigallia, by launching what they called a "Guerriglia Marketing" campaign. A critical component of the campaign was to broadcast for free on SpegnilaTV an important Italian championship soccer game between two of the leading teams (Juventus and Rome) by rerouting the live signal from SkyItalia, the only network with broadcasting rights for Serie A soccer ("Telestreet Rome," 2003). The producers of SpegnilaTV used the incredible ferment that usually precedes decisive soccer games in Italy to draw attention to local social causes. Before the game started, a communiqué was read in support of a hundred Italian and migrant families threatened of eviction from their homes in the neighborhood. In addition, the 15-minute interval between the first and second halves of the game, which is devoted to commercials on mainstream television, was creatively used by SpegnilaTV to protest the growing commercialization of sports in Italy through limiting public access to sports events. Throughout the game, a logo at the bottom of the screen read: "Turned off in Senigallia, Disco Volante lights up again in Rome."

Not all the broadcasts of Telestreet are a direct affront to institutional power, but the mere existence of these channels is an indication of the growing intolerance of some Italians for the lack of discretion they have in public affairs, particularly at the local level. The proliferation of street television across Italian cities enabled by cheap analog and digital video technology reveals a desire for a participatory culture that had been repressed by years of an irreverent corporatization of Italian politics and media.

TELESTREET AS MEDIA CONVERGENCE

In his book *Convergence Culture* (2006), Jenkins urges readers to think of convergence less as a technical process bringing together various media technologies and more as an unpredictable cultural dynamic that is shifting the old patterns of media production and consumption (3). In doing so, Jenkins further argues, media convergence potentially expands the field for a participatory culture and eventually helps solidify a process of much needed deliberative democracy. Critics of convergence, however, describe this optimism as populist idealism primarily because the control mechanisms of older corporate media are still in place and will never be fatally challenged despite occasional forays of grassroots resistance through the work of political bloggers, committed YouTubers, and other cyber activists. Of course, the old corporate media barons have been touting convergence as a way to monitor and shape consumer behavior, but as Jenkins argues, consumers have been advocating participation in a convergence media system to force old media players to listen more to their information needs and entertainment interests. Eventually, the impact of this transitional media order might not amount to corporations relinquishing control over media content, but to regular consumers developing more complex and creative ways to interact with that content. The most significant change might be, as Jenkins put it, that we are moving from an "individualized and personalized media consumption toward consumption as a networked practice" (244).

The work of Telestreet, as described above, with its corrective potential of traditional news, its function as an alternative to homogenization in conventional media content, and its competing role as a knowledge community, is a telling example of how consumption is becoming a collective process of revising and rewriting the rules of media production. The coverage of the Naples trash debacle in mainstream news sources, for example, was, despite its relative frequency, excruciatingly inconclusive. The efforts of Insu^tv may not have lead to immediate remedying action either, but its grassroots coverage went places traditional journalists often ignore and eventually provided affected citizens and also immigrants a public platform where they can come together to identify common problems and deliberate on effective solutions.

The convergence of individual efforts in the case of Telestreet is sustained beyond moments of crisis in their communities. In fact, these bottom-up channels are creating a social network of experts, activists, volunteers, and other neighborhood leaders who constantly map the socio-economic and cultural changes within their communities. The consistency of their work is a direct reaction to the hit-and-run coverage typical of corporate media. This kind of old and new media-based activism at the community level is also creating a wired version of the informed citizen who rises above the limitations and exclusive expertise of political parties and elite governance and cultivates their own critical skills to challenge existing power structures.

This new wired citizen is crucial to the ongoing debate on whether the digital/convergent media can make it easier for the practice of democracy. I do not wish to assume readily that Telestreet and its audience are by virtue of their existence successful and better exercises of democracy than previous attempts with older, more conventional media. Michael Schudson (1998) cautions against an idealization of the informed citizen in the era of do-it-yourself journalism, and a brief summary of his argument is helpful in discussing the democratic potential of the Telestreet phenomenon. In his historical analysis of civic life in the United States, Schudson argued that the emergence of various media technologies helped people transition from an aristocracy and political party-based citizenship to an informed individual-based citizenship, but an abundance of information also complicated the individual's capacity to process at times highly complicated information. For Schudson, the digital era with its self-help media should produce "monitorial" citizens, not an informed and expert citizen who may or may not act on the wealth of information they have access to. Digital democracy, he argues, is overrated:

> most thinking about citizenship [in the digital era] is confined to the model of the individual informed citizen, and employs a rather rigid version of that model. I would like to offer an alternative. I propose that the obligation of citizens to know enough to participate intelligently in governmental affairs should be understood as a "monitorial" obligation. Citizens can be "monitorial" rather than informed. A monitorial citizen scans (rather than reads) the informational environment in a way so that he or she may be alerted on a very wide variety of issues for a very wide variety of ends and may be mobilized around those issues in a large variety of ways (http://web.mit.edu/comm-forum/papers/schudson.html).

To a large extent, monitorial citizens are not aloof observers, or "absentee citizens" as Schudson says, nor are they necessarily committed activists, but they are active participants in political life in as far as they are conscious of the importance of shared knowledge in a deliberative democracy. The same technology that has complicated their processing capacity is also helping them develop new skills in seeking and assessing existing information as well as producing competing information sources to challenge the interests of elite groups. In the case of Telestreet, some channels offer easy-to-follow kits on how to create grassroots television channels, while others provide technical tips on how to make effective videos using minimal technology. These attempts are meant to help citizens understand better the need to monitor public daily life and learn how to serve their own interests. As mentioned above, for many immigrant communities in Naples, for example, Insu^tv may be one of the rare options to have a window of representation and counter a stereotyped image in mainstream media of criminality and clandestine immigration. A peaceful street protest in 2007 by Ghanian and Nigerian immigrants in one Neapolitan neighborhood was fleetingly covered in the local media as yet another episode of inevitable violence of African immigrants. The protest, which was instigated by a shootout targeting a group of immigrants during a neighborhood party, was a peaceful attempt to complain about the lack of police intervention in cases where immigrants are the victims of violence. Insu^tv's migrant section broadcast many videos of the incident and featured long interviews with immigrants who were detained and subsequently released by the police. This kind of reporting provides a much-needed alternative perspective on vital issues affecting local communities, which are either ignored or caricatured by conventional media.

These individual-based initiatives of grassroots media production constitute new communication networks where power relations and the supremacy of political opinion are challenged. Telestreet is an example of what Manuel Castells calls "mass self-communication," a horizontal network of socialized communication that reaches wide audiences through the use of peer-to-peer media (2007). For Castells, this is the new stage where institutional power structures will be contested. While political battles in the pre-Internet era took place in the mass-media public sphere, today these battles for informational power are waged in peer-to-peer communication like blogs, wikis, social networks, and other creative digital platforms. As an extension to his theory of the "network society," Castells sees in the development of these citizen-generated media evidence that people in the network era do not merely have access to more information, but they use that wealth of information to create new competing knowledge cultures, increasingly forcing old media players to share a heretofore exclusive territory of information production.

There are many examples of this arguably leveled field of media power in various contexts: the popularity of blogs in France was crucial in mobilizing more people to vote against the ratification of the controversial European Union constitution. After the 2005 suburban riots in France, mainstream journalists were scrambling to understand a long-marginalized urban space beset by deep structural social and economic problems. Bondy Blog, a grassroots citizen journalism initiative in one of the Parisian suburbs, provided unprecedented access to daily life in these largely unknown and heavily caricatured neighborhoods. In the United States, viral videos through Youtube and other online video platforms have either embarrassed political candidates or rallied critical support behind Barack Obama's historic campaign for the presidential elections. Like Telestreet, such initiatives are creating a new category of networked publics whose critical importance is most likely to increase as more youth grow up more conversant in digital media in post-industrial societies.

CONCLUSION

In an era of globalization it seems more fitting to look at the edges to track down value in political and social action by individuals and small groups. The proliferation of small-scale initiatives on the margin continues to compete with the powerful presence of institutionalized political and media structures, complicating in the process the relationship between information producers and consumers. Some argue that this decentralization in the source of information is leading to a digital balkanization whereby people seek niche cultures they identify with and converge less and less in public spaces where democracy can be practiced through deliberation and consensus. The risk of fragmentation is not unfounded, and we can easily add to that the danger of the rampant conglomeration of previously individual sites in the hands of big corporate media, as in the case of News Corp. acquiring strategic social networks like MySpace or the growing use of copyright law by big media to limit competition from popular grassroots sources. But perhaps what is striking about this emerging network of new wired information producers and publics, and more particularly with cases like Telestreet, is the fact that people still show a profound sense of creative resistance even when the mechanisms of corporate control seem overwhelming. I do not wish to presume here an inherent liberating quality of technology, but the people who are using it creatively and outside of the structures of the market are reaping the benefits of their action, albeit in minimal fashion.

In the heavily conglomerated Italian media landscape Telestreet constitutes a refreshing beacon of hope despite its marginal position both geographically and in terms of audience reach. Its marginality, however, does by no means discount its strategic work within local communities. Given its simple means of production and small footprint its impact has been rather important, particularly when it filled the information gaps left by conventional media.

In conclusion, the Telestreet project forces us to re-center our research objectives around the important position of the local within the national. In Italy, the local is indeed a critical locus of major social, economic, cultural, and political action; and this local vibrancy is often obscured by the simplistic representation it meets in mainstream media. My focus on Telestreet is an attempt to redeem the local as a revealing paradigm of analysis of media globalization.

NOTES

1. For more technical details about the set up, see: www.radioalice.org/nuovatele street/index.php?module=subjects&func=viewpage&pageid=28.
2. For more historical background on Italian alternative media in the 1960s and 1970s and "free radios" in particular, see: Downing, 2000.
3. "Franco Berardi Bifo is a contemporary writer, media theorist, and media activist. He founded the magazine *A/traverso* (1975–1981) and was part of the staff of Radio Alice, the first free pirate radio station in Italy (1976–1978). Like others involved in the political movement of Autonomia in Italy during the 1970s, he fled to Paris, where he worked with Felix Guattari in the field of schizoanalysis. During the 1980s he contributed to the magazines *Semiotexte* (New York), *Chimerees* (Paris), *Metropoli* (Rome) and *Musica 80* (Milan). In the 1990s he published *Mutazione e Ciberpunk* (Genoa, 1993), *Cibernauti* (Rome, 1994), and *Felix* (Rome, 2001). He is currently collaborating on the magazine *Derive Approdi* as well as teaching social history of communication at the Accademia di Belle Arti in Milan." http://www.generation-online.org/p/pbifo.htm.
4. Personal interview with author, November 2007.
5. This percentage omits the number of illegal immigrants in the area, which is estimated to be around 40 percent of the overall immigrant population. For more details on the nature of migratory flows in Naples, see: Fusco Girardi, L. and Ian Chambers, "Il caso di Napoli, Italia: un modello spontaneo di integrazione," www.unhabitat.org/downloads/docs/Media/italian/WHD%20CS4%20-%20Naples%20(I).pdf.
6. The 2006 Censis Report on Immigration offers a detailed analysis of the media's representation of immigrants.

REFERENCES

Agrisano, Nicola. (2007). Personal Communication. November.
Andreucci, Giacomo. (2007). Personal Communication. November.
Castells, Manuel. (2007). "Communication, Power and Counter-power in the Network Society." *International Journal of Communication* 1: 238–266.
Downing, John. (2000). *Radical Media: Rebellious Communication and Social Movements*. New York: Sage.
European Union Parliamentary Assembly. (2004). "Monopolisation of the electronic media and possible abuse of power in Italy." Resolution 1378. http://assembly.coe.int/Documents/AdoptedText/ta04/ERES1387.htm.
Jenkins, Henry. (2006). *Convergence Culture: Where Old and New Media Collide*. New York: New York University Press.
Insu^tv. http://www.insutv.it/.
International Federation of Journalists. (2002) "Journalists Call for European Union-Leaders to Act over Media Mogul Berlusconi's Conflict of Interest." January 29.

http://www.ifj.org/en/articles/journalists-call-for-european-union-leaders-to-act-over-media-mogul-berlusconis-conflict-of-interest.

Radio Alice. http://www.radioalice.org/.

Schudson, Michael. (1998). "Changing Concepts of Democracy," http://web.mit.edu/comm-forum/papers/schudson.html.

Telecitofono. http://www.telecitofono.it/mambo/.

Teleosservanza. http://www.teleosservanza.it/.

"Telestreet Rome." *ZNet: The Spirit of Resistance Lives.* Oct. 4, 2003. www.zmag.org/znet/viewArticle/9746.

Chapter Ten

Web-Based Technologies in Media and Cultural Production: Emerging Evidence from Italian Web-TVs and Web-Radios

Lorenzo Mizzau, Federico Riboldazzi, and Fabrizio Montanari

INTRODUCTION

The aim of this chapter is to study the effect of the diffusion of web-based media technologies in Italy, and in particular, web-radios and web-tvs, on the issues of access and diversity in media and in cultural production. Our aim is to give a snapshot view of the situation of Italian web-radios and web-tvs, in order to shed some light on the potential for increased access and diversity through the use of new ubiquitous technologies. In other words, we will try to answer the following questions: do web-radios and web-tvs in Italy increase access and diversity of the media and cultural production and distribution systems? In which way does it happen? By web-radios and web-tvs, we mean those websites whose main activity is to deliver audio or video content to Internet users prevalently through the streaming technology (Barberini 2006; Bonini 2006). Aggregators of several single initiatives (e.g., Pandora, live365.com) are thus excluded, as our inquiry concentrates on single, individual initiatives with a distinct editorial function.

In this paper, we want to combine the debates on new media with those on the global and the local characters of media and culture products. On the one side, globalization stimulates different types of convergence (of corporate ownership, cultural forms, and communication systems), which seems to increase the potential for globalising media and cultural production by the entertainment multinationals, eliminating the specificities of each local context (e.g., Hesmondhalgh 2002; Tunstall 1994). On the other, media and cultural artifacts seem in many cases to be still grounded in particular geographic, social, and cultural contexts (e.g., Coyle 2006; Mizzau and Montanari 2008; Peterson 1997; Scott 1999). Our basic claim is that web-radios and web-tvs constitute an efficient and flexible means of communication that enhances the possibility for local media and cultural "actors" to come into existence, develop and reach their (local and global, actual and potential) audiences. The evidence about Italian web-radios and web-tvs, in fact, seem to indicate that while this particular means of communication allows for global transmission, its low-cost, high-flexibility features made it an ideal means to stimulate local, small-scale, and "marginal" initiatives, that would have been impossible to set up with the traditional technology and economic structure of broadcasting radio (because of, for example, the overcrowding of frequencies).

Our evidences will be drawn from Italian web-radios and web-tvs, through a qualitative analysis based on multiple case-studies methodology (Eisenhardt 1989). In particular, we combine data deriving from a previous research based on in-depth interviews of Italian web-radios and web-tvs founders and managers (Ordanini, Mizzau, and De Leonardis 2007), secondary data and web search methods to carry out a census of the web-radios and web-tvs operating in Italy, and a textual content analysis of the websites of several web-radios and web-tvs aimed to classification purposes. These techniques are all directed to demonstrate how web-radios and web-tvs are able to enhance both the diversity of content offered by the media and the access to the media by both the "supply" (i.e., founders and professionals) and the "demand" (i.e., users) sides. The paper is divided in three sections. The first section illustrates the theoretical background and motivations behind the study. The second section presents some empirical evidences and examples of web-radios and web-tvs in Italy. The last section discusses the results and draws a few theoretical conclusions that map the role of web-radios and web-tvs in the general discussion of global and local media in Italy.

WEB-BASED TECHNOLOGIES: ACCESS, DIVERSITY AND DYNAMICS OF GLOCALIZATION IN MEDIA AND CULTURAL PRODUCTION

There is significant evidence that illustrates why web-based technologies can play a critical role in increasing access and diversity in media and cultural production. The first factor is cost reduction. By reducing economic constraints and facilitating production and transmission of content, web-based technologies open up new opportunities to a larger number of potential 'senders.' As we will show in the case of web-radios and web-tvs in Italy, the investment required to set up a high-quality web transmission is considerably lower if compared with an over-the-air transmission. The first scenario only requires a pc connected to the web, a microphone or stereo equipment interface, and a portion of Internet bandwidth (Coyle 2006; Mühlenfeld 2002).[1] According to Menduni (2006: 91), "an internet radio does not require licenses, frequencies or authorizations, it allows for avoiding administrative hurdles, saving costs and overcoming censorship, and can be heard worldwide at extremely low costs." Web-radios and webt-tvs give the possibility to overcome the bottleneck of the limited availability of frequencies, which enormously raises the costs of access for every over-the-air media system operating within a regulated environment.

In particular, financial advantages increase access for local, small or marginal operators, for example community-based radios, which are faced with difficulties in both fund raising and operating costs, since they lack huge financial resources and cannot count on extensive advertising markets given their limited audiences. As Coyer (2006) asserts, internet radio addresses the problems of scarcity, as "a means for circulating information and culture irrespective of geographic boundaries and as a means of subverting the dilemma of scarcity within the limited analogue bandwidth" (2006: 129).

The positive impact of the Internet on access and diversity also relies on potential advantages in terms of diffusion and consumption of cultural products. One of the most influential accounts in this respect, Anderson's (2006) theory of the "long tail" concentrates on the opportunities offered by the massive digitalization of cultural products combined with the widespread diffusion of the Internet. His key point addresses the issue of diversity and choice, and the "democracy" of the tools of production, distribution and connection, which depend on the "tyranny of locality." This means that audiences are geographically dispersed and thus required to be reached by physical distribution. The problem here is the necessity for every cultural product to have a potential audience within a narrow geographical area. "It's not enough for a great documentary to have a potential national audience of half a million; what matters is how much of an audience it has in the northern part of Rockville, Maryland" (Anderson 2006: 17). In this view, this problem has the same consequences as the limited frequency availability of broadcasting: "The radio spectrum can carry only so many stations, and a coaxial cable only so many TV channels. And, of course, there are only twenty-four hours of programming a day. The curse of broadcast technologies is that they are profligate users of limited resources" (Anderson 2006: 18). The cultural products market has responded to these limitations by offering products with a great potential for filling theatres, fly off shelves, and create fidelity in the radio and TV audiences (i.e. music hits, blockbusters movies, and best sellers). Of course, this represents a great limitation to diversity in cultural production, since a few titles (the most promising ones) tend to fill all the physical space for cultural products, leaving apart myriads of commercially less appealing, yet potentially valid products. According to (Anderson 2006: 18), however, times are changing: "now, with online distribution and retail, we are entering the world of abundance." In fact, thanks to the Internet, access (for niche products to distribution and for consumers to niches) is facilitated, because niche titles become profitable just as their demand expands due to the fact that they are acquired in aggregate high volumes.[2]

Positive accounts on the effects of the global interconnectedness (Hendy 2000) favoured by the Internet are supported by several influential approaches in sociology and sociology of culture (e.g., Beck 1997; Robertson 1992), cultural studies (e.g., Featherstone 1990), and economic geography (e.g., Mizzau and Montanari 2008; Scott 2000). These studies, that somewhat counterbalance the approaches that emphasize the possible negative effects of the enhanced globalization process of the last years, include Power and Scott's (2004) comments on the two last trends occurring in the field of cultural industries: the localization of cultural production, on one hand, and the globalization of cultural distribution and consumption, on the other. Power and Scott see these two processes as complementary, with the positive effect that "many different cultural styles and genres become accessible to far-flung consumers so that highly specialized niche markets are also proliferating alongside the blockbuster markets in which major corporations largely participate" (Power and Scott 2004: 11). In sum, according to these argumentations, the Internet-enhanced "globalization does not appear to be leading to cultural uniformity so much as it increases the variety of options open to individual consumers" (Power and Scott 2004: 13). This aspect of globalization supports our idea of increased diversity in media and cultural productions. In other words, web technologies seem to open up new opportunities to local actors and, thus, improve access and diversity in media and cultural production.

WEB-RADIOS AND WEB-TVS IN ITALY

The goal of this paragraph is to give a snapshot view of the situation of Italian web-radios and web-tvs, in order to shed some light on the potential for increased access and diversity through the use of new ubiquitous technologies. In other words, we will try to answer the following questions: do web-radios and web-tvs in Italy increase access and diversity of the media and cultural production and distribution systems? In which way does it happen?

Before coming to web-radios and web-tvs, it might be useful to analyze some peculiar features of the Italian radio and TV industry at large. The Italian media context has been characterized since the 1980s by a progressive increase in the price of licences requested to transmit (Menduni 2001). In the last years, the number of radio broadcasters with a national license has ranged between 15 and 20, while the panel of local authorized radio stations monitored by Audiradio (2007) comprised in 2006 less than 100 organizations of some relevance. Nonetheless, Italy has traditionally been characterized by a vibrant community of radio founders (Menduni 2006) and by large, supportive and loyal audiences, as the same Audiradio inquiries testify. Italian radio broadcasting experts (Menduni 2006; Fenati and Scaglioni 2002) argue that Italy hosted the largest number of radio enterprises in the world after the United States, but the saturation of FM frequencies since the 1980s has considerably limited the possibility for small organizations to gain access to a regular frequency, thus increasing the level of the entry barriers for this kind of medium. Moreover, even though the Italian law on communication grants some financial support to all media, there are no "alternative" models for local, small, or niche media, such as, for example, the öffene Kanale in Germany—a particular institutional form of media which is granted financial support by federal and regional governments and requires particular licences, aimed at supporting minorities or community needs (Mühlenfeld 2002).

As far as national TV broadcasters, Italy is characterized by a duopoly in which RAI (the Italian public radio and television company) and Mediaset (the largest Italian private television company) are the most important players. The influence of these two companies and their ability to gather most of the financial resources available both from public funds and advertising, leave very little space to new potential competitors to gain access to the market. As a result, national TV in Italy offers very little diversity. Nevertheless, the landscape of local TV seems to be more vibrant, since local TV channels are increasingly playing a relevant role. In 2006 there were in Italy more than 1,000 local TV channels, and while the national broadcasters have experienced a period of economic stagnation, local televisions in the last ten years have more than doubled their income from advertising—while the total revenue from commercials for local channels in 1994 was around 190 millions euros, in 2004 it has exceeded 400 million Euros (Pedrali 2005; Grasso 2006).

The main reason for the increasing role played by local radio and TV is to be found in their ability to answer local audiences' needs. Local TVs seem more able to understand and value local identities by producing programs (e.g. shows, news, music, etc.) consistent with the specific needs of their local audiences. For example, if national broadcasters mainly produce generalist programs targeted for a national audience, local TVs differentiate themselves by addressing themes more relevant for their specific audiences. This is consistent with the regionalist forces that have always characterized Italy from a cultural, historical, and social point of view, as a very fragmented nation.

Moreover the local could be interpreted not only in a geographical sense, but also, to some extent, as a synonym of community-based, marginal, niche, emergent, new, innovative—anything that is not established, non-mainstream and, thus, not (yet) global. Consistently with this broader interpretation of the sense of local, we analyze the emerging scenario of the Italian web-radios and web-tvs highlighting how such localism can be deployed in such different ways, different from a purely interpretation. In doing so, we will present some examples of web-radios and web-tvs according to the classification proposed by the work of Ordanini et al. (2007). In particular, we will underline some general features shared by different categories of players such as: (1) players driven by personal/amateur/social aims (i.e., the need for expression or sharing of content and ideas); (2) players driven by institutional aims, such as to promote, extend, or facilitate communication among participants to an institution; and (3) players driven by commercial aims, such as those pursued by new established for profit companies or by traditional broadcasters, which create a new web division in order to expand their customer base beyond the constraints of the over-the-air frequencies, to extend their brand, or develop a community of customers.

THE CASE OF ITALIAN WEB-RADIOS

It is hard to determine the exact number of web-radios in Italy, because of the relative novelty of the phenomenon and the rapidly changing rates in industry players' birth and mortality typically associated with such businesses. According to recent reports (Ordanini et al. 2007), however, in 2007 it ranged between approximately 150 and 300.

Among the web-radios with personal, amateur, and social aims, Radio Officina Talenti Emergenti was founded by three friends with the aim of "creating something new in the Italian musical panorama," because most Italian radios are "totally undifferentiated: they talk about horoscopes, weather and stuff like that, and they transmit always the same music" (www.radiofficina.com). For this reason Radio Officina Talenti Emergenti deliberately excludes mainstream music and uses the web-radio as a complement to other activities such as concerts, interviews, and music reviews. Among the most famous amateur stations is also Lolli Radio, founded by Marco Lolli, an experienced professional director of radio programmes on the national public channel RAI-Radio2. Marco Lolli has developed his personal idea of an "easy" or "happy" format, covering "trash" music such as cartoon soundtracks. In an interview reported by Ordanini et al. (2007), he reveals how experimentation of new formats is intrinsically inhibited by the over-the-air context, due to the cost of licenses that, for example, amount to several millions of Euros for a local frequency in Rome. Thus, these two examples seem to support our thesis that web-radios can improve the level of access and diversity of content.

In the case of institutional web-radios, Radio LUISS (powered by LUISS, Libera Università Internazionale degli Studi Sociali, a private university based in Rome), was founded with the aim to "contribute to the vitality and the social life of the university through a 'place' where the students can meet each other in every moment" (Ordanini et al. 2007). Radio LUISS transmits via cable every weekday for seven hours throughout the university spaces such as corridors, restaurants, etc., and is streamed via web all day, seven days a week, reaching students that are, for example, at home in the evening and on the weekends, or those that are studying abroad as exchange students. Radio LUISS is one of the radio stations joining the inter-university web-radio initiative Unyonair. The Unyonair project started at the beginning of 2007 and was promoted by Radio24 (a national FM broadcaster derived from the newspaper Il Sole 24 Ore), in 2007 comprising 40 university web-radios all over Italy. The main goal is to help universities build their own web-radios to "stimulate debates, socialization and active participation to the life of the campuses, reinforcing the sense of belonging to a more vibrant university community" (www.unyonair.it), and to provide them with the necessary organizational, economic, editorial, and technical skills. The enthusiastic response by many Italian universities testifies to the needs of identity enforcement, "artistic expression and promotion of culture," as the students of Milano Bicocca University declare (www.b-radio.net), and external visibility of the institutions, which is made possible by the setting up of a web-radio.

Not only can universities reach their students even when they are at home as we have just seen; arts institutions are to benefit from the cost- and flexibility-related advantages of web-radios and web-tvs. This is the case, for example, of Radio Papesse, the web-radio of the renown contemporary art center Papesse di Siena, which takes part in the international web-radio network live365.com, whose aim is to follow "the life of the museum: the artists' voices, the moments of creativity, the interviews, and the literary and musical events organised by the Center" (www.radiopapesse.org). Radio Papesse, then, becomes "a community radio, but with an enlarged target: the casual visitor and the art expert, the art hobbyist and the profane" (www.radiopapesse.org). The possibility to reach an enlarged target for a content niche is evident also in the case of Indisound, whose manifesto asserts that it is pursuing "the promotion of independent Italian and European music" (www.indisound.net), which finds it difficult to be programmed on traditional, over-the-air channels. To this aim, the association is financed through private donations, a model usually uncommon in Italy, except for certain political media outlets (Menduni 2001). In this way, Indisound supports niche, emergent musicians that are able to reach enlarged audiences, and give the latter the possibility to follow their preferred emergent artists bypassing the popularity-based selection criteria of major radios and media in general. Other examples include web-radios of municipal and regional governments, and opinion and political movements, particularly minority political parties such as Radio Umanista. In sum, these Italian institutional web-radios prove to be efficient and flexible tools for increasing access and diversity in the Italian media landscape, since they satisfy important institutional needs of communication and participation unattended by traditional media.

Finally, as far as commercial web-radios are concerned, Radio SNJ is one of the most heard among the pure webcasters[3] (with around 10,000 listeners per average day). Radio SNJ is a Milan-based venture, whose founders declare that "we made it because we were radio fans, and we were not standing any more the kind of music on the traditional programmes" (Ordanini et al. 2007). This position echoes the one from the director of Radio Rana, Patrick Domanico, another commercial web-caster who appeared on the Italian scene in 2001. When founding this Bologna-based web-radio, his main preoccupation was "to give visibility to emerging artists," who find it hard to be programmed on mainstream circuits (Ordanini et al., 2007).

According to Bonini (2006), who interviewed several pioneers of Italian web-radios (such as Samuele Agosti, co-founder of SNJ Radio)), these are typical motivations for the foundation of web-radios all over the world. Apart from economic concerns, many commercial web-radios are directed to the enhancement of the musical diversity through programming niche content, which would not have the chance to be listened to on mainstream media (e.g., Radio SNJ and Radio Rana above). Other examples of commercial niche web-radios include Orion radio (emerging artists), radioPromoClassica (classical), Onda Tropical (latin), and the FM-derived multi-channel web-radios 105 (e.g., Hip-Hop/R'n'B, Rock, Classics) and Radio MonteCarlo (Chill-out, Love songs, Film), which expand and differentiate their offer through the web.[4] These cases, also, seem to demonstrate that web-radios constitute an effective means for increasing the diversity of content programmed also among the commercial, for-profit organizations, thus benefiting to the overall community of Italian listeners.

THE CASE OF ITALIAN WEB-TVS

When analysing the most prominent examples of Italian web-tvs, we will use the same classification based on the aims of the organizations employed for web-radios and proposed by Ordanini et al. (2007).

The spread of web-tvs with personal/amateur/social aims in Italy originates in the diffusion of personal blogs and videoblogs (Tessarolo 2007). Among them, the blog of Italian comedian Beppe Grillo represents the main example of the capacity of the web to valorize counter-institutional contents. Beppe Grillo started his career in RAI in the late 1970s. Through his satirical monologues about politics, economy, and environmental issues he became the most famous and controversial Italian comedian. His personal blog and videoblog (www.beppegrillo.it) deal with social and political issues, and have quickly become among the most popular ones not only in Italy, but also internationally. According to his founder, the Internet is the place for doing "true politics, connected to work, school, health, safety, the family, water and energy management" (www.beppegrillo.it). Thanks to his blog, Beppe Grillo has supported many campaigns to make Italian citizens aware of social and political issues usually ignored by traditional broadcasters.

In September 2007, for example, Grillo organized a national "protest day" (the V-Day) during which he collected over 300,000 signatures to promote the approval of a new law called "Clean Parliament." One of the aims of the law is to deny eligibility for members of the Italian parliament to those officially convicted of crime. The success of the event did not depend on any massive promotion through traditional broadcasters, but on Grillo's ability to create a web-based national and international community of users. Furthermore, during V-Day, the public speech that Beppe Grillo held to present the 'Clear Parliament' initiative was video-streamed live by Ecotv.it, a web-tv recently born in Milan, while being completely ignored by any other traditional TV channels. Despite this lack of "official media" coverage, the show was watched by Internet users in more than sixty-five countries all over the world, and in Italy it gained more audience than Al Gore's international hit Live Earth (Unknown 2007).

Beppe Grillo's initiatives and the activity of Ecotv.it provide evidence about the possibility for niche (or amateur) social media to become national information outlets and to reach larger audiences, drawn by the relevance of the themes discussed that are difficult to reach through traditional broadcasting platforms (Grillo's initiatives are often counter-establishment and critical about the policies of many telecommunication corporations, which are the owners of many of the large broadcasters in Italy). This is very much to the fore when it comes to politics, since many Italian web-tvs are very related to the goal of spreading political ideas. Nessuno.tv, for example, was founded in 2005 with the aim of gathering personal blogs and videoblogs in one website. Initially, Nessuno.tv distributed generalist content both on the web and on a digital TV channel. Then, in 2006, it changed its core activity, and specialized in politics, becoming the "first political television in Italy" (www.nessuno.tv).

Similarly, the web-tv of the non-profit organization Arcoiris aims at being an alternative to RAI and Mediaset for political shows and news. On Arcoiris .tv there are no commercials, and movies, short films, and documentaries are downloadable for free by the users. Recently Arcoiris.tv has also begun to offer online lessons where amateur directors are trained to produce high quality short movies and documentaries addressing social and political issues, generally not covered by national broadcasters. Again, the main goal of such initiatives is to increase the number of user-generated content and to ease the access of minor political movements to larger audiences.

As far as institutional players are concerned, Italian Municipalities constitute a clear example of how web-tvs can benefit institutions' needs mainly dedicated to inform users about any kind of news related to their local environment. In web-tvs such as florence.tv, messinawebtv.it, or fvg.tv (the web-tv of the Italian Autonomous Region Friuli-Venezia Giulia), users can find news on the weather, interviews of local politicians, as well as reportages of the main events occurring in their respective geographic areas. These initiatives gained large audiences since they responded well to the localist attitude of Italian audiences, which is not satisfied by national broadcasters. Such web-tvs, in order to reach the valorization of local identities, try also to strengthen the relationships with their audience by asking their users to upload videos that document any kind of relevant event they paricipate in. This is the case of c6.tv, a web-tv specialized in the production of content generated in Milan, with daily materials (i.e. videos, interviews) uploaded by its users.

Also several universities have launched institutional web-tvs with the aim to develop a strong organizational identity through a virtual socializing place where students can find news about classes, events, and everything related to the life in the university (e.g., bocconi.tv, the web-tv of Bocconi University, and unimore.tv, the web-tv of Modena and Reggio Emilia University). As far as web-tvs with commercial aims, many of them are influenced by the model of successful Internet companies that promote the sharing of user-generated content. One of the first to appear in 2000 was mytv.it. This website became popular in 2001 thanks to the cartoon series Gino il Pollo (Gino the Chicken). The cartoon was originally a parody of Bush's war against Bin Laden and the terrorism in Afghanistan, and after its success, it became a cartoon series for children co-produced by RAI, the public media company in Italy. In 2006, the website mytv.it underwent some drastic changes increasing the importance of user-generated content and interactivity, with a new layout of the website that clearly resembles the one of YouTube. The main goal of this initiative is to imitate a model that has succeeded in the global scenery, the YouTube format, promoting at the same time local contents (i.e. videos produced mainly by Italian users). Similar intents can be noticed also on TheBlogTV, another example of Italian web-tv focused on user-generated content. For example TheBlogTV has launched an initiative called Il mio paese (My country). The initiative consists of asking users to produce home-made videos that document their everyday lives in their local contexts. The best videos will be edited together in a unique feature documentary by popular Italian director Daniele Vicari. This example also supports our thesis that web-tvs contribute to enhancing the possibility of success of, in particular, local players. By getting inspiration from global successful websites like YouTube, Nessuno.tv and TheBlogTV succeed in increasing the participation and sharing of local content, which would have been difficult to replicate on traditional media channels.

Web-tvs are also becoming powerful instruments of brand extension for private companies. In 2006, Telecom Italia (the biggest Italian telecommunications company which also owns the majority of shares of M-Tv Italia channel) launched a web-based project named Flux. The intent of Flux was to alternatively promote young artists and musicians—who are usually not programmed by traditional broadcasters—by collecting user generated content to be shown on a specific TV channel. In November 2006, Flux became QOOB, and the TV channel was moved to the digital television of Telecom Italia Media while the website qoob.it keeps collecting user generated videos to be shown on digital television.

In sum, it seems that web-tvs are as effective as web-radios in promoting the interests of existing organizations and increasing the level of access and participation to the life of them, otherwise limited by the rigidity and cost of traditional broadcasting media or the cost of dedicated alternative media (e.g., satellite, digital terrestrial transmission).

SUMMARY AND CONCLUSIONS

In this paper, we demonstrated how web-based technologies allow media and cultural products to become more accessible and diversified, enhancing, thus, the overall diversity of information and cultural offer. As we showed, this scenario is favoured by several factors, such as lower costs and increased efficiency in the selection processes (Anderson 2006; Coyle 2006). Accordingly, web-radios and web-tvs seem to constitute an effective means of communication, that can enhance the possibility for relevant media and cultural players to come into existence and reach their audiences, and particularly those who have difficulties in reaching the public necessary to their economic survival (local, niche, marginal, or minor actors).

This issue may be considered of particular interest in Italy, given the characteristics of its media and cultural context. On one side, the Italian broadcasting market presents a high degree of concentration and consolidation: national radios are only 18 among hundreds of limited-coverage stations, while television is characterized by a duopoly between the publicly funded RAI and the privately owned Mediaset, just scratched by the presence of Telecom Italia-owned 'third pole' (La7 and M-Tv Italia). On the other, local TVs and radios are increasingly playing a relevant role by producing programs consistent with the specific identities and needs of their local audiences—an important issue in Italy where regionalism is particularly present.

In such a context, in which alternative media channels (e.g., satellite and digital terrestrial) do not prove to be successful in meeting the audience's needs (Grasso 2006), the web appears to open up new opportunities for local actors, which, in turn, improve the overall degree of access and diversity in the media. Drawing on examples from the continuously evolving world of web-radios and web-tvs, we claim that this can happen not only for local actors who share a common geographic territory or live in close proximity, but also, for community-based, marginal, niche, emergent or innovative forms of media and cultural production. In this way, we believe that such advantages apply to local (e.g., Radio Capri, Amiata Radio, Sorrento Radio), marginal (Rete Gay and Radio DeeGay), niche (LolliRadio, Indisound), and community-based (Radio LUISS and other university web-radios, Arcoiris) actors.

However, some issues are posed for web-radios and web-tvs, regarding in particular the possibility to be effective in increasing access and diversity. First, although the number of Italian households with broadband connections grew notably over the last years, an intra-national digital divide between those accessing the web and those who cannot is still highly significant (ISTAT 2006). Second, as Ordanini et al. (2007) conclude, the economic sustainability of the commercial independent web-radio and web-tv model is a matter of discussion, until advertising and rating agencies will shift to more web-oriented metrics. Thus, high-quality niche initiatives will be difficult to implement, not allowing for a full exploitation of the medium potential. Operating cost issues, for both web-radios and web-tvs, lead us also to consider that the commercial business model does not differ much from that of a traditional broadcaster, since economies of scale in editorial and marketing costs persist. Further, we agree with Mühlenfeld's (2002) idea of the web-radios 'success trap,' namely, the proportional growth of bandwidth costs with the increase in the number of visitors (and the same is true also for web-tvs).

Nevertheless, as far as our explorative study indicates, it seems that the Italian situation allows for more access and diversity than, for example, the U.S. situation after the CARP fee model release in 2002 (Lessig 2002)—further exacerbated by the May 15, 2007 decision to heighten the fees for the operation of web-radios—which constrained many web-radios to shut down.

The Italian context seems also to leave open more possibilities if compared to the German situation depicted by Mühlenfeld (2002), in which economic constraints affect the survival possibility of all kinds of web-radios, due to the particular license to be obtained by webcasters. This holds even if Ordanini et al. (2007) report that the situation of Italian web-radios is far from being stable from a regulatory point of view: they report that some agreements between the two Italian copyright collective societies (SIAE and SCF) have been reached and are on the way to be attended by an increasing number of operators.

Finally, it seems important to highlight that, even though we concentrated particularly on single, independent web initiatives here, future scenarios let us foresee an increasing importance of "automated channels" (e.g., automatic playlist construction tools such as last.fm or Apple's iTunes webradio services) and user-generated content websites, however with an apparently contradictory tendency. On one side, multinational web-services providers have launched and refined their musical services based on multiple web-radios' aggregation, such as Pandora or live365.com, obtaining significant audience responses (Arbitron 2006). On the other, user-generated content sites such as YouTube or mySpace.com have grown enormously in popularity and share value—just consider the costly acquisitions of the two websites, respectively, by Google and News Corp. All these examples, anyway, suggest in our opinion that local- or independent-originated innovation and diversity of content is sustained by new technologies and globalization forces (Mizzau and Montanari 2008), rather than being hampered by them, and will never be suppressed as vital stimuli are constantly requested by large operators and particularly multinational conglomerates, to gain visibility and market shares in a ceaselessly competitive media and cultural consumption world.

NOTES

1. The same argument is true also for operating costs, with some important differences which we will treat in the concluding paragraph of this paper.
2. Recently, it seems that the time is ripe for a modification of the gatekeeping traditional theories, developed for both media and cultural products in the realms of sociology of media (McQuail, 2000) and cultural economics (Hirsch, 1991). Their basic assumption is that the supply of any kind of content (information, cultural products, etc.) has to be mediated from its source to the recipient(s) by some entities (typically mass media): accordingly, this process of filtering is necessary because of oversupply, specialization of audiences and limited attention spans (Hesmondhalgh, 2002; Kretschmer et al., 1999). What seems to be changed in the new, web-technologies scenario, is that the gatekeepers are in the final parts of the value chain, and often

coincide with consumers themselves, who influence each other through (specialized) user communities made available by Internet. Examples can be blogs, peer-to-peer and file-sharing websites such as Youtube or mySpace, recommendation lists, and web-radios and web-tvs (Anderson 2006).

3. Another useful classification of web-radios, apart from the one proposed by Ordanini et al. (2007), distinguishes between "pure webcasters" and "broadcasters that transmit also through the web," identifying differences in the approach to the web by each of these categories (Ordanini et al. 2007). While pure webcasters are often amateurial and cannot count on relevant investments, traditional broadcasters transfer their expertise on the web, drawing on their financial resources; however, it seems like traditional broadcasters consider, so far, the web as an accessory tool, to be used for aims of consolidation of the existing audience or offer of extra-content such as recordings of past programs, etc. Therefore, pure webcasters exhibit more innovative models, based on a consideration of the web as a medium with its own specificities and completely different from the "air" (Ordanini et al. 2007).

4. 105 Classics, for example, is transmitted on a single FM frequency available in Milan, Turin, and Genua. On the web, 105 and 105 Classics offer 10 different channels.

REFERENCES

Anderson, Chris. *The Long Tail: Why the Future is Selling Less of More*. New York: Hyperion, 2006.

Arbitron. "ComScore Arbitron Rated Online Radio Networks." 2006. www.arbitron.com/onlineradio/home.htm (accessed October 12, 2006).

Beck, Ulrich. *Was ist Globalisierung? Irrtüumer des Globalismus—Antworten auf Globalisierung*. Frankfurt/Main: Suhrkamp Verlag, 1997.

Bonini, Tiziano. *La Radio nella Rete. Storia, Estetica, Usi Sociali*. Milano: costa & nolan, 2006.

Coyle, Rebecca. "Ether to 01. Digitizing radio" (Editorial). *Convergence*, 12, no. 2 (2006): 123–127.

Coyer, Katie. "Community Radio Licensing and Policy." *Global Media and Communication*, 2, no. 1 (2006): 129–134.

Eisenhardt, K. M. "Building Theories from Case Study Research," *Academy of Management Review*, 14, no. 4 (1989): 532–550.

Featherstone, Michael. "Global Culture: an Introduction," in *Global Culture: Nationalism, Globalisation, and Modernity*, edited by M. Featherstone. London: Sage, 1990.

Grasso Aldo. La TV del sommerso. *Viaggio nell'Italia delle TV locali*. Milano: Mondadori, 2006.

Hendy, David. *Radio in the Global Age*. Cambridge: Polity Press, 2000.

Hesmondalgh, David. *Cultural Industries*, London: Sage, 2002.

Hirsch, Paul. M. "Processing Fads and Fashions: An Organization Set Analysis of Cultural Industries Systems," 313–34 in *Rethinking Popular Culture: Contempo-*

rary Perspectives in Cultural Studies, edited by C. Mukerji and M. Schudson. Los Angeles: University of California Press, 1991.

ISTAT. "Annual report on the diffusion of technological devices among Italian people." 2006. www.istat.it (accessed September 19, 2006).

Kretschmer, Martin, George Klimis, and Chong Choi, "Increasing Returns and Social Contagion in Cultural Industries." *British Journal of Management*, Vol. 10 (1999): 61–72.

McQuail, Danny. *Mass Communications Theory*. London: Sage, 2000.

Menduni, Enrico. *I Linguaggi della Radio e della Televisione*, Roma-Bari: Laterza, 2006.

———. *Il Mondo della Radio: Dal Transistor a Internet*, Bologna: Il Mulino, 2001.

Mizzau, Lorenzo and Fabrizio Montanari. "Cultural Districts and the Challenge of Authenticity: The Case of Piedmont, Italy," *Journal of Economic Geography*, 8 (September 2008): 651–673.

Mühlenfeld, Hans. "Mass Communication as Participation: Web-Radio in Germany: Legal Hazards and its Contribution to an Alternative Way of Mass Communication," *European Journal of Communication*, 17, no. 1 (2002): 103–113.

Ordanini, Andrea, Lorenzo Mizzau, and Marta De Leonardis. *Le Webradio in Italia*. Research report. Milano: Centro di ricerca ASK, Università Bocconi, 2007.

Pedrali, I. "Televisioni Locali e Minimal TV," 123–147 in *Neotelevisione: Elementi di un Linguaggio Catodico Glocal/E*, edited by M. Pecchioli, Milano: costa & nolan, 2005.

Peterson, Richard .A. *Creating Country Music: Fabricating Authenticity*. Chicago: University of Chicago Press, 1997.

Power, Dominique and Allen J. Scott, eds. *Cultural Industries and the Production of Culture*. London: Routledge, 2004.

Scott, Allen J. *The Cultural Economy of Cities—Essays on the Geography of Image-Producing Industries*. London: Sage, 2000.

———. "The US Recorded Music Industry: on the Relations between Organization, Location and Creativity in the Cultural Economy." *Environment and Planning*, 31 (1999): 1965–1984.

Tessarolo, Tommaso. *Net TV. Come Internet Cambierà la Televisione per Sempre*. Milano: APOGEO, 2007.

Unknown. "Grillo Fa Tremare la Politica Italiana," *La Stampa*, September 10, 2007.

Part Four

IMMIGRATION AND DIVERSITY

Chapter Eleven

Missed Opportunities: The Debate on Immigrants' Voting Rights in Italian Newspapers and Television

Cristian Vaccari

This chapter addresses the way in which the Italian mainstream media covered a policy proposal advanced in late 2003 by Gianfranco Fini, who was then Vice Prime Minister of a center-right government led by Silvio Berlusconi. During a conference on European immigration policy held at the Italian National Council of the Economy and Work (CNEL), a public institute that provides consulting to the Government and Parliament, Fini said that legal immigrants should be given the right to vote in local elections, a policy apparently inconsistent with the center-right coalition's alleged hard-line stance on immigration. The statement spurred a bitter controversy, which lasted for about a month. Although eventually no legislative overhaul occurred, Fini's proposal could have significantly changed the dynamics of the country's public discourse if it had been taken as a starting point to debate crucial substantive issues such as globalization, national identity, the coexistence of different ethnicities and cultures, and long-term immigration policies. With a little help from politicians, the media could have provided a crucial contribution to such a debate. This study, however, shows that, quite to the contrary, journalists and politicians, bound by the collusive relationship that is typical of the Italian system, turned the debate on Fini's proposal into a matter of political posturing, and thus missed an opportunity for a substantive public policy discussion that is long overdue in Italian society.

To prove such an argument, this article starts by offering a brief overview of immigration in Italy and its representation in the media, then analyzes the implications of Fini's proposal and addresses the way in which three Italian newspapers and four television channels covered it. Results clearly show that most of the media coverage adopted a "political" framing of the story, rather than a "policy" framing, and focused mostly on relationships between political parties and leaders, treating Fini's proposal as an attempt to gain influence in the coalition and a more appealing image among voters. If coverage had focused on policy, however, it could have elicited a substantive discussion on how immigration should be dealt with in the long run and how political rights should be conceived and granted in an ever-changing world. Our evidence suggests that the media did very little to promote a public conversation on the meaning of immigration for national identity and citizenship. The Italian political communication system is still poorly equipped to deal with complex issues related to globalization.

IMMIGRATION IN ITALY: CITIZENS' ATTITUDES, POLICY RESPONSES, AND MEDIA COVERAGE

After being a country of emigration in the nineteenth and a large part of the twentieth century, Italy is now undoubtedly a country of immigration (Colombo & Sciortino, 2004). According to the Italian Institute of Statistics (ISTAT), on January 1, 2006 foreigners living in Italy amounted to 2,670,514, about 4.5 percent of the whole Italian population. Other studies, which include estimates of irregular immigrants, set the figure at almost four million, or about 7 percent of the population (Fondazione ISMU, 2007). As figure 11.1 shows, Italy did not experience significant inflows of immigrants until the early 1990s, when many Albanians landed on its South-Eastern coastline after the collapse of their country's national-communist regime (Mai, 2005). Since then, the number of documented immigrants in Italy has grown almost tenfold. The first significant law regulating immigration was passed in 1990, followed by reforms in 1998 and 2002. Although immigration in Italy increased steadily from 1993 onwards, the number of legal residents experienced large fluctuations due to large-scale amnesties in 1990, 1995, and 2002.

Immigration in Italy displays five distinguishing traits (Grillo, 2002). First, unlike in France and Britain, there is not one single major group in terms of ethnicity or country of origin that constitutes the bulk of immigrants in the country. Currently, the five most represented countries of origin are Albania, Morocco, Romania, China, and Ukraine. Sixteen nationalities comprise slightly less than fifty percent of total immigrants, thus making this population very diverse in terms of language, religion, ethnicity, and customs. Second, immigration from former Italian colonies is a marginal factor, as the country's role in colonialism was limited compared to other European former empires. Italy's colonial possessions included Eritrea (1884–1941), Somalia (1890–1941), Libya (1911–1943), Ethiopia (1936–1941), Albania (1939–1943), and the Dodecanese, a group of Greek islands (1912–1943). Third, a

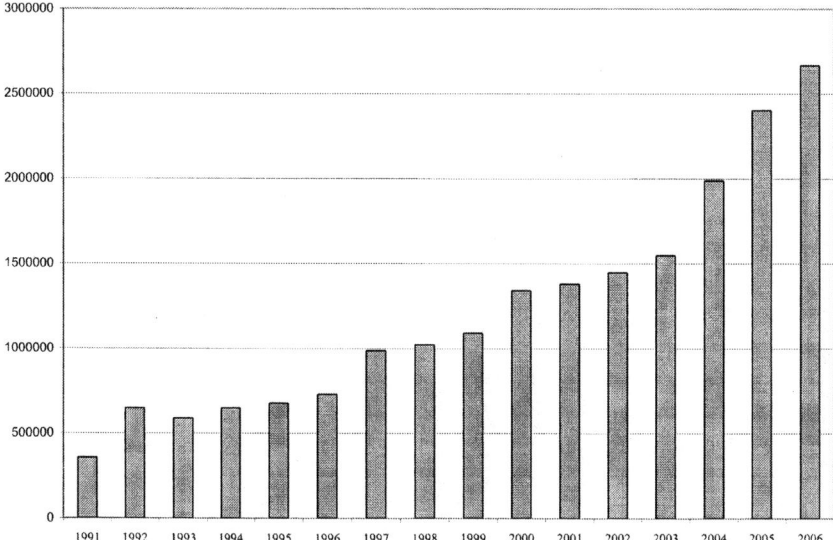

Figure 11.1. Documented Foreign Residents in Italy, 1991–2006.

significant part of the immigrant population in Italy consists of people from Eastern Europe and Asia who entered the country after the end of the Cold War. Fourth, the immigrant population in Italy is demographically different from that of other European countries, as it features fewer families and children and more single mothers, although family reunions are becoming more common and the picture is rapidly changing due to immigrants' high fertility rates. Finally, immigration has taken place almost entirely in a world where globalization is developing on a full scale and the ease of and right to mobility for every human being are commonplace.

However, as in most countries of immigration, the phenomenon has been met with unease and suspicion by the vast majority of Italian citizens, media, and political actors. Since the nineties, concern has grown over the relationship between immigration and crime, largely as a result of media framing. While there was no evidence of an increase in crime rates, the press embarked in a "feeding frenzy" on crime stories, many of which prominently featured immigrants and thus forged a symbolic link between the two. Fear of and opposition to immigration played a key role in the electoral successes of the center-right coalition, as voting research shows (Itanes, 2001). After September 11 2001, with the help of the media, some Italian politicians, most notably the populist Lega Nord, a crucial component of the coalition supporting the Berlusconi government, attempted to exploit the misleading equivalence between Muslim immigrants and terrorists. Local communities often rally against increased immigrant presence in their areas, especially when immigrants attempt to establish their own public spaces, such as mosques (Saint-Blancat & Schmidt di Friedberg, 2005).

Italian citizens' opinions of immigrants are multifaceted, possibly masquerading latent attitudes unexpressed due to their social undesirability. Overall, the majority of the population claims sympathetic feelings toward immigrants and realistic assessments of their necessary role in the economy and society, but large percentages also manifest negative impressions and agree that Italian society is still far from being discrimination-free. A Eurobarometer (2007) survey, which measured attitudes toward immigration, ranked Italian citizens nineteenth out of twenty-five member countries in terms of tolerance toward immigrants and acceptance of their integration. Another Eurobarometer study (2006) shows that Italians assess inter-racial integration and tolerance in their country quite bleakly: 68 percent agreed that being from a different ethnic origin is a disadvantage in Italy and 77 percent believed that discrimination against those groups is commonplace, with 57 percent claiming that it is more widespread than five years before, compared to 49 percent among all EU citizens. Data on individual attitudes, presented in table 11.1, show that substantial percentages of Italians explicitly consider immigrants a threat to their identity, employment, and security. On the other hand, recognition of immigrants' economic and cultural contribution is far from absent and attitudes toward inclusive policies for legal immigrants, such as voting rights and access to public healthcare, reveal that there is substantial consensus for greater social and political integration.

The political system has responded to, and attempted to leverage on, the ambivalent feelings of many Italians. The alternation of permissive and restrictive measures over the last two decades did little to change the dynamics of immigration, which respond to the demands of an advanced economy in a country affected by declining birthrates and large imbalances in the age

Table 11.1. Italians' Attitudes Regarding Immigrants and their Rights (% agree)

Immigrants are a threat to our culture, identity, and tradition	26.6
Immigrants constitute a threat to employment	35.1
Immigrants endanger law and order and people's personal safety	39.2
Immigrants are a resource for our economy	46.9
The presence of immigrants stimulates the opening of our culture	51.4
Legal, tax-paying immigrants should be allowed to vote in general elections	65.3
Legal, tax-paying immigrants should be allowed to vote in local elections	73.9
Legal, tax-paying immigrants and their families are entitled to public healthcare	97.1

Source: Fondazione Nord Est (2005).

composition of the population, thus making the addition of young workers willing to accept low-paying jobs necessary for sustaining economic growth and balancing public finances. Thus, political institutions were much more effective in limiting immigrants' political rights than in countering their inflow. Italian laws on citizenship acquisition are among the most restrictive in Europe, except for people of Italian origins. Legal immigrants from outside the European Union can apply for Italian citizenship only after ten years of residence,[1] the longest term in Europe. As a consequence, the Italian Institute of Statistics certifies that as few as 180,000 foreigners became Italian citizens from 1995 to 2006. According to Pastore, Italy "has among the lowest rates of nationality acquisition on an annual basis (0.9 percent of its foreign population)" (2004, p. 39) by comparison with other European countries. Such a blockade in political rights greatly impedes the full civic integration of law-abiding immigrants.

Since immigration constituted a new and unexpected phenomenon for most of the population in the nineties, the media played a crucial part in shaping Italians' perception of immigrations. According to Campani, the press adopted a "strategy of anticipation" by which they "spread pre-formed images of foreigners before the Italian population as a whole could have a direct experience of them" (2001, p. 38). Journalists, however, do not operate in a vacuum. Wood and King (2001, p. 2) observe that they often act "as the mouthpiece of political parties or other powerful groups" and Tsoukala claims that the media "play a crucial role in the process of construction of the migratory threat, especially by objectifying the definitions advanced on the matter by politicians and the security agents" (2005, p. 180). The images of immigration provided by the media are "part of political battles and the fight for specific power interests" (Campani, 2001, p. 39) and thus power brokers strive to shape them in order to fulfill their own goals. Italian journalists have thus been accomplices of politicians and political entrepreneurs in producing and reproducing stereotypes of immigrants, rather than being the main initiators of such representations.

That the media would behave as little more than an echo chamber for politicians comes as no surprise given the history of media-politics relationships in Italy. Historically, the Italian newspapers have been weak as business enterprises, and thus controlled either by political parties (party press) or by economic powers who employed them as public relation tools. The public broadcasting radio was created in the 1920s by the Fascist regime to indoctrinate the masses and its television branch, born in the 1950s, has always been controlled by the dominant parties and seen by them as a more or less direct instrument of propaganda and influence on society, despite various reform laws that were supposed to free the public service of any undue external influence, but overall have left the political control on its personnel and programming almost unhindered (Mazzoleni, 2000; Padovani, 2004). As for the private broadcasting television, it has always been dominated by Silvio Berlusconi's three-network group, Mediaset, and thus, while it surely contributed to the modernization of Italy's political communication in the 1980s and 1990s, it is effectively under the control of the leader of the center-right coalition. The fragility of the media and, consequently, their choking embrace with the political system make Italy a fitting example of the "Mediterranean" or "polarized pluralist" model of media systems (Hallin & Mancini, 2004), where the relationship between politicians and journalists tends to be collusive and political actors have more influence on the contents of the news than in "liberal" systems, where the press is more autonomous from politics. As we will see shortly, this arrangement of media-politics relationships came into play also in the case analyzed in this article.

Most of the literature on how the Italian media have portrayed immigrants and immigration since this issue entered the public agenda is laden with strong criticism of media coverage. The most widespread complaint has to do with bias in the selection of the news. The media cannot be fully blamed for applying their "news values" (Gans, 1979) to immigrants as well as Italian citizens, which leads them to heavily cover crime stories where immigrants happen to be involved; yet, the fact that journalists limit their coverage of immigration almost exclusively to criminal matters is less understandable. For instance, Corte (2002) studied the news feeds on immigration produced by the main Italian news service and found that 92 percent focused on irregular immigrants, while only 8 percent dealt with regular immigrants. This is in stark contrast with the actual proportion of illegal versus legal immigrants in Italy, which estimates set at about one illegal immigrant for every four legal ones (ISMU, 2007). More generally, information in the media tends to be superficial and focused on isolated events. Most articles about immigration deal with the facts of the day and very few in-depth analyses are published that could help readers better understand the background and lifestyle of immigrants. On television, immigration is regularly reported on in the news, but is seldom discussed in more lengthy programs such as talk shows and reportages, which could enable more complex readings of the phenomenon (Censis, 2002; Binotto & Martino, 2004). Very little attention is paid to the problems and practices of immigrants' integration in Italian culture and society (Cotesta, 1999). Immigration is covered solely when it represents an emergency, described with metaphors such as "invasion," "wave," and "flood." When there is no such a crisis, immigration as a normal, ordinary phenomenon is absent from the media agenda. Immigrants' views and concerns are thus not voiced proportionally to their presence and relevance in the country. Among the media's shortcomings, the most consequential is probably their avoidance of the issue of the role of immigrants in the Italian economy. According to Sciortino and Colombo (2004), in the early stages of the growth of immigration the media covered the issue quite substantively, but in the 1990s they abandoned these topics and directed their coverage mostly to crime stories. The quality of public debate on immigrants' economic role was thus undermined, as Sciortino and Colombo contend: "a country that imports large numbers of foreign workers but does everything to avoid talking about it could be considered rather bizarre" (2004, p. 110).

Other studies offer an even more critical perspective and charge the media with full-fledged bias in the representation of the issue. According to this research, journalists implicitly or explicitly equate immigration with deviance and confuse deviance with crime. In particular, Alessandro Dal Lago (1999; see also Ghirelli, 1990) concludes that the media help reproduce the "tautology of fear," which stems from the mutually reinforcing hostile discourses by political-moral entrepreneurs, public authorities, law enforcement agencies, and citizen groups. Journalists reproduce the image of the "angry citizen" who reacts "naturally" to the imminent threat of immigrants' invasive presence in his/her territory, and consequently present politicians' and law enforcement agencies' tough stands on immigration as a democratic response to such arousal among their constituencies. Even when immigrants are victims of aggressions, journalists often refrain from fully denouncing these offences and instead strive to explain them as understandable consequences of the presence of foreigners in a certain area and of the social unease that immigrants are supposedly bound to cause. Xenophobia and racism are hardly ever imputed to Italians who insult or assault immigrants, although they are mentioned when similar incidents occur against immigrants in other countries. On the other hand, foreigners who commit crimes in Italy are explicitly tied to their nationalities: "An Italian thief is a thief, a Moroccan thief is a Moroccan" (Pratt, 2002, p. 38). Finally, unlike the quality press in most European countries, Italian media often fail to properly "police" racist or xenophobic language adopted by citizen groups and politicians.[2]

The literature summarized here clearly shows that, on an average day, one should not expect the Italian media to provide a very accurate and neutral picture of immigration and immigrants. Crime stories featuring illegal immigrants and news about citizen protests against the "invasion" of foreigners, possibly with some reference to terrorism and other threats, are the norm of what the Italian public is offered by the mainstream media. However, it would not be unreasonable to expect that, if the right political conditions ensued, the media could indeed address the issue in a more substantive, less emotional way. If political leaders, rather than just arousing fear of and anger toward immigrants in order to gain popularity among a diffident public, opened a debate on a serious policy issue related to immigration, journalists could be expected to follow suit and enrich such a discussion. If politicians began talking about immigrants not as an emergency and an intrusion to be tackled in the short run, but as generally law-abiding people who contribute to the Italian society and who could fulfill the duties and claim the rights of any other citizen, journalists could be expected to delve into these issues and at least partially adopt the same frames and narratives. Such an unlikely set of circumstances did indeed materialize in late 2003 in the form of a controversy among parties to the center-right governing coalition, which we now describe in order to contextualize our study.

GIANFRANCO FINI'S POLICY PROPOSAL AND ITS MEDIA COVERAGE

On October 7, 2003, Gianfranco Fini, president of right-wing party Alleanza Nazionale (AN) and Vice Prime Minister of the Italian center-right government led by Silvio Berlusconi, claimed that legal immigrants residing in Italy for a long enough time, even though not Italian citizens yet, should be granted the right to vote in local elections.

The proposal struck most as unexpected, given the hard-line stance on immigration that Fini's party and the whole center-right coalition had taken during the previous legislature, when the center-left had the majority in Parliament (1996–2001). Moreover, a proposal similar to that advanced by Fini had been included in an early draft of the immigration reform passed by the center-left government in 1998, but had quickly been discarded because it did not achieve consensus within the center-left coalition itself. It thus seemed all the more puzzling that Fini and his right-wing party would dare where a progressive coalition had not. Indeed, Fini himself had said in 1998 that the right for immigrants to vote in local elections was one of the "negative aspects" of the government's draft (Zincone, 2006, p. 368). Furthermore, Fini had just authored, together with Umberto Bossi (Minister of Reforms and leader of the xenophobic and populist party Lega Nord), a law on immigration claimed to be much more restrictive than the 1998 legislation.

However, the political environment clearly indicated that Fini had taken this initiative as a tactical move that was intended to change the balance of power within the center-right alliance. Fini and his party had long been critical of Prime Minister Silvio Berlusconi's management of the relationships within the coalition. Critics thought that AN, in spite of being the second coalitional party in terms of votes and seats in Parliament, was not fairly rewarded in terms of power and visibility by comparison with Lega Nord, whose leader was thought to thrive on good personal relationships with Berlusconi and ruthless political and media tactics that helped his party gain more clout than its electoral and parliamentary strength could justify. Fini was thus trying to break the isolation he saw himself and his party falling into.

A second target of Fini's move was his own party. In 1993, AN had been founded on the ashes of an older party (Movimento Sociale Italiano) that explicitly claimed to be the proud carrier of Fascist heritage. Fini had based his career and leadership on the mission to transform his party from the standard-bearer of post-fascist nostalgia into a modern conservative subject, which included bleaching it of the racist stands the party often used to adopt. After Berlusconi's Forza Italia had joined the European People's Party in 1999, Fini repeatedly claimed that AN should follow the same path and in this light the proposal regarding legal immigrants' right to vote could be presented as a "centrist" move demonstrating democratic maturity, solidarity, and willingness to address the requests for more active integration policies voiced by some components of the Catholic Church.

For all its political subtext, Fini's was also a serious and path-breaking policy proposal that could enrich the stale debate on immigration in the country. Italian politicians and opinion-makers over time have tended to focus on what Dell'Olio calls "immigration policy," which "addresses the question of who should be allowed to immigrate and in what numbers," rather than on "immigrant policy," which "addresses the question of what to do about immigrants once they are here" and "focuses on what to do about the effects of immigration upon society" (Dell'Olio, 2003, p. 107). In Italy, there had always been plenty of discussions on how to control the country's borders and regulate the entrance of foreigners, but very little had been said, let alone done, about immigrants' civil, social, and political rights, which limited the nation's ability to fully come to terms with the real challenges posed by immigration as a daily reality. Fini's proposal could thus start filling the gap between immigrant and immigration policy.

Italian journalists fully and immediately recognized the ambiguity of the situation and the intertwining of policy and political motives in Fini's statement. In an editorial in *Corriere della Sera* on 14 October 2003, political scientist and commentator Angelo Panebianco wrote: "The proposal advocated by Fini to allow immigrants to vote in local elections offers our country a great opportunity. That is, the opportunity to seriously discuss our strategies to integrate non-communitarian workers. Let us hope that such necessary debate will not be spoiled by the usual old, and quite miserable, coalitional bickering." By contrast, six days earlier, *La Repubblica*'s political editor Massimo Giannini opined: "A serious proposal for managing the issue of the coexistence of different cultures in a context of shared and respected rules becomes a tactical move that ends up just destabilizing the [governing] coalition en route to the local (if not political) elections." Well aware of the various implications of Fini's proposal, the press was in a position to influence how the debate on the issue would be framed, whether in "policy" terms, that is, as part of a strategy to integrate immigrants and their cultures without threatening Italians' sense of security, or in "political" terms, that is, as just one more battle in the trench warfare on leadership, power, and legislative clout within the ruling coalition. Since both elements were clearly present from the beginning, the decision on how to frame the debate was to a great extent in the lap of the journalists.

To assess how the Italian media covered Fini's proposal and the following debate, an empirically-based theory of the contents of political news coverage is necessary. Patterson's (1980) classification of four types of issues covered by the media provides the theoretical framework and methodological toolkit required for this study. Patterson identified four issue types: policy, political, campaign, and personal. "Policy" issues stress the concrete problems that lawmakers and government officeholders address and for which citizens demand solutions. "Political" issues comprise the dynamics of the political system and the relationships among its key players, including ideological debates, internal fights, and negotiations. "Campaign" issues deal with propaganda, the state of public opinion, and the electoral repercussions of any decision or political event. Finally, "personal" issues entail politicians' lives on both the public stage and the private backstage. Whereas the U.S. literature has for a long time lamented the preponderance of campaign vis-à-vis policy coverage (Patterson, 1993; Farnsworth & Lichter, 2003), research on Italian elections has shown that the media tend to devote much more attention to policy issues than to any other kind of topic (Marini & Roncarolo, 1997); this might be related to the decline of Cold-War ideological alignments and the crisis of the party system that was based on those cleavages, which in turn resulted in journalists' adopting a more practical, less ceremonial approach to politics.

Scholars to a large extent agree that media coverage of policy issues is normatively preferable to political, campaign, or personal coverage, or at least that policy aspects should be the main ingredient of a healthy information diet for the public. For example, Patterson compares the effects of the "game" schema, which presents politics as a sports competition and politicians as players focusing on winning and thus results in coverage based on political and campaign issues, with those of the "governing" schema, which focuses on the practical task of solving collective problems by elected officeholders and thus elicits coverage of policy issues (1993, p. 89):

> When voters encounter game-centered stories, they behave more like spectators than participants in the election, responding, if at all, to the status of the race,

not to what the candidates represent. On the other hand, stories about the issues and the candidates' qualifications bring out the politics in voters, eliciting evaluations of the candidates' leadership and personal traits and of their records and policy positions. These stories also cultivate more involvement, which is evident in the voters' greater reaction to such stories.

On this theoretical and empirical basis, Patterson's typology can be applied to the way Italian media covered the controversy that stemmed from Fini's proposal. Although Patterson devised this typology for studying election coverage, it can be applied also to political and policy discussions among governing and opposition parties. Moreover, as in other countries, Italian politics experiences a state of "permanent campaign" (Ornstein & Mann, 2000), whereby politicians rely on the media to speak directly to citizens and create consensus on their policy goals rather than, or in addition to, negotiating legislation behind closed doors.

METHODOLOGY

The purpose of this research is to assess whether the Italian newspapers and television news programs framed Fini's proposal as a policy or as a political issue, or rather as an issue of some other kind (campaign or personal). In order to answer this question, we analyzed news stories and opinion articles that appeared in the three national independent newspapers that enjoy the largest circulation in Italy (*Corriere della Sera*, *La Repubblica*, and *La Stampa*).[3] *Corriere della Sera* has always positioned itself as the newspaper of the record in Italy and, since the collapse of Cold-War alignments, it has rarely sided with any coalition, although it openly endorsed the center-left alliance during the 2006 general election campaign. On the other hand, *La Repubblica* is explicitly aligned with the center-left coalition, while *La Stampa*, though generally sympathetic to progressive positions, tends to be less explicitly aligned. Newspaper articles were analyzed between 8 and 24 October 2003, that is, from the beginning of the controversy until it essentially waned from media coverage because it had become clear that no concrete legislative action was to be undertaken on the issue. Furthermore, to study how television covered the debate, the sample included the day-time and prime-time editions of the four television news programs with the highest ratings[4]—three on the public service network RAI (TG1, TG2, TG3) and one (TG5) aired on Berlusconi's network.[5] The time frame for television news stories is shorter (7–14 October 2003) because the controversy withered from television much sooner than from newspapers, as could be expected given the different space and time constraints under which print and television journalists operate.

Overall, 226 newspaper articles (30 of which appeared in front pages) and 64 television news stories were coded.

Patterson's scheme was applied as follows. Stories and articles were coded as framing the subject as a policy issue when they stressed the implications of Fini's statement (and those by other politicians related to it) on the governance of immigration in Italy, the role of immigrants in the country from an economic, social, or political standpoint, the technical and practical issues that would have to be dealt with in order to implement the proposal, the relationships between Italy and the rest of the global society, and the changing nature of Italian citizenship. On the other hand, stories were coded as framing Fini's proposal as a political issue when they focused on the political goals that Fini was thought to pursue through his legislative initiative, the reactions by Fini's governing allies and fellow partisans, and their implications on the balance of power between parties. The controversy could also be framed as a campaign issue when journalists emphasized its possible electoral repercussions, while a personal issue framing focused on Fini's personality and his development as a leader.

RESULTS

We will first analyze the data on newspaper coverage. Table 11.2 shows the incidence of the various types of issues in the three newspapers' front pages between 8 and 24 October 2003.

As the data show, only *La Stampa* equally balanced its front-page coverage between policy and political considerations. On the other hand, both *Corriere*

Table 11.2. Coverage of the immigration debate on newspapers' front pages, 8–24 October 2003

Newspapers	Policy	Political	Total
La Stampa	5	5	10
%	50	50	
La Repubblica	1	9	10
%	10	90	
Corriere della Sera	4	6	10
%	40	60	
Total	10	20	30
%	33	67	

Note: no front-page articles were coded as featuring "campaign" or "personal" issues.

della Sera and especially *La Repubblica* overwhelmingly presented Fini's proposal and the ensuing debate as a matter of politics related to dynamics of party politics. A good example of such politically-framed coverage are the three newspapers' front-page titles on 9 October 2003, the second day since the controversy had started. *Corriere della Sera* chose an utterly political title, referring to the implications of Fini's move for his own party: "Fini goes on: Beyond this right." *La Repubblica* focused on internal disputes within the center-right coalition and portrayed the subject as a dispute between the Prime Minister and the Vice Prime Minister: "Berlusconi stops Fini." *La Stampa* centered more on the legislative process resulting from the proposal: "Berlusconi back-pedals on immigrant vote, but Fini insists that AN will present a draft law proposal." Examples of policy-related front-page stories can be found in *Corriere della Sera*'s 12 October 2003 title: "We must abolish quotas for immigrants," which referred to a proposal by the Unione dei Democratici Cristiani e di Centro (UDC), a centrist party of the governing majority, to reform the system of legal access for immigrants, and, especially, in editorials, such as *La Stampa*'s comment on 8 October 2003, titled "A look toward Europe," which emphasized the accordance between Fini's proposal and most European legislation on the matter.

The aggregate data show that the three main Italian newspapers covered the debate in political rather than policy terms by a factor of two to one. Most articles focused on the bitter contrast between the leaders of center-right parties, some of whom, most notably Bossi, threatened to leave the alliance if Fini's proposal were passed, while Berlusconi was often reported to be mediating between his most recalcitrant allies. A final point of equilibrium was found by the Prime Minister when he proclaimed that, were a parliamentary vote on the proposal to be held, there would be no "majority bond" among center-right parties, which meant that each could vote freely without submitting to any coalitional discipline and without engendering a political crisis. While these political developments were surely crucial for the ability of the ruling coalition to endure the conflict among its components, the policy substance of the matter was largely left overlooked in news coverage.

Data on internal articles, shown in table 11.3, offer results that are remarkably similar to those regarding front-page stories, and to some extent paint an even more disappointing picture, as the percentage of policy-related articles decreases by comparison with front-page coverage. Newspaper journalists, though surely influenced by politicians' portrayal of the matter as an internal political fight rather than a genuine debate on immigrants' rights, did very little to frame Fini's proposal as a substantive policy issue. Rather, journalists' eyes were set on negotiations and power-brokering.

Some examples from the first day of the controversy (8 October 2003) clarify the different types of perspectives adopted by journalists. A rare instance of policy-focused stories on *La Repubblica* was a series of in-depth articles on how immigrant communities had integrated in various local economies, the first of which focused on Sikh workers in rural Northern Italy. *La Stampa* offered a short article that reported some figures on immigration flows in Italy and an even shorter note on the number of immigrant small-business owners in the country. *Corriere della Sera* published an analysis of the number of immigrants that would have been able to vote if Fini's proposal had passed and mentioned the case of the newly instituted immigrant delegation in Rome's City Council. Political framing mainly consisted in reports of politicians' reactions to Fini's statement and background stories on the relationship between and within parties and coalitions. Thus, *Corriere della Sera* featured two stories that presented Fini's move as a "warning to" and a "duel with" Prime Minister Berlusconi. Two other stories were centered on Lega Nord's leader Umberto Bossi, the advocate of the hardest stance on immigration within the center-right, who reacted vigorously against the proposal. Similarly, *La Repubblica* described Prime Minister Berlusconi as "infuriated" by Fini, claimed in an editorial that the latter was forcing an "ultimatum" on the former, and featured an interview with Bossi titled "If [Fini] makes a deal with the center-left on immigration, I will take everyone to the polls," implying that Lega Nord would have withdrawn parliamentary support to the government, which would likely have led to anticipated elections to restore a governing majority. *La Stampa* similarly reported reactions by leaders in both coalitions and employed a "campaign" perspective in an article titled "The Vice Premier's strategy to boost his party," which speculated on how Fini's move could entice moderate conservative voters. Similarly, an editorial

Table 11.3. Coverage of the immigration debate on newspapers' internal pages, 8–24 October 2003

Newspapers	Policy	Political	Campaign	Other	Total
La Stampa	28	42	3	0	73
%	38	58	4	—	
La Repubblica	10	40	6	0	56
%	18	71	11	—	
Corriere della Sera	17	42	6	2	67
%	25	63	9	3	
Total	55	124	15	2	196
%	28	63	8	1	

Note: no internal articles were coded as featuring "personal" issues.

on *Corriere della Sera* called the proposal a "shock to voters" and claimed that it was a sign that Fini had decided to engage citizens directly through the mass media rather than negotiating legislation behind closed doors with his fellow coalition members.

It is important to stress that, although Fini's proposal was certainly not unrelated to political dynamics and was probably launched as a "dog whistle" to upset the coalitions' internal equilibrium, political elites quickly engaged the issue in a way that was far from devoid of policy substance and certainly constituted legitimate content for media coverage. Soon after Fini's announcement, his party presented a heavily debated draft law on the subject, which, in order to counterbalance its "inclusive" goal, proposed that voting rights be granted only to those legal immigrants who could prove that they were able to adequately support themselves and their families. Most experts claimed this proposal was unconstitutional as it would discriminate among individuals of different economic conditions in the provision of a fundamental right. Lega Nord then responded with its own draft law, which curiously stated that immigrants could acquire the right to vote only if they knew the local dialect of the area they lived in. As previously mentioned, the centrist component of the governing coalition called for a complete overhaul of the legislation on immigration, proposing to abolish entrance quotas. Another draft law had already been issued by the main center-left party, the DS (Democratici di Sinistra), that also advocated a less restrictive regime. On October 12, Romano Prodi, then Chairman of the European Commission and former Prime Minister of a center-left government (1996–1998), stated that the Commission was favorable to granting voting rights to legal immigrants in local elections, and that this could be the first step toward allowing them to vote in general elections, too. Mayors and other local officials commented on the ways in which they were trying to include legal immigrants in local representative and governing bodies, thus adding context, examples, and potentially new stories and characters that the media could feature to make their coverage of the issue more iconic and interesting.

In short, although Fini's announcement clearly had political as well as policy motives and implications, it also forced most leaders and parties to make some public statements as to where they stood on the issue and what alternative proposals, if any, they would advance. Thus, there is no doubt that a substantial amount of different public policy options was made available to the public by all relevant political actors. Newspapers, however, by and large preferred to focus on political aspects of the controversy rather than helping their readers understand the substantive implications of a complex and sensitive subject. In Patterson's terms, journalists presented the debate on immigrants' voting rights as a game that political leaders were playing among themselves, rather than as a governing dilemma that required enlightened understanding of concrete problems and adequate solutions to citizens' demands. This, as we will see in the discussion, is a common syndrome in the Italian political communication system, mostly related to the close ties between politicians and journalists, but in this case the effects on public debate have been particularly dismal given the potentially unique opportunity provided by the circumstances and the pressing need for a substantive debate on this particular issue.

After this somber assessment of newspapers, we now turn to television coverage. Given the time constraints placed on television journalists, and especially the need for compelling images and stories in order to attract and sustain the attention of an increasingly volatile audience, television news can hardly provide a more suitable arena for substantive debate than newspapers. In a way, such expectations can be easily confirmed by examining the amount of coverage provided by television news programs. While the three newspapers featured a total of 99 stories on immigrants' voting rights in the week after Fini's statement, the four TV newscasts covered in this study produced only 64 total segments on the issue in their day-time and prime-time editions combined.

More than the sheer amount of coverage, however, it is the content and quality of reporting that is worth considering. As shown in table 11.4, the aggregate data on TV newscasts are quite similar to those on newspapers, with roughly one-third of the stories framed as policy issues and little less than six out of ten framed as political issues. However, a comparison between the public service and the main private network reveals an exception to the pattern encountered so far.

Of all the media analyzed, TG5 is the only one that framed the issue of Fini's proposal more in policy than in political terms, although the number of stories it featured is too small to warrant unqualified generalizations.

Table 11.4. Coverage of the immigration debate in television news programs, 7–14 October 2003

TV Network	Policy	Political	Campaign	Total
TG1, TG2, TG3 (RAI)	15	33	2	50
%	30	66	4	
TG5 (Mediaset)	8	4	2	14
%	57	28	14	
Total	23	37	4	64
%	35	57	6	

Note: no television news stories were coded as featuring "personal" issues.

However, it is safe to assume that the private channel stands in clear contrast with the public service newscasts, whose coverage closely resembled that of newspapers. Such difference between RAI and TG5 can be explained by the different approaches to politics by public and private television networks. On the one hand, because of the strong political influence on RAI's programming and personnel that was mentioned above, the coverage of politics in public television has historically been tied more to the political elites rather than to citizens, often giving the viewer a sense that politicians use the medium to talk to each other over people's heads. Thus, the fact that RAI newscasts framed two-thirds of the stories in political terms comes as no surprise given the general outlook on politics adopted by public service journalists. By contrast, commercial newscasts usually give a more practical portrait of politics. Their stories tend to be shorter, place lesser emphasis on political matters, and require less political knowledge by the viewer. Such characteristics contributed to making TG5's coverage of Fini's proposal more issue-oriented than that of RAI.

DISCUSSION

It is important to recognize the limitations of our findings as well as their strengths. A case study always requires further research before any generalizations can be made beyond the events and actors involved in the particular situation and timeframe under investigation. The present research is also limited in that it only focused on mainstream, generalist media. Although the vast majority of Italians still rely solely on these outlets for information and entertainment (Censis, 2006), it would also be worth studying the potentially different perspectives provided by niche, alternative, and grassroots media, especially on the internet. Furthermore, the coverage that was analyzed dealt with a top-down policy process, activated and pursued by high-ranking government officials and party leaders, with no engagement on the part of citizens and grassroots activists. The outcome of media coverage and public debate might be different in the case of bottom-up policy-making, initiated and implemented with at least some active contributions from citizen groups and immigrants' networks. Such an effort, which could be feasible at a local level, would deserve careful scrutiny in terms of both its policy construction and outcome, and the public discussion that would ensue.

Still, once we have recognized the limits of this study, our findings are quite clear and consequential. The debate on immigrants' voting rights was not centered on the substance of the problem, but it mostly focused on internal political battles within the ruling coalition. The larger questions of citizenship, rights and duties in a multicultural, genuinely global society were sometimes mentioned, but were generally confined to the background. Citizens who turned to the mainstream media with an appetite for a policy debate, or simply with the desire to better understand the issue and its implications, were largely disappointed, while those who cared little about the subject or had never considered the possibility of immigrants' enjoying political rights in Italy, or, for that matter, the many complex issues related to their integration in society, had very few chances to be introduced to such matters.

Such findings, it must be stressed, are in accordance with the literature on the representation of immigration by the Italian press, but also in stark contrast with studies on media coverage of politics and elections in general, which claim that Italian journalists tend to focus on policy issues as opposed to political or campaign matters (Marini & Roncarolo, 1997). Italian journalists might not yet be knowledgeable, resourceful, or sensitive enough to provide their publics with substantive coverage on immigration, while at the same time they are now able to provide reasonably specific coverage on issues such as the economy, healthcare, or foreign policy, which are more integrated into their skills, competence, relationships, and professional routines.

However, a fair assessment of the case studied here cannot overlook the role of political actors in shaping the debate. The controversy was a fitting example of how Italian politics is now immersed in a permanent campaign, where parties and leaders constantly court public opinion not to rally support for their policy proposals, but to increase their bargaining power within and between coalitions. The debate on Fini's landmark announcement thus confirms Roncarolo's (2002, p. 145) evaluation of the permanent campaign in Italy:

> at the core of the permanent campaign Italian-style there are more strategies aimed at playing the political game in the party arena than there are forms of political marketing and appeals to citizens. We could therefore say that Italian politics has taken on the formal character of the permanent campaign—its length—while emptying it of substance.

Therefore, political actors bear a substantial share of responsibility for the dominant "political" framing of the issue. Fini himself was often reported as seeing his proposal as a tactical move aimed at shaking the balance of power within the ruling coalition and promoting his own image as a reliable, modern, European conservative leader. The press cannot be blamed for "inventing" such political subtext per se, since it was widely publicized by Fini himself and by both supporters and opponents of his proposal. The political system did not just set the agenda, but it also defined the frame for the discussion, which the media largely followed and voters acknowledged:

according to a poll published by *Corriere della Sera* on 11 October 2003, 56 percent of voters agreed that "Fini made his proposal in order to enhance his international image, aiming at the European elections."

The media thus responded and adapted to the external political climate and largely mirrored the frames adopted by political elites rather than shaping the debate on their own terms. Journalists also chose not to challenge the frames proposed by the elites because such frames satisfied their appetite for conflict among political players. The media outcome of Fini's proposal thus offered an example of what Wolfsfeld (2004) has termed the "politics-media-politics" circle, where the media respond to the elites' agenda-setting and framing efforts, but in the process they also partially shape the public environment, to which political actors in turn have to respond. However, the peculiarity of the Italian politics-media complex, as it emerged from this particular case study, is that the political system tends to have more clout than in other Western democracies not only in creating events and controversies that set the public agenda via media coverage, but also in defining languages, frames, and narratives through which issues are discussed both at the elite and at the media level.

While a more active, autonomous, or adversarial posture by Italian journalists vis-à-vis politicians could hardly be expected given the peculiar morphology of the country's political communication system, and while there is no empirical basis to believe that the outcome of such an unlikely turnaround would be normatively more desirable, this study clearly highlights some worrisome tendencies. One can hardly doubt that there is a physiological circle of influence between the elites, the media, and public opinion. The question, especially in those rare occasions when crucial and sensitive issues such as immigrant policy are debated, is whether such circle turns out to be virtuous or vicious. The evidence offered here strongly suggests that the latter was the case and that Italy still has a long way to go on the path to a public sphere that can adequately address immigration, which is one of the most pressing issues related to globalization.

NOTES

1. A draft law approved by the Council of Ministers in August 2006, but not yet passed by Parliament at the time of this writing, would reduce the term to five years of residence.

2. A case in point is mentioned by Campani, who deserves to be fully quoted: "Irene Pivetti, former president of the Italian Parliament, was allowed to get away with saying that the Albanians should be thrown into the sea: she was not prosecuted, she is still a parliamentary deputy, is still invited to speak on television, and the present center left

government still tries to court her vote" (2001, p. 46). Since the quoted article was written, Mrs. Pivetti's career has taken another twist, as she left politics and started working as a talk show host in one of Berlusconi's television channels.

3. According to industry data, in 2003 the three newspapers combined for a 1.67 million circulation, or about a fourth of the overall 5.76 million total daily newspaper circulation in the country. Data source: www.primaonline.it.

4. According to audience ratings, in 2003 the four networks studied had about 17 million average viewers in the prime-time bracket (from 8:30 to 10:30 PM), which amounted to about 70 percent of the total television audience. During the time the news programs are broadcast, the audience share held by the four networks can be estimated to exceed 75 percent. Data source: http://www.primaonline.it.

5. I wish to thank CARES—Osservatorio di Pavia for providing the data on television coverage.

REFERENCES

Binotto, Marco, and Valentina Martino (eds.). *Fuori Luogo: L'immigrazione e i media italiani*. Rome: Rai Eri, 2004.

Campani, Giovanna. "Migrants and Media: The Italian Case." Pp. 38–52 in *Media and Migration: Constructions of Mobility and Difference*, edited by Russell King and Nancy Wood. London, New York: Routledge, 2001.

Censis. "Tuning Into Diversity: Immigrati e minoranze etniche nei media." 2002. http://www.censis.it (accessed 19 March 2009).

———. *Quinto rapporto sulla comunicazione in Italia 2001–2005: Cinque anni di evoluzione e rivoluzione nell'uso dei media*. Milan: Franco Angeli, 2006.

Colombo, Asher, and Giuseppe Sciortino. "Italian Immigration: The Origins, Nature and Evolution of Italy's Migratory System." *Journal of Modern Italian Studies* 90, no. 1 (March 2004): 49–70.

Corte, Maurizio. *Stranieri e mass media: Stampa, immigrazione e pedagogia interculturale*. Padua: CEDAM, 2002.

Cotesta, Vittorio. "Mass media, conflitti etnici e immigrazione: Una ricerca sulla comunicazione dei quotidiani nell'Italia degli anni novanta." *Studi Emigrazione* 36, no. 135 (September 1999): 387–394.

Dal Lago, Alessandro. *Non-persone: L'esclusione dei migranti in una società globale*. Milan: Feltrinelli, 1999.

Dell'Olio, Fiorella. "Immigration and Immigrant Policy in Italy and the UK: Is Housing Policy a Barrier to a Common Approach Towards Immigration in the EU?" *Journal of Ethnic and Migration Studies* 30, no. 1 (January 2003): 107–128.

Eurobarometer. "Discrimination in the European Union—Country report on Italy." 2006. http://ec.europa.eu/public_opinion/archives/ebs/ebs_263_fiche_it.pdf (accessed 19 March 2009).

———. "European Social Reality." 2007. http://ec.europa.eu/public_opinion/archives/ebs/ebs_273_en.pdf (accessed 19 March 2009).

Farnsworth, Stephen, and Robert Lichter. *The Nightly News Nightmare: Network Television's Coverage of U.S. Presidential Elections, 1988–2000*. Lanham: Rowman & Littlefield, 2003.
Fondazione ISMU. *Dodicesimo Rapporto sulle migrazioni 2006*. Milan: Franco Angeli, 2007.
Fondazione Nord Est. "Migration and Citizenship Rights in Europe." 2005. www.fondazionenordest.net/uploads/media/english_version.pdf (accessed 19 March 2009).
Gans, Herbert. *Deciding What's News*. New York: Pantheon Books, 1979.
Ghirelli, Massimo. *Razzismo e Media*. Rome: Il Passaggio, 1990.
Grillo, Ralph. "Immigration and the Politics of Recognizing Difference in Italy." Pp. 1–24 in *The Politics of Recognizing Difference: Multiculturalism Italian Style*, edited by Robert Grillo and Jeff Pratt. Burlington: Ashgate, 2002.
Hallin, Dan, and Paolo Mancini. *Comparing Media Systems: Three Models of Media and Politics*. Cambridge: Cambridge University Press, 2004.
Itanes. *Perché ha vinto il centro-destra*. Bologna: Il Mulino, 2001.
Mai, Nicola. "The Albanian Diaspora-in-the-Making: Media, Migration and Social Exclusion." *Journal of Ethnic and Migration Studies* 31, no. 3 (May 2005): 543–561.
Marini, Rolando, and Franca Roncarolo. *I media come arena elettorale: Le elezioni politiche 1996 in Tv e nei giornali*. Rome: Eri, 1997.
Mazzoleni, Gianpietro. "The Italian Broadcasting System between Politics and the Market." *Journal of Modern Italian Studies* 5, no. 2 (July 2000): 157–168.
Ornstein, Norman, and Thomas Mann (eds). *The Permanent Campaign and Its Future*. Washington, DC: American Enterprise Institute and The Brookings Institution, 2000.
Padovani, Cinzia. *A Fatal Attraction: Public Television and Politics in Italy*. Lanham: Rowman & Littlefield, 2004.
Pastore, Federico. "A Community out of Balance: Nationality Law and Migration Politics in the History of Post-Unification Italy." *Journal of Modern Italian Studies* 9, no. 1 (March 2004): 27–48.
Patterson, Thomas. *Out of Order*. New York: Knopf, 1993.
———. *The Mass Media Election: How Americans Choose Their President*. New York: Praeger, 1980.
Pratt, Jeff. "Italy: Political Unity and Cultural Diversity." Pp. 25–40 in *The Politics of Recognizing Difference: Multiculturalism Italian Style*, edited by Robert Grillo and Jeff Pratt. Burlington: Ashgate, 2002.
Roncarolo, Franca. "Virtual clashes and political games: The campaign in the print and broadcast media." Pp. 143–161 in *The Italian General Election of 2001: Berlusconi's Victory*, edited by James Newell. Manchester, New York: Manchester University Press, 2002.
Saint-Blancat, Chantal, and Ottavia Schmidt di Friedberg. "Why are Mosques a Problem? Local Politics and Fear of Islam in Northern Italy." *Journal of Ethnic and Migration Studies* 31, no. 6 (November 2005): 1083–1104.

Sciortino, Giuseppe, and Asher Colombo. "The Flows and the Flood: The Public Discourse on Immigration in Italy, 1969–2001." *Journal of Modern Italian Studies* 9, no. 1 (March 2004): 94–113.

Strozza, Salvatore, and Nicoletta Cibella. "Elementi e caratteri dell'integrazione." Pp. 75–162 in *L'immigrazione straniera: Indicatori e misure di integrazione*, edited by Antonio. Golini. Bologna: Il Mulino, 2006.

Tsoukala, Anastassia. "Looking at Migrants as Enemies." Pp. 161–192 in *Controlling Frontiers: Free Movement into and within Europe*, edited by Didier Bigo and Elspeth Guild. Burlington: Ashgate, 2005.

Wolfsfeld, Gadi. *Media and the Path to Peace.* Cambridge: Cambridge University Press, 2004.

Wood, Nancy, and Russell King. "Media and Migration: An Overview." Pp. 1–22 in *Media and Migration: Constructions of Mobility and Difference*, edited by Russell King and Nancy Wood. London, New York: Routledge, 2001.

Zincone, Giovanna. "The Making of Policies: Immigration and Immigrants in Italy." *Journal of Ethnic and Migration Studies* 32, no. 3 (April 2006): 347–375.

Chapter Twelve

Globalization vs. Localization: Anti-immigrant and Hate Discourses in Italy

Rinella Cere

INTRODUCTION

In the context of globalization, national and transnational borders appear to have a new meaning in our times: they seem doubly important when discussion of immigration is concerned, but dismissed when the rhetoric of globalization of a world increasingly connected economically, socially, and culturally is at stake. Discussions about globalization have abounded in recent years as many theorists and commentators have tried to make sense of these rapid economic, social, and cultural changes. More importantly an uneasy relationship has developed between the forces of globalization and those of localization. Migration movements and their media coverage have been at the center of the discussion of an increasingly globalized world. In scholarly circles this movement of people has brought about a critique of the more "celebratory" definitions of globalization. One can think about Featherstone, Giddens and Robertson who argue in turn that globalization should not be conceived as a homogenizing process (Featherstone, 1990: 2); that globalization-localization is a dialectical process (Giddens, 1990: 64) and that globalization is bringing about a more united world, although Robertson qualifies his statement by suggesting that this does not necessarily mean united in an "integrated in naive functionalist mode" (Robertson, 1992: 18).

Conversely writers such as Ferguson, Mattelart, and Sparks have been especially critical of globalization. Ferguson has described globalization as mythology with attendant problems of meaning, evidence, and evaluation: "Myth, in the context of globalization, is not used here in the sense of an untruth, but rather as a way of classifying certain assumptions about the modern world . . . [myths] taken together they explain and justify much about the topography of a shifting global political and cultural economy" (1992: 74).

Mattelart's criticism is particularly useful in unravelling some of the contradictions within globalization, and seems especially relevant to the reading of media discourses of "migration flows": "The world is a contradictory system made up all at once of interdependencies and interconnections, of schisms, fragmentations, and exclusions. If the new global configurations are marked by the logics of globalization and homogeneity, they also harbor contrary and interfering logics" (1994: ix).

This "contrary and interfering logic" is especially visible on the question of borders. The European Union and its members are an important example in this respect: on the one hand we have increasingly "free-exchange areas" between countries and people which have signed the Schengen agreement[1] and on the other, a restoration of those borders for migrants and refugees. This is where the first major paradox of the global economy unfolds: market deregulation and an opening to international investments clearly have come to invalidate more and more the role of national governments and the control of national borders. Yet, in terms of immigration controls and representations, the practices and discourses in place are still very much based on the traditional nation-state (Sassen, 1996: 16–17; my translation) even if as in the case of Italy national identity is generally characterized as "weak."[2] In this chapter I want to discuss some of the contradictions and tensions at the heart of the globalization-localization phenomena; in particular I want to look at representations of immigration and immigrants circulating in the Italian media, looking at examples from press and terrestrial national news broadcasts. In doing so, I will concentrate on one main theme which has surfaced regularly: the criminalization of immigrants, with special attention to the representations of hate campaigns against Muslims, one of the major immigrant groups over the last six years.

NEW POLITICAL FORMATIONS AND NEW IMMIGRANTS

Hate campaigns, examples of which will be discussed below, have been normally instigated by relatively new political formations such as the Lega Nord and Forza Italia as well as by more traditional right wing parties, such as Alleanza Nazionale (National Alliance). The latter was renamed from the former Italian Social Movement (MSI-Movimento Sociale Italiano), which in turn was the party born out of the ashes of the Fascist party, following the Second World War. The Northern League (Lega Nord) is a more recent political and cultural phenomenon which began in the 1980s and refuelled debates around national identity vs. local and regional identity, debates which have often been at the center of the history of Italy. It enjoyed high electoral support in the 1980s (18 percent) mainly through its extreme populist politics and language but has since lost much of this support settling at 4 to 5 percent nationally.[3] It has also abandoned its former secessionist claims in favour of a federalist model. Forza Italia was the title adopted by the party established by the media tycoon Silvio Berlusconi when he first entered the electoral political race in 1994, which he subsequently won in coalition with the Lega Nord and Alleanza Nazionale. Berlusconi's Forza Italia, in fact the very name,[4] stands for much of Italian contemporary culture: football, television, entrepreneurial spirit, and free-market. Not surprisingly it has also been called a television party: "Television breaks up the places where democracy is formed, it mixes candidates with porno-stars, comedians with members of parliaments, biscuits adverts with adverts of ideas, the electoral poll card is substituted by the remote control" (Corsini, 1994: my translation). These political parties have often been active protagonists of the development of "institutionalised racism" that Rusconi has described as the "depositary of democratic ethnocentrism . . . a soft surrogate of racism" (Rusconi, 1993: 11). Before the general election of 2008, Forza Italia and Alleanza Nazionale formed a single party called the Popolo della libertà (Pdl). It went on to win the 2008 general election, again headed by Berlusconi, also in coalition with the Lega Nord.

In the last fifteen years, the immigrant population has grown exponentially in Italy, like in other Western European countries (Cesareo, 2006). Immigrants in Italy now number at nearly three millions and the largest immigrant community is Romanian, followed by Albanian, Moroccan, Chinese, and Ukrainian; these last two communities have grown at a greater pace in the last ten to fifteen years, in 1992 Chinese immigrants were only 15,000 while Ukrainians did not even appear in the first twenties.

The largest concentration of immigrants is to be found in Lombardy with over 800,000 residents, followed by Veneto (just over 400,000), Lazio (390.000), Emilia Romagna (365,000), Piedmont (310,000), and Tuscany (275,000). Over half of the total immigration is concentrated in the north, followed by just under a million in the center and the rest in the south and the islands.[5] In terms of occupation, the immigrant population is for the largest part employed on a permanent full-time basis (66.4 percent) and the rest on a part-time basis; a large proportion is employed in the service and tertiary sector (55.1 percent), mainly in three areas: domestic service, commercial, and catering. The other dominant occupation is concentrated in industry, which in the statistics includes the building industry, respectively at 23.3 percent and 16.8 percent. To note here is how these manual occupations are dominated by immigrants in comparison to occupational statistics available for the Italian population, in spite of the fact that half of the immigrant population has attained tertiary education; a fact which indicates a highly unequal context of opportunities (Istituto Nazionale di Statistica, 2009).

The increase in immigration in recent years in all countries of the European Union has also brought about new legislation on immigration. The most recent legislation passed in Italy is the Amato-Ferrero (April 2007) which has modified the Bossi-Fini, passed by the previous center-right government, a legislation which had been unable to stop illegal immigration or to channel into a legal set up increasing migration flows. The Amato-Ferrero legislation includes the abolition of detention centers, the CPT (Centri di permanenza temporanea), formerly introduced by the right wing-coalition and the Bossi-Fini legislation. The Amato-Ferrero law is more liberal in its approach to immigration but also claims to be more realistic: in some ways, it adopted the measures and formulas first seen in the 1991 Maastricht Treaty, where discourses of "reason and tolerance" (e.g. integration of immigrants legally resident in the European Union) were articulated alongside discourses of "realism" (e.g. tighter controls on clandestine immigration from all member countries, especially from Mediterranean countries) (Cere, 2000: 67).

Sassen (1999) suggested that this kind of draconian legislative measures to stop immigration is not necessarily a new phenomenon as empires in Europe attempted to protect their borders from incomers before, with the distinctive difference that those were truly "armies pressing at the borders" not metaphoric ones of small groups of individuals; as recently as two hundred years ago there were no frontiers' controls at the border within or around Europe. Therefore much has changed in recent times: firstly, through the construction of a myth about mass migration and secondly, in the way migration is perceived as threat:

> Migration flows have always been limited in terms of space, time and numbers ... collective fantasies from large sections of the host society evoke images of inundations, flows of immigrants and refugees from all over the world, which seem never ending. But these images do not correspond to contemporary reality as it did not in the past, when borders were not yet controlled. (Sassen, 1999: 127, my translation)

This dual discourse of protection of and from is intrinsic to the ideology of the European Union and its member states: the EU is caught in the dilemma of retaining its liberal ideology, at the base of which is the concept of assimilation, yet proclaiming itself as a multicultural society. In short, the contextual background in which news discourses about immigrants are embedded is both global and local: it draws from contradictory ideas at the heart of European liberalism and the unresolved question of multiculturalism or assimilation (Modood and Werbner, 1997; Barry, 2001; Habermas, 2006).

The unresolved question about multiculturalism vs. assimilation is also increasingly present in discussion and writings about racism in the media as well as part of news discourses about immigrants, who have increasingly become target of racist discourses.

Work on media and racism (Balbo and Manconi) has brought attention to the way prejudice and racism operate in Italian society and media. The immigrant communities which have moved to Italy in the last twenty years are a central "new subject" within the Italian background of different regional identities. Immigrants in Italy are often described by an inaccurate word "extracomunitari" (external to the European community) which immediately defines the Italians as part of Europe and immigrants as "extra," outsiders and external. In relation to the adoption of this term Balbo and Manconi asked whether the Swiss, the Scandinavians or the Canadians could also be addressed as "extracomunitari." Yet Italians use this term only to connote people from the East and South of the world (Balbo and Manconi, 1992: 60).

Balbo and Manconi's first study brought some evidence of the racisms/ different kinds of racism (described in the plural by the authors) which were beginning to circulate in parts of Italian society. These racisms were studied and described as part of the "white-centerd" model present throughout western countries and in particular European ones. This model constructs a well-known process based on "the hierarchies of periphery and center, western culture and 'other' cultures, us and them" (Balbo and Manconi, 1990: 11). They argue that these discourses then sediment slowly within everyday life and become part of a potential discursive racist imaginary, what they term: "i razzismi possibili" (latent racisms). Their second study, written two years after "I razzismi possibili," entitled "I razzismi reali" (Balbo and Manconi, 1992) examines how Italian society, which has often considered itself hostile to openly racist ideologies, has in fact changed dramatically and this is particularly visible in the discourses of political formations of recent years mentioned earlier on, such as the Lega Nord and Forza Italia (now Polo della libertà). Something that will become apparent in the next section where I am going to focus on one of the central themes mentioned in the introduction which is regularly covered and discussed in the Italian news media: the criminalization of immigrants and the emphasis on the strife between immigrant communities, law enforcement agencies, the Italian population, and Islamophobic representations of Muslim immigrants.

THE CRIMINALIZATION OF
IMMIGRATION IN THE MEDIA

Although the news agenda in relation to immigration is still largely dictated by national-based events, the case of Italy (with the ongoing movement of people from parts of Africa, especially from Morocco and Senegal, and their often fateful attempt to reach the coast of Italy, principally Lampedusa and Sicily) indicates that global criminal gangs are now increasingly part of European immigration movements: "The creation of an impregnable outer border has given new scope for criminal fraternities like the mafia to add the traffic in human cargo to their traffic in drugs" (Fekete and Webber, 1997: 67). This has also resulted in the coupling of immigrants with criminal activities and a conflation between "ethnic gangs" and "ethnic victims" (Fekete and Webber, 1997: 72).

The romanticism often attached to earlier immigration movements, especially at the turn of the 19th century (often captured in photography and early documentaries) has now been replaced by the notion that immigration is not solely about deserting poverty and seeking a better life. This transformed view of immigration results in ambivalent representations of immigration: either to be "tolerated" if economically useful or to be stopped and combated, both literally and legislatively if it is not. This transformation in how immigrants are viewed and represented has brought about increasingly tight border controls, which in turn has resulted in the increase of criminal activities around immigration movements and a consequent criminalization of immigrants themselves. This process has changed their status from people in search of a way out of poverty to people in search of a way out of poverty for equivocal purposes. In Italy these kinds of views are promoted regularly by the Lega Nord and the newly formed Popolo della libertà especially through their daily newspapers, respectively *La Padania* and *Il Giornale*.[6] Other media owned by the Lega Nord, the television station Telepadania and the radio station Radio Padania Libera also contribute further to the ongoing negative discourses about immigrants. These in turn, create a climate of intolerance and harassment. An example of this kind of intolerance is evident in the clashes between the Chinese community and the municipal police in Milan (Thursday 12 April 2007), sparked off by the maltreatment by traffic wardens towards Chinese shop owners using trolleys to deliver goods during daytime. The Chinese business community has argued that restrictions have been applied exclusively in the area where they operate and not in other business areas of Milan, thus accusing the police of discrimination. A particular violent altercation between a traffic warden and a Chinese woman sparked off tensions and protest ensued. The protest in Milan provided some of the conservative media with a pretext to criminalize the Chinese community, and many more themes other than the more specific one about the incident in Milan surfaced as a result. Arguments ranged from rules not being followed to a perceived lack of commitment to the host community. In an article from *Il Giornale* entitled "L'autoisolamento di una comunità" (The self-isolation of a community)[7] an argument is made about absolute "cultural difference" alongside a provocative coupling of Chinese and Muslim culture: "Chinese and Muslims, although so different, have in common a sense of superiority. For Muslims, the Koran guarantees them that they are the best nation in history. Among the Chinese there is a belief that the word 'culture' is only meaningful if applied to Chinese culture."

Emphasis on "cultural difference" brings to the fore issues which have been core to the ideology of exclusion, often converging on notions of legality and illegality. The anti-spitting legislation introduced in Prato (Tuscany), where the largest Chinese community resides (*L'Unità*, 14 April 2007) is another example of this and is clearly rooted in what Sibley called "spatial purification" (quoted in Gabriel, 1998: 97). This concept justifies the basis of white fears about territory and identity and about "defilement and pollution." For Gabriel it is also important not to underestimate how such fears "work at a number of levels, including the personal or local, national and the global" (1998: 98). The Chinese community has argued that it is exclusively and solicitously asked to follow rules which are not imposed on Italians in the same way, and that this is tantamount to racist practices.

The worst criminalization discourse has undoubtedly been addressed towards the Roma groups. Roma have always being singled out as "objects of prejudice, hostility and persecution" (Gatti et al., 1997:114). If stereotypes about the Chinese in the West often revolve around them being entrepreneurial and very successful in their business (Cohen, 1997), the opposite is true of the Roma. The latter, like the Muslim immigrants discussed below are undoubtedly the groups of migrants most caught up in the negative dynamics produced by the forces of globalization and localization. Roma and Muslims are very rarely mentioned in the mainstream conservative media except in connection with negative events and crime.

ISLAMOPHOBIA AND THE MEDIA IN ITALY

Muslim communities have diversified in recent years with the Moroccan community still the largest group. There are however many other Muslim nationalities resident in Italy; in numerical order, Albanians, Tunisians, Senegalese, Egyptians, Algerians, Somalis, Pakistani, and Bangladeshi (Cesareo, 2006). Their occupational data is very similar to that of other immigrant groups. Muslim immigrants are now a third of the total immigration population in Italy, and they have become increasingly targets of political right-wing graffiti. Political graffiti on public walls have always being part of Italian culture; this "tradition" has often combined the irreverence of radical politics with a poignant ideological message. These have been used widely by the left in the 60s and 70s as well as by the extreme right. Some Lega Nord's members have adopted graffiti (although clearly not an official policy) right from the beginning of the party's formation. Touring Northern Italy it is impossible not to come across graffiti in support of the Lega Nord and their slogans about "Padania libera." These kinds of sub-cultural activities are in recent years increasingly addressed towards immigrants and their places of worship. Recent anti-Islamic graffiti have appeared near a building which doubles as a mosque in Milan's Viale Jenner.[8] This mosque and the incorporated institute of Islamic Studies have been at the center of attention for a considerable time as suspicion has spread about its alleged terrorist activities. As the example below of *AnnoZero* highlights, little proof has emerged about these so-called terrorist activities, and to date only one individual has been successfully prosecuted.[9]

Prejudice and stereotyping have reached new proportions in the constant association between Islam and terrorism and the consequent criminalization of Muslims. Immigrants from Muslim countries, or mixed faith countries (Kurdish people from Iraq and Turkey, Northern and Sub-Saharan Africans, especially Senegal, Eritrea, Somalia and in recent times more frequently from Asia, especially Bangladesh) make up the largest immigrant group in Italy. These communities are often in the news due to anti-Islamic feelings constantly being whipped up by the Lega Nord and other center-right forces alongside sections of the Catholic Church. The phenomenon of the "War on Terror" led by the United States has undoubtedly compounded the problem. Issues covered often revolve around the building of new mosques and activities in mosques, what may appear to be "non-events" in news and informational culture. The opposition to mosque building is an ongoing trope in Italy as mosques are increasingly seen as terrorist centers rather than places of worship. Over the years research has shown that in Italy as elsewhere much news coverage has centerd on "fears of mosques," "Islamic invasions," and "threats to civilization" (Cere, 2002; Macdonald, 2003; Triandafyllidou, 2006).

TELEVISION NEWS, THE CATHOLIC CHURCH AND ISLAMOPHOBIA

One important case of this kind of reporting was in 2000 (well before 9/11) for the building of a mosque in Lodi.[10] The news item selected by the public service channel RAI1 at this time is very significant for the understanding of new alliances being forged between conservative Catholicism and new right-wing xenophobic movements such as the Lega Nord. Paradoxically the Lega

Nord, at least in its earlier history declared itself to be an anti-clerical party, and many of the earlier campaigns not only were they directed against the power of Rome in the state sense but also against the power of the Vatican.

The news item in question concerned a statement made by Cardinal Giacomo Biffi about Muslims and how they are not "part of our humanity": "Muslims are strangers to our humanity. Catholicism remains our historic religion and we need to worry about our national identity." This public statement was covered in some details by the national public service news broadcast, Tg1, on their main evening news at 8 pm.[11] The selection of the story was undoubtedly linked to the news event about the building of a mosque in Lodi which was happening concurrently and which was fiercely opposed by the Lega Nord, although that was never stated directly in the news item itself (RAI 1, Tg1, 30.09.00). The structure of the news item appears to be "balanced": it is framed in such a way that we are provided in turns via indirect interviews with the views of Cardinal Giacomo Biffi, the views of the leader of the Muslim Community and at the end of the news item with a different view from the Catholic camp. Nonetheless, the role of the journalist/reporter is never critical; rather he acts as a "paraphraser" of the Catholic views. The contextual background of this news about Muslim immigrant communities in Italy is interwoven with nationalism, Europeanism, theologocentrism, ethnocentrism, and at no point throughout the item does the journalist attempt to unravel some of the contradictions. Biffi's statement to TG1 is extremely problematic in suggesting that there is a vast difference between Muslims and the rest of humanity, as well as in its assumption that Catholicism is the state religion. It is the contradiction at the heart of Biffi's statement which is commented on by Hamza Piccardo, the leader of the Muslim Community in Italy. His emphasis is particularly in relation to the Italian Constitution which states that people are free to practice different religions, and Catholicism, although the majority religion cannot be equated with being a state religion. This statement is worth quoting in full:

> Truly this refuelling of the controversy with Cardinal Biffi as its protagonist does surprise me. The Cardinal seems to forget some important things, firstly that Italy is a secular state, secondly that Italy is not only made up of Catholics but also of Jews, Protestants and now of Muslims; the fact remains that our community has full rights to live in this country and experience the best relations of communal life and reciprocal respect with all the other communities. Biffi's insistence on our inability to fit in, to homogenize with Italian society, I think represents a huge problem on the part of certain sections of the Catholic Church. (Tg1, 30 September 2000)

In terms of the item's "apparent" objectivity what is very important is the final interview of the news item with another member of the Catholic

Church, Vinicio Albanesi, religious leader of Capodarco Community,[12] not a conservative but an ecumenical representative this time, which nonetheless seems even more ideologically problematic, in its historical reference to the crusades: "I think Cardinal Biffi articulates fears we all have, but we have an evangelical rule which tells us to welcome rather than discriminate. The Church has had many challenges, in the year thousand, and today has a challenge from new populations, maybe we can resort to Jesus' evangelical words which tell us to have courage and not fear." The reference to "fears we all have" is extremely problematic in its assumption that these fears exist in the first place and are at the same time collective fears. Very little evidence is presented about these presumed fears. This kind of discourse is a good example of anti-Islamic views receiving airtime on the main Italian public service channel. A recent controversy surrounding the comments made by the new pope Benedict XVI on Islam at the University of Regensburg has compounded this view about Islam as a religion to be feared (for a full critical discussion of the Pope's speech see Coury, 2008).

LEGA NORD AND POPOLO DELLA LIBERTÀ AGAINST ISLAM

In fact, discussions of anti-Islamic views recur regularly in the news; one was particularly well known at the European and international levels as it involved former Prime Minister Silvio Berlusconi on a trip to Berlin on 26 September 2001 when he publicly claimed that western culture was superior to Islamic culture: "We should be conscious of the superiority of our civilisation, which consists of a value system that has given people widespread prosperity in those countries that embraced it and guarantees respect for human rights and religion . . . this respect certainly does not exist in the Islamic countries" (Luzi, 2001). Other discourses have ranged from calls to close mosques mentioned above, to extreme suggestions always by Lega Nord politicians to bar Muslims from entering the country (Passalacqua, 2001). What is important to consider about many of these news events and respective representations is that they are not unconnected single incidents but a clear example of how ideas continue to circulate in the west and in this case in Italy about "the clash of civilisations." Berlusconi used the term "clash of culture," adapted from Huntington's original phrase (Huntington, 1996), a thesis which provided Americans with a new explanation on "the new phase" of international politics' and which Said described as the "Clashes of Ignorance" (Said, 2001). After news of this kind, a host of claims and counter-claims are set in motion, but there is little analysis of the specific context in which such racist views originated, a context which in Italy is linked to fears about religious identity especially from the Catholic quarter. As Eco has argued, it would not even be of much importance if these views were not based on "lengthy and passionate articles, which have legitimated them" (Eco, 2001). Many published in the mainstream Italian press as well as in more specialised publications such as the Quaderni Padani.[13]

When councillors from the former Forza Italia and Alleanza Nazionale called on the closure of two mosques in the center of Naples because, according to them, "mosques in the center of Naples are a public danger" and "people are frightened, there are too many Muslims around here," (Russo, 2001) they are calling on centuries-old prejudices, but also prejudices which have global resonance in contemporary times. More problematically these assertions are claimed to be made in good faith and in "trying to avoid any clashes between the two communities" (the Muslim and Neapolitan), which in fact have been coexisting quite peacefully for centuries (Salierno, 2001). As a way of "reparation" to Muslims, these publicly elected officials suggest moving the mosques to the countryside ("meglio creare nuovi luoghi di culto in provincia"), where according to them, there is less tension and less possibility of conflict. These anti-Islamic views which echo others around Europe based on the same notion of the mosque as "threatening space" where "images of men at prayer in the mosque, together with shots of its external architecture, constitute one of the most frequently iterated visual tropes of Muslim separatism, matched in audio form by the repeated "call to prayer" (adhan) (Macdonald, 2010). Another frequent anti-Islamic view, which was first aired on the Lega Nord's own television station, Telepadania and subsequently on TeleLombardia (a regional television station) was that Muslims should be denied entry into countries of the European Community. Speroni, a Lega Nord's Member of the European Parliament, then proceeded to circulate and expose his racist idea at a meeting of the European Parliament in Strasbourg, and in addition added what could appear as a "folkloric and spectacular" element (Lega Nord members are much inclined to these kind of excesses) but is in fact a degrading parallel; he suggested that we should treat Muslims the way we have treated the "Fiorentina": "The European Community has decided that we cannot eat 'Fiorentina' [a thick steak on the bone of cows from the Chiana area banned by the European Union during the BSE crisis], not because it tastes awful or because it is harmful, but because there is a danger. In the same way we should behave with Muslims." This particular news item was picked on by different countries' news media and represented as a folkloric feature of Italian politics rather than as a more serious suggestion that Muslim people should be barred from entering Europe, simply on the basis of their religious identity. Even more dubious is the final part of Speroni's argument, again picked on by the news media in the same way, which states that "Muslims" already in Italy (and Europe) who are good and well behaved ("buoni e bravi") can stay, emphasising the other racist development described by Taguieff (1994) as "tolerant racism." In his book on prejudice and racism Taguieff explains that xenophobia, of the kind practiced by the Lega Nord, is a form of latent racism and it never manifests itself directly, either in the rejection of one particular group, or stranger or immigrant, but it operates by creating a myth about identity with an obsession about hybridity ("mixofobia") alongside the construction of a hierarchy of the groups rejected (Taguieff, 1994: 426). The above mentioned discourses are of course symptomatic of the direction the Lega Nord has taken over the years, further and further into right-wing racist and xenophobic ideology, to encompass not just Southern Italian people, their original hate target, but all immigrants, and now especially Roma and Muslims, thus confirming Taguieff's explanation of the hierarchical ordering of xenophobic discourses.

TELEVISION AND ISLAMIC TERRORISM

More recent discourses analysed in the Italian news have concentrated increasingly on Muslims and terrorism activities. *AnnoZero*,[14] a current affairs program on public service television channel RAI 2, dedicated one of its episodes to domestic violence against women within Muslim communities in Turin; however, alongside it also introduced the topic of presumed Jihadist activities in a Turin mosque. Although this program is generally considered a serious attempt to report on events in Italy, in this particular instance there was a clear "sensationalist" approach to the topic partly due to lack of evidence about the Jihadist activities. The only evidence about these subversive activities was based on the finding of some pamphlets and magazines perceived to belong to Al Qaeda. In addition all the guests invited although more qualified to comment on the section on violence against women, were not in any way qualified to comment on the second part about Islamist extremism. The guests were writer Veronica De Laurentis, Fahrat Wael, president of the Islamic Community in the province of Venice, Khalid Choucki, member of the youth section of the advisory body on Islam, Marco Pinti, member of the youth section of Lega Nord, Samira (no surname provided), a young Muslim woman of Moroccan origins who has suffered domestic violence and whose son was abducted by her husband; other guests included the parliamentary political representatives Katia Belillo from the Italian Communist Party (Comunisti italiani) and Carolina Lussana of the Lega Nord. The choice of guests seems also somewhat problematic, as there are a disproportionate number of guests from the Lega Nord, given their very small political constituency, in comparison with other Italian political forces. To insert a badly researched news report about Islamic extremism alongside a programme dedicated to violence on women in the Islamic community, apart from the direct association which it conjures up, it also shows a polemical and sensationalist approach to journalism.

These kinds of unfounded information instigate a climate of fear and fuel further tension between immigrant communities and what has been described by Younis Tawfik (a Muslim writer and university lecturer resident in Italy), president of the cultural center Al Hikma, in an interview by Cassarà of *L'Unità*,[15] as "la caccia al musulmano" (the hunt for Muslims). In this interview Tawfik has also pointed out that there is no such thing as a journal for Al Qaeda (discussed in the programme); what does however exist is a website in Iraq from which some of the material found at the mosque may have been downloaded. Tawfik's final comment was especially critical of the presentation of the news item; this was constructed as an exclusive journalistic document about the propaganda distributed by the Islamic Jihad in a mosque of the city of Turin while in fact it was a poorly researched and executed journalistic piece (*L'Unità*, 1 April 2007). This programme, although having much of value in terms of the main investigation, was nonetheless problematic in his coupling of violence against women in the Muslim world with Jihadist activities; it was also a clear example of negative stereotypes being reinforced by the media, and which are today part of both a local-global circulation of ideas about Muslims and Muslim culture.

CONCLUSION

Many of the themes which surfaced above take us back to questions of "assimilation" vs. "multiculturalism" and the problems associated with it which Taguieff defined as "the substitution of the much discredited racial superiority with the acceptable version of difference between traditions" (Taguieff, 1994: 423). Although for Taguieff this is just as problematic, as he sees differentialism as a new clandestine racism, he nonetheless asserts that western tradition is nonetheless seen as superior. News about immigrants are often covered either in the context of "spectacular news," such as those above instigated by extremist utterances by members of the Vatican hierarchy or by the former Prime Minister Silvio Berlusconi or of "deviant" activities such as the graffiti by supporters of the Lega Nord: extremist views seem very palatable to the news machinery world over, and Italy is no exception. Positive news about immigrants is still rare in the news media, with some notable exceptions as the corrective article about *AnnoZero* published by *L'Unità* mentioned above exemplify.[15]

When it comes to Islam, the "classical" polarisation of orient vs. occident, Islam vs. Christianity is much in evidence, a polarisation discussed at length by Said (1991) in his book *Orientalism* and subsequently in *Covering Islam*: "Insofar as Islam has always been seen as belonging to the Orient, its particular faith within the general structure of Orientalism has been to be looked at first of all as if it were one monolithic thing, and then with a very special hostility and fear" (1997: 4). Said does not think Orientalism and the sentiments of hostility and fear are as severe today as in the "Middle Ages and the early Renaissance, when in Europe Islam was believed to be a demonic religion of apostasy, blasphemy and obscurity" (1997: 5), nonetheless many uncritical news media pronouncements evoke similar judgements towards Muslims today. These are reinforced by political forces such as the Lega Nord, which harps back to an earlier anti-Islamic culture (that of the Crusades for example). Muslim culture as a whole is in turn seen as a threat to Italian national identity and to Italian customs, with the inevitable conflation of Catholic identity with Italian identity. This is much in evidence in the word of Cardinal Giacomo Biffi discussed above: "Catholicism remains our historic Italian religion and we have to worry about safeguarding our national identity" (Tg1, 30 September 2000). This conflation is especially problematic in relation to immigrants' rights as citizens and its particular role in forging alliances between conservative forces within Italian society, and the contradictions which surface as a result. After all the Lega Nord is promoting a northern regional identity which stands in opposition to the Italian nation-state identity and certainly in opposition to global or cosmopolitan identity formation.

Rodinson argued when he wrote about nineteenth century imperialism and attitudes to Islam that: "The campaign against Islam became as fierce as ever, fortified as before with arguments dating back to the Middle Ages, but with modern embellishments" (Rodinson, 1981: 66). In Italian terms it reintroduces the old problem of whether the Italian state is a truly secular state, whether the media are in fact still the same "Christian videocracy" as it was first defined in a 1970s study[16] and whether a multicultural society, with all the distinctions that the concept entails, is actually in existence in Italy: "If similarities and assimilations are often valuable by and for themselves, and if one must be careful not to exalt the role of diversity and differentiation, one must nevertheless recognize the reality of differences" (Taguieff, 2001: 308–309).

Since September 11 we can detect two different and antithetical positions in the media in Italy: on the one hand, more caution in reporting negative views of Islamic cultures and, on the other, an exacerbation of the racist essentialism seen above. In the intensive global circulation of news some sections of society and the media are cautious about promoting and representing Muslim immigrant groups as anti-modern while center-right political forces, parts of the press and an uncritical televisual media have already laid the "ground" for further prejudiced views against immigrants. Thus migrants become both "victims of globalism" as well as "nationalism" (Jordan, 2003: 60) and are increasingly caught in the tension between local-national and global interests.

NOTES

1. Britain is the only country which has not signed the agreement.
2. What Ginsborg has called "nazionalizzazione debole" (weak nationalization) in Paul Ginsborg, ed. *Stato dell'Italia* (Milano: Mondadori, il Saggiatore, 1994), 643–644.
3. In 2006 national elections the Lega's overall vote was 4.6 percent. *The Economist*, 30 July 2007.
4. Forza Italia is the slogan used in football grounds when the national team is playing. It means Go on Italy.
5. For more detailed statistics as at 1 January 2008 see Istituto Nazionale di Statistica, La presenza straniera in Italia: caratteristiche socio-demografiche (National Statistics Institute, The Immigrant presence in Italy: socio-demographic characteristics), http://demo.istat.it/altridati/rilbilstra/, accessed 12 April 2009.
6. *Il Giornale* is owned by Silvio Berlusconi.
7. *Il Giornale*, 14 April 2007.
8. The Milan Council, run by Il popolo della libertà and Lega Nord has yet to grant permission to build a mosque.
9. Many myths circulate about Abu Omar as he resided at the center for a short time, before he disappeared under mysterious circumstances. Abu Omar is an Egyptian Imam who had sought political asylum in Italy. He was kidnapped in 2003 by covert CIA agents with the help of the Italian security services.
10. Lodi is geographically very close to Milan and at the heart of Lombardy, which along with Veneto and Piedmont is one of the richest regions in Italy with its strong ideology of industriousness, hard work, etc. normally posited against southerners (Italians and immigrants).
11. To date Tg1 (Telegiornale) has still the largest audience of all news provision in Italy.
12. The Capodarco Community is a religious voluntary organisation established to help people with disabilities with employment and social integration, www.comunitadicapodarco.it/, accessed 22 February 2008.
13. The Quaderni Padani is the "academic" journal of the Lega Nord.
14. *AnnoZero* is a current affairs program broadcast on the second public service channel Rai2 every Thursday at 9 pm. It is led by a longstanding journalist/talk show

host Michele Santoro. It began broadcasting in 2006 and the very first program on the 14th of September discussed the issue of immigration in Milan. *AnnoZero* is generally considered a serious and critical political program.

15. *L'Unità* is the daily founded by Antonio Gramsci and aligned today to the Democratic Party.

16. A Bianco (1974) La Videocrazia Cristiana. Rai-Tv, cosa, chi, come. Rimini, Guaraldi. A term widely used in Italy, in the past it used to refer to the political control of the Christian Democratic Party over the public service broadcaster RAI (Radiotelevisione italiana).

REFERENCES

Afshar, Haleh, and Mary Maynard. *Gender and Ethnicity. Special Issue of Ethnic and Racial Studies* 23, no. 5 (2000).
Allievi, Stefano. *Islam italiani*. Torino: Einaudi, 2003.
Allievi, Stefano, and Jorgen S. Nielsen, eds. *Muslim Networks and Transnational Communities in and across Europe*. Leiden Boston: Brill, 2003.
Balbo, Laura, and Luigi Manconi. *I razzismi possibili*. Milano: Feltrinelli, 1990.
———. *I razzismi reali*. Milano: Feltrinelli, 1992.
Bunglawala, Inayat. "The demonising of Islam." *Press Gazette*, 2002.
Barry, Brian. *Culture and Equality: An Egalitarian Critique of Multiculturalism*. Cambridge: Polity Press, 2001.
Campbell, Christopher P. *Race, Myth and the News*. Thousand Oaks: Sage, 1995.
Cardini, Franco. *Europe and Islam*. Oxford: Blackwell, 2001.
Cassarà, Tonino. "Annozero preoccupante, ma ora rischiamo la caccia all'islamico. Interview with Younis Tawfik." *L'Unità*, 1 April 2007.
Cere, Rinella. *European and National Identities in Britain and Italy: Maastricht on Television*. Lampeter: Edwin Mellen Press, 2000.
———. "'Islamophobia' and the media in Italy." *Feminist Media Studies* 2, no. 1 (2002): 133–136.
———. "The Body of the Woman Hostage. Spectacular Bodies and Berlusconi's Media." Pp. 235–256 in *The War Body on Screen*, edited by Karen Randell and Sean Redmond. London: Continuum, 2008.
Cesareo, Vincenzo, ed. *The Eleventh Italian Report on Migration 2005*. Monza: Polimetrica International Scientific Publisher, 2006.
Clifford, James. *Routes: Travel and Translation in the Late Twentieth Century*. Cambridge, MA: Harvard University Press, 1997.
Cohen, Robin. *Global Diasporas. An Introduction*. London: UCL Press, 1997.
Coury, Ralph M. "Syllabus of Errors: Pope Benedict XVI on Islam at Regensburg." *Race and Class* 50, no. 3 (2008): 30–61.
Downing, John, and Charles Husband. *Representing 'Race': Racisms, Ethnicities and the Media*. London: Sage, 2005.
Esposito, John L. *The Islamic Threat: Myth or Reality*. Oxford: Oxford University Press, 1992.

Fairclough, Norman. *Media Discourse*. London: Arnold, 1995.
Featherstone, Mike, ed. *Global Culture: Nationalism, Globalization and Modernity*. London: Sage, 1990.
——. *Undoing Culture: Globalization, Postmodernism and Identity*. London: Sage, 1995.
Featherstone, Mike, Scott Lash, and Roland Robertson. *Global Modernities*. London: Sage, 1995.
Fekete, Liz and Frances Webber. "The Human Trade." *Race and Class* 39, no. 1 (July–September 1997): 67–74.
Ferguson, Marjorie. "The Mythology about Globalization." *European Journal of Communication* 7, no. 1 (1992): 69–93.
Gabriel, John. *Whitewash. Racialized Politics and the Media*. London: Routledge, 1998.
Ghalioun, Bhuran. *Islam e Islamismo. La modernità tradita*. Rome: Editori Riuniti, 1998.
Gatti, Uberto, Daniela Malfatti, and Alfredo Verde. "Minorities, Crime and Criminal Justice in Italy" in *Minorities, Migrants, and Crime: Diversity and Similarity across Europe and the United States*, edited by Ineke Haen Marshall. Thousand Oaks: Sage, 1997.
Giddens, Anthony. *The Consequences of Modernity*. Cambridge: Polity, 1990.
Gilroy, Paul. *Between Camps: Nations, Cultures and the Allure of Race*, 2nd ed. London: Routledge, 2004.
Ginsborg, Paul. *Storia d'Italia dal dopoguerra a oggi. Società e politica 1943–1988*. Torino: Einaudi, 1989.
——. ed. *Stato dell'Italia*. Milano: Mondadori, il Saggiatore, 1994.
——. *L'Italia del tempo presente. Famiglia, società civile, Stato 1980–1996*. Torino: Einaudi, 1998.
Golini, Antonio. "La questione migratoria e il quadro demografico italiano." *Il Mulino, Rivista bimestrale di cultura e politica, anno XLVIII*, n. 381 (Jan–Feb 1999): 117–122.
Gordon, David A., John Michael Kittros, and Carol Reuss, eds. *The Ethics of "Correctness" and "Inclusiveness": Culture, Race and Gender in the Mass Media*. New York: Longman, 1996.
Gritti, Roberto, and Magdi Allam. *Islam, Italia. Chi sono e cosa pensano i musulmani che vivono tra noi*. Milano: Guerini e Associati, 2001.
Guolo, Renzo. "I nuovi crociati: la Lega e l'islam." *Il Mulino, Rivista bimestrale di cultura e politica, anno XLIX*, no 391 (Sept–Oct. 2000): 890–901.
——. "La Chiesa e l'Islam." *Il Mulino, Rivista bimestrale di cultura e politica, anno XL*, no 393 (Jan–Feb 2001): 93–101.
Habermas, Jürgen. *Dopo l'Utopia*. Venice: Marsilio Editori, 1992.
——. "Non possiamo rispondere 'la barca è piena'." *L'Unità* (4 June 1993).
——. *Times of Transitions*. Oxford: Polity, 2006.
Hafez, Kai, ed. *Islam and the West in the Mass Media*. Cresskill, NJ: Hampton Press, 1999.
Hall, Stuart. "Interview. Culture and power." *Radical Philosophy* 86 (Nov–Dec. 1997): 24–41.

———. "Questioning Multiculturalism." Keynote lecture at Crossroads Conference, Birmingham, 2000.
Huntington, Samuel P. *The Clash of Civilizations and the Remaking of World Order.* New York: Simon and Schuster, 1996.
Hardt, Michael, and Antonio Negri. *Empire.* Cambridge, MA: Harvard University Press, 2000.
Hartmann, Paul G. *Racism and the Mass Media: A study of the role of the Mass Media in the Formation of White Beliefs and Attitudes in Britain.* London: Davis-Poynter, 1974.
Hesse, Barnor, ed. *Un/settled Multiculturalisms, Diasporas, Entanglements, Transruptions.* London: Zed Books, 2000.
Husband, Charles, ed. Race in Britain. *Continuity and Change*, 2nd ed. London: Hutchinson, 1987.
Jewkes, Yvonne. *Media and Crime.* London: Sage, 2004.
Jordan, Bill and Franck Düvell, eds. Migration. *The Boundaries of Equality and Justice.* Cambridge: Polity Press, 2003.
Kymlicka, Will. *Politics in the Vernacular: Nationalism, Multiculturalism, and Citizenship.* Oxford: Oxford University Press, 2001.
Lazarus, Neil. "Charting globalisation." *Race and Class* 40, no. 2/3 (March 1999): 91–109.
Lull, James. *Media, Communication, Culture: A Global Approach.* Cambridge: Polity, 1995.
Macdonald, Myra. *Exploring Media Discourse.* London: Arnold, 2003.
———. "Muslim Women and the Veil. Problems of Image and Voice in Media Representations." *Feminist Media Studies* 6, no. 1 (2006): 7–23.
Marletti, Carlo. "Immigrati extracomunitari e razzismo nei programmi televisivi." Rai, Servizio verifica qualitativa programmi trasmessi (1990).
———. "Extracomunitari. Dall'immaginario collettivo al vissuto quotidiano del razzismo." *Nuova Eri* 106, Roma (1991).
Marshall, Ineke Haen, ed. *Minorities, Migrants and Crime: Diversity and Similarity across Europe and the United States.* Thousand Oaks: Sage, 1997.
Mattelart, Armand. *Mapping World Communication: War, Progress, Culture.* Minneapolis: University of Minnesota, 1994.
Meeks, Brian, ed. *Culture, Politics, Race and Diaspora: The Thought of Stuart Hall.* London: Lawrence & Wishart, 2007.
Melloni, Alberto. "Sguardi nello specchio: tre modi cattolici di percepire l'Islam" Limes. *Rivista Italiana di Geopolitica, Quaderno Speciale* no. 4 (2001): 173–182.
Miles, Robert, and Malcom Brown. *Racism*, 2nd ed. New York: Routledge, 2003.
Modood, Tariq, and Pnina Werbner, eds. *Debating Cultural Hybridity: Multi-cultural Identities and the Politics of Anti-racism.* London: Zed Books, 1997.
Modood, Tariq, Anna Triandafyllidou, and Ricard Zapata-Barrero, eds. *Multiculturalism, Muslims and Citizenship: A European Approach.* London: Routledge, 2006.
Morley, David and Kevin Robins. *Spaces of Identity: Global Media, Electronic Landscapes and Cultural Boundaries.* London: Routledge, 1995.

Moses, Jonathon W. *International Migration: Globalization's Last Frontier*. London: Zed Books, 2006.
Pace, Enzo. "Cittadinanza e nazionalità nell'Europa degli immigrati." *Il Mulino, Rivista bimestrale di cultura e politica, anno XLVIII*, no. 382 (March–April 1999): 367–373.
Poole, Elizabeth. *Reporting Islam: Media Representations of British Muslims*. London: I. B. Tauris, 2002.
Poole, Elizabeth, and John E. Richardson, eds. *Muslims and the News Media*. London: I. B. Tauris, 2006.
Ramadan, Tariq. *Essere musulmano europeo. Studi delle fonti islamiche alla luce del contesto europeo*. Enna: Citta Aperta Edizioni, 2002.
Randell, Karen, and Sean Redmond, eds. *The War Body on Screen*. London: Continuum, 2008.
Rattansi, Ali, and Sallie Westwood, eds. *Racism, Modernity and Identity*. Cambridge: Polity, 1994.
Robertson, Roland. *Globalization*. London: Sage, 1992.
Robinson, William I. "Globalisation: nine theses on our epoch." *Race and Class* 38, no. 2 (1996): 13–31.
Rodinson, Maxime. *Marxism and the Muslim World*. London: Zed Press, 1979.
——. *Europe and the Mystique of Islam*. London: I B Tauris, 1988.
——. *Muhammad*. London: Tauris Parke, 2002.
Rusconi, Gian Enrico. *Se cessiamo di essere una nazione. Tra etnodemocrazie regionali e cittadinanza europea*. Il Mulino: Bologna, 1993.
Said, Edward. *Orientalism. Western Conceptions of the Orient*. London: Penguin, 1991, 1st ed. 1978.
——. Covering Islam. *How the Media and the Experts Determine How We See the Rest of the World*. London: Vintage, 1997, 1st ed. 1981.
Saint-Blancat, Chantal. *L'Islam in Italia, una presenza plurale*. Roma: Edizioni Lavoro, 1999.
Sardar, Ziauddin Islam. "Resistance and Reform." *New Internationalist*, no. 345 (May 2002): 9–13.
Sassen, Saskia. *Losing Control? Sovereignty in an Age of Globalization*. New York: Columbia University Press, 1996.
——. *Migranti, coloni, rifugiati. Dall'emigrazione di massa alla fortezza Europa*. Milano: Feltrinelli, 1999.
Shohat, Ella, and Robert Stam. *Unthinking Eurocentrism: Multiculturalism and the Media*. London: Routledge, 1994.
Smith, Anthony. *Nations and Nationalism in a Global Era*. Cambridge: Polity, 1995.
Spencer, Sarah, ed. *The Politics of Migration: Managing Opportunity, Conflict and Change*. Oxford: Blackwell, 2003.
Taguieff, Pierre-Andre. La forza del pregiudizio. Saggio sul razzismo e sull'antirazzsmo. Bologna: Il Mulino, 1994. English version: Taguieff, Pierre-Andre. *The Force of Prejudice on Racism and Its Doubles*. Minneapolis: University of Minnesota Press, 2001.

Triandafyllidou, Anna. "Religious diversity and multiculturalism in Southern Europe: the Italian mosque debate." Pp. 117–142 in *Multiculturalism, Muslims and Citizenship: A European Approach*, edited by Tariq Modood, Anna Triandafyllidou, and Ricard Zapata-Barrero. London: Routledge, 2006.

Van Dijk, Teun. *Communicating Racism: Ethnic Prejudice in Thought and Talk*. London: Sage, 1987.

——. *Racism and Press: Critical Studies in Racism and Migration*. London: Routledge, 1991.

——. *Elite Discourse and Racism*. London: Sage Series on Race and Ethnic Relations, vol. 6, 1993.

Vitale, Ermanno. *Liberalismo e multiculturalismo. Una sfida per il pensiero democratico*. Roma-Bari: Laterza, 2000.

Waters, Malcom. *Globalization*. Routledge: London, 1995.

Zincone, Giovanna. "Immigrati: quali politiche per l'integrazione." *Il Mulino, Rivista bimestrale di cultura e politica, anno XLIX*, no. 387 (gennaio–febbraio 2000): 81–90.

——. *Secondo rapporto sull'integrazione degli immigrati in Italia*. Bologna: Il Mulino, 2001.

Chapter Thirteen

Multiculturalism in New Italian Cinema: The Impact of Migration, Diaspora, and the Post-Colonial on Italy's Self-Representation[1]

Alberto Zambenedetti

REDEFINING THE NATION BY REFRAMING ITS CINEMA

The co-existence of multiple peoples and cultures on the Italian peninsula and its islands is an historical fact. Before unification, Italy was understood more as a geographic location than as the territory of a nation, and if the Risorgimento brought political unity and led to the birth of a new country, it was the Fascist regime that attempted cultural unification through its coercive strategies of nation formation. Nevertheless, the diverse regional traits that characterize the multiple identities of the peoples of Italy were never entirely obliterated by the homogenizing efforts of the State. Diversity amongst citizens in post–World War II Italy was marked by language, food, local traditions, clothing, and—to a much lesser degree—religion.

As historian Paul Ginsborg writes, the "economic miracle" that took place between 1958 and 1963 "meant much more in the history of Italy than a booming economy and rising standards of living. It meant an unparalleled movement of the peninsula's population," especially—but not only—from the agricultural south to the industrialized north (Ginsborg 1990: 218). This displacement contributed to bringing the regional traits in contact and sparked reactions in the resident population that spanned from tolerance to assimilation to ghettoization. In this respect, the Italian people could be reframed both in the context of the national and the international discourse in terms of a multicultural/diasporic nation, endowed with diversity rather than doomed to fragmentation. As a consequence, the films that are embedded in the narrative of the Southern Question,[2] such as *Rocco e i suoi fratelli/Rocco and His Brothers* (Visconti, 1960), or *I Fidanzati* (Olmi, 1963), can be recontextualized and interpreted as *protomulticultural* films inasmuch as they deal with issues of tolerance, integration, and assimilation. Of course, in the sixties diversity in terms of race was almost entirely absent from the screens because the face of the country was largely uniform, even if Elio Vittorini, in his proto-resistance novel *Conversazione in Sicilia/Conversations in Sicily*, registers the presence of Chinese itinerant traders in Sicily as early as 1937.

Many factors contributed in the last thirty years to bring to the fore the need for a new representation of the Italian nation in the media. They span from the aforementioned local economic boom to the combination of global political events—the widespread process of de/counter-colonization, the demise of communist/socialist/dictatorial regimes in Eastern Europe, the poverty and the climate of terror in North Africa, the dissolution of the Yugoslavian federation, the ratification of the Maastricht Treaty, and so forth—and they all contributed to the formation of a wave of mass immigration in the peninsula. This relatively new phenomenon is best epitomized by the episode of the cargo ship Vlora, which on August 6, 1991 transported over 20,000 Albanians to the coasts of Puglia (Apulia), in the vicinity of Bari. The impact of that dramatic episode on the imagination of Italians is so resilient that in 2004 twenty-three-year-old filmmaker Roberto De Feo reconstructed those tragic moments in his short film *Vlora 1991* by editing fictional and documentary footage.

On a daily basis, since the early nineties, mass immigration prompts the country to rethink its identity in terms of culture, religion, heritage, and to re-situate itself in a European and global context:

> The increasing conflict over what Italians call *extracomunitari* (non-European immigrants) is tied to a central aspect of European integration: the development of a new conception of citizenship. Although a shared sense of European identity and the institutions to legitimate that identity remain notoriously difficult to consolidate, it has proven far easier to forge a common conception of *those who do not belong*. (Dawson and Palumbo, 2005: 166; my italics)

At the same time, the still largely multifarious nature of the "native" population in terms of regional differences often translates into an ambivalent attitude toward the processes of integration and/or assimilation of the immigrants and refugees. On the whole, mass immigration is often regarded as a large-scale contemporary version of the Southern Question and handled in a very similar fashion: this "new" cross-section of the population provides cheap labor for the industries of the North-East and the North-West, as well as for the regions whose economy is still driven mainly by agriculture. However, immigrants are largely looked at as an alternate population, destined to serve the needs of the country but not to partake in the enjoyment of its resources: B-class individuals, when individuals at all, posited as "others" against the alleged uniformity of the citizens by birthright.

The media and cinematic representation of this phenomenon is just as problematic as the phenomenon itself. At the inception of the nineties, the country presented to the European Union a seemingly optimistic image of itself, thanks to its growing economy and a period of civil and political stability. However, the bubble of confidence was destined to burst soon. While ridding the country of its closeted skeletons (oftentimes with questionable techniques of intimidation and blackmail), Tangentopoli—the all-embracing investigation carried out by a pool of judges based in Milan and also known as "Operazione Mani Pulite/Operation Clean Hands"—destabilized Italy both on a political and economic level, further widening the division between left and right, and the gap between the poor and the wealthy. With the rise of the neoconservatives to power, and the beginning of the Berlusconi era, the country has grown progressively more ideologically divided, and the strengthening of the national secessionist parties such as Lega Nord and their local constituencies has exacerbated the polemics revolving around the question of national identity vis-à-vis immigration. The language of the parties at power—and oftentimes of the ministers themselves—was tainted with tones of intolerance and racism: the leaders intentionally turned the clock back to 1934, when "the Duce worried aloud that the 'numeric and geographic expansion of the yellow and black races' meant that 'the civilization of the white man [was] destined to perish.'" (Ben-Ghiat, 2001: 128) The main ideologues of the Roman Catholic Church did not miss the opportunity to echo this Counter Reformation language: when musing on the "missed opportunity" of referencing the alleged Judeo-Christian roots of Europe in the European Constitutional Treaty of 2004, Cardinal Joseph Ratzinger (now Pope Benedict XVI), wrote that "Europe, in the hour of its greatest success, seems to be emptied from the inside, as if paralyzed by a circulatory crisis, a crisis that endangers its life by relying on transplants that efface its identity. The yielding of the supporting spiritual forces tallies with an increasing ethnic decline" (Pera and Ratzinger, 2004: 60; my translation).

If the official culture is still overall infused with intolerance and provincialism, it is by looking through the interstices of the fairly globalized Italian pop culture that one can find a better representation of these issues and their impact on the way Italians perceive themselves and their identity. This chapter looks at cinema, advertisements, and popular music, as these art-forms seem to offer a much more refined and subtle understanding of the effects of the phenomenon of mass immigration and the issues it raises in a country that is relatively young and that cannot reductively be equated with a single, united, and homologous nation. Specifically, a significant number of books and articles of recent publication have called attention to a very minor trend, a peripheral—albeit significant—category existing within the already loosely defined "New Italian Cinema":[3] films about migratory phenomena. From Gabriele Salvatores' Italian émigrés to Ferzan Ozpetek's Turkish refugees, many directors have tackled the topic of migration, seemingly covering every angle of this broad and multifaceted subject. In their book *Migranti in Celluloide*, Luisa Cicognetti and Lorenza Servetti compile an extensive inventory of these films from 1985 through 2003, dividing them into two categories: films about emigration, and films about immigration. In the first category, Cicognetti and Servetti lump together films on the Italian Diaspora and the Post-Diaspora, films that depict contemporary travelers, tourists, exiles and émigrés, as well as films about Italians moving across the peninsula; in the second, they group films about all sorts of immigrants coming to Italy, independently from their respective countries of origin and the means of transportation they employ for their displacement. To this day, English language scholarship is still grappling with this rough categorization, and it is struggling to improve the terminology employed in researching and analyzing this uneven, imperfect, yet fascinating group of films. In order to fully understand the complexity of this phenomenon and its significance in the construction of the image of the migrants, first and foremost it is necessary to provide satisfactory definitions and a general theoretical grid from which to start. Therefore, the most important step taken here is to attempt a full revision of the terminology: as a whole, the sub-genre can be straightforwardly referred to as *migration cinema*; within this, some categorizations are necessary. In fact, many films before the advent of New Italian Cinema had already dealt with migrations: the recent *Preferisco il Rumore del Mare / I Prefer the Sound of the Sea* (Calopresti, 2000), for instance, is a prime example of a postmodern version of the aforementioned *protomulticultural* films, inasmuch as it is embedded in the same, continuing narrative of the Southern Question. Not surprisingly, a close analysis of *Rocco e i Suoi Fratelli* and *I Fidanzati* reveals that their impact on the New Italian Cinema directors is visible beyond issues of style, technique, and authorship. As early examples of cinema about *internal migrations*, these well-known masterpieces established a number of thematic, linguistic, and narrative templates that find an application in the discourse on the later *de/counter-colonization cinema*[4] as a whole.

A new critical approach needs to be developed for cinematic representations of the Italian Diaspora[5] as well, since films such as the recent *Nuovomondo* (Crialese, 2006) are nowadays attempting to redress and reconsider historical oversimplifications and oversights with regards to the massive migrations to the Americas. Undoubtedly, the classic films on this topic have been discussed extensively, especially in relation to the metropolitan areas that welcomed, or simply tolerated, the waves of immigrants from the old world. However, what seems to be missing from the picture is an attempt to devote scholarly attention to *post-diasporic* cinema or, in other words, to the films of the new generations of migrants/tourists that cross the Atlantic in both directions in search of their fortune and/or their origins. Examples of these are *My Name is Tanino* (Virzì, 2002)—which tells the story of a young Sicilian man, Gaetano "Tanino" Mendollia, who travels to the United States in order to find meaning in his life—and *Ciao America* (Ciota, 2002) in which the main character reverses Tanino's trajectory.

Enveloped within the large folds of the post-diasporic blanket, yet another trend can be detected: films that tell the stories of Italians who leave their fatherland for destinations that are (in the majority of the cases) not inscribed in the historical narrative of the Diaspora. Neither fully migrant nor simply tourists, these travelers reject the well-explored paths established by the latter and position themselves at the margins of the "diasporic public spheres" (Appadurai, 1996: 147). As their motivations are very rarely of financial nature, they seek for alternatives that befit their existential restlessness, their thirst for diversity and less homogenized cultures, and their disillusionment with post-industrial, metropolitan, European/Communitarian Italy. Without the pretense of being exhaustive, this chapter attempts to shed some light on the multifaceted issues presented by the oxymoronic postulation of a *Multiculturalism Italian Style*, i.e. a national way to deal with an inter/trans-national phenomenon that, we argue, has permeated the culture and its cinema and rocked its already shaky foundations to their core. In four large brushstrokes, we focus on several examples of migration cinema and its iconography, investigating the representations of "self" and "other" between stereotype and glamour, eroticism and ideology, politics and aesthetics.

CINEMA, FASHION, AND COMMERCIALS: *VLORA AND LAMERICA*

The spring-summer 1992 campaign designed by Oliviero Toscani for *United Colors of Benetton* featured photographs of strong social content: an AIDS patient on his deathbed surrounded by his family in a *pietà*-like composition, a victim of a mafia killing covered by a white sheet and lying in a pool of his own blood—in his turn mourned by women in traditional Southern Italian black attires, and the aforementioned arrival of the Vlora cargo ship in Puglia. In her book on the shocking, thought-provoking, and controversial campaigns that Toscani created for the clothing manufacturer from Treviso,

Lorella Pagnucco Salvemini comments on the picture of the Albanian odyssey as follows:

> A ship is besieged by hundreds of wretched people, who are chasing a chimera of freedom and economic dignity, oppressed in their own country and refused entry elsewhere. "It looks like a timeless photograph but it nevertheless belongs to days which we have only just experienced, while we were all on the beach enjoying Italian good-will," Oliviero Toscani wrote not sparing to blame himself as well.
>
> It was inevitable that this impressionist vision of hordes of starving people looking for a crumb of bread and a crumb of hope should powerfully recall the memory of the great, tragic migrations across the ocean in the early 1920s and 1930s, when there was a mass exodus of Italians degraded by poverty and ignorance to the United States, South America, Australia and Canada. But they were also reminiscent of the compulsory transfer of crowds of Italian workers to Belgium, Germany, and Switzerland after World War II, albeit traveling by rail rather than by sea.
>
> It is possible, therefore, that these sad stories of misery and desperation, given international exposure by the Benetton campaigns, transcended the Italian-Albanian context of the images, referring to the drama of earlier exoduses including the Cuban one. (2002: 91)

Avoiding facile accusations of exploiting social issues at the advantage of rampant capitalist agendas, Salvemini touches on a point that is crucial in the discussion of how the Albanian exodus impacted Italy: she notes that Toscani is holding up a mirror for Italians to look at the history of their own migration in order to understand the motives behind such humiliating, desperate acts. In fact, the photographer's "in-your-face" aesthetics, albeit inherently demagogic, seeks to transcend the logic of commerce and blow a whistle for the international community to hear, reaching peoples all over the world through the powerful vehicles of pop culture.

The issue of the Albanian exodus was addressed by Gianni Amelio in his 1994 film *Lamerica*. The film tells the story of a fraud concocted by two ill intentioned Italians, Gino and Fiore, who pretend to open a shoe factory in Albania with the actual purpose of embezzling emergency aid funds from the Italian government. In order to succeed with their plan, they need an Albanian figurehead to pose as the president of the company. Their choice falls on Spiro, an elderly man who they believe they can easily manipulate. Their patronizing ways with the locals, their ignorance of the history of the country, and their limited understanding of the situation they are trying to exploit will ultimately sentence their plans to failure.

The opening credits are juxtaposed with an Istituto Luce[6] newsreel from April 1939 that shows the arrival of the Italian troops in the harbor of Durrës (Durazzo in Italian) on the occasion of the annexation of Albania. While squads of soldiers are deposited to shore, the voice-over illustrates the grand plans that the Fascist regime has for the colony, which, since 1925–1926, had been tied to Italy under an informal agreement of protectorate. The invading forces are seen marching in the streets of rural Albania, saluted by men and women as liberators and bearers of progress. The director then cuts to a shot of the same harbor in 1991, where men in rugs, hoping to board a ship to Puglia, are battling the police while chanting "Italy, Italy, you are the world!"

A series of vicissitudes in the course of the film lead the younger of the two phony entrepreneurs, Gino, to be incarcerated and to have his Italian passport confiscated. This emasculating plot-twist levels the disparity between him and the undistinguishable hordes of Albanians who are desperately trying to flee the country and reach Italy. Gino's loss of the ability to assert his national identity and therefore his "otherness" from the people he so much despised and looked down upon in his odyssey across the barren, hungry, forsaken country, causes his gaze—and ours with his—to be sutured with that of the refugees when he finally manages to board the Partizani, an Italy-bound cargo ship that the director clearly modeled on the Vlora. In other words, if through the Benetton campaign Oliviero Toscani forced consumers to look at people who had lost their purchasing power and, as a consequence, their own identity in the post–Cold War world, Gianni Amelio forces viewers to align with them, to look through their eyes. Hence, the spectacle offered by Italian television—that bleeds into Albanian houses, hospitals, and bars in all its superficiality and sex/money driven programming—becomes the illusory notion of the world beyond communism and dictatorship, a kaleidoscope through which the disenfranchised can look and pine for the alluring riches of the West.

On the deck of the ship, Gino comes across Spiro. At this point in the narrative, the viewer is aware that the old man turned out to have been an Italian soldier who had participated in the 1939 invasion, had been traumatized by the tortures he suffered under the communist dictatorship that followed the end of the war, and believes to be still in his twenties. Spiro delivers the melodramatic speech that concludes the film and seals the director's argument: mistaking the world around him and the perception of his own self, the infantilized man believes to be on a ship to the United States, and expresses his concern for not speaking English. He also underlines the failure of the Fascist language policies—of imposing the national standard code over the regional dialects—by confessing his inability to speak Italian too. The closing of the circle (the conflation of 1920/1930s Italian Diaspora with 1990s Albanian Diaspora) is juxtaposed with swelling music and an emphatic montage of faces of Albanian refugees. In the attempt to be noticed and acknowledged, the prospective immigrants look into the camera, thus returning the condescending gaze of the Italian spectator and rejecting the objectification of the cinematographic eye. Rodica Diaconescu-Blumenfeld offers a harrowing critique of this equation:

> A paradigmatic axis is to be set-up: the Italians went to America, the Albanians go to Italy; the old man had been made into an Albanian; and while he re-becomes Italian, the young Italian (almost) becomes Albanian. But the point is that in setting up a taxonomy of sameness that enables you to recognize the existence of something, you are also occluding difference. In Lamerica, the Italian's suffering displaces the story of the real hunger of the dispossessed Albanians. (2003: 95)

DE/COUNTER-COLONIZATION CINEMA: *SLAVI, NEGRI, MAROCCHINI, ALBANESI*, AND THE FLATTENING OF THE IMMIGRANT'S BODY

The migratory fluxes that started to target the Italian peninsula in the mid-1980s provoked sudden and deep changes in the fabric of Italian society: they flooded the job market with meek and inexpensive labor force, hence redistributing capital and oiling the wheels of the already thriving submerged market; they increased the level of cultural heterogeneity of the main metropolitan areas or even brought ethnic diversity where it was previously unheard of; ultimately, they catapulted Italian culture in the stream of globalization in a sudden and unapologetic fashion. The responses of the Italian people(s) varied greatly, spanning from intolerance to assimilation, from acceptance to hatred, from understanding to the grimmest nostalgia for overtly racist discourses.

As an almost completely new cross-section of the population, this "alien body" of migrants revitalized the question of defining the Italian identity: by rehashing the narrative of the Southern question on de/counter-colonial lines, the migrants reminded the Italians of issues that were still very close to home in post-1989 Europe. Hence the reiteration of the stigmatizing rituals that had accompanied the internal migrations during the economic boom, and the widespread usage of stereotyping discourses in the media.[7] For the Parondi family in Visconti's *Rocco e i suoi fratelli* the primal ethnic scene—when the individual is marked as "other" with respect to the hosting culture—corresponded to their labeling as *terroni* (racial slur for "Southerners") by their Milanese countrymen; the word, together with identifying their geographical provenance, bore many other stereotypical traits generally associated with Southerners: generalized backwardness, a penchant for melodrama, a strong emphasis on the body rather than on the intellect, and so forth. Similarly, the label is utilized to mark—and reaffirm—regional distinctions amongst the community of blue-collar workers in Olmi's *I Fidanzati*. In the case of de/counter-colonial migrants, their degree of difference from the natives is greater, thus greater is the stigmatization of their "otherness": the word *extracomunitari* has become an umbrella term that identifies non-natives of every provenance, thus flattening their individual ethnic and cultural identity. More specifically, Sub-Saharans, East and West Africans are grouped by their blackness and homologized by the racially inflected epithet of *negro* ("black person"; not to be translated with the English n-word); people from the Maghrib are conflated into the category of *Marocchino/ Moroccan*; Eastern Europeans are erroneously all considered *Slavi/Slavs*; finally, being *Albanese/Albanian* becomes reason enough to be considered lazy, worthless, or even contemptible. On the patterns of these stigmatizing practices, historian Paul Ginsborg writes: "The humiliations and suffering of the Italians in northern Europe in the 1950s and 1960s are now those of the Africans in Italy. And if there are no signs telling them to keep out of public gardens (as there were in Switzerland for the Italians), incidents of intolerance and aggression have certainly not been lacking" (1990: 412).

The group of filmmakers that are usually associated with New Italian Cinema has grappled with the representation of de/counter-colonization and migrations for almost twenty years. The films they have produced vary greatly in many respects; however, two major trends in this migration cinema sub-genre can be identified: films that deal with dark-skinned immigrants—grouping together *negri* and *marocchini*—and films that portray the trajectories of light-skinned immigrants—*slavi* and *albanesi*. However, the issues attached to migration films seem to show recurring patterns, and in many ways the interpretive categories elaborated for their predecessors can be productively applied. In his article "African Immigration on Film: *Pummarò* and the limits of vicarious representation," David Forgacs brings to the fore the vexing question of voice and highlights the shortcomings of Michele Placido's directorial debut:

> Ostensibly a film showing the experience of a black African migrant from his point of view, it was in reality a text addressed by a white production team to a white audience using black actors to perform white-scripted roles. A black audience already knew about these problems and did not need to be told about them. [. . .] At best the film allowed a partial identification with black immigrants on the part of the white viewer. At worst it reproduced [. . .] some of the very racist categorizations which on a conscious level it sought to repudiate. In this way the film raises important questions about the limits of this type of vicarious representation of black people's experience by white people. (in King and Wood, 2001:86)

Pummarò[8] tells the story of Kwaku Kwalaturé, a young doctor from Ghana, who travels to Italy in order to reunite with his brother Kwala (aka Pummarò). Once in Naples, Kwaku learns that Kwala has left the tomato fields where he was employed as a picker because of a quarrel over the exploitative wages. The film is structured around the protagonist's symbolic voyage towards an increasingly cold and inhospitable North, following the traces left behind by Kwala. The doctor partially replicates the narrative in which his brother had fallen: he gladly accepts meek employment in Naples, where he works shoveling manure on the fields; he gets involved with the underworld in Rome, where he tries to rescue Nanù—an African prostitute who is pregnant with Kwala's baby; he finds a position in a foundry in Verona, where he romances Eleonora, a white divorcée teacher; finally, he reaches his brother in Frankfurt, Germany, only to discover that he had died in unspecified circumstances.

The film's attempt at creating social awareness on the perils and tribulations of the African migrants is very straightforward: for instance, Kwala's journey across the Italian peninsula highlights the various exploitive practices to which the immigrant labor force is exposed—from the compensation of tomato pickers in the South, which is based on skin color, to the systematic lowering of the immigrants' wages in the Northern factories. In addition, *Pummarò* explains some episodes of racial intolerance and the general resentment towards Africans by displacing racist thinking onto socio-economical issues, such as the unequivocal fact that the phenomenon of mass immigration gave way to the devolution of unskilled workers' rights, thus turning the clock back to pre-1968 factory conditions. Furthermore, the film attempts to foreground several taboo-breaking issues, such as interracial unions, while at the same time depicting less obvious effects of assimilation: in Verona, Kwaku meets Isidoro, another Ghanian émigré who inducts the protagonist to foundry work. Like *Rocco and His Brothers*'s Ciro Parondi, Isidoro's two daughters have lost the language of the father; in fact, among them they speak the northeastern vernacular, and they resort to standard Italian when addressing their ISL father.

As Forgacs noticed, *Pummarò*'s "vicarious representation" of the migrant's experience is very problematic, because it does not allow for the individual to 'talk back' to the hosting society. In fact, the result is quite the opposite: the dominant culture reifies and objectifies the minority by expropriating it of its rights of self-representation:

> As a focalizing black character, Kwaku may be looked at by the white viewer in two contrasting ways: with a look of vicarious identification, whereby the white viewer is drawn to merge in fantasy with him and empathize with his plight, as if he were undergoing it in the viewer's place; and with a distancing and

alienating look by which Kwaku is held at bay by the camera, made an object of contemplation and eroticized as a body. (2001: 87)

According to him, the film falls short when depicting the interracial affair, because it mitigates the differences between Eleonora and Kwaku to an almost parodic degree: the immigrant is handsome, mild-mannered, highly educated, has an uncanny mastery of Italian language, is able to quote Shakespearean verse at length, and yet he retains the seducing features of African exoticism and mystery. In other words, the film refused to address the taboo of miscegenation in all its explosive potential by softening the differences between the characters. Frantz Fanon recalls the much less poetic nature of post-colonial interracial sexual relations: "Talking recently with several Antilleans, I found that the dominant concern among those arriving in France was to go to bed with a white woman. As soon as their ships docked in Le Havre, they were off to the houses. Once this ritual of initiation into 'authentic' manhood had been fulfilled, they took the train for Paris" (1967: 72). According to Fanon, the economy of this particular exchange is driven by a mixture of sentiments, amongst which we can detect vengeance—with the colonized subject acting sexually upon his former colonizer—and discovery—the "otherness" of the white-skinned mistress.

With regards to the Italian case, the issue of miscegenation is addressed by another film of the same period, *Teste Rasate/Skinheads* (Fragasso), depicts the downward spiral of a young man, Marco, into neo-Nazifascism[9] in 1993 Rome. Here, the theme of the contemporary de/counter-colonizing migrations is more apparent, since the young woman who romances the protagonist is a Somali maid named Zaira. Marco's nostalgia for Fascist Italy is made even more repugnant because it rehashes colonial discourses in the context of the metropolis, where the black migrant/colonized seems to be more at peace with the world than the clueless white native/colonizer.

The film's Manichean universe reverses the color scheme universally—and problematically—associated with notions of good and evil: the whiteness of the skinheads is defined against Zaira's blackness, their evil project is counterpoised by the woman's willingness to sacrifice her dreams, her aspirations, even her family for the man she loves. However, this is not to say that the character is endowed with any agency or even with a full-blown consciousness: in fact, Marco often refers to her as the *negra*, and what fuels his desire for her is nothing more than a morbid fascination for her exotic black skin, of which he is intimately ashamed. He also repeatedly corrects Zaira's Italian, thus reaffirming his superiority and dominance while mocking and infantilizing her. Finally, her body is repeatedly fetishized and eroticized through strategies of animalization and primitivism. According to Fragasso, it is impossible for a black woman to hear some music without feeling the uncontrollable desire to dance—barefoot—to its mystical beat. Similarly, according to Placido, every black man is a skillful percussionist. Forgacs points out that in these sequences the black characters are suddenly flattened to erotic spectacles by the objectifying gaze of the white spectator, which is made to align with the white character for whom these performances are enacted. Therefore, even if most of *Pummarò* is focalized through Kwaku, when he "starts playing a pair of hand-drums to demonstrate to Eleonora how they can be used to communicate in 'his culture' and then gets up to play the large drums on the stage" (Forgacs, 2001:89), the spectatorial alignment switches, and the Ghanaian immigrant's "vicarious representation" displays all its limitations.

The proliferation of films on de/counter-colonial migrations by Italian filmmakers began in the early 1990s, when the fall of the dictatorial regime in Albania caused an enormous wave of white-skinned immigrants who, in thousands, traveled to the peninsula on boats and ships. Although having set the standards for the category, *Lamerica*, like *Pummarò*, adopts practices of "vicarious representation" in depicting the plight of this cross-section of the immigrant population, and attempts to revert the imbalance between Italian and Albanian voice only in the celebrated closing sequence. A step further is Matteo Garrone's 1998 *Ospiti*, which depicts a handful of days in the lives of two young Albanian immigrants, Gheni and Gherti, in suburban Rome. In this movie, the anthropologically oriented director focuses on a set of characters he had already introduced to his audience in a segment of his installment film *Terra di Mezzo* (1996). Garrone focuses on the relationship of the two protagonists with two Italians who befriend them, a stuttering photographer and a Southern retiree. The photographer, in order to obtain a show in a restaurant, accepts the request of the owner to provide the two cousins—who are employed as busboys in the business—with lodgings for a few days. Shot entirely with a hand-held camera, the film utilizes techniques of "reality effect" in order to minimize the objectification of its subjects, the only exception being a mental flashback that is made to look like a home video. The very title of the film provides an ironical comment on the notion of natives as "hosts" and immigrants as "guests": in fact, the Italian word *ospiti* can be used interchangeably to signify both. This intelligent pun is supported by the coupling of the Albanians with the Italians, and by the mutual relationship of trust and respect that they slowly build.

Gheni and Gherti represent two ways in which migrants can respond to the hosting culture: situated at the bottom of the social ladder by their status of (probably) illegal immigrants, the two need to win their bread in the submerged market like Kwaku and Kwala. Just like the two brothers, they have different reactions to the infantilization and exploitation to which they are constantly exposed. On the one hand, Gheni trusts that the only way to social mobility is through work, and he dreams of returning to his country with enough money to open a mechanic's shop. This project is what differentiates him from Gherti who, on the other hand, rejects the ethics of work because of his troubled inner world. During one of his nocturnal walks in the neighborhood, Gherti triggers a flashback of his family sending him a video message in which they complain about the poverty and the war that are sweeping his homeland. Furthermore, Gheni and Gherti are allowed a natural speech, unlike Kwaku and Zaira: their Italian is accented, their mistakes and imperfections are genuine, and when speaking to each other they use the Albanian idiom. Neither Corrado—the photographer—nor Lino—the retiree—are endowed with superior oratory qualities: the former stutters heavily and the latter betrays, through his words, the lack of a formal education. The men are in fact exceptions in a world that looks diffidently at Albanians: in the opening scene, the boys try to make conversation with two girls at a train stop. Initially, the girls are nice to them, but when asked if they want to ride in the same car with Gheni and Gherti, they shy away and rush in the opposite direction. In the same way, Corrado's bourgeois neighbors approach him in the parking lot of the building where they reside and ask him politely to go to the police and register the immigrants. The flattening of the sociocultural—but not economical—distance between Corrado and the young Albanians is conveyed through the dialogic relationship of their wardrobes: in two occasions, the photographer wears t-shirts with global symbols of American consumerism (Coca-Cola and Batman) printed on them. The Albanian "West" (or "North"), Italy has produced its own metonymical icons, and Gherti wears them proudly on his chest: Leonardo, Michelangelo, but also the global Lion King and Bryan Adams.

Interestingly, *Ospiti* also offers a commentary on the eroticizing gaze of which black women are subjects in many de/counter-colonization films: although dating a white woman, Corrado goes out with some friends and ends up dancing with a beautiful woman of color. The director cuts from the heated dance scene to Corrado coming home and waking up Gheni; the two talk about the night, and the photographer confesses that he had sex with the woman, but that her sexual voracity and passion caused him to get excessively aroused and to ejaculate prematurely. Although the treatment of this bonding moment amongst men shows the possibility of (white) multicultural friendship, it is impossible not to notice that it is staged at the expense of the (presumably) African, animalized woman: she is scapegoated on the altar of the repudiation of a colonial relationship between the Italian (former colonizer/present native) and the Albanian (former colonized/present immigrant).

Artan Minarolli's *Nata pa hënë* /*The Moonless Night* (2004) is an even better example of de/counter-colonization cinema because it depicts the plight of

Albanian migrants from their country of origin, and not solely as "others" in relation to Italians and/or westerners. Naturally avoiding the pitfalls of "vicarious representation," the film stands as a sort of antidote to the trend that films like *Lamerica* started: its characters are granted individuality, consciousness, and motivations. To put it into words of post-colonial scholarship, *Nata pa hënë* can be productively interpreted through the theoretical grid offered by Mary Louise Pratt in her definition of "autoethnographic expressions":

> If ethnographic texts are a means by which Europeans represent to themselves their (usually subjugated) other, autoethnographic texts are those the others construct in response to or in dialogue with those metropolitan representations. [. . .] Autoethnographic texts are typically heterogeneous on the reception end as well, usually addressed both to metropolitan readers and to literary sectors of the speaker's own social group, and bound to be received very differently by each. (1992: 7)

This autoethnographic representation of the Albanian emigrants tells the story of Rudina and her grandfather, who board an overcrowded train in the attempt to reach the coast and escape from the impoverished country. On the night of their departure, a friend of Rudina's approaches her with a large poster of Leonardo Di Caprio, and asks her to kiss him on her behalf. The Italian-American Hollywood star is utilized metonymically to refer to a generalized West—the equivalent of the North to the African migrants—the steppingstone to which is the Italian peninsula. Several vicissitudes mar their trip, but eventually Rudina, her grandfather, and the boy with whom she falls in love along the way reach the coast. There, a number of prospective refugees wait for their turn to undertake the perilous crossing. Ready to give up their identities in the hope of a better future in the hosting culture and society, the migrants are photographed with a Polaroid camera, given the picture, and told to hold on to it. In other words, while they lose their passports and their national affiliation, their tri-dimensional bodies are stripped down to two spatial coordinates, in a flattening paradigm that is duplicated (image/word) by the aforementioned, stigmatizing label of *albanesi*.

Minarolli's depiction of this "waiting crowd"—an assembly of disenchanted souls who are marooned to the Adriatic shore by the waves of dissatisfaction with their land—seems to provide a counterpoint to the second to last episode of Nanni Moretti's *Aprile* (1998). In the latter, the director and his crew wait for a ship of refugees on a beach in Apulia. Before the actual arrival and disembarkation of the refugees, the melancholic landscape is almost empty, sparsely punctuated by the few, darkly-clothed figures. Its apparent barrenness and inhospitableness—which Moretti relates metaphorically to the alarming rise of neoconservative and secessionist parties in the country—evokes narratives of colonial memory, in which Italians were the ragged colonizers of seemingly deserted and uncultivated lands:

> There follows an interview where Moretti, as interviewer, asks a group of Albanians about the recent election result, and their opinion of its significance for their situation. In the ensuing embarrassing incomprehension on the part of the refugees Moretti labels his questions "half-witted questions, completely inappropriate." [. . .] The camera then cuts to documentary footage of another boatload arriving at the eastern port of Brindisi. The protagonist, usually so voluble, is uncharacteristically silent as the camera rolls. This silence is that of Italy, and of the West in general, unresponsive of the Albanians' plight. (Small, in Andall and Duncan, 2005: 243)

Ultimately, *Nata pa hënë* draws a parallel between the attempts at escaping/emigrating from Albania in the years of the communist dictatorship and the present time, therefore allowing for a historicized reading of what seems reasonable to call the "Albanian Diaspora." If such a postulation is deemed historically viable, then the post-colonial theoretical apparatus can be productively applied to the experience of the current Albanian migrants. Hence, the cinematic representations of their plight, such as *Lamerica* and *Nata pa hënë*, have to be interpreted in a dialogic relationship not only with one another, but also with other instances of migration cinema, such as exilic, accented, diasporic, and post-diasporic filmmaking.

THE SOPHISTICATED OTHER: THE CASE OF FERZAN OZPETEK

Istanbul-born director Ferzan Ozpetek moved to Italy at the end of the 1970s to pursue a college education in cinema studies at the university of La Sapienza in Rome. In the course of the 1980s he worked with several theatre companies in the country and as assistant director of a number of films. Using Hamid Naficy's terminology, the Turk could be defined as an exilic filmmaker: he is part of those "individuals or groups who voluntarily or involuntarily have left their country of origin and who maintain an ambivalent relationship with their previous and current places and cultures" (2001: 12). Ozpetek's feature debut *Hamam/Steam—The Turkish Bath* (1997) is the story of a young designer who is bequeathed property in Istanbul by his long-forgotten aunt. Wanting to quickly sell the unexpected legacy, Francesco flies to Turkey and stays with the family that his dead relative had befriended. When he finds out that the property he inherited is an old hamam, a Turkish bath, and that his prospective buyer plans to tear it down to replace it with a mall, he decides to keep it, refurbish it, and run it. The length of his stay in Istanbul becomes undefined, and the experience changes his life, first prompting him to loosen up on his efficiency-driven lifestyle and later to come out as a homosexual.

Italy and Turkey, and more specifically their respective capital cities, are posited as two dramatically beautiful ancient sites that cannot be fully grasped. Rome is always seen through the ribbon-windows of the modern house on the hill where Francesco and his wife Marta live. The geometric lines and the glazed surfaces contrast and complement the panorama of the ancient city, which the protagonist can overlook but not possess. In fact, the Italian identity is alien to him, even if he can gaze at its supposed cradle from a high vantage point. On the contrary, Francesco finds pleasure in roaming aimlessly through the old streets of Istanbul, discovering its hidden beauties, its colors, its smells, and its inhabitants. Through its protagonist, Ozpetek portrays and inverts his own trajectory: just like the director "went West" and found a career in the withering Italian industry becoming one of its prime directors, Francesco needs to "go East" and assimilate the Turkish culture, learn the language and so forth, in order to come to terms with his sexuality and ultimately to define his own identity. He moves across four main locations/locales: from his cold, aseptic house overlooking Rome he travels to Istanbul, where he finds shelter in a much warmer and darker, almost murky house. The latter is connected to the hamam by a little door, a threshold that leads to the final stage of his voyage.

Opzetek's third feature, *Le Fate Ignoranti/His Secret Life* (2001), is set entirely in Rome. Antonia and Massimo are a seemingly happy couple of professionals in their late thirties. After a car runs over her husband and kills him, Antonia accidentally learns about the man's seven-year-long infidelity. Devastated by the two-fold loss, the woman starts looking for answers, and discovers that her husband's lover was in fact a man named Michele. Once the initial shock is overcome, she befriends Michele and enters his world.

If the obliviousness of Antonia's bourgeois mentality is established as the normalcy of the Italian people, the "otherness" of Michele's community constitutes a submerged alternative at the core of which the complexity of one's identity can be unveiled and embraced. Through means of color palette and décor, Ozpetek initially depicts these worlds as irreconcilable and colliding, and slowly scrambles the boundaries that separate them, pointing at the recognition and acceptance that the gay community claims for itself (which is sealed in the end credits, where the cast of the film joins the annual Gay Pride parade). The director's glamorization of queerness does not neglect to expose his target spectator—the middle-class after-pizza Sunday night Italian moviegoer—to some common issues related to homosexual and trans-sexual life, while at the same time he "orientalizes" the community—and indexes his own roots—through the characters of the Turkish political refugees Emir and Serra.

La Finestra di Fronte/Facing Windows (2003), Ozpetek's fourth feature, tells the story of Giovanna, a twenty-nine-year-old mother of two who is married to Filippo. Despite being burdened by the mundanity of their routine and their financial troubles, the couple decides to take care of a Jewish holocaust survivor who enters their life by accident. While helping the amnesiac, senile man Giovanna befriends the handsome young professional who lives in the apartment facing hers, whom she sometimes spies from her kitchen window during her nightly reveries. The two become romantically involved, but Giovanna shies away from the escapade before it becomes adultery and rejoins her unaware family.

Giovanna lives in the same building of her co-worker Eminè and her family. The woman—presumably a Turkish immigrant, since the character is played by Ozpetek's regular Serra Yilmaz—lives with the African Jumbo (short for "Giovanni Battista") and his (their?) two children. In the course of a pizza dinner with Giovanna and her family, Emirè scolds her little girl for having dropped food on her shirt and says: "Remember, you always need to be cleaner, better mannered, and tidier than the others" (my translation). Without directly wording it, the character addresses the issue posed by the children's colored skin in a still predominantly white society. In order not to be looked down on as little primitives—a trope that recurs in the Italian brand of racist discourse—the children are suggested to assimilate the culture and outsmart it by being better players at its own game, an attitude towards life that, inevitably, entails the suppression of the influence of the cultures of origin of their own parents on their new, hyphenated identity, and the distancing from their heritage. In fact, as David Ward notes,

> racist arguments against immigration no longer bear on the question of the biological inferiority of the immigrant, for that is now untenable in scientific terms. Rather, racist strategies bear now not so much on the fear of difference, but the fear of equality. For racist groups, the threat now posed by the immigrant is to the integrity of the host country's culture, which they fear risks being diluted by the bearers of other, antithetical cultures. (1997: 91)

The subversive potential embodied by second-generation immigrants and their interaction with white Italians is explored more significantly in the two feature films of a screenwriter-turned-director who is preoccupied with issues of multiculturalism and identity: Marco Ponti.

MULTICULTURALISM ITALIAN STYLE: MARCO PONTI AND THE BENETTON YOUTH

In 1997 and 1998 Oliviero Toscani exhibited a series of photographs in Florence and Copenhagen. Here is how Giovanni Agosti, in the introduction to the volume that gathers these pictures, comments on the shows:

> On pylons, among which one wanders as in a wood, the images are displayed—each printed more than three meters high. Hundreds of faces stare straight into the camera lens, reducing the presence of the photographer to nothing. Contravening all photographic norms, the aim is to make a huge identification photo, like the ones issued by photo booths in train stations: the result has the usual cleanness of the images that characterize Toscani's work. White background, lit from front and behind, a rudimentary use of technology—the same principles as the snapshot—and always shot from the same angle. In this way, objectivity becomes poetic. [...]
>
> For him [Toscani], the faces almost make up a map of the beauty of today's youth, where whoever is photographed isn't there just to be looked at, unlike professional models, but is directly addressing us. And, despite the fact that the photos have all been taken in exactly the same way, saying much the same thing, it's not a homogeneous, canonic kind of beauty set in stone. Instead, it's like topography that is still tangible, where one town might be famous for its cathedral, another for the parish church, yet another for the cemetery: before everything becomes the same.
>
> Compared to Toscani's most recent work, the novelty here lies in the deliberate introduction of the concept of beauty, in all its ethnic possibilities. [...] [T]here's the almost illuminist aspiration to create an anthropological atlas. (Toscani, 1997: 8–9)

Toscani's photographs construe, rather than represent, a typology of the modern youth that Douglas Coupland, in his novel *Shampoo Planet,* labeled *Benetton Youth,* and that Henry A. Giroux defines as "global kids whose histories, memories, and experiences began in the Reagan era of greed and conspicuous consumption" (1993–1994: 11). The photographs initiate a movement of de-localization of the Benetton product, from the foggy plateaus of the Veneto where the company is based to the metropolis of the globe that the consumers inhabit. Caren Kaplan comments on the Toscani/Benetton paradigm by noticing that "Benetton offers us a 'united world' of different, ethnically inflected models all wearing virtually the same product" (1995: 50). This model is criticized for its political shallowness by Giroux, who argues that "the harmony and consensus implied in these ads often mock concrete racial, social, and cultural differences as they are constituted amid hierarchical relations of struggle, power, and authority" (1993–1994: 10).

More specifically, Karen Pinkus addresses the tense relationship between the residues of Fascist culture in contemporary Italy and the globalizing movement of the Benetton campaigns: "the positive, youthful association of the Benetton name with a new world order of global unity is also another way of forgetting the colonialist legacy, and then, by association, the very mechanism of power forged under the regime that may still persist at some level in Italy today" (in Allen and Russo, 1997: 149).

In his first two feature films, writer and director Marco Ponti tells the story of metropolitan, post-Reaganite youngsters who closely resemble the *Benetton Youth*. The opening credits of his debut *Santa Maradona* (2001) are juxtaposed with a montage of the goals of the famous Argentinean soccer player Diego Armando Maradona, a global icon of success and self-destruction, of stubborn individualism in the context of a team game, and of multiple falls and comebacks. The soundtrack to this montage is the eponymous song *Santa Maradona* by Mano Negra. The legendary Franco-Spanish band named after an Andalusian anarchist group is on the forefront of anti-globalization counter-culture, and in the nineties it has been politically active across Europe and the Americas: we can argue that the band stands in as a signifier for the aesthetics of cross-contamination that permeate the film. The unmistakable, hybrid sound of the band, collated onto the images of Maradona—who also synecdochically evokes the world of soccer and its global reach—lead the viewer into the life of Andrea and his friend Bart(olomeo), two unemployed graduates in the humanities affected by arrested development and who cannot find a satisfactory placement in the post-college world. Their story is set in Turin, one of the most diverse cities in Italy. The protagonist falls in love with the girly and beautiful Dolores while his friend and roommate secretly dreams of Lucia, the exotic Indian-Italian student who completes the quartet.

The references to popular culture—mainly Italian and American—are many and multi-layered, and they constitute the foundations on which the hypertrophied language of the youngsters is based. Their creativeness, impeded by the superstructure of the capitalist society, is let loose in their profuse profanities, their word mongering, and their hyperbolic loquaciousness. Bart—the lazy couch potato who cannot find a reason to leave the apartment—desires Lucia—the exotic woman whose otherness is comfortably dimmed through hyphenation. However, this sexual tension is not addressed directly, but it is mitigated through its dissemination in the media. After Lucia's boyfriend publishes some pictures of her nude in the *Photo* magazine, Bart is seen gazing at them and telling Andrea that he is going to "dedicate a melancholic wank to our friend Lucia." The man is then seen coming out of the bathroom and pretending to talk to the girl through her photograph. Bart sits on the couch, turns on the TV, flips through the channels and stares at a dance scene from a

Bollywood film in a mixture of arousal and catatonia. The director then cuts to Lucia, who is shaving her legs and watching the same movie. The girl's exoticism and sexuality—she is one of the very few instances of a non-one-hundred-percent white character in New Italian Cinema—are fetishized and filtered within the same cinematic/televisual shot.

A/R (2002), Marco Ponti's second film—a heist comedy with a romantic core—features more ethnic characters, the most prominent of them being Tolstoj, a middle-age, gentle, charismatic, and soft-spoken Indian bellboy played by legendary actor Kabir Bedi, who has been working in Italy since 1976, when he starred in the TV miniseries *Sandokan*, which was based on the colonial novel by Emilio Salgari. The boundaries of the Italian culture are once again teased out in the conversations between him and Dante, a disenchanted Benetton Youth who is about to embark on a trip around the world in the attempt of escaping from an existence that he perceives as meaningless. Dante and Tolstoj—as their names cry out—have a penchant for word mongering and storytelling, although their pacing and deliveries are very different. If Dante's sarcasm is often conveyed through surreal punch-lines, urban slang, and staccato jokes, Tolstoj's velvety voice and composure lend themselves to mesmerizing anecdotes and words of "oriental" wisdom.

AS A WAY OF CONCLUDING A NON-CONCLUSIVE ARGUMENT: THE EXAMPLE OF *BELL'AMICO*

In the early nineties popular culture began to offer representations of the migration question. While in literature the hyphenated identities of the new diasporic writers begin to emerge,[10] their televisual and cinematic correlatives are still missing. The patriarchal eye of the Italian director is still the privileged lens through which immigrants, refugees, and ethnic minorities are seen by the Italian audiences. However, as Graziella Parati underscores, "the ongoing process of the creation of nonessentializing concepts of sexual, racial, cultural, and ethnic difference is reflected in the national and narrative contexts that the immigrants have created and continue to create" (in Allen and Russo, 1997: 187). Some filmmakers, displaying a more perceptive sensibility than their peers on the changes that occur around them, manage to offer multicultural openings within the ongoing narrative of a national cinema. The cases of Michele Placido, Gianni Amelio, Ferzan Ozpetek, and Marco Ponti are to be taken as exemplar of a trend that is still in the formation process and that is starting to produce films such as *Lezioni di Volo* (Archibugi, 2007), in which ethnically inflected characters take center stage. A prime instance of the de-nationalization of Italian Cinema is *Bell'Amico* (D'Ascanio, 2002), the story of the love/hate relationship between Angolan director Mariano Bartolomeu and Nicola (Luca D'Ascanio), an anthropologist who offers him room and board in contemporary Rome. During his stay in Nicola's apartment, Mariano borrows his camera and starts filming his host; the short film he authors narrates the unraveling of Nicola's psyche after a traumatic break-up with his girlfriend, Laura. In addition, many vicissitudes mar the director's sojourn, resulting in a fall-out between the friends that precipitates Nicola into a depressive state. All ends well when Mariano enters the short in a film festival and wins, securing a contract for a feature that allows for him to pay back Nicola the money he borrowed and for the friends to finally understand, and reconcile with each other. An intelligent Chinese box, the film literally "frames" both D'Ascanio and Bartolomeu as narrators and narratees, and functions as a metaphor for the modes of racial division/interaction in upper-middle class, urban Italy. If D'Ascanio's signature over the film can be understood as appropriation of authorship—'whitewashing' the film—it is also true that in *Bell'Amico* Bartolomeu has a voice in the first-person. As Hamid Naficy points out, "[t]he authority of the exiles as filmmaking authors is derived from their positions as subjects inhabiting interstitial spaces and sites of struggle" (Naficy, 2001: 12); within this framework, the *mise-en-abîme* of Mariano's short can be interpreted as a signifier for his position of external exile from the former Portuguese colony, and his "otherness" from the narrative of Italian white bourgeois professionals. His present and previous work, just like his body, is narrated/contained by the work of the Italian director, but slowly takes over the reins of narration and "talks back" to the hosting society, refusing the stigmatization of his blackness/otherness/exoticness and asserting his own right of self-representation. Bartolomeu transforms Nicola's patronizing gesture into counter-anthropology, and takes advantage of his newly found insider's position in order to turn the camera onto his host and therefore obliterate any attempt at a racial hierarchization of storytelling.

If *Bell'Amico* cannot be considered a conclusive statement in the de/counter-colonial struggle for cinematic representation in the North/West mainstream, it certainly indicates a way to the future. In some way similar to the collections of short stories authored by immigrants but edited by natives,[11] this film is also a step forward inasmuch as it succeeds in avoiding—at least internally—the racist practices of labeling, stereotyping, flattening, and stigmatizing that have flawed so many works of migration cinema.

As a way of conclusion, let us quote Naficy once again: "[d]iaspora, exile, and ethnicity are not steady states; rather, they are fluid processes that under certain circumstances may transform into one another and beyond" (2001: 12). And if neither of these states can be fully embraced as identity defining, nor can the old-fashioned concept of Nation State. In fact, too often this notion is utilized as an ideological haven in opposition to the reality of the ever-shifting European multiplicity, and it is especially faulty when referred to the case of the multifarious peoples who currently inhabit the Italian peninsula.

NOTES

1. This chapter is an extended and revised version of an essay titled "Multiculturalism in New Italian Cinema," which appeared in *Studies in European Cinema* 3: 2, pp. 105–116, doi:10.1386/seci.3.2.105/1

2. The Southern Question, or *Questione Meridionale*, is a long-running debate—the definition was first employed in 1873—around the social and economic developmental cleavage between Southern and Northern Italy.

3. With "New Italian Cinema" critics identify the wave of films by young and not-so-young directors that followed the departure of the great masters such as Visconti, Rossellini, De Sica, and last, Fellini. Chronologically speaking, it began in the late 1980s and is still ongoing.

4. This coinage provocatively groups together films about processes of reverse colonization—i.e., when former colonized peoples migrate to the former colonizer's land—that may be triggered by an array of different motives. In the case of Italy, this includes territories that have never been under its formal colonial control, but for whose peoples the peninsula represents—pardon the conceptual generalization—either the civilized North/West or a steppingstone to other First World countries.

5. Strictly defined, the Italian Diaspora took place between the unification of the country in 1861 and the outbreak of World War I in 1914. However, large-scale migrations phenomena did not recede until the late 1920s, well into the Fascist regime, and one last wave can be observed after the end of World War II.

6. Istituto Luce is the oldest public institution dedicated to the production and distribution of didactic and informative cinematographic materials in the world. It was created in Rome, Italy in 1924, and it soon became a powerful instrument of propaganda of the Fascist regime. Today, the archive of the Luce is available online at www.luce.it.

7. See Belluati, Marinella, Giorgio Grossi, and Eleonora Viglongo. *Mass Media e Società Multietnica*. Milano: Anabasi, 1995; and Marletti, Carlo. *Extracomunitari. Dall'immaginario collettivo al vissuto quotidiano del razzismo*. Roma: RAI, 1991.

8. Literally, *Pummarò* (short for *pummarola*) means "tomato sauce" in Neapolitan dialect. Of course, the title is a sarcastic pun on the job that Kwala must perform, dawn to dusk, in the pursuit of his and Kwaku's happiness.

9. Of course, the formulation of "Nazifascism" is historically very problematic; however, the word effectively highlights the youngsters' limited understanding of the models on which their political creed is based.

10. See, for instance, Parati, Graziella. (ed.) *Mediterranean Crossroads: Migration Literature in Italy*. Madison: Teaneck, 1999.

11. See for instance, Maspoli, Emanuele. (ed.) *La loro terra è rossa. Esperienze di viaggio di migranti marocchini*, Torino: Ananke, 2004.

REFERENCES

AAVV. *The Outsider: Prejudice and Politics in Italy*. Princeton: Princeton University Press, 2000.

Allen, Beverly and Mary J. Russo, eds. *Revisioning Italy: National Identity and Global Culture*. Minneapolis: University of Minnesota Press, 1997.

Bellinello, Pier Francesco. *Minoranze Etniche e Linguistiche*. Cosenza: Editoriale Bios, 2000.

Ben-Ghiat, Ruth. *Fascist Modernities. Italy, 1922–1945*. Berkeley: University of California Press, 2001.

Bocca, Giorgio. *Gli Italiani sono razzisti?* Milan: Garzanti, 1998.

Braccini, Barbara. *I Giovani di Origine Africana: Integrazione socio-culturale delle seconde generazioni in Italia*. Turin: L'Harmattan, 2000.

Colors, sample issues.

Dawson, Ashley and Patrizia Palumbo. "Hannibal's Children: Immigration and Antiracists Youth Subcultures in Contemporary Italy." *Cultural Critique*, no. 59 (Winter 2005): 165–186.

Diaconescu-Blumenfeld, Rodica. "The Desire of the Other: Balkan Dystopia in Western European Cinema." Pp. 90–104 in *Moving Pictures, Migrating Identities*, edited by Eva Rueschmann. Jackson: University of Mississippi, 2003.

Gatti, Sergio. *Lamerica di Gianni Amelio*. Piacenza: Morpheo edizioni, 2007.

Giroux, Henry A. "Consuming Social Change: The 'United Colors of Benetton.'" *Cultural Critique*, no. 26 (Winter 1993–1994): 5–32.

Ginsborg, Paul. *A History of Contemporary Italy. Society and Politics 1943–1988*. London: Penguin, 1990.

Goldberg, Vicki. "Benetton and the Uses of Tragedy." Pp. 166–71 in *Light Matters: Writings on Photography*, edited by Vicki Goldberg. New York: Aperture, 2005: 166–171.

Gómez-Reino Cachafero, Margarita. *Ethnicity and Nationalism in Italian Politics. Inventing the Padania: Lega Nord and the northern question*. Burlington, VT: Ashgate Publishing Company, 2002.

Grillo, R.D. and Jeff C. Pratt, eds. *The Politics of Recognizing Difference: Multiculturalism Italian-Style*. Burlington,VT: Ashgate Publishing Company, 2002.

Kaplan, Caren. "'A World Without Boundaries': The Body Shop's Trans/National Geographics." *Social Text*, no. 43 (2005): 45–66.

Mantle, Jonathan. *Benetton: The Family, the Business and the Brand*. London: Little, Brown and Company, 1999.

Naficy, Hamid. *An Accented Cinema: Exilic and Diasporic Filmmaking*. Princeton: Princeton University Press, 2001.

Pera, Marcello and Joseph Ratzinger (Pope Benedict XVI). *Senza Radici. Europa, Relativismo, Cristianesimo, Islam.* Milan: Mondadori, 2004.

Rivera, Annamaria. *Estranei e Nemici: Discriminazione e violenza razzista in Italia.* Rome: DeriveApprodi, 2003.

Salvemini, Lorella Pagnucco. *United Colors: The Benetton Campaigns.* London: Scriptum Editions, 2002.

Small, Pauline. "Immigrant Images in Contemporary Italian Cinema: A Nation with a Clear Conscience?" Pp. 239–254, in *Italian Colonialism: Legacy and Memory*, edited by Jacqueline Andall and Derek Duncan. New York: Peter Lang, 2005.

Toscani, Oliviero. *Facce*. Rome: Castelvecchi, 1997.

Index

ABC, 140
Åberg, Frida, 132, 134
Accolla, Tonino, 110
adaptation, xvi–xvii, 32, 60, 81, 91, 101–4, 109–11, 115–17, 121, 125–26, 135–36, 141–42
Afghanistan, 194
AGCom, 12–13, 62. *See also* Competition Authority (AGCM)
Al Hikma, 237
Alleanza Nazionale (National Alliance), 32–33, 210–11, 215, 226–27, 235
All in the Family, 104
Al Qaeda, 236–37
Al Shamshoon, 101–2
Amato-Ferrero Law, 228
Amato, Giuliano, 123
Amelio, Gianni, 250–51, 264
Americanization Paradigm, 80–81
Andreucci, Giacomo, 177
animation, 65, 71, 104–5, 125
Annozero, 232, 236, 238
Antena 3, 70
AntTV, 178
Apple, 197
Aprile, 258
Arbore, Renzo, 109
Arcoiristv, 194
Argentina, 69, 132

Australia, 37, 69, 156, 250
Austria, 132

Balibar, Etienne, 29–30, 33
Belgium, 132, 250
Belillo, Katia, 236
Bell'Amico, 264–65
Berardi, Franco (Bifo), 175
Berlusconi, Silvio, vii, xi–xiv, 10, 12, 14–15, 17–18, 32, 38, 41–43, 46, 49, 172, 203, 205, 210, 216, 234, 237, 247
Bertelsmann, 4
Bewitched, 104
Biffi, Giacomo (Cardinal), 233–34, 238
Big Brother, 130, 135–36, 140
The Bill, 93
blog(s), 177, 181, 193, 198; blogger, 179; TheBlogTV, 194–95; videoblog, 73, 193; weblog, 154
"Bologna Noi," 162
Bond, James, 92, 95
Bondy Blog, 181
border, 28–30, 137, 228, 230
Bossi, Umberto, 121, 210, 215–16, 228
Brancaccio, 96
brand, 63, 68, 83, 108–9, 114, 190, 195, 261
Brazil, 132

Britain, 11, 204. *See also* UK
Burnett, Mark, 132, 134

cable, xiii, 8, 13, 21, 23, 26, 47–48, 191
Cagney and Lacey, 90
Camera dei deputati, 32
Canadian Radio Telecommunications Commission (CRTC), 27
Canale 5, xi, xiii. *See also* Mediaset
Canal Plus, 4–9
capital, xiv, 27, 31, 58, 64, 68, 71, 75, 252, 260; capitalism, 25; social capital, 152–53, 162, 164
Carabinieri, 93
Cardinale, Salvatore, 46–47
cartoon(s), 80, 83, 104–5, 190, 194
Catholic Church, 109, 211, 232–33, 247
CBS, 130, 132, 133, 140
Cecchi Gori, Vittorio, 7–8, 43
Celebrity Survivor, 141
Centro Europa 7, xi
China, 120, 204
Choucki, Khalid, 236
Christian Democratic Party, xii–xiii
Christianity, 238
"Christian videocracy," 238
Ciao America, 249
citizenship, 29–30, 112, 120, 158–59, 180, 204, 207, 214, 220, 246. *See also* digital citizenship
colonialism, 30, 204
colonization, 8
Columbus Center, 23
commercial television, xiv, 82–83, 86, 89
Commonwealth, 157
communication networks, xvi, 22, 58, 181
Communist Party, 236
Competition Authority (AGCM), 6–7. *See also* AGCom.
conflict of interest, xiv, 172
Constitutional Court, xii, 13, 41, 43
convergence, xvii, 130, 172–74, 176–77, 185; media convergence, 173, 179

Conversazione in Sicilia, 246
corporate media, xiv, 179, 182
Corriere della Sera, 43–44, 211, 213–17, 221
The Cosby Show, 105
counter-colonization, 246, 248, 252–53, 257
CSI, 93
cult, 90, 126
cultural: diversity, 27–28, 142; domination, xiv, 126; industries, 188; production, xiv, 28, 185–88; proximity, xiv, 81; studies, vii, viii, xvii, 188

Dallas, 80, 84, 88
Dark Justice, 90
De Agostini Group, 67, 70, 76
De Feo, Roberto, 246
De Laurentis, Veronica, 236
De Mita, Ciriaco, 123
Democratici Cristiani e di Centro (UDC), 215
Democratici di Sinistra (DS), 217
democratization, 18, 159
deregulation, xii, xiii, 59, 226
dialect, 114, 118, 121–22, 127, 217
diaspora, 23, 245, 248–49, 251, 259
di Carlo, Elena, 112, 115, 127
Di Felice, Aldo, 24, 27
digital, viii, xvi, 5–7, 9–13, 16–18, 21, 28, 37–47, 49–51, 174, 178, 180–182, 193; broadcasting, xi, 11, 18; citizenship, 157–59; democracy, 180; digitization, xvi, 37–38, 41; divide, 39, 196; networks, 57–58; platform, 6–8, 43, 46–47, 181; revolution, xvi, 6; satellite pay-TV, 4–5, 8–10, 17; technology, xi–xii, 38, 178; (terrestrial) television (DTT), xvi, 3–4, 10–18, 37–50, 195–96; transmission, xi, 195
Distretto di Polizia, 93
documentary, 65, 133, 138, 140, *144–45*, 187, 195, 246, 259

docusoap, 132, 142
Dogma, 134, *144*
Domenica In, 46–47
domestication, 104, 115
Duce, 247
duopoly, 26, 38, 40–42, 44, 46–47, 50, 57, 64, 74, 189, 196

e-government, 40, 157–58
Eastern Europe, 120, 205, 246
Ecotv.it, 193
Edwards, Marion, 101–2
Einstein Multimedia, 73, 141
Endemol, 60, 65, *67*, 71–72, 130, 135, 138, 141
epic, 82, 134
The Equalizer, 89–90
ethnic absolutism, 27
Eurobarometer, 206
European Commission (EC), 5–9, 15–17, 61, 217
European Union (EU), xi, xvi, 3, 5, 9–11, 15–16, 18, 37, 39, 58, 60–63, 157, 163, 172, 181, 206–7, 226, 228, 235, 247
Expedition Robinson, 130–31, 133, 137, *143*
extracomunitari, 229, 246, 253

fascism: Fascist Italy, 30, 255; Fascist Party, 226; Fascist regime, 122, 207, 245, 251
Fastweb, 9
fiction, 82, 85, 115, 123, 145
Fini, Gianfranco, 203, 210–11, 214–17, 220–21, 228
Fininvest, xiii–xiv, 61, 79, 83–84, 86. *See also* Mediaset
Finland,156
The Flintstones, 104–5
flow, 26–27, 73, 134, *144*, 175–76, 216; communication, 81, 154; global, 59; international, xii, 151; media, xii, xiv, 94, 126; migration, 226, 228; television, xvi; transnational, 31, 80

Flux, 195
format(s), 58–59, 65, 68–*69*, 75, 93, 130–32, 135, 137, 139–*43*, 145, 190, 194; global format, xvii; reality TV format, 129, 135, 140, 142; reformatting, xii, xvi, 126
Forza Italia, 211, 226–227, 229, 235. *See also* Berlusconi, Silvio
FOX, *72*, 101–2, 105, 127
FOX International Television, 101
France, 3, 29, 43, 57, 60–61, *66, 69*, 71–72, 80, 84, 110, 181, 204, 255
Free Trade Act, 27
Fremantle, 60, 65, *67*, 71–*72*
Frulla, Liza, 28

game show(s), 59, 70, 129–31, 133–34, 137–42, 173
Garrone, Matteo, 256
Gasparri, Maurizio, 48; Gasparri bill, 13–14; Gasparri Law, 14, 42–43, 48
genre, xiv, xvi, *45*, 63, 71, 79, 81–83, 93, 95, 104–5, 111, 129, 132, 134, 137, 140–41, 145, 188, 248, 253
Gentiloni, Paolo, 42; Gentiloni bill, 42–44, 49
Germany, 3, 5, 7, 43, 61, *66, 69*, 72, 132, 189, 250, 254
global markets, 22, 27, 58
global media, xv, 16, 21–22, 26, 30, 33–34, 126, 172
globalization, viii, xii, xiv–xvi, xviii, 21–22, 30, 57–60, 65, 74–75, 139, *143*, 151, 154, 165, 173–74, 176, 182, 185, 188, 203–5, 221, 225–26, 231, 252, 263; effects, 59; forces, 197; processes, viii, 3, 173
global television, 129–30, 142
glocalization, 59, 91, 129, 135, 142, 186
Google, 197
Gore, Al, 193
Gracie Films, 101–2
Grande Fratello, 140. *See also* Big Brother
Grillo, Beppe, 193

Groening, Matt, 102
guerrilla: broadcasting, xiv; media, xii

Hanna-Barbera, 104
Hill Street Blues, 90
The Honeymooners, 104

I Dream of Jeannie, 104
identity, xv, 28–29, 106–8, 120, 122, 174–75, 177, 191, 194, 206, 231, 236, 238, 246–47, 251, 260–61; American, 103; cultural, xvi, 22, 110, 120, 253; ethnic, 107; European, 246; identity formation, 34, 238; Italian, xv, 238, 252, 260; local, 75; national, 22, 29, 63–64, 75, 121, 203–4, 226, 231, 238, 246, 251; political, 106–7; regional, 226, 238; religious, 235
I Fidanzati, 245, 248, 253
Il Giornale, 230
Il Maresciallo Rocca, 93
Il Musichiere, 59
Il Sole 24 Ore, 191
immigration, xii, xviii, 33, 111–12, 120, 122–23, 157, 177, 203–11, *214*, 216–*18*, 220, 225–31, 247–48, 261; African, 253; European, 203, 230; illegal, 181, 228; immigrants, xii, xviii, 122, 209; mass immigration, 246–47, 254
imperialism, xiv, 30, 80–81, 94, 238
imperialist paradigm, 126
import/export, xv, 68
indigenization, xvii, 81, 91, 104–5, 107–11, 113, 115, 125; paradigm of, xv
Indisound, 191–92, 196
Insu^TV, 175–77
interactivity, 48, 153, 159, 194
international distribution, 21, 101, 125
internationalization, 58, 60, 69, 72
International Journal of Cultural Studies, vii
Internet, xviii, 39–40, 57, 73, 152–55, 159–60, 174, 178, 181, 185–88, 193–94, 219

Iperbole, 153, 158–63
Islam(ic), 101, 229, 231–32, 234–38
Istituto Luce, 250
Italia 1 (Italia1), xi, xiii, 130, 135, 140. *See also* Mediaset
italiani all'estero, 23, 31–32

jihad, 236–37
The Jetsons, 104–5

Kirch, 4

La Finestra di Fronte, 261
Lamerica, 249–50, 252, 256, 258–59
La Omicidi, 93
La Padania, 230
La Repubblica, 211, 213–16
Lascia o raddoppia?, 59
La7, 196
La Squadra, 93
La Stampa, 213–16
Le Fate Ignoranti, 260
Lega Nord (Northern League), 121, 205, 210, 216–17, 226–27, 229–30, 232–38, 247
Lezioni di Volo, 264
Linden, Johan, 132
L'isola dei Famosi, 130, 140–42
localization, 60, 91, 107, 112, 142, 188, 225–26, 231; de-localization, 262
Lolli Radio, 190
Lollobrigida, Gina, 122
long tail, 187
Loren, Sophia, 122
Loribel, 71
L'Unità, 237–38
Lussana, Carolina, 236
Lux Vide, 67, 71

Maastricht Treaty, 228, 246.
Maccanico, Antonio (Communications Minister), 8–9, 41; Maccanico Law, 41
Mafia, xvi, 81–83, 85–89, 91–96, 112, 115, 230, 249

Magliaro, Massimo, 23–25, 27
Magnolia (Group), 60, *67*, 70–73, 130, 141
Maradona, Diego Armando, 263
MBC, 101–102
media industry (media industries), xii, xv–xvi, 44, 57–60, 126, 151
Media Program, 62
Mediaset (Group), xi, xiii–xiv, 7, 11–17, 38, 40–44, 47, 50, 57, 64–65, *67*, 70–71, 79, 86, 90, 101, 122, 125, 141, 145, 172, 189, 194, 196, 208, *218*
Méndez, Denny, 122
Migranti in Celluloide, 248
migration, ix, 30, 42–43, 47–48, 58, 63, 132, 174, 176–77, 225–26, 228, 245, 248, 250, 253, 264. *See also* immigration
migration cinema, 248–49, 253, 259, 265
Minarolli, Artan, 257–58
Ministry and Department for Innovation and Technologies (MIT), (DIT), 156–58
Miss Italia, 122
Mondadori, xiii
Mondo TV, 71–72
MO-Net/Unox1, 153, 158, 160–63
monopoly, viii, xi–xiii, xvii–xviii, 9, 14, 16, 46–47, 85
Moretti, Nanni, 258–59
MSI (Movimento Sociale Italiano), 226
M-Tv Italia, 195–96
multiculturalism, xviii, 28, 33, 123, 228, 237, 245, 249, 261–62
Munafò, Stefano, 96
Murdoch, Rupert, 8–10, 17, 43
My Name is Tanino, 249
MySpace, 73, 182, 197
mytv.it, 194

NAFTA, 27
Name That Tune, 59
Nata pa hënë, 257–59

National Center for Public Administration Informatics (CNIPA), 156
nationalism, 21, 28, 233, 239,
nationality, xv, 29, 119, 207,
nation-state, 21, 25, 29, 31, 33, 226, 238
NBC, 59, 90, 132
neotelevisione, xiv, 79, 82, 84–88, 93
Nessuno.tv, 193, 195
the Netherlands, 69, 129–30, 132
New Global Vision, 174
New Italian Cinema, 245, 248, 253, 264
new media, viii, xii, xiv, xvii–xviii, 60, 64, 73, 151–54, 157–59, 165, 174, 177–79, 185
News Corporation (Newscorp), 4, 7–9, 14–16, 18, *67*, 172, 197
New York Police Department, 93
Non Solo Nero, 122–23
North America, 29, 165
Northern Italy, 9, 86, 171, 177, 216, 232
Nuovomondo, 248

Obama, Barack, 181
Omar Shamshoon, 101
Onda Tropical, 192
on demand, 9, 73
Operazione Mani Pulite (Operation Clean Hands), 247
Orfeo TV, 171, 173, 175
Orientalism, 238
Orion radio, 192
Ospiti, 256–57
"otherness," xii, xvii–xviii, 111, 114, 251, 253, 255, 260, 263, 265
Ozpetek, Ferzan, 259–60, 264

Palomar, *67*, 71–72
Pardo, Denise, 24–25
Parliament, European, 235–36
Parliament, Italian, xiii, 6–7, 11, 13–14, 24, 28, 32, 42, 44, 49, 96, 193, 203, 210–11, 215–16, 227
Parsons, Charlie, 131, 140
Partecipa.net, 153, 158, 160–63

Payne, Don, 105–6
Pinti, Marco, 236
Placido, Michele, 87, 264
pluralism, xii–xiii, 40–41, 48–49, 172
policy, xvi, 4–6, 8, 10–12, 16, 18, 28, 58, 65, 68, 74–75, 151–52, 157, 161–62, 203–4, 210–21, 232; broadcasting, 3, 28; cultural, 17–18, 29–31; EU, 10, 60–61; immigration, 120, 203, 211, 221; media, 17; national, 17–18; policy-making, xii, 10, 152–53, 155–56, 158–59, 162–63, 219; public, 57, 155, 217
Pope Benedict XVI, 234, 247. *See also* Ratzinger, Joseph
Popolo della libertà (PDL), 227, 230, 234
Porta a Porta, 48
postmodern(ism), 103, 108, 248
Preferisco il Rumore del Mare, 248
Prime Minister (of Italy), xi, xiii, 32, 41, 121, 172, 203, 210, 215–17, 234, 237
prime time, 104, 134
Prodi, Romano, xiii, 5, 31, 41–42, 49, 172, 217
proxyvision, 176
public service broadcaster, 5, 38–39, 42–43, 50, 62, 64, 72, 132, 240
public sphere, xvi, 38, 82, 159, 162, 165, 176, 181, 221
Pummarò, 253–54, 256

Radio Alice, 174–75
Radio Città Futura, 175
Radio LUISS, 191, 196
Radio MonteCarlo, 192
Radio Officina Talenti Emergenti, 190
Radio Padania Libera, 230
Radio Papesse, 191
radioPromoClassica, 192
Radio Radicale, 175
Radio Rana, 192
Radio SNJ, 192
Radiotelevisione Italiana. *See* RAI
Radio Umanista, 192

RAI, xii–xiii, xvi, 5–8, 11–12, 21–28, 34, 38, 40–45, 47–49, 57, 64–65, 71–72, 83–86, 90, 96, 122, 141, 172, 175, 189, 193–94, 196, 213, *218*–19, 233, 236; RAI Fiction, 96; RAI International, xvi, 23–29; RAI Trade, 72
Ratzinger, Joseph, 247. *See also* Pope Benedict XVI
reality (TV, shows, program, format), viii, 70, 129–30, 134–35, 137–*43*, 145, 173
Regional Competence Centers (RCCs), 157
regionalism, xv, 121, 196
Rete 4 (Rete4), xi, xiii, xvi, 13–14, 17, 41–43, 47–48; Salva Rete 4 (Amendment), xi, 43. *See also* Mediaset
re-territorialization, 115–16
Ris, 93
Rocco e i Suoi Fratelli, 245, 248, 252
Roseanne, 104

Salgari, Emilio, 264
Salvatores, Gabriele, 248
Sandokan, 264
Santa Maradona, 263
Sartori, Carlo, 48
Schengen agreement, 226
SDS, 8
Serie A, 8, 24, 43, 178
Shukran, 122–23
sitcom, 59, 80, 82, 84, 104–5
The $64,000 Question, 59
Sky Italia, 4, 9, 14–17, 43, 64, 172
soap opera, 59, 80, 82–84, 88
social realism, 88, 92, 94–95
"the South," 31, 87, 121, 125, 227, 254. *See also* Southern Italy
South Africa, 37
South America, 250
Southern Italy, 87–87, 123, 125. *See also* "the South"
Southern Question, 245–46, 248, 252

Spain, 60, 69–72, 132, 140
SpegnilaTV, 178
stereotype(s), 90, 92, 103–4, 106–7, 110–11, 113–15, 118–19, 121–22, 125, 136, 181, 207, 231, 237, 249
Stream, 8–9, 64
Strix Television, 131
SVT, 131–32
Sweden, xvii, 11, 66, 69, 130, 132–33, *143*, 156
Swift il giustiziere, 90

tautology of fear, 209
Tawfik, Younis, 237
Teleaut, 178
Telecinco, 70
Telecitofono, 175
Telecom Italia, 5–8, 43, 46, 195
Telegiornale (Tg), 44, 46–49, 177, 213, 218, 233, 238
Telelatino (Network), 21–29
telenovelas, 80, 83
Teleosservanza, 177–78
Telepiù, 5–9, 14–15, 64
television network(s), vii, xvii, 219
Terra di Mezzo, 256
Teste Rasate, 255
Tg Migranti, 177
Toscani, Oliviero, 249–51, 262
The Tracy Ullman Show, 105
transculturation, xvii, 81, 91, 94
transnational communication, xvi, 22
transnational media, 29
transnationalism, 30

trash TV, viii–ix
The Turkish Bath, 259
TV drama, 58–59, 63–65, 71–72, 80, 82–83, 85, 90, 93, 95

UK, 3, 16, 57, 66–68, *72*, 89, 92, 129–31, 156. *See also* Britain
Un Mondo a Colori, 122–23
Unimedia, 71
United Colors of Benetton, 249
United States of America (USA), xvii, 10, 37, 69, 90, 102, 111, 130, 132, 152, 156, 180–81, 189, 232, 249–51
Unyonair, 191

Van Miert, Karel (Commissioner), 5, 7, 9
Vatican, 24, 233, 237
V-Day, 193. *See also* Grillo, Beppe
Vengeance Unlimited, 90
Vicari, Daniele, 195
virtual communities, 164
Vita, Vincenzo, 47
Vittorini, Elio, 246
Vivendi Universal, 9
Vlora, 246, 249, 251

Wael, Fahrat, 236
Western Europe, 4, 9, 29, 89, 129, 227
White Paper (proposal), 12
Winx, 65
WTO, 27

YouTube, 73, 181, 194–95, 197–98

About the Contributors

Michela Ardizzoni holds a PhD in Communication and Culture from Indiana University–Bloomington. She is an assistant professor at the University of Colorado at Boulder. Among her most recent publications is the book *North/South, East/West: Mapping Italianness on Television* (Lexington Books, 2007). Her research interests include media and identity politics, transnationalism, migration and mediatic spaces, alternative and urban media, gendered politics of media representation.

Flavia Barca is a media economist, and has been working on the following topics, among others: the local TV sector in Italy and in Europe; the Indies sector in Italy and the United Kingdom; small and medium-sized enterprises in the communication sector; new business models for content delivery on the web. She is Professor of Economics and Management of Communications Companies in the Department of Communication Sciences at the University of Teramo. She is also Coordinator of the Institute of Media Economics-Iem of "Fondazione Rosselli" (www.fondazionerosselli.it) and Member of the Board of "Fondazione Bordoni" (www.fub.it).

Rinella Cere is Senior Lecturer in Media and Communication Studies at Sheffield Hallam University, UK. She has researched and taught extensively in Media Studies and her publications include a monograph: *European and National Identities in Britain and Italy: Maastricht on Television* (2000) and numerous articles and chapters on the media and popular culture in Italy. The most recent publication is "The Body of the Woman Hostage. Spectacular Bodies and Berlusconi's Media," in *War Body on Screen*, K. Randall and S. Redmond eds., due out in 2008 for Continuum.

Alessandro D'Arma is a former research consultant for media companies. In 2007, Alessandro D'Arma received his PhD from the University of Westminster with a thesis on "Broadcasting Policy in Italy's Second Republic 1994–2006." His academic research interests are in media policy and regulation and the political economy of media. He is currently working as a postdoctoral researcher on an AHRC-funded research project on "The Production Ecology of Pre-School Television in Britain."

Chiara Ferrari is an Assistant Professor of Mass Communication in the Department of Communication Design at California State University, Chico. She received her PhD in Cinema and Media Studies from the UCLA School of Theater, Film and Television in 2007, and her Master's Degree in Media Arts from the University of Arizona in 2003. A native of Italy, she earned her Bachelor degree in Philosophy from Università degli Studi di Genova in 2000. Her work focuses on the negotiations between local and global factors in the international import/export of television programs, with particular attention to reformatting and audiovisual translation.

Mark Hayward is Assistant Professor in the Department of Global Communications at the American University of Paris. His primary research interests are cultural policy, television, and technology.

Andrea Marzulli is a researcher in the field of media and creative industries. With a degree in Cinema History from the University of Rome and a Master's in audiovisual management and digital television management, he planned and managed several research and consultancy projects on the Italian and international television markets for local and national institutions and for the leading Italian broadcasters. He wrote papers in business magazines and contributed to collective books on the media market. He also coordinated various editions of the IEM annual report *L'industria della comunicazione in Italia*. Presently he is responsible for market studies at the Istituto di Economia dei Media of the Fondazione Rosselli.

Lorenzo Mizzau is a PhD student in Management at the University of Bologna, Italy. He is also an affiliated researcher at ASK Centre for Research on Management and Economics of Arts and Culture Institutes, Bocconi University, Milan. His specialization concerns the economics of media industries with a particular emphasis on the music industry. He is editor of the webjournal ticonzero.info.

Fabrizio Montanari is an assistant professor at the University of Modena and Reggio Emilia, where he coordinates the OPERA Research Unit (Gluno

Research Center), specializing in cultural industries. He is also a lecturer at Bocconi University and Chief Editor of the web-journal ticonzero.info. His main research interest regards the analysis of networks in cultural industries.

Giorgia Nesti (PhD in European and Comparative Politics) is Assistant Professor in the Department of Historical and Political Studies (University of Padova, Italy), where she teaches Communication Policy and Institutions and Governance of Communication in Europe. Her research interests focus on European Integration, regulation in communication market, issues related to media and the information society.

Cinzia Padovani holds a Masters in Philosophy from the University of L'Aquila, Italy, and a PhD in media studies from the University of Colorado Boulder. She is currently an Assistant Professor in the Department of Radio and Television, Southern Illinois University Carbondale. Her publications include *A Fatal Attraction: Public television and politics in Italy* (Lanham, MD, Rowman & Littlefield, 2005), also published as *Attrazione Fatale: Televisione pubblica e politica in Italia* (Trieste, Italy, Asterios Publisher, 2007). She has published extensively in peer reviewed international journals such as *Javnost/The Public, Television and New Media, The International Journal of Media and Cultural Politics*, and *The Asian Journal of Communication*. Her current research focuses on the transition to digital TV and the impact of this transition on public service broadcasting institutions in various countries.

Marta Perrotta is a post-doc fellow at Dipartimento Comunicazione e Spettacolo, University Roma Tre, Italy. In the same University she is Lecturer in Television Formats. Her research interests range across the aesthetics of television genres, global formats and local adaptations, the uses and languages of contemporary radio. She is the author of two manuscripts, ìIl format televisivoî (Quattroventi, 2007) and *L'ABC del fare radio* (Audino, 2003). Her writings appear in such journals as *Media, Culture and Society* and *The Radio Journal* (forthcoming).

Federico Riboldazzi is a PhD candidate in Management at the University of Bologna, Italy. His specialization concerns the economics of the cultural and media industries with a particular interest for the Internet, the movie industry, and the videogames industry. He is also editor of the web-journal ticonzero.info.

Cristian Vaccari is assistant professor in the Department of Political Science of the University of Bologna. He also was a visiting fellow at Columbia University Massachusetts Institute of Technology, and American University in Washington, DC. His research focuses on political communication in comparative perspective with particular attention to the Internet and new media. He has published three books in Italian and his research has been published in several journals, such as *Political Communication, European Journal of Communication, French Politics*, and *New Media & Society*.

Chiara Valentini, PhD, is assistant professor at the Department of Language and Business Communication at the Aarhus School of Business, University of Aarhus, Denmark, where she teaches both B.A. and M.A. level courses in communication management and public relations. Previously, she has worked and consulted with organizations and public institutions of several countries, including the Italian Representation of the European Commission in Rome and the European Movement International Secretariat in Brussels. She is the author of a book on EU communication strategies and co-author of two books on Italian PR-journalist perceptions. She has written various articles on public communications, relationship management in international contexts, and media relations, both in Italian and international journals. Her research interests focus on public relations and relationships management; public and political communication; public affairs and public diplomacy; international and intercultural communication; and the European Union.

Alberto Zambenedetti was born and raised in Venice, Italy. He has a Laurea in Foreign Languages and Literatures from Universit‡ degli Studi di Venezia, Ca'Foscari, a Master's degree in Cinema Studies from New York University, and he is currently pursuing a PhD in Italian Studies from the same institution.

Breinigsville, PA USA
06 December 2009
228635BV00004B/3/P